To Chris —
For greater understanding.

CopShock
Second Edition

Surviving Posttraumatic
Stress Disorder (PTSD)

Allen R. Kates

Foreword by
LAPD Detective William H. Martin (Ret.)

HOLBROOK
Street Press

Published by
Holbrook Street Press, Tucson, Arizona USA

Second Edition Printing History
September 11, 2008
Copyright © 2008 by Allen R. Kates

Printed in the United States of America

First Edition Printing History
May 1999, January 2001, October 2001, May 2004
Copyright © 1999 by Allen R. Kates

Publisher's Note
This book is designed to provide information about the subject matter covered. It is sold with the understanding that the publisher and author are not engaged in rendering psychological, financial, legal, or other professional services. If expert assistance is needed, the services of a competent professional should be sought.

Cover design and illustration by Lightbourne Images
Copyright © 1999, 2008

Publisher's Cataloging-in-Publication

Kates, Allen R.
  CopShock, second edition: surviving posttraumatic stress disorder (PTSD)/ Allen R. Kates; foreword by William H. Martin.
  p. cm.
  LCCN: 2008920136   ISBN: 9780966850123

  1. Post-traumatic stress disorder. 2. Police—Job stress. 3. Police—Mental health. I. Title.

RC552.P67K38 2008   616.85'21   QBI99-901849

"No arsenal...is so formidable as the will and moral courage of free men and women."

—President Ronald Reagan

CopShock, Second Edition
was published on September 11, 2008
to commemorate the anniversary of the attack on America.

CONTENTS

Preface to the Second Edition

Less than a month after the devastation of 9/11, I was in New York City, staggering through what was left of the World Trade Center complex.

Cop2Cop, the peer support group running a police helpline in New Jersey, had invited me to speak to their volunteers and staff, but they said there was no way I could truly understand what police officers were feeling without going down to the pile.

They were right.

Horror does not adequately describe the scene—the twisted blackened metal beams sticking out from compressed debris that reached more than two stories, the fires and black smoke... The makeshift memorials: hasty letters pinned to a post, photographs from happier times, crayon drawings of daddy in his police or firefighter uniform, poems stained with tears.

What I also saw were the faces of police officers, firefighters, soldiers, steel workers and civilians determined to lift our country out of shock and despair. In their eyes, I saw the spirit, will and courage of our people. And I was reminded that no matter what happens to us, we will step through the flames together better than we were.

After leaving the World Trade Center site, I had the privilege of meeting many officers from the New York City Port Authority who were hurting over the loss of friends and co-workers. But despite their pain, they were on the job.

Many were helped back to work by a peer support organization called POPPA that talked them through the grief and uncertainty, an organization that has helped thousands of cops cope with the horror of 9/11, and the day-to-day raw emotions of police work. POPPA is the ideal model for what peer support units throughout America should strive for, and for what police associations and departments can do to improve the quality of life for officers.

Like POPPA, *CopShock* focuses on *resiliency*, our ability to bounce back from adversity, and the will to overcome any obstacle. The stories of police officers in the book take us to the depths of their hopelessness and, in most cases, show

how they clawed out of the darkness, and back to good mental health. They show us that feeling overwhelmed is normal. Despairing is normal. Developing PTSD is a normal reaction to an abnormal amount of stress. And healing and recovery are also normal, possible, and empowering.

In the years since the first edition of *CopShock* came out, I've learned a lot. I've presented seminars around the country and in Europe, and have met hundreds of police officers. What impressed me the most was their "will and moral courage," their desire to do good, their determination to make the world a better place.

As a result of those experiences and the countless telephone calls and emails I've received, I've revised, updated and expanded more than 50 percent of *CopShock*, and added five new chapters. Many readers speak of the police officers featured in the first edition with reverence. Consequently, I have included their stories in their original form.

In this second edition, I've added a series of self-tests on Posttraumatic Stress Disorder, Stress, Anxiety, Depression, Resiliency and Panic Disorder that will help focus your thoughts and feelings. In addition, I've included a piece called *Please Listen*, which tells your loved ones or friends what they can do for you when you are feeling over-whelmed.

You will notice that the National Law Enforcement Officers Memorial Fund (NLEOMF) has an important presence in the book. It is the keeper of the police culture and knowledge. It is the guardian of all police officers have done and learned, of their achievements, of their sorrows, of those who have given their lives, of those who hit the streets each day to make things safe. This remarkable non-profit organization maintains records of the past so we will know what to do with the future.

The NLEOMF has been given the honor of building and maintaining a National Law Enforcement Museum in Washington, DC. This museum will be a constant reminder of the sacrifices police officers make, of the values they represent, and what they contribute to society.

Thank you for being cops. Stay safe...

Allen R. Kates, MFAW, BCECR

Foreword

As police officers, we have a very real problem. We don't recognize how what we see, hear, smell, taste and feel affects us on a daily basis. Our responses to violence are so subtle and long-term that we do not realize what is happening to us until we begin to lose what is most important in our lives: our families, friends, health, spirituality, honor, commitment, and sense of self-worth.

We identify who we are by what we do, and when that begins to unravel, it shakes us to our core. We become uncertain and wonder if anything matters anymore. We stop communicating with our families. We may experience panic attacks, relationship breaks, suicidal thoughts, uncontrollable anger and an inability to control actions.

We wake up in the morning and say, "I don't want to go to work anymore." We develop coping skills that are unhealthy for us and those we love. We begin to look for relief through alcohol, drugs, sex, food, gambling, and shopping for new "toys" that will help us feel better. I know. I've done it all, and none of it works.

We continue to sink deeper and deeper into whatever compulsive or addictive behaviors we have adopted. The panic attacks grow. We begin to get "sick" more often to avoid work. We find excuses not to go home to our families because we can't admit the sexual, sleep, and other dysfunctions present in our lives. We don't want our loved ones to see our pain. Their "knight in shining armor" isn't shiny any more. We don't recognize how trauma affects us, both in our professional and personal lives.

Many of us have horrible nightmares. We have flashbacks and feelings of being irritable and on edge. Nothing we do is enjoyable anymore. We're always critical of everything and everybody, because everybody is the enemy. Sadly, most of us are unaware that we may be suffering from Post-traumatic Stress Disorder (PTSD) or its associated conditions.

CopShock provides the tools necessary for those of us in law enforcement to recognize and survive the effects of trauma. It reinforces the dangers inherent in police work while reassuring there is hope for psychologically wounded cops. The book's extensive chapters on support sources are major resources for self-help, PTSD management and recovery from addiction. They describe where to find immediate assistance to get our lives, families and careers back, and where to obtain help for loved ones, friends, or coworkers. The book serves as a worthwhile aid for peer counselors and therapists trying to help traumatized clients.

This book's value is not limited to law enforcement alone. It is equally useful for anyone in other emergency services professions such as firefighters, paramedics, nurses, dispatchers, disaster workers and hospital emergency room personnel. The stories and detailed references will also significantly benefit combat veterans and civilian victims of trauma.

The author Allen Kates has spent several years documenting the research and resources. The stories within these pages demonstrate graphically what happens to those who did not have these support sources available to them at the time of their traumatic encounters. *CopShock* shows police officers how to establish effective support to inoculate themselves against trauma or, once traumatized, to recover from its consequences.

For over thirty-three years, I have served as an emergency services provider—two years in ambulance service, two years in volunteer fire service, four years in the United States Coast Guard as a medic, four years as an LAPD police officer and twenty-one years as a detective. I am now a chemical dependency and intervention counselor.

For most of my police years, I was addicted to alcohol and prescription drugs. I often had suicidal thoughts and once tried to kill myself. I didn't realize that my exposure to frequent trauma was causing PTSD. Fortunately, I have benefited from counseling and am now in recovery. But if I had had this book when I was a rookie cop, maybe the quality of my life would have been better.

I have never read a book with so much truth, honesty, eye-opening emotion and problem identification as *CopShock*. This book will begin the healing process for thousands of dedicated, active-duty officers. These officers have decades of service left to perform, yet do not know that the cumulative effects of PTSD have taken a heavy toll on them. Even retired officers, once they identify their symptoms, will begin to heal.

The general public, those we have sworn to protect and to serve, will also gain valuable insight from this book into the lives of law enforcement officers. They will see how confronting life-threatening or hopeless situations causes changes in our personal lives, marriages, careers and families. They'll see why some of us behave the way we do in our contacts with them.

It is my prayer that this informative, inspiring book assists law enforcement, their family members, emergency services people, war veterans and the general public in recovering from trauma.

William H. Martin

Detective William H. Martin (Retired)

**Former Coordinator,
LAPD Drug and Alcohol Rehabilitation Program**

Introduction

The detective led me to the door of a rat-hole called the interrogation room. He sat in a chair against a window, I with my back to the door. Between us was a gnawed, wooden table barely large enough to set up the tape recorder and microphone. The only other objects crammed into the tiny room were a punched-out, green metal filing cabinet and a black telephone.

The detective's white dress shirt, sleeves rolled to the elbows and unbuttoned at the throat, was decorated with a scrawny print tie and a black 9mm pistol dangling from a right shoulder holster. He was round-faced, as big as a fullback, the smallness of the room making him seem all the bigger. After he began his story, tears came to his eyes, and he wept silently in the tiny cubicle. He told me of flashbacks and nightmares, of reliving scenes as if from horror movies.

"The mother tied the hands of the two children with phone cord and stabbed them as they ran around the apartment..."

But this was not a movie. The detective had lived the dreams. The crime scenes he had investigated were real and the victims, he said, haunted him in his sleep and pursued him while awake.

"The infection turned to gangrene. So when I walked into the crime scene and saw the body, the ankle was rotted away and full of maggots..."

In a gush of words he described his drinking, drugging and uncontrollable crying fits, reactions sometimes associated with a dangerous psychological condition with which he was diagnosed called Posttraumatic Stress Disorder (PTSD).

"Do many cops suffer from PTSD?" I asked him.

"In this country, probably a third of the police force."

While astonished by his estimate, later I was to learn from research the detective was right. As many as a third of the cops in this country are impaired by PTSD and cannot function well, if at all.[1]

Posttraumatic Stress Disorder was first diagnosed in Vietnam veterans years after the war. They developed it from combat situations. Today PTSD may well be the most significant reason cops become emotionally crippled.

After interviewing the detective, I spoke to two other police officers that day who were diagnosed with PTSD. Both were Vietnam War veterans. One of them spoke indifferently about stressful effects the war had had on him, as if underplaying the effects would make them tolerable. The other, his eyes tearful, his voice breaking, couldn't talk about the war at all. He said he hadn't even told his therapist about what happened in the war—now decades later.

This same man told me what happened to Vietnam veterans who were cops during the 1992 Los Angeles riots. Riot conditions were similar to a battlefield with automatic gunfire, snipers, fires, smoke, screams and explosions. Some officers felt they were reliving their war experiences and, overwhelmed, had to leave the scene to seek help from counselors.[2]

By the end of the day of interviewing at the Los Angeles Police Department, I had solid information for writing a newspaper story about cops with PTSD. I went to say goodbye to the detective when he motioned me into his office and shut the door.

The detective, William H. Martin, the LAPD's Drug And Alcohol Rehabilitation Program Coordinator, said traumatized cops were calling him in the middle of the night. Yet cadets at the academy and even seasoned officers didn't believe anything could happen to them. They need a book, Bill said, to explain how PTSD ruins lives.

"I've gone to too many funerals of cops who ate their guns because they couldn't take it," he said. "A book is part of the solution."

"Wouldn't a doctor be more suited...?" I began.

"Cops need a book from a layperson's point of view," Bill interrupted, "a book from somebody who reports facts in an impartial, objective way without psychological jargon."

After I got home, I called several treatment centers and police peer supporters (cops trained to look after cops) in other cities. I learned that even though most police departments do not experience as high a rate of suicides as Los Angeles and New York, the consequences of trauma can devastate officers' lives. And the lives of their families.

The counselors I talked to thought a book about how cops handle the effects of trauma and PTSD from a journalist's unbiased standpoint—something they'd never seen before—would be valuable in their work helping law enforcement officers cope.

My resistance vanished. I spent the next six years researching and writing *CopShock*—stories of how cops prevent or manage psychological trauma.

Those six years took me to places I had never been before. Dark streets in big cities, drug dens, scenes of shootings and beatings. In the back of police cars, I hung on as they careened, sirens wailing, through streets and alleys. I wore a bulletproof vest that made me drench my shirt with sweat. I witnessed cops stonefaced and people weeping in grief as their friend, shot, was carried out on a stretcher.

I walked the corridors of police power, meeting administrators and politicians. And I talked to over a hundred police officers, their spouses and friends, union representatives, counselors and combat war veterans.

I listened to police officers' tales of the toll it takes on them to wear a stone face. They told me how anger and despair held inside turns against them, eating away at faith and hope.

The stories in this book tell the cops' stories in their words. Of what it's like to shoot another human being and to be shot, knifed and beaten. The book tells of police officers' struggles with treacherous administrators and hostile doctors. Of the day-to-day buildup of "routine" events that can break an officer down. Of sleepless nights, horrifying flashbacks, drinking binges, drug taking and suicide.

The stories explore the dark recesses of the mind, in which violent thoughts and loss of control crash into each other. And the stories show how police officers pull themselves out, how they survive psychological trauma and Posttraumatic Stress Disorder.

Rather than immediately taking the reader through the definitions of trauma and PTSD, I begin this book with the first story. Giving psychological trauma a human face illustrates, better than any explanation, where PTSD—*copshock*—begins and how it progresses and changes lives.

Chapter 1

Assaults

"I asked God, 'Please take my life.'"

Bomb squad detective Tony Senft warned me the meeting place was hit or miss. Not having an assigned room at the medical center for their monthly meetings of the New York Police Self-Support Group, members took what space they could get. Sometimes they met in a cramped hallway.

After wandering around, I found the support group in a small office, which was crammed with about forty to fifty men and women, one on crutches, most incapacitated from shootings, assaults and accidents. As few chairs were available, many people had lowered themselves to the floor and sat with their backs against the walls.

During the meeting, officers shared stories and advice on how to cope with injuries. Tony and his partner were severely injured when they tried to dismantle a bomb in the early 1980s. Tony was blinded in one eye and still has bits of concrete embedded in his body. He suffers from incessant medical problems including PTSD.

Before long, Tony introduced me, and I explained what I was writing about. After the meeting, a few officers drifted over to talk. A short, blond woman, very thin, with large hazel eyes said she was a recently retired transit cop. She wore a white blouse and brown narrow pants, further accentuating her slender figure. She must have weighed less than a hundred pounds. Although I had trouble imagining her a cop, her handshake was strong and her approach forthright.

Her voice, however, gave something away. It was a plea, a hint of vulnerability. She told me she had developed Posttraumatic Stress Disorder as a result of an attack on the subway. It left her with massive physical injuries that nearly destroyed her psychologically. To me she looked perfectly fine.

It was after we left the meeting and began the interview in my hotel room that Christine McIntyre told me how she acquired PTSD and how she chose to ignore it, a decision that nearly killed her.

The Transit Officer's job is similar to a patrol officer's, but the venue, instead of a street, is usually a subway platform, a train or a dark tunnel. Transit cops encounter the homeless, the mentally ill, people with lice, tuberculosis, AIDS and other diseases. They tangle regularly with crack addicts, panhandlers, turnstile jumpers, vandals, thieves and pickpockets.

Christine was well suited to her job. She ran six to eight miles a day. She worked out and lifted weights. At a couple of inches over 5 feet and weighing 115 pounds, she was a ball of energy and a bundle of trouble for anyone who messed with her. She was trained at self-defense and regularly honed her skills at the shooting range.

After finishing the police academy, she was assigned to District Four in Manhattan. For a twenty-six-year-old rookie it was exciting work. Almost every night she went on a gun run, a man-with-a-gun-in-the-subway call. Sometimes there were stickups on trains, sometimes gunmen in the tunnels.

Accompanied by a training officer wherever she went, she wasn't allowed to make arrests until she had more experience. Like many female cops, Christine was plagued with indifferent bosses, only a few of whom treated her as an equal. Most of her training officers "couldn't have been more miserable to me. They'd sit in the back of the train and close their eyes."

After five weeks, a couple of those weeks in training and the rest solo on night tour, Christine received a transfer notice from District Four to District One, known as the Crystal Palace for the high rises that housed large companies in the area. She was also notified on that Friday that on Monday she was to attend fire zone training. That meant she wouldn't actually start patrolling in District One until Tuesday night.

Happy with the new duty, she cleaned out her locker and took her uniforms to the dry cleaners to be fresh for her first patrol in the new district. How could she know this innocuous chore would change the course of her life?

On Monday morning, dressed in a business suit, she went early to fire zone training and relaxed with a coffee in the empty classroom. By eight, she was getting nervous. Where was everybody? Eventually, someone stepped in to tell her the training was canceled.

When she called her new command, the sergeant on duty wanted her to come in right away and finish the day tour on the trains. Not having a uniform, she couldn't. He instructed her to rush down to the dry cleaners and come in instead for the 6:30 P.M. roll call. Having been up since before five that morning, she knew it was going to be a long night.

It took hours to get home. When she got there, she sat down at her piano bench and began her favorite Chopin piece— *Waltz in E flat.* Classically trained and a former music teacher, she still played for fun and relaxation.

But she was too charged up to play more than a few bars. It was Christmas time, she had a new job and a new boyfriend, Robert, whom she knew was "the one." He was a Secret Service agent and former NYPD officer. He understood her love for the job and would never ask her to quit. Although he was Jewish and she Catholic, they were readily accepted into each other's families.

As a surprise for his birthday, she sneaked into his apartment a few days before her transfer with a Christmas tree and decorated it. He loved it and loved her. "I had everything I wanted," she said. "Great job. I wanted to be a police officer and I was. I wanted to help people. And I had the man I waited for for months. My life was never going better."

That night, the sergeant assigned Christine to a District 20 train run on the R line. Though not familiar with the route, she convinced herself it was not going to be bad, despite her fatigue. But what she heard at roll call troubled her.

The roll-call sergeant said the public was not too happy with the Transit Authority. Subway patrons were complaining that the homeless, many of them mentally ill, were sleeping in the subway, throwing trash everywhere and using the floors as toilets. The odor was appalling and people wanted the police to do something about it.

When the transit police attempted to remove the homeless from the subway, citizens from "nice" areas of New York who rarely, if ever, rode the subway attacked the police department in the press. Some, those who usually traveled the clean, heavily patrolled downtown routes, would badmouth Transit Officers to their faces. It was a no-win situation. The sergeant advised his officers to stand back and avoid confrontation if possible.

This warning confused Christine. In the academy, she was taught she was supposed to control a situation. How do you control a situation by doing next to nothing? The contradiction preyed on her mind as she prepared to board the train at 59th Street and Lexington.

Contrasting the ominous feeling in her heart, the subway was cheerful. She saw several friends from District Four with whom she had graduated, and they exchanged a few laughs. Christine loved to joke. She tapped her boot to the music a saxophonist played on the subway platform, a jazzy blues version of *Silent Night,* the notes bouncing brightly off the walls. Shoppers, party-goers and commuters were in a holiday mood, chatty and friendly.

Christine was wearing a crisp, clean uniform. Her coat was warm against the bitter cold of the platform. Down at her side, her service revolver was freshly oiled, and she could feel the hug of a spare gun in a shoulder holster. Her bulletproof vest was comfortable and, for a change, the heavy utility belt, about 20 pounds of equipment, wasn't digging into her. She felt good, in control. This was Monday, December 14th, 1987, her first tour in District One. Nothing was going to ruin it.

She boarded the train in the middle, presenting herself to the conductor. She wanted him to know she was close by if he needed her. The car was packed, moving sluggishly at first as it gained speed entering the tunnel heading toward Fifth Avenue. When the entire train was in the tunnel, it suddenly lurched to a stop. Christine heard the conductor's buzzer. He needed her.

Poking his head out of the booth, he said, "Okay, officer. I guess it's time to do your job. We got some lowlife out on the rightside catwalk."

Barely the width of an average man's shoulders, the catwalk is a narrow concrete pathway along one or both sides of a tunnel where subway workers move from station to station. Christine saw light from the train reflected on the tunnel wall, illuminating a ghostly figure gliding from the front of the train toward her car.

Christine's plan was to get the man on the train before he got hurt, take him out at the next stop and either arrest him, which was unlikely in view of the roll-call instructions, or escort him from the subway system and let him go. She spoke quickly into the microphone attached to a cuff on her collar.

"This is 1549. I got a report of an individual on a catwalk..."

There was no returning sound, no reassuring *shhhhhhhh*, no crackling noise like cellophane on a Christmas present that signifies a connection to Communications. Christine's radio was silent. The tunnel cocooned her in a dead spot.

The conductor slid open the rightside door and Christine leaned out, one foot on the catwalk. The man whose face was shrouded in darkness crept toward her.

"Excuse me, sir, would you mind stepping into the train?" she said, her voice non-threatening.

She could see in the gloomy light his coat was rumpled and dirty. His pace did not change.

"Sir, you're not supposed to be out here. Please get into the subway car."

The man brushed against her as he passed, and then stopped, turning to face her. His beard was matted and he smelled bad. The brief physical contact made her uneasy. Did he mean to touch her? She suppressed a momentary revulsion.

"This is dangerous. Please get onto the train."

He did not respond, appearing to study her as if he hadn't made up his mind what she was. He wasn't very big, and he was short, an inch or two over five feet. Christine wasn't very big either, but she knew she could handle him if it came to that. Able to lift her own weight, she assumed he would be easy to subdue and drag in.

She stepped onto the catwalk. Immediately, she sensed something wrong. His cold stare was predatory. As if on the hunt, he was searching for an advantage.

Drawing the baton from her utility belt and tucking it under her arm, she slid a couple of steps closer to him on the catwalk.

"Sir, get on the train."

He pushed her hard, knocking her off balance. Her hat flew off.

"You're under arrest," she said, "for attempting to assault a police officer. Turn around and put your hands up."

Bending toward the train, he pressed his hands against the car's window. Christine's heavy winter coat and bulky utility belt prevented her from getting behind him in the narrow width of the catwalk. She thought, *It'll be okay. He's cooperating.*

She was clamping a cuff on his left wrist when he twisted toward her, folding his left arm around her head. He grabbed her by the hair, yanking her head back. His other hand skated down the left side of her face, a shiny object between his fingertips. The object slashed a path from the tip of her scalp, down behind her ear, across her neck, severing veins, nerves and muscles.

Christine felt the pressure of the object against her throat, then an immediate tingling and sharpness. Touching her neck, her hand came away bloody.

"You son-of-a-bitch!" she cried.

Dropping the cuffs, she drew the baton and bashed him twice, once on the neck, then on the head. The next time she hit him, the stick bounced off and flew onto the tracks.

Issued by the academy, her nightstick proved to be an ineffective weapon. According to Christine, it was about as hard as rolled up gift wrapping paper.

Rather than deterring the man, Christine's defense enraged him. Lunging at her face, he tried to slash the other side of her throat. When she dipped back to dodge the attack, she saw in his eyes a feral bewilderment.

He went wild, hacking at her coat and vest. The vest prevented him from puncturing her heart and lungs. But he managed to slice through the arms of her coat, gashing her arms and shoulders. Throwing up her hands to block his renewed advance, he focused his anger on the soft tissue of her palms, flailing and cutting.

Despite her wounds and the shock of the assault, Christine backed up to draw her service revolver. The more she retreated, the more he went after her.

Defending herself with one hand, she closed the bleeding fingers of her other hand around the gun butt and tried to pull the gun from the holster. Her gun would not let go. It was stuck.

Her holster had a specially constructed notch that served as a safety mechanism. Too many people had stolen officers' guns from their holsters during fights, and the notch was designed to prevent suspects from getting the weapons. The notched holster required an officer not to pull up on the gun so much as twist it out. Only the maneuver required space to twist the weapon out, something she didn't have. To get it out, she'd have to use both hands, possibly a fatal course of action.

Her thoughts racing, she went for a spare gun, an off-duty five-shot in a shoulder holster under her left armpit. It wasn't there. During the struggle, the holster and harness had twisted around her back. The gun was behind her, unreachable, humped under her uniform jacket and heavy coat.

As the man pressed his attack, Christine felt a sticky wetness down her uniform. Light-headed, losing blood, she grabbed at the concrete wall. Her hand fell on a rusted metal handrail. What drew her attention, and remains a recurring memory today, was the image of her own blood blackening the painted, yellow, rotted steel.

With unexpected strength, she wrenched the handrail from the wall and thrust it at him. Now she was on the attack. Still trying to retrieve the spare gun with her right hand, she swung the four-foot pole from side to side with the other hand to keep him at bay.

She struck the wall, then the side of the train, missing the man, yet driving him back. The next blow made contact, bludgeoning him on the neck and the shoulder. She clubbed him again in the neck. Jerking the pole back to gain momentum, she struck the train car, snapping the shaft in half.

Taking advantage of the sudden shift in the struggle, her assailant scooped up the broken half of the handrail and hammered her in the shoulder and hands.

As long as he isn't cutting me, she thought, *I can try again for the gun.*

Using both hands as he pummeled her, she finally freed her service revolver from the holster. But then he turned around and walked away, toward the rear of the train.

"Police, don't move!" she shouted, pointing her gun at his back. He didn't stop.

She could have shot him. But a New York cop could only shoot a fleeing felon if he posed further threat. She regrets she didn't fire. Shooting might have given her some measure of control. Shooting might have prevented her from seeing herself in the months and years to come as a victim.

Not aware how badly she was hurt, Christine followed him toward the back of the train. She called the central dispatcher again. The radio was useless.

Her heart pounding, she tasted what she thought was copper in her mouth. She watched the man jump down onto the train tracks and cross to the other side, heading toward the 59th and Lexington subway station, from where she came.

Her feet, hands and head tingled. She couldn't open or close her hands nor raise her arms. Aware she was weakening, Christine accepted that the battle was over.

She staggered to the open door of the train car. She told me she thought the man, the fight and what happened next were all a dream, and she could only remember fragments of the dream.

Fragments like...

> Calling on the radio, "1013, 1013, officer down." The radio dead.
> Floating into the car.
> Faces of people screaming.
> Blood dripping down clothes.
> Bloody bootprints on the floor.
> The radio suddenly working. *Shhhhhhhh...*

In the dream, a woman orders people off a seat and says, "Lay down, officer."

Faces appear before her like apparitions. Hands press a scarf against the wounds. A man plays with the dial of her microphone.

"I'm a passenger on the train. We have an officer that is slashed, and she's in real bad shape. She's starting to pass out."

Christine describes the attacker, what direction he was going in. The man repeats what she says. A woman's face bends down into the helpers trying to stop the bleeding and says, "Why are you helping her? She's gonna die anyway."

To her horror, Christine realizes the train is not moving. It's sitting in the dark tunnel like a dug-in beetle afraid of the light. Five minutes or five hours pass. She thinks she's dying. The motorman won't budge. He is afraid the suspect is still on the tracks. He might run him over.

After an eternity, the train inches forward into the next station.

It was all a dream, wasn't it? If only she hadn't taken her uniforms to the cleaners, she would have reported for work earlier, and she wouldn't have been on this train, and this wouldn't have happened. If only, if only, if only...

Suddenly the car door rumbled open and in rushed a transit cop. The cop and a passenger picked Christine up and ran her out of the train up two long flights of stairs.[1]

Near the top, the rescuers lost their balance, almost dropping her. Not one to let a joke go by, even in a desperate situation, Christine said, "Hey, wait 'til I get to at least street level. Then you can drop me."

At street level, Christine told me she thought she saw "millions of lights and cops," touching her, pushing her toward the ambulance's open doors. News cameras poked their lenses at her, capturing the drama. _SEE COP BLEED TO DEATH, STORY AT ELEVEN..._

She was in and out of consciousness. She recalls sirens blasting as they raced to the hospital, police car lights surrounding her, strobing through the windows of the ambulance, an attendant shouting her vital signs over the din into a microphone. Then, nothing.

Infinite black space.

A piano tinkling _Waltz in E flat._

A saxophone hooting out _Silent Night._

Screaming awake into a sea of noise, she fixed her eyes on the ambulance's ceiling. She tasted copper in her mouth.

Emergency attendants scissored up the arms of her uniform coat. They sliced through socks, pants, searching for a vein to accept an IV tube, all the time talking to her, trying to keep her awake.

"Christine, Christine, stay with us," she remembers one of them saying over and over. "Do you know your arm is cut too?" She didn't know.

To keep her alert, they told jokes. But when she said in a stern voice, "Don't ruin these pants," it took them a moment to realize she didn't mean it. They laughed. She laughed and closed her eyes. And the world darkened and disappeared.

Waking up, she gasped for air. She was in motion, sailing down a long corridor. Ceiling lights rushed by like luminous frosted clouds. Someone in green held her wounds shut. Someone in white jabbed her with a needle. And around her spun a tempest of blue, white and green uniforms and a wall of jumbled sound.

Then the face of her attacker appeared like a ghost on a subway wall. She wasn't hallucinating. It was him. The cops had caught him and brought him to Bellevue Hospital for a "show up." Parading the assailant in front of the victim was standard procedure for making an identification. When she said, "That's him," he laughed. In his pocket police found the razor blade he used to slash Christine.

Her gurney resumed its stormy journey into the Emergency Room where hands lifted her onto a shimmering, metal table. Someone in green washed the blood away. Doctors fussed over her wounds and prepared anesthetic. Though they were ready to sew her up, she refused to go under. She wanted to see Robert, to hear his voice.

What seemed like seconds later, he appeared. She told him she loved him, and he said he'd be here for her always, a promise he meant and kept. She accepted the medication and, with insensibility swelling over her like waves, floated away into deep blue as they wheeled her into surgery.

In the recovery room, she woke up to screaming. It was not her voice. In the bed next to her lay a homeless man whose leg was severed by a train. She told me, "He was not someone I wanted to wake up to."

For hours, she listened to the man's screams. When the nurses tended him, she caught flashes of bloody bandages, and the vision sickened her. "In a hospital as large as Bellevue," she said, "they could not find a private room for a wounded cop."

In the recovery room, also, were Robert, an officer assigned to watch out for her, and the chief of the transit police. She had boarded the train at nine in the evening. It was now four and a half hours later.

"Hi, Christine. How ya doing?" asked Chief Del Castillo. "Are you okay?"

Still drifting on the anesthetic, she said, "Boy, Chief... Lookit, it's only one-thirty. I could still finish my tour. Come on, let's go out..."

For several days following the slashing, daily papers and television news programs sensationalized the story, sometimes distorting facts. Most newspapers incorrectly reported Christine was on her first solo patrol. She had actually patrolled alone for weeks. The worst blunder, which came from the police department, happened several months after the incident. Christine pulled the records of what happened to her and read she was listed as deceased.

For Christine, the first few days after the wounding were a blur of get-well cards, fruit baskets and visits from reporters, family and friends. The police department commended her bravery by conferring on her the "Cop of the Month" award.

A Secret Service agent mentioned to President Ronald Reagan that Robert's friend was hurt in-the-line-of-duty, and Reagan immediately wrote Christine a letter of sympathy and encouragement. The President ended by saying, "Please know that Nancy and I will be keeping you in our thoughts and prayers." Christine "always felt touched by his compassion."

But with the support also came the politics of injury. At the time, the Transit Authority and the New York Police Department were separate entities, harboring petty jealousies and mistrust. Although NYPD Police Commissioner Benjamin Ward was in the hospital visiting a wounded cop in a room right next to Christine's, she believes he did not visit her because she was from a different department. "I was not one of his guys."

In contrast to the Commissioner's snub, the ambulance attendants who worked on Christine came to see her and brought her a gift. Then Mayor Edward Koch's assistant barged in, announcing that the mayor was about to arrive and insisted that everyone except immediate family leave the room. That meant the paramedics, having driven for an hour across town on their own time, had to get out. Annoyed at the intrusion, Christine refused to have her friends pushed out the door. Upon departing, the assistant said that the mayor would probably not stop by.

Moments later the mayor walked in. "He was not his happy self," said Christine. Nor did he bring a cheesecake. Koch's chef usually made one for injured officers. A well-wisher said she had missed out because she had irritated the mayor. Two days later, a cheesecake arrived. Christine never found out why he sent it then instead of handing it to her in person when he had the chance. Maybe he forgot to give it to her.

Christine didn't understand why people who should know better seemed not to comprehend how badly she was injured, physically and psychologically. Having received many food gifts, Christine asked the nurses to set up a table so cops working the hospital could help themselves. She was trying to open a fruit basket when a police officer guarding a prisoner at the end of the hall dropped by. He extracted a razor blade from his pocket and waved it in front of her face. "Hey, doesn't this remind you of something?" he said.

Someone pulled him from the room. She didn't see him again, but she never forgot him. She's asked herself ever since why a fellow officer would be so insensitive. A theory is that if he had treated the situation thoughtfully, then he would have had to face the possibility that a life-threatening assault could happen to him, too.

For a few years Christine would have to adjust to her injuries and to people who could not grasp what she was experiencing. Muscles that were severed from her scalp all the way down behind her ear to her throat had to be reattached. Her left forearm had cuts and bruises everywhere and muscle there, too, was severed.

Although her hands sustained surface wounds not requiring stitches, they bear permanent defense scars, branding the progress of the slashing. To close the wounds, she required thirteen staples across her neck and ten on her left forearm.

Following the surgery were three years of physical therapy, three times a week, then another year of twice a week. She sees a chiropractor, probably forever. Nerves that were sundered cannot be repaired. Consequently, she still endures numbness in the left leg, left arm and left side of her face, especially the jaw.

While Christine described the damage, I shifted in my chair and gazed at her across the table in amazement. The tape was spinning, but whom had I recorded? Surely, not the person sitting across from me. She looked healthy. The surgeon did a marvelous job hiding the wounds. When people looked at her they wondered what all the bother was about. No one could tell she had been hurt. And that's the whole point. On the surface, I couldn't see, and neither could most other people, the wounds that were much deeper.

Listening to Christine, I thought, *It's a miracle she survived the brutal attack.* I soon learned that it was more a miracle she survived the convalescence.

For seven months after the assault, Christine was off work. She spent a week in the hospital, about a month at her parents' home and then felt compelled to stay at Robert's. She said she couldn't rest at home. She was getting too many phone calls and visitors.

Was it a case of too much concern, having too many friends? She thinks it was the expectations of others for her to be well that put stress on her. Her friends, although genuine in their love, did not grasp the magnitude of the injuries nor her growing fear. Their mere presence compelled her to retell the story of the attack, to relive it day after day in all its terror.

At night, every night, she woke up thinking about the incident. "The nightmares," she said, "at first, they were not too bad." She was able to get back to sleep. But that would not last.

Christine was feeling disconnected from the assault. She knew it had happened, but she felt it had happened to someone else. Even when she spoke to cadets at the police academy about her encounter, she described it as if talking about a person she knew as an acquaintance, someone outside herself, a person living down the street she didn't dare visit.

"This whole thing was like somebody else lived it," she said. "I mean, after everything I've been through, all the pain and all the trauma, it really still stands like it was a dream, almost like a movie. Like it never even happened to me, but I'm feeling all the after-effects."[2]

Paradoxically, she questioned what she had done, examining the details again and again, blaming herself to see if somehow she was at fault. Initially, everyone told her she'd done everything right, by the book. Rule number one, she got out alive. Then friends turned on her.

"A cop I worked with up in Operations told me the story he had heard. He said I got a call on the radio of some perp in the tunnel and, because I was a rookie, wanted to be a hero so I ran into the dark tunnel to get him out. And he believed it was true. I wasn't trying to be a hero. I was doing my job. I thought he knew me as a person who would not be stupid, but I guess I was wrong.

"Another wild story had me on top of the train. Because of these stories they were cold to me up in the Operations Unit. I felt betrayed, and I lost respect for my fellow officers from that point on and no longer trusted them.[3]

"They were second guessing me and that hurt me because I knew I did everything right. I couldn't imagine myself doing anything other than what I did."

Second guessing by brother and sister officers is not unusual. Whenever a cop is shot or hurt, roll-call sergeants often critique what happened. This permits officers to learn from the incident. The process helps both fellow cops and the officer who was involved. Sometimes, however, the effect of reliving the horror so soon after the incident can cause lasting injury.[4]

Not long after Christine got home from the hospital, her brief, troubling dreams escalated into full-blown homicidal nightmares. When she closed her eyes, she saw herself descending the dark stairs to the platform, getting on the train and being attacked by the razor-blade man. She told me her desire was to stop thinking about it because she wanted to get better and return to work. Then, a cop friend unwittingly helped her sabotage herself.

"Christine, listen," he said. "If this stuff has upset you emotionally, you better not say anything to anybody because they'll get you off the job."

"There's no way," she responded. "This is my life, this is my career."

From that moment on, Christine clammed up. She refused to tell anybody how she was feeling or even admit to herself she had major problems because she feared her bosses would take away her job.

Oddly, once she made the decision to hide her feelings, the nightmares stopped almost completely. When she did have a bad dream, it was minor and controllable. This change reinforced her belief that she was doing the right thing. In that mind-set, she attended the mandatory two meetings with the police department psychiatrists.[5] Convincing them nothing was wrong, her determination to appear psychologically healthy backfired. After seven months convalescing, the Transit Authority doctors gave her an ultimatum.

"'We're putting you back so you won't become too mentally detached from work,' the doctors told me. 'Otherwise, you might become afraid to go back.' I said, 'How can you put me back to work? I'm still not feeling well.' I didn't say emotionally I was not well. I was still on probation and afraid they would fire me."

At the prospect of being forced to leave, Christine tasted copper in her mouth. Pains shot across her chest. She couldn't get air. Her left arm tingled. Yet she agreed to return to work immediately.

Still enduring physical therapy, she performed light-duty jobs in Operations for a couple of months, answering phones, handing out guns, and disbursing money for toll booths. "I put 110 percent into it no matter how menial the job. I wanted to prove I'm fine. I'm just as good as anybody else."

Christine struggled to keep up. To not forget instructions from her superiors, she wrote everything down on "many little pieces of paper." After awhile, the lieutenant assigned her to the Operations Desk to perform high-profile tasks working with the Chief of Police, Transit Authority officials, inspectors and the press. The job was considered a plum assignment and usually only officers who performed well and had spent considerable time in the unit merited it.

She felt proud of herself that her boss had confidence in her ability. Those who believed the job should have gone to them and not to a rookie treated her with hostility. And the pressure started to mount.

Around this time, about ten months after the attack, Christine, along with other police officers, was honored during Medal Day in a ceremony at police headquarters. As she climbed the stairs of the stage to receive the Distinguished Medal of Honor and the packed auditorium burst into clapping and cheering, she had conflicting feelings. She had heard that some of her fellow officers were not convinced she deserved the medal, but others concluded she earned it. The result was that rather than feeling heroic for what she did, she worried that she "was not worthy of the award."

Uncertainty contributed to growing anxiety when, a few months later, she was moved again, this time to Dispatch, a part of the Operations Unit. She told her supervisors she "needed to feel capable and useful." She got more than she wished for in a job that became more frightening than the subway.

She sat in front of an immense board pinpointing where police officers allocated to her were located in the subway system. Sometimes she would cover all of Manhattan or all of Queens, Brooklyn or the Bronx. Receiving calls for help from 9-1-1 Emergency operators, she would radio the jobs to the nearest police officers. She was their life-support system. If cops were in trouble, they called her. She was their only hope, and the responsibility was crushing.

While her other police department tasks provoked little stress, this job became a source of dread. Contradictory stories were still circulating about what happened in the subway tunnel, and Christine felt she had to prove to other cops and to herself that she was capable of doing anything anybody else could do. "A nervous wreck," she was forced to take sick leave several times to escape the intolerable pressure.

Whenever she heard a "1013, Officer Needs Help," coming from another dispatcher's station, Christine would "freeze up" with fear. The calls made her flash back on her own life-threatening attack, now one year past, and relive it. The nightmares returned stronger and stranger than before.

"Some nights when I would have the nightmares, I would be in the subway system, in the same place where it happened. But then it didn't have to happen in the subway. I mean, I'm dreaming I'm in a store and all of a sudden I would be fighting with this guy like I was in the subway."

Christine's nightmares occurred almost every night around two or three in the morning, preventing her from getting back to sleep. She would go to work by six-thirty, exhausted. Her ability to function began to fail. She started to stutter. When she had to concentrate on a call or watch the board, without warning a flashback would completely distract her. She had difficulty remembering things.

"I couldn't remember simple things, like they would say, 'Call him and tell him to be there at four instead of one.' I couldn't remember what I was supposed to tell them. I would have to write everything down.

"Sometimes I would go through a day and wonder if I got a phone call or went to the store or dreamed that I did. I couldn't distinguish the difference. I couldn't remember what was real and what was a dream. The taste in my mouth... the coppery taste, I'd get that all the time."

Other police officers I talked to have described similar tastes when they've been under stress. One described it as metallic, another as iron and another as the taste of blood. A couple of officers said they could taste the greasy brake linings from the black and white cruisers or sometimes smell decaying flesh when they were nowhere near a dead body. During flashbacks, people who suffer from PTSD often report they taste something that reminds them of a traumatic event.

Realizing it was more than a year since the attack and her ability to cope was deteriorating, Christine turned to a police friend for help. He advised her to see a counselor outside the force. After two to three months of tests and therapy sessions at the Diagnostic and Counseling Services Center, the doctor gave his assessment.

"He said, 'You are destroying yourself. You have Posttraumatic Stress Disorder, and it's totally taking over your life. I don't think you should be performing as a police officer. You should commit yourself to a psychiatric hospital.'"[6]

Christine told me she stood up and said, "Sal, if you ever bleed a word of this to anybody, I will sue you, because I won't do anything else but this. Nobody's going to take this job away from me. I'm going to be okay. I'm just stressed, that's all."[7]

I asked Christine, "After you were diagnosed with PTSD, were you able to function?"

"I had something to take my mind off it," she said. "Robert and I were going to get married in about ten months. We were planning the wedding ourselves and it took a lot of time out of my day, off time, on time. I was excited and I was able to force down all my feelings."

Christine's method for suppressing feelings worked. The nightmares became occasional again. Nearly two years had passed since the assault and everything seemed better. But with the wedding over and nothing to distract her mind, a tidal wave of feelings washed her away. The nightmares intensified. Accompanying them were cold sweats and a racing heart. She was up every night for months. Everyone at work noticed she was worn out. She couldn't concentrate, and they couldn't depend on her. At home, she was irritable and short-tempered.

"Every little thing would bother me. Robert was having trouble accepting what was happening to me, and it was hurting our marriage. And I stopped doing things. I stopped cleaning the house. The wash was piling up. I stopped cooking, which was something I loved to do. I stopped playing piano. After I'd gotten hurt, I went on shopping sprees and I was still doing it, only more. I had enough of everything, but I would buy and buy and buy. I have clothes I haven't worn that still have tags on them. I have shoes that are still in boxes."

I asked Christine why she went on shopping sprees.

"Depression and the necessity to feel something. I mean, this had taken away every bit of self-esteem. Shopping made me feel good."

"Did depression affect the way you acted in other ways?"

"One time I was on my way to work, going up the stairwell from the subway..."

"How were you on the subway?"

"The first thing I did once I was able to walk was go out on the subway platform. When Robert was available, he would walk me to the turnstile and come back for me after work. But I thought if I waited any period of time, I would grow frightened of it. So by the time I went to work, I was okay."

"You were going up the stairwell..."

"I was anxious every time I rode the subway... There was this young guy. You know, it's five-thirty in the morning, the subway's totally empty. I'm the only person there, and a guy wants fifty cents? I don't think so. He wants my whole wallet."

"Were you in uniform?"

"Civilian clothes and I had my gun on me. And he goes, 'I want fifty cents.' And I say, 'No, my man. No money.' His shoulders move up and down and he's positioning himself like in a dance so he can have leverage. And he says, 'Yo! Just gimmie fifty cents, okay.'"

"What did you do?"

"My gun was in a belly band and I went to get it. Like, they know. They already know if somebody's going into their jacket, what you're gonna take out. You're not going to take out a 'Congratulations! You're a winner!' card. And I told him, 'Step back. Get the hell away from me!'"

"Did you pull your gun on him?"

"No, but I almost did. Then the copper taste came into my mouth and like this whole thing dropped from my head to my toe, like a blood rush. I was also angry because I realized I was unable to make a clear decision. Afterwards, I kept asking myself, *What should I have done?*"

Christine attributed her overreaction—going for the gun—to depression and being anxious. She felt less in control, vulnerable to attack and more prone to act quickly to disable a perceived threat without considering the consequences of her actions.

"Were there other times when you felt threatened?"

"It would happen all the time," she said. "I was consumed by people. Especially in the subway. I was taking the subway every day to work and these homeless people, they were... they were destined to kill me."

She laughed. "It sounds crazy, but some of these people would leave that impression on me.

"If a homeless person came near me," she went on, "I would get the copper taste. I couldn't get air. My hands would start to tingle and sweat. I'd lose feeling in my fingertips and get lightheaded. I'd feel my heart pumping and get really bad migraine headaches."

"Had you had migraines before you were attacked?"

"Never. And I was getting them so badly I was vomiting."

"In these encounters with homeless people, what were you thinking?" I asked.

"I was saying to myself, *Oh my God. Am I ever going to be able to do this?* I mean, look at the way I'm reacting. Just a homeless person. As time went by, I was slowly getting worse."

"Did you try to alleviate your stress? You were a runner. Did you work out again?"

"I tried running again, but I was hurting myself. Probably because I wasn't healed enough yet. I tried a lot of things. You see, I wanted to be the same person that I was before. You know? I was battling myself because I couldn't understand why I was going through this. I was looking at myself as a loser. I saw myself as a weak person, and I could not face not being a cop. I've asked myself, *Why can't I accept this damn thing that's happened and let it go?* No, it was taking me under."

"Did your friends try to help?"

Christine sighed. "I couldn't talk to people anymore. Nobody could understand. I have friends who are female cops. It frightened them to hear about this, and I was embarrassed to admit I was having problems. And I have friends who aren't cops. They couldn't understand it. And how could I relate my feelings to them when they couldn't even comprehend what I was feeling?"[8]

"Before the attack, were you a strong person?"

"Very strong. And I felt I had to work harder because just by looking at me, people didn't take me seriously as a cop."

"Because you were a woman?"

"Yes. People would try to make me appear as if I wasn't intelligent. It was important I knew where I stood. To let people know I was feeling vulnerable, this would acknowledge something I didn't want to admit. I didn't want people to think I was damaged. I wanted them to feel I was strong."

"What about your husband?"

"We were having a lot of problems in our relationship. For a long time I felt dead inside. Robert did everything for me. He paid the bills, did housework, went grocery shopping, everything. But he couldn't understand either. Who could? If I myself couldn't, how could I expect him to?"

"And your family?"

"My parents were supportive, but there was nothing they could do to help."[9]

Now married and back at work with no wedding to plan for, Christine made an error in Dispatch for which she cannot forgive herself, and even today it makes her hands shake when she thinks of it. A female officer called in a "1013, Officer Needs Help," but the transmission was fuzzy...and Christine wasn't sure what the officer said.

"I'm not sure I didn't hear it because the transmission was poor or because of the fear it caused in me."

Having no way to contact the officer who made the call, Christine panicked. Fortunately, the officer called back, informing Christine that the problem resolved itself and there was no emergency. Christine's lieutenant castigated her for not responding. Missing a "1013," the call that saved Christine's life, was a little too close to home.

Christine said she felt sick after that and couldn't continue working. "It killed me to think that, God forbid, if anything had happened to her I would be responsible. It was a very bad thing, very shameful for me. I never wanted to hurt any of my fellow cops. This makes me feel like I wasn't a good cop. In reality, I wasn't well."

The 1013 incident brought back violent memories of the slashing. Her mind replayed the images continuously, giving her little sleep or respite from pain. One week later, her feelings reached a climax. The Police Self-Support Group, which Christine had attended sporadically, invited her to join several injured police officers on NBC's the _Today_ show. "Before this, my mental breakdown was very hush-hush. This was the first time I outright expressed myself on how I felt."

During the interview, one of the other officers described PTSD reactions similar to hers. Tommy said he couldn't concentrate or remember. He cried for no reason. He had nightmares, cold sweats and was always irritable, exhausted. Although he experienced flashbacks, he denied he had problems. Like Christine, he overreacted to innocent situations and people. And like Christine, he was in an intermittent state of unreality. He wept openly on the television show, and his account made her realize the unreal was real.

"After the television interview, I went home and broke down," she said. "That unleashed everything, like opening Pandora's box. All of these feelings that I had suppressed all this time. Everything was exposed. Within a week or so, I wouldn't go outside the house. I lay in bed all day and I cried."

I asked Christine, "You didn't go to work?"

"I had to go out sick from work because I wouldn't leave the house, and I was crying all the time. I was totally withdrawn. I didn't want to go shopping for clothes or even food. My mother or Robert would have to bring food in. I didn't want to socialize. And I was drinking a lot too. Drinking at night to fall asleep."

"Did the alcohol help?"

"No, and during the day I didn't sleep either. I sat in bed and cried and I had the blinds closed and rocked myself. Sometimes I would sit in a chair or sit on the floor in a corner of the room, in the dark room, rocking and crying. You must realize that I was the person who everyone would call to ask 'What do I do?' or 'What do you think of this or that?' I would always give advice. I was the strong one. I was the capable one. Now what was I?"

Knowing she was in trouble, Christine called Tony Senft from the support group. Tony could not drive because of his injuries, and he couldn't get a driver at such short notice. He convinced Christine to come to him.

"I can't tell you what it was like to get into the car," she said. "I fought with Robert. He had to take me by the arm and then pick me up and carry me to the car. I was paranoid about everything. Every little noise startled me. Even the sun, the sun was hurting my eyes."

Christine put the front seat down so no one would see her in the car. "I lay down crying the entire way there while Robert drove."[10]

Realizing she needed professional care, Tony advised Christine to see his psychiatrist, a therapist experienced in helping veterans with PTSD. The next day her mother drove her to see his doctor.

"I sat in front of him and cried," she said. "I couldn't tell him what happened to me for almost three sessions. And then he told me he was going on vacation and I came apart.

"I really feel like I want to kill myself," she told Dr. James J. Cavanagh. "I can't stand crying anymore. I can't stand what this is doing to my life. I'm killing my marriage. I'm killing everything. I don't know how much more I can take."

"If you feel as though you're a danger to yourself," the doctor said, "I think you should let me admit you to the hospital."

"The hospital! Absolutely not," she said. "If I was hospitalized, I would never be a cop again. They'd consider me mentally unstable."

The doctor and Christine decided it was better if she made the decision to go. "Can you imagine what would have happened if they forced me? It would be like being arrested. They'd have to call the police and order an ambulance. People would come and take away my gun and shield."

Christine returned home to her dark room, crying and rocking to try to soothe herself. Suicidal, she called a friend who sent her to another psychiatrist. Dr. Joseph Benezra advised hospitalization. Again, she refused.

"I went home from that session and had a terrible argument with Robert, and he left to go to work. He could not comprehend what I was going through. I was scared to death of everything and I was afraid to go out. I was a prisoner of something that happened to me and he couldn't understand that. I wondered why that guy didn't just kill me and save me and my family from all this.

"After Robert left, I went into an hysterical fit of crying and couldn't stop. I took medication the doctor gave me to sleep and some Scotch. I was hallucinating. I took my gun and I sat down on the couch in the living room with the TV blasting and I was crying, rocking back and forth, and I brought it up to my mouth and I was screaming—

"'God please take my life from me! I've been through enough. Please help me. I didn't do anything to deserve this. I failed as a person and I failed as a police officer and I failed at my marriage and there's nothing else in this life I want. Forgive me for what I'm about to do. Please help me take my life.'"

The phone rang.

At first she wasn't going to answer it. She did, and the call saved her life. It was Tommy, the officer from the Police Self-Support Group who spoke of his PTSD reactions on the *Today* show, calling to see how she was.

She said to him, "I'm sorry I can't help anybody else because I can't help myself. The pain is too much for me to take. Everyone will be much better off without me around."

He listened, and he talked to her until she promised to put down the gun. He wanted to drive out to see her, but she said no. He told her next time he might not be there to stop her. This motivated Christine to return to the psychiatrist. In tears, she told Dr. Benezra she wanted to go back to work. He told her he wanted her to go to the hospital.[11]

Once again, she fought the doctor, unable to accept that she had moved from care-giver to care-needer. A few days later, she finally agreed to be voluntarily committed to North Shore University Hospital. On the way, she took several antidepressant, antianxiety and sleeping pills. She said, "I didn't want it to be a reality for me."

Before admission to the psychiatric unit was granted, Christine was required to subject herself to a medical examination in the emergency room. "This was the greatest humiliation," she said. The resident performed a gynecological exam. Christine felt it was an offensive and unnecessary intrusion but didn't think she was in a position to protest.

Afterwards, an aide took her upstairs to the eighth floor, the Psych Unit. She's not sure what she expected, but when she saw gray, steel doors with tiny windows, doors that required keys or beepers to open, doors that slammed shut behind her, she felt panic. She couldn't reconcile how a cop could be locked up like a criminal.

More indignities were to follow. The nurses directed her to undress and then took her clothes away. Ironically, her attacker, an escapee from a Connecticut mental institution, had failed to kill her, but succeeded in reducing her to his level, and she couldn't do anything about it.

Locked away, stripped of everything she associated with the outside world—clothes, shoes, a pen, a telephone—she felt abandoned. "I felt like I lost my battle. I lost my career."

It was two in the morning. For a few hours, loaded with drugs to fight off the reality of where she was, Christine slept.

The next morning, she met with a room full of doctors, nurses and aides. Weeping, she told them the little she could remember of the incident. By this time she was blocking out many details. Never looking up from the table, she had no idea what the staff members looked like. She sat there, hunched over, plucking tissues from a box.

The days in the hospital passed slowly while she received medication, one-on-one counseling and engaged in group therapy. She kept a diary of her ups and downs. Rereading the entries gave insight into her frightening misadventure. After earning "points of improvement" for following rules like taking medication and attending counseling, she was allowed to watch television, do crafts and use an exercise bike. From the moment she was assaulted, she started losing weight and was now down more than 25 pounds, weighing 88 pounds.

Christine said the staff was very protective, too protective. "I couldn't shave my legs without a person outside the shower watching me. They were afraid I'd hurt or kill myself."

She was angry that her attacker had put her here, locked in with people like him. "It was horrifying," she said. "I was in with a lot of really sick people who were chronically mentally ill, people who had been in and out of mental institutions their entire lives. It was very degrading."

The status of the people locked up with her affected how she responded in group therapy. She would not open up because several patients were under arrest for drug offenses. They were people she was ordered to apprehend and here she was facing them as an equal.

Her shame and powerlessness revealed themselves in headaches and troubled sleep. After the first night, the nightmares returned. During the day, despite taking several medications, migraine headaches caused her to throw up repeatedly.

The indignity she endured as a psychiatric patient was not limited to the shower. "I couldn't make a phone call, I couldn't leave the floor until I'd earned privileges, like in a jail. Eventually, I was allowed to go off the floor and make calls and go on day trips.

"Once I went on a day trip to a museum, and the people at the museum know who you are. You're with the psycho ward at North Shore University and they keep an eye on you. It was terrible. It was like *One Flew Over The Cuckoo's Nest.* This is the humiliation I had to endure because of what happened to me.

"Once I was actually allowed to go home and sleep at home, and I was a mess. I was a mess because I was out of that security and I didn't know how I was going to act. I didn't know what was going to happen. I was dreadfully afraid to go home to my husband. The thought of having to take on responsibilities like cleaning the house, cooking and living a normal life again scared the hell out of me. That's how bad I was for the month I was in there."[12]

Since the attack, Christine talked incessantly about the slasher. In the hospital, she was obsessed with him, wondering what he was doing, what kind of treatment he was receiving. She hated him and wanted "to see him suffering."[13]

About two weeks into her hospital stay, Christine's doctor suggested a method for breaking her mental block about the attack. He wanted to administer sodium amytal, a short-acting barbiturate. It was supposed to help release inhibitions. Although she was still having nightmares, they were not about the incident itself. She wanted to relive it one last time. She thought, *If I can get it out, then that will be the end of it.*

The day the drug was to be given, the medical staff and several interns assembled in a room to observe the procedure. She said she felt like a laboratory specimen under a microscope. An IV bottle dripped solution into her arm. The doctor told her to recite numbers backwards. After the drug took effect, the doctor asked her questions about herself. Then he asked her about the incident, questions like, "Do you know you did everything you could to come out of there alive?" She cried and answered *Yes* and wanted him to go on. He hesitated.

She pleaded with him, "Please don't stop. Please take me back."

He refused to delve into the details of the assault, and for two days after the procedure, she sobbed uncontrollably.

"I was angry because I felt he left me hanging. He made me think he was really going to help me and he didn't. I couldn't understand why he did that. And I was angry because it was like I didn't live it. Do you know what I mean?

I thought that if I went back there subconsciously, maybe when I awoke it would have been more realistic to me, and I would be able to deal with it."

I asked her, "Did the doctor tell you why he didn't take you back?"

"He said he didn't feel it would have done any good."

Coming to terms with the unreality of the attack was one of many hardships Christine tolerated in the hospital. The news that she was hospitalized in a psychiatric unit caused her disgrace in the eyes of her friends and family.

"I've lost friends over this. I've lost cousins," she said. "When I was in North Shore, a cousin of mine had a baby. She was on the maternity floor of the same hospital, and I went to visit her. They looked at me like I had some infectious disease or I was going to pull out a gun and kill everyone in sight. They were frightened over where I had been."

After a month in the hospital, Christine was allowed to leave. Initially, while still on medication, she saw her main therapist, Dr. James J. Cavanagh, three times a week. However, her therapy seemed unsuccessful. She had waited such a long time before seeking help, denying her problems, that the symptoms of Posttraumatic Stress Disorder held on tenaciously.

Christine told me she left the hospital with more "unexplainable" issues than when she went in. She was overly suspicious and forgetful. She'd forget what she was saying in the middle of a conversation and while driving would become lost.[14]

But she had made progress in the hospital. At last she was facing the aftermath of the assault. Feelings she previously ignored were in turmoil. She was getting better, only it felt worse.

Thinking a vacation might help relieve her suffering, Robert took her to Europe. Away from familiar surroundings, she became paranoid and suicidal. And rather than improving their relationship, the trip increased the tension between them. She had little interest in sex and kept turning her husband away. When Robert talked of police work, she couldn't bear to hear about it. And even when he accompanied her to therapy sessions, he couldn't understand why talking about police work was such a problem for her.[15]

From time to time, Robert's job required him to work in other cities, and when he was away Christine's fears surfaced dramatically. She slept with a knife under her pillow, listening for noises. She was afraid somebody would break in and rob her or that someone was in the basement waiting to attack her.[16]

Christine told me her nightmares, along with other reactions, accelerated in intensity. "When I got out of the hospital, that's when the nightmares got really bad. I dreamt I was fighting with this man... and I'd wake up hitting my husband when he was asleep. I was punching him in the side, around the head."

"How did he react to this?" I asked.

Christine chuckled. "He wasn't too happy about it."

We both laughed. Then her face saddened. "I still see and can feel the horrifying times when I'd wake up hitting Robert. Punching with all my might, missing his head by inches and hitting the pillow. That memory is awful.

"He'd wake up and I would start crying and he would hold me. He'd hold me until I fell back to sleep.

"Sometimes I feel very guilty about the whole thing. I feel my problems spilled onto him, destroying parts of his life that were important to him."

"What do you mean?"

"He was so involved in helping me, he left a job he loved. He waited years to get into the Secret Service. This was his life-long dream. And when he finally got in, I got hurt and he took responsibility for my life."

"What did he do?"

"He took me to the physical therapist three times a week. I mean, he did everything for me. I was able to get into the shower, but other than that I couldn't move my neck for months. On top of working full-time and traveling, he took care of me. When he traveled, he didn't comprehend the emotional problems I was having... I was having nightmares and trying to hide them. I was drinking a lot. My drinking caused a lot of problems.

"He felt that he might be transferred out of state and he didn't want to leave me. At this point, I still wanted to stay a cop in New York. This guy was more devoted to me than to his job. At times our marriage was really rough. I mean, the time when I was in the psychiatric hospital, I had him physically thrown out."

"What happened?"

"It was the night before I was getting the sodium amytal. He was tired... He had left the Secret Service and was back in the NYPD. He joined them to do investigative work. But they wanted him in the legal department because he was an attorney. He refused, so they sent him to Bedford-Stuyvesant, a bad place to work as a patrol officer.

"He also had to go home, feed the cats, see me at the hospital and do all the paperwork with my Workers Compensation and with my job. He was sending letters and talking to people back and forth because they weren't going to pay the medical bills. They didn't believe I was sick. It was nonstop for him...

"The night before the sodium amytal, I wanted him to be with me because I was scared. He was very tired, and I didn't accept that as a good reason. I got angry. When he came to the hospital, I went totally berserk. I started screaming...

"I don't remember this, Allen. This is what he told me. A lot of things have happened to me, I don't remember. Big chunks of my memory are gone...

"I remember being angry with him but I don't remember him coming down and me having him thrown out."

More than anything else, Christine wanted to be a cop again. She also wanted to start a family. But she didn't see how she could attain those goals because of her physical and mental conditions. A neurologist told her the nerve damage was irreparable. The left side of the face and the left ear would always be numb. As far as being a cop, she said she couldn't "take on any responsibility."

Resigned that she could not return to police work, Christine applied to the Transit Authority for a disability stress pension. Dr. Benezra reported that her PTSD symptoms were directly related to the assault and that she could never again function as a police officer.[17]

Two other outside doctors agreed with his evaluation. Then Christine had to face the Transit Authority doctors. They had a different point of view. The transit doctors, their allegiance to the administration, challenged her request. They didn't believe she had PTSD.

"I would go to my doctor and he would say I was damaged psychologically. Then I'd go to their doctors and they'd say I wasn't, except for one who agreed with my doctor and they never let me see him again. His report was not taken seriously. The transit doctors said I was lying, as if I was making all this up. It was ludicrous."

The transit doctors forced her to visit the Transit Authority clinic sometimes once a week for months, questioning her endlessly about the traumatic events. Christine believed they wanted her to make a mistake. In addition, they sent her to outside doctors, whom they hired, to duplicate the process.

In spite of Dr. Cavanagh informing the transit doctors that their harassing interviews were making Christine worse, they insisted she attend the many redundant, often contradictory examinations. In a letter to the transit doctors, Dr. Cavanagh wrote that she was "in a near panic for days prior" to an examination, and "in a state of high agitation for at least a week to two weeks afterward."[18] Nevertheless, they sent her to doctor after doctor, frequently into the city from her home on Long Island, at least a one hour drive, making it impossible for her to go by herself.

As well as distressing Christine, the process mystified those who took her to the interminable meetings. For hours, her husband, mother or friend, Andy Helbling, sat in the waiting room. A police officer shot in-the-line-of-duty, Andy had been hospitalized a few floors above Christine. Andy, Robert, her mother and other friends and relatives could not fathom what was going on.

"It was a mind game," Christine told me, "and they thought they were going to win. What did they care what harm they did to me? What they were trying to do is make me so crazy that I'd quit or, because I was still on probation, do something wrong to get fired."

At the clinic, she was required to see the transit doctors at 6:30 in the morning. She was the first on their sign-up sheet. "I wouldn't get out for hours and hours. People who came hours after me were out hours before me. Sometimes after I'd been waiting a long time they'd tell me that a report from one of their outside doctors wasn't in yet and to come back next week. It was torture."

During one evaluation, Christine was examined by a transit doctor who "didn't know what to do with me." The doctor left the cubicle to consult next door with her superior, a doctor who seemed to act like Christine was faking her illness. Christine listened in on their conversation, and this is what she said she heard.

"We've taken enough from Christine," said the supervisor. "How long does she think she can go on with this fiasco? Put her back to work. I'm tired of her lies."

"Oh, my God, I was ready to throw him out the window. I stood outside their room while they looked at me like I was some crazed maniac. I started lunging at this doctor and screaming, 'Why are you doing this to me?'

"A sergeant and other workers came running in and pulled me away from this idiot. He said he was going to press charges. He didn't, but that was the last time I saw the doctors alone. From then on I had to be escorted by a union rep and someone from the Employee Assistance Unit."

Still searching for a reason to dispute her stress claim, a transit doctor then concluded Christine suffered from a brain tumor and planned to send her to a neurologist for a CAT scan. It didn't happen, because by then the Pension Board was processing her application for retirement.

Why, when presented with compelling evidence of PTSD, even suggest a brain tumor? It was a cunning speculation. Not a line-of-duty injury, a brain tumor was not likely a pensionable illness, and the police department, the doctors' boss, would be off the hook.

In the end, the Transit Authority, out of excuses, approved Christine's disability pension. From the day she applied for a pension to when she was finally approved took about nine months. For Christine, it was nine months of mistreatment and torment. A transit doctor, not the one she lunged at, apologized for their conduct. "He apologized for the constant abuse I endured. He said he was glad I had won my case." Then, to her astonishment, he volunteered that his job was to discredit applicants for stress pensions regardless of the legitimacy of their claims.[19]

Christine retired from the police force in December 1992. A few months after her official departure, we met and talked for the first time. In one of our many long follow-up telephone calls, she told me that after the first time I interviewed her she didn't sleep for several nights. The terror and bitterness flooded back, and she had to work her way through the pain. I hated being the catalyst for her nightmares. At least she takes some solace in warning others that you can't get away with burying feelings.

"They're going to knock at your door," she said, "and it's not going to be lilacs and roses."

After years of suffering, Christine's life has moved in a more positive direction. On April 28, 1994, she gave birth to a girl, 6 pounds, 11 ounces. Her name is Victoria. She has dark brown eyes and, like her mother, an explosive smile. Then, on February 20, 1998, Christine delivered a healthy 6 pound, 15 ounce boy named Matthew James. Like his sister, his big blue eyes are turning chocolate brown. Instead of arrest reports and gun runs, Christine thinks about diaper changes and birthday parties. Christine told me her children have given her life new meaning.

On a doctor's advice, Christine and her family moved to a southern Florida city where the warmer climate is helping her neck and arm improve. On occasion, she feels tingling in her hands and fingers and down her left leg. Despite the loss of sensitivity in her hands, she has resumed playing piano. She still has no feeling on the left side of her face—a nagging physical reminder that sometimes triggers PTSD reactions.

For psychotherapy, she sees Dr. Harley V. Stock, a police psychologist for many years and an authority on PTSD. "He helps me tremendously," she said. The cousin who acted fearfully when Christine visited her in the maternity ward lives nearby, and they have revived their friendship.

"Things are good between us, and I do love them very much," says Christine, "but I wonder if she really understands what happened to me."

Christine McIntyre's story is about a vicious assault and its destructive consequences. Assaults on-the-job have become for all of us, cops and civilians, commonplace. About a fifth of civilian workers, one in five people, say they've been attacked at work.[20] Postal workers, government employees, apartment and hotel managers, storekeepers, sales clerks, cabdrivers, gas station attendants, restaurant managers, lawyers—no one seems immune. Police officers are especially vulnerable.

Justice Department reports suggest that nearly every second cop can expect to be attacked in any one year.[21]

Why so many assaults? The reasons are varied—a breakdown in respect for cops, an increase in violent criminals, teenage hoodlums and gang members. In some instances, self-destructive acts by cops provoke assault.

People assaulted in the workplace, whether civilians or police officers, run a high risk of developing PTSD if they don't get help. Christine is one of thousands of people whose lives are jeopardized every year. A gun and training did not prevent her from becoming a victim of crime.

I asked Christine what her PTSD reactions are like today. She told me she is still having nightmares although, thanks to continuous counseling, not too frequently. She wakes up suddenly in the middle of the night with some sense of fighting but has no clear picture of where or with whom. She doesn't hit her husband anymore, something he appreciates. Her migraines are gone, and she doesn't feel the urge to shop until she drops.

Sometimes she feels anxiety, anger, fear, not to the same extent as years before, yet the intense feelings have not dissolved into thin air as she had hoped they would. They surface when she least expects them, disguised as cold sweats, headaches and forgetfulness. They come when she sees a homeless person, hears a siren or learns of an officer getting hurt.

Chapter 2

What Is CopShock?

"I faked an attack of Posttraumatic Stress Disorder."

In the movie *The Client* based on John Grisham's novel, an eleven-year-old boy is traumatized after witnessing a suicide. Two days later, locked in jail because he refuses to tell what he saw, he falls on the floor, hyperventilating and sucking his thumb. Paramedics rush him to hospital where he manages to sneak out undetected.

When he calls his lawyer, he tells her, "I faked an attack of Posttraumatic Stress Disorder. It was easy as pie."

This is nonsense. Although PTSD sometimes reveals itself differently in children, the movie implies you can get it in a couple of days, and everybody will know you've got it. The American Psychiatric Association suggests that therapists should not even attempt a diagnosis of PTSD until a sufferer has experienced "disturbance" for more than one month.[1]

As far as it being "easy as pie" to fake—meaning, the child convinced the doctors he had it—that is also absurd. PTSD is hard to diagnose. Doctors are loath to suggest it as its symptoms look too much like other complaints. For instance, nightmares may be a symptom of PTSD, but they may be occurring for other reasons. The movie bends the truth, giving a false view of what PTSD is and is not.

Does PTSD mean mental illness? No. It is a normal reaction to an abnormal amount of stress. "...you are not crazy... PTSD is a normal reaction to being victimized, abused, or put in a life-threatening situation with few means of escape."[2]

Then what is PTSD—what I call copshock? It is a psychological condition comprised of a few groups of symptoms, like clusters of stars in the sky. And there is no simple description.

First, some history. Posttraumatic Stress Disorder is a fancy term for a condition we've been aware of for many years. More than three thousand years ago, an affliction resembling PTSD was observed in soldiers who fought in the Trojan War. In the American Civil War, Union soldiers, in shock from killing and burying other young Americans, were diagnosed with "nostalgia."

In World War I, it was called "soldier's heart," "effort syndrome," "trench neurosis," or "shellshock." Over 250,000 British troops alone are known to have developed shell-shock. In World War II, shellshock became "combat fatigue."

From the Vietnam War evolved its present label—PTSD. From the first war with Iraq, veterans' officials suspect Persian Gulf War Syndrome contracted by American soldiers could be a form of PTSD.[3] In all wars, the common factors are exposure to extreme violence and PTSD's ability to overwhelm and disable its victims.

Initially, psychologists thought only combat soldiers became overwhelmed by horrible incidents. For instance, more than sixty years after World War II, veterans who saw combat are still coming forward with PTSD. Professionals realized soon, however, that anybody exposed even once to grave injury, illness, crime or death could be shocked into a psychological stupor from which some never recover.

People not involved in combat can develop PTSD symptoms. Survivors of Hurricane Andrew in Florida suffered from "combat-like symptoms." They startled at noises, couldn't sleep and had nightmares and flashbacks of the hurricane. After the Kobe earthquake, many Japanese victims, used to keeping feelings inside, were overwhelmed by fear, anger and despair. Effective counseling by foreign therapists convinced the Japanese to start a research center on Posttraumatic Stress Disorder.[4]

Murders, rapes, assaults... In the United States, more than 17,000 people are murdered each year, and their families are psychologically shattered by the brutal acts. Every year, almost 300,000 women, children, adolescents and men are raped, and some never heal. Many female illegal aliens develop PTSD after experiencing rape or robbery during their fearful run over the border. After tennis star Monica Seles was stabbed by a deranged fan, she recovered quickly from her injuries, but became a recluse for over two years while undergoing treatment for PTSD. The loss and carnage were so great in the Oklahoma

City bombing, that survivors, witnesses *and* psychologists were treated for extreme posttraumatic stress.[5]

But not every occurrence of PTSD is as a result of combat, murder, rape, assault, earthquakes, hurricanes or other natural or human caused disasters. For instance, of the millions of people who undergo surgery every year, a quarter million wake up during the ordeal, and from the shock of what they see or hear, some develop PTSD. In a Detroit area survey of traumatized people, a sudden, unexpected death of a loved one accounted for almost one third of PTSD cases. A study shows that the diagnosis and treatment of breast cancer may hasten the development of PTSD.[6]

Although it is generally accepted that 1 percent of the population has PTSD at any one time, the American Psychiatric Association estimates that at some time in our lives, as many as 14 percent of us may develop PTSD. For people who are "at-risk," like combat veterans and victims of crime, the prevalence of PTSD shoots up to as high as 58 percent.[7] With such high numbers, we will likely come into contact with someone who has PTSD. We could develop it ourselves.

How do we make sense of the statistics? Why do some of us get PTSD and others who experience the same trauma do not? Mental health professionals don't know all the answers. The American Psychiatric Association only designated PTSD a disorder in 1980. PTSD research is still in its infancy. Fully understanding the workings of a disorder takes many years.

Some medical experts believe that upbringing may determine who is vulnerable to getting PTSD and who isn't. Genetics may also play a role, but many trauma specialists believe it is unfounded, an excuse to blame the victim.

People with a past history of unresolved traumas may be vulnerable to PTSD when a new trauma, no matter how minor, strikes. Yet, the opposite may also be true. Past horrifying events may strengthen our ability to cope with new ones. Not every explanation applies to everybody. But chances are high that suppressing feelings will get us into trouble.

Like John Wayne in cowboy movies, some of us prefer to suppress our turbulent feelings after a very distressing experience. We shut our eyes and say everything's okay. For many, emotions build up and explode in inappropriate ways like crying, expressing anger or committing violent acts months or years after the trauma—when we've often lost sight of what caused the emotional outburst in the first place.

Embarrassment and fear may prevent us from seeking support from family, friends or outsiders like therapists. In our society, mental problems are still considered signs of weakness and perhaps lunacy. Judging ourselves harshly, we rarely recognize that our reactions are normal. The situations that caused the traumas, not us, are abnormal. We need to give ourselves a break.

Why do some of us seem to cope better than others? One of the main reasons has to do with perception. A first century AD Greek philosopher, Epictetus, noted, "Men are disturbed not by things but the views which they take of them." Hans Selye, who coined the word "stress," said, "it is not what happens to you that matters, but how you take it."[8] How we perceive or view a situation is everything.

In defining Posttraumatic Stress Disorder, it is helpful if we know what *stress* and *trauma* mean.

* * *

Trauma? Few of us have not experienced trauma in our lives. It's a shock, a sudden kick to the body or mind that sends us into a spin. Trauma is, in part, "An emotional shock that creates substantial and lasting damage to the psychological development of the individual..."[9]

Stress? Stress is not a thing. You cannot hold it in your hand. You can't carry it in your pocket. Psychologists say it is a process, as intangible as happiness, anger, love, fear and pain.

I'm certain you've heard people say, *I'm done in, At the end of my rope, Going to pieces, Over the edge, Having a nervous breakdown.* Human beings have an endless inventory of expressions that mean the same thing. Stress results when we fail to adapt to a situation. Any change can lead to stress. Stress is also the feeling of being faced with demands that cannot be met.[10] These are demands we *believe* are beyond our capability of fulfilling.

PTSD? Posttraumatic Stress Disorder is called a *disorder* because it disrupts the normal functioning of our lives. It disrupts sleep, relationships, work and physical health. PTSD is called an *anxiety* disorder because some of its chief attributes are anxiety, fear and avoidance of anything—feelings, people, places—we feel may cause us pain.[11]

The definition of PTSD according to the American Psychiatric Association starts with two key elements. To become candidates for PTSD, first we must have experienced or witnessed a traumatic event "that involved actual or threatened death or serious injury." Secondly, we must respond with "intense fear, helplessness or horror."[12]

But the way in which police officers react to shocking scenes may not accurately fit this definition. Cops rarely respond to horrible events with "intense fear, helplessness or horror." At crime scenes, officers usually appear calm and in control. That is because they have been trained "to dissociate from their emotions or suppress their emotions in order to be able to endure the scene."[13]

Regardless of whether cops at first satisfy the definition for PTSD or not, they sometimes develop the condition. They set themselves up for PTSD if they suppress their emotions after a traumatic incident and do not get proper support. "They get stuck and life for them is changed."[14]

Nevertheless, PTSD is not an inevitable consequence of trauma for cops or anybody else. Nobody develops it automatically. Most people do not acquire it at all. For those who develop PTSD, however, they often don't know they have the condition because it can take months or years for a precise diagnosis.

An accumulation of several traumatic or violent events may lead to PTSD. But one major traumatic event is sufficient to cause the disorder in some people.[15] Police, like combat veterans, are especially prone to developing it because they see so much despair, misery and harm done to others. Sometimes the harm is done to them, like the injury done to Christine McIntyre.

* * *

After being severely injured, Christine suppressed her emotions and developed PTSD. She had nightmares, couldn't sleep and drank to try to sleep. Even at work when occupied, she flashed back on the man with the razor blade, couldn't concentrate and had trouble completing her tasks. She forgot many of the details of the assault and couldn't remember simple orders. She avoided returning to the subway until she finally forced herself to face her fears. Unable to cope with her inner turmoil, she attempted suicide.

At times she felt nothing for her husband, the person she loved most. She can't account for why she overreacted and had him thrown out of the hospital.

We can trace the origin of Christine's PTSD back to one single traumatic incident, the subway attack. She endured subsequent secondary injury from accusatory officers at work, panicked relatives and callous transit doctors.

Like Christine, many of us respond to trauma with anxiety, impulsive behavior, hostility, depression, drinking and suicide attempts. These reactions may start the process that produces PTSD. But what distinguishes Posttraumatic Stress Disorder from other stress responses and syndromes and makes it particularly hard to manage are these clusters of symptoms:[16]

Reliving of the trauma

➤ persistently reexperiencing the trauma in episodes like flashbacks and nightmares
➤ feeling as if the traumatic event were invading or intruding on thoughts

Avoiding reminders of the trauma

➤ inability to remember important aspects of the trauma
➤ avoiding thoughts, conversations about the trauma or places that might remind us of it
➤ numbing of responsiveness like becoming detached, uninvolved in family or work, withdrawing, having difficulty actually feeling anything for anybody

Experiencing arousal, agitation as a result of the trauma

➤ problems in concentrating, falling or staying asleep
➤ being irritable or bursting out in unexplainable anger
➤ becoming easily startled, overreacting to situations as a consequence of being super-alert or hypervigilant about people or places

Chapter 3

9/11

"I thought I was the only one left."

James (Jimmy) Brown got his "chops broken in high school" for having the same name as the pompadoured soul singer and reformed armed robber. But Jimmy couldn't sing a note, wore his hair short, and instead of joining a band, saw himself in law enforcement, and joined the New York City Police Department.

"I loved playing cops and robbers, I loved chasing the bad guys, foot chases, pursuits, and everyday was different," said Jimmy, a 5 foot 9 inch former police officer.

"But I hated working for the police department, dealing with all the bureaucracy and the politics, that stuff I hated."

Jimmy was a cop for nine years, from 1992 to May of 2001, the whole time at the 72nd precinct in Sunset Park, Brooklyn. Among other things, he worked Patrol, and the equivalent of highway public safety on the precinct level, working solo for a few years doing car stops.

"When you needed a day off, you had to request a vacation day," said Jimmy. "The holidays were out of the question. Christmas was not going to happen."

He accepted that. There was a lot of crime during the holidays, and the department needed officers on the street. "But if you needed time off for a christening, you needed a Saturday, that was hard."

Even when he finally got off Patrol, and got a solo detail, which gave him steady weekends off for a home life, he still found it difficult to work for the department.

One of the reasons was car stops. He was required to write a certain number of summonses per month. He said they were called "performance objectives," but by any name they were quotas, and an added burden.

For example, he said that when he was on radio patrol, he had to write a minimum of 25 summonses each month— 20 parkers, 5 movers, and one criminal summons. When he was in the summons detail, he was obligated to write 15 movers a *day*, and when on OT tour, it was 25 just for the one tour.

"If you didn't meet that quota, you weren't getting the days off when you requested them," said Jimmy. "If you continued not meeting the quota, the department would move you off the shift. If you were on day tours, which was better for your home life, they would threaten you with putting you on midnights or with sending you to the 75th precinct."

Compared to the 72nd precinct, the 75th precinct had three to four times the number of violent crimes.[1] "That was considered the shit-hole of Brooklyn," Jimmy said. "You couldn't get any worst than that."

Sometimes Jimmy did the 4 to12 or midnight shift in order to earn overtime for his upcoming wedding in 1999. Working alone was not the safest, and occasionally he stopped cars full of men for traffic infractions and discovered the cars were stolen. He was involved in a few car pursuits, but the majority of his work was writing summonses.

In Jimmy's opinion, the police department was a revenue generating agency. It was a business, and each year he had to beat last year's numbers.

Jimmy said that the city was reactionary, and things happened in cycles. Sometimes there was a push on red light summonses, another time it was stop signs. Then there was passing a school bus with flashing lights summonses. This was always done in reaction to the bad accident of the week that was making news.

"There were guys on the force who were desperate to get their numbers. There was one guy who stopped a school bus on one of the major thoroughfares, 4th Avenue, which is three lanes in each direction. Technically, everybody on both sides has to stop. He would have a driver with an empty bus turn on the flashing red lights, and everybody who passed, he'd pull over.

"They called it *flakin'* people. That's what a quota does. It drives you to worry about getting your numbers."

After awhile, Jimmy couldn't stand it anymore, and decided to leave the police department, and see if he could join the fire department.

"The fire department was not trying to generate revenue. You weren't penalized if there weren't enough fires that month. And you could always get your days off by switching with another guy."

However, Jimmy's wife didn't want him to leave the police department. "She was convinced it was more dangerous."

Jimmy's wife, a social worker at the time, felt that no matter what situation you got yourself in as a cop, you had some control and could pull back. "If I'm in a car pursuit and I feel like it's too dangerous, I can always slow down and drop back or call off the pursuit. If I'm chasing a perp with a gun on foot, and I'm getting into an area where I feel I'm losing my tactical advantage, I can pull back."

But in the fire department, there was no pulling back. You couldn't call off trying to put out a fire or rescuing somebody trapped on the upper floor of a burning building.

However, he also knew that if a cop feels that Patrol is too dangerous, he could get an inside job. "You can become a house mouse."

And that's what he became. In the last couple of years he was in the police department, he didn't want to risk getting injured, or jammed up, so he took a job as the domestic violence officer while waiting to see how his plans for joining the fire department panned out.

Jimmy initially thought that anybody who wanted to be a firefighter had to be crazy. One day when he was a cop, he was heading back to the station house for his meal, and he saw smoke a couple of blocks away. He was the first unit on the scene, and the fire department wasn't there yet. A house was fully engulfed in flames, and people on the street said there were people trapped upstairs in the back.

"I tried to go in the house. It was so bad I couldn't even step on the sidewalk. And I watched the firemen run into that burning building. I thought they were idiots. I'd never do that."

The prospect of having a better home life, and less stress, overrode his feelings of caution, and, at the age of 34,

Jimmy entered the fire academy. He said the training was nothing like the police academy. The police academy was six months of mostly classroom work and a gym period. Fire academy was eight weeks of mostly outdoor physical stuff with a small amount of classroom lecture.

After completing the first part of the fire academy training, Jimmy became a probie, and was assigned to a Manhattan training house, Engine 10/Ladder 10, on Liberty Street, right across the street from 5 World Trade Center, for another fourteen weeks.

The joke at the fire academy was that he was going to a *slow house* where they "roll down the gates at 6 o'clock because everybody goes home after work. Manhattan just doesn't see as much fire duty as some of the poorer neighborhoods in the outer boroughs."

"10 House" was a double firehouse, with an engine and a ladder truck. Jimmy was to do seven weeks on the engine side, and seven weeks on the truck side. Then the captain was to evaluate his performance and send the results to the academy. What was to follow was another two or three weeks of training at the academy, and then graduation.

Jimmy never did complete his training.

On Monday, September 10th, 2001, he was in the middle of his fourteen week stint working a 24. He started at 6 PM, worked all that night, and because he'd swapped a tour with somebody else, was scheduled to work the coming day shift to 6 PM.

Early that Tuesday morning, September 11th, 2001, there was a transformer fire, and both the truck and engine went out. Jimmy was in the engine. They put out the fire, and had to sit on it until ConEd came out. Then they left, and backed into quarters about 8:30 AM.

Three or four of the firefighters hung out on the apron at the front of the firehouse with the apparatus doors open waiting for the 9 o'clock roll call. Jimmy was sitting in *housewatch* inside near the front. His duty, among other things, was to observe anyone entering or leaving the firehouse.[2]

Suddenly, everbody heard a plane descending rapidly.

From his vantage point, Jimmy couldn't see outside, but he could hear the jet.

"Holy shit, here comes a plane," he heard a firefighter say. "It's gonna hit the Trade Center."

"And me being a probie, I thought they were breakin' my balls," said Jimmy.

He heard the plane's engines rev up, and he got up from his seat...

...and then there was a booming explosion.

He described it as "a concussion wave that goes right through you." The housewatch had large plate glass windows that shook so much he expected them to shatter. But they didn't. Not yet.

He moved quickly to the apparatus floor, looked up, and saw a huge fireball enveloping the top of the Trade Center towers, emanating from around the 94th to 98th floors of the 110 story buildings. The fireball was so immense, he couldn't tell which tower was hit. It was 8:46 AM.

"I could actually feel the heat. And I watched the debris start coming down."

One of the firefighters got on the mic to alert the others in the firehouse they were going out on a run. Another picked up the phone to inform the dispatcher, and everyone plunged into gear and jumped on the rigs. The truck started out first.

Suddenly, flaming debris showered down on the firehouse, the street, and on the rigs. Civilians walking by ran into the firehouse to get out of the way. Jimmy didn't know what he was supposed to do with them and ushered them out toward safer buildings, shut the door, and he was the last man hopping on the rig.

The truck and then the engine dropped off its firefighters in front of the Marriott Hotel on Liberty Street. There was so much smoke, the men thought the plane had hit 2 World Trade, the south tower, and they went to the front of the building to get a position on the fire. Even the men who watched the crash couldn't tell which tower it was.

Jimmy asked what kind of plane it was. There were three different responses that ranged from a small plane to a large jet. "So the guys that actually watched it happen didn't know."

They soon realized that the south tower was okay, and the firefighters ran into the street to get to the entrance of 1 World Trade, the north tower on West Street.

Outside the north tower, he saw another probie he worked with from the truck. His friend was getting off duty, about to go home, and had grabbed a ride on the other rig. Since they'd been riding heavy, they didn't have an extra mask and air tank for him, so the chauffeur told him not to go inside the building.

When Jimmy came upon him, he was helping a female burn victim that had staggered outside, and was lying on the ground. He was kneeling, and with a fire extinguisher, watered the victim down. As Jimmy ran toward them, he could see the woman, pink and burned down the entire length of her body.

Jimmy thought, *Oh, good. This is a training exercise. It's not for real.* Because she had the same color as the dummies they used at the fire academy to drag out of fires. They were a pink, fleshy color.

Then he remembered... He remembered feeling the firehouse shake from the plane strike. He remembered seeing the fireball. And he realized this was no training exercise.

He entered a doorway in the north tower that led to a foyer, and on the floor was a burn victim screaming in pain.

How did this person survive the fall from the airplane? Jimmy wondered. His mind was playing tricks on him.

He found out later that when the plane exploded, the jet fuel flashed down the elevator shaft, and blasted a fireball into the lobby. Anyone in the lobby got hit.

In order to get through the foyer doorway into the lobby, Jimmy would have to step over this terribly injured person who was in the way. He wanted to stop and help, but he told himself that medics were behind him. He was carrying a hose roll up, and he had to get up those thousands of stairs and put the fire out.

"I had to consciously tell myself to move. It took everything I had to step over this person and go into the lobby of the building."

Jimmy's firehouse used to do building inspections at the twin towers, and he knew what the lobby of the north tower looked like. But it now looked nothing like what he remembered. Much of the marble that was once on the walls now lay shattered on the floor. The marble that remained was cracked, and all the plate glass windows were blown out. The walls were scorched and black from the fireball.

Jimmy and the other firefighters had rushed to get into the lobby, but now they had to stop. They had to wait for the chief to "give us our marching orders."

So Jimmy stood there and waited, and listened, and heard things he could not have imagined. He heard elevators screeching down the shafts and crashing somewhere down below. He heard something thud outside onto the concrete, and then another, and another.

"The units coming in told us what it was. People were jumping, bodies were dropping. That gives you a state of mind—If people are willing to jump to their deaths rather than stay and wait for us, *Shit, it's not good up there.*"

Jimmy waited, and the tension continued to build. A senior firefighter with at least fifteen years was standing next to him, and kept muttering.

"Jimmy, Jimmy, it's gonna be bad. It's gonna be bad. People are gonna die today. It's gonna be bad..."

Jimmy thought, *Shutup.* "You know, I'm friggin nervous, and it'll be as bad as it is, you're just making it worse. That was his way of dealing with the situation. It just didn't make things any better for me in my head."

Then the chiefs went into action and decided to pair up the engine companies. Engine 10 was paired with Engine 5, and the idea was that their personnel would go up together, one company carrying the hose roll ups to start, and they would switch off and on so nobody got worn out by the time they reached the fire floor.

The roll ups were heavy, rubber-lined, canvas hoses, and each one weighed about 50 pounds and was 50 feet long. To make them easier to carry, each hose was "rolled up" or folded, one segment over another segment, so a firefighter could hoist the whole thing like a big bundle onto his shoulder.

Once the firefighters got up to the floor below the fire floor, they planned to connect three roll ups to make 150 feet of hose. Then they would hook one end to the standpipe system, and lug the hose up the stairwell to fight the blaze.

Unfortunately, the firefighters only got part of the message, and *every* firefighter in both companies ended up carrying their hose roll ups on their shoulders, as well as wearing their bunker gear, tanks and other equipment, for the trek up to the fire, which was 90 something floors above them.

Before heading into the stairwell, the firefighters huddled together and one of them said, "Look, everybody stay together. We don't leave each other."

They turned around, and their lieutenant wasn't there. He had gone in ahead of them and missed the huddle.

"We already lost somebody. We tried to make radio contact with him," said Jimmy, "but it was impossible because there were so many units on the scene, and so much radio traffic that you couldn't reach anybody. And if you did, you got cut off by somebody else before you got a message through."

Then they tried to enter the stairwell, which was near the elevator shafts, but ran into a bottleneck. It was not a fire door or even a double door, just a regular doorway opening. Civilians were walking down the stairs and out the door, and the firefighters had to use the same door. One civilian would come out, and then one firefighter would go in. The process of getting two companies of firefighters, each with a hose roll up over his shoulder, through that doorway was long and tedious.

While Jimmy waited for his turn to go through the doorway into the stairwell, he noticed that a couple of the elevator doors were askew, and he had to tell himself not to lean on them or he might go down the shaft. Then he heard an elevator car scream and crash through a shaft. He didn't know if anybody was in it, it just kept falling to the basement level.

"You heard crashes, you had bodies falling outside, and you could smell jet fuel, you could smell burnt flesh. Your senses were overloaded."

Jimmy said that he tried to concentrate on what was in from of him, and what was in front of him was so overwhelming, he had a hard time grasping it. "Things that were in the periphery, I ignored. I had guys come up to me afterwards that said they spoke to me in the lobby and I don't remember it."

Jimmy and the others started up the stairwell and kept trying to reach the lieutenant. They were going up, and the civilians were still coming down.

"It was a surreal experience," said Jimmy. "Because the stairwell was in the core of the building, and you didn't hear anything from outside anymore. Which was a relief, but now it was very quiet, churchlike. You didn't talk too loud."

The civilians coming down the stairs were calm, and descended in an orderly fashion, one behind the other. They tried to give the firefighters encouragement. They said things like—

"God Bless you..."

"Good luck..."

"You guys got a tough job ahead of ya."

Jimmy said that some handed the firefighters water they took from vending machines. "We would take it from one civilian, climb a couple of steps, and hand it to another civilian, and then the civilian would hand it to another fireman. It was a game. Because everybody thought that the other guy needed it more."

The scene that transpired was not something you'd see in a movie. Moviemakers often like to portray chaos, they like to show shouting, fear, anger, fistfights—something to make more drama. But that's not what happened.

What happened was peaceful, and, for all of us, humbling. It's what makes us believe that there is hope for humanity after all.

Some of the civilians making their way down were injured with sprained ankles, burns, and cuts, and were being helped down by other civilians. But because they were injured, they couldn't move too quickly, and it took them longer to get down the stairs. As a result, as the firefighters went up, they would find long gaps in the line with no civilians coming down.

"There was one line to the right of firemen, and one to the left side of civilians," said Jimmy. "That's all that could fit on the stairwell, it was so narrow. There were able-bodied civilians behind the injured, just waiting their turn, not jumping in front of the injured, just waiting behind them patiently, even though the line was slow and people were dying only several floors above them. And they came down calmly, and nobody was panicking. This was amazing."

Jimmy was concerned about the senior firefighter who told him things were going to be bad. Although they were both in their mid-thirties, the man was not in good shape, and as they were on their way up, he was lagging behind. Jimmy kept looking back to make sure he wasn't having a heart attack. That was the biggest concern in the fire department. "You're carrying so much gear, it's such a physical job, a lot of guys would drop dead from heart attacks."

Jimmy was concerned about himself, too. "My doctor is always trying to put me on medication for high cholesterol. My overriding concern was a heart attack for both the senior guy and myself, which, that day, ultimately, was the least of my worries."

To try to prevent overexertion, the firefighters would take breaks about every ten to fifteen floors. At one point, they moved out of the stairwell into an office area, sat down for awhile and drank water. Jimmy looked out the window and saw paper flying everywhere.

Then he felt... *something.*

"It was very subtle," he said. It was a thump and rumble, and likely the south tower being hit by the second hijacked plane. But there was no way Jimmy could know for sure. The radios weren't working.

The failure of the radios was no surprise. During building inspections, the radios didn't work properly in non-emergency situations, so why should they work now?

"They were good if you were a couple of floors away, but you wouldn't be able to communicate with the chief on the ground. You were cut off from the outside world. When I was looking out the window in that office area, I got a garbled transmission about a third plane. A third plane?"

He thought they must be imagining things.

From his position on the south side of the building, Jimmy could see the big sphere sculpture down in the courtyard. The square was usually swarming with people, but now there were none, only flying papers.

Jimmy stepped back from the window, and noticed phones on the desks. He picked one up, hoping it was working, heard a dial tone, and phoned his wife at work. There wasn't much he could tell her. He knew a plane hit the building, but didn't know how bad it was. He didn't know about the second plane.

"She was a mess," he said. "I tried to calm her down. I said, 'Don't worry, we're still pretty low in the building and just waiting to go up farther.' She thought I meant that I was outside the building waiting to go in. I told her I'd call again if I got the chance, and hung up. And that was the last time I talked to her for several hours, long after the towers came down."

Jimmy and the other firefighters were up in the teens to 20s in the building, not that high yet. It was slow going, trudging up the stairs with about 100 pounds of gear each, and having to take rest periods or they would pass out from exhaustion.

A firefighter in the other engine company, Engine 5, was having chest pains, and everyone stopped at least twice to let him rest, but then he got them real bad. "We were waiting for the medics coming up behind us to take him back out. We didn't want him to keep going and then actually have a heart attack when we would be too high to save him."

Engine 10 finally made radio contact with their lieutenant who had started up ahead of them. He was up around the 40th floor, and said he was going to wait for them. The lieutenant from Engine 5 said that Jimmy and the other four members of his company should go ahead. Engine 5 would wait for the medics, and then they'd be right up.

The company from Engine 10 resumed their ascent. They mounted another two floors on the staircase when the north tower shook and swayed for about ten seconds.

That was the shock wave from the south tower as it collapsed. Even though the north tower was hit first, the south tower had sustained more structural damage, and the firefighters and police officers in that building had no warning that death was imminent.

A cloud of what looked like smoke ballooned up the stairwell of the north tower from below. The firefighters donned their face pieces and turned on their air tanks. Then the lights went out, throwing them into a hushed blackness.

A few seconds later, the emergency lights in the stairwell flickered on. Then they realized the smoke was not smoke at all, it was dust, and they took off their face pieces. They didn't know the south tower was down, but instinctively knew their rescue mission was over.

"We assumed another plane had hit our tower and we were a target. We decided to drop everything that wasn't attached, and get the hell out of the building."

Free of the hose roll ups and other equipment, they moved quickly down the stairs. They met some cops that said, "Get the hell out."

Then as they passed firefighters from a different company taking a break sitting on the floor in the stairwell, one of them said, "We didn't get an evacuation order, where the hell are you going?"

"I'm sure a lot of guys were thinking, 'Look at the friggin' cowards, running out of the building.' But I don't know any guy who is gonna willingly give up his life and make his wife a widow when he can't save anybody, not even himself."

Most of the civilians who were physically able to get out of the building were out by now. Jimmy was at the end of his company on the way down when two Port Authority cops pushed in front of him from a landing, and they were carrying an obese man down the stairs, his feet dragging on the steps. Because they were all abreast, Jimmy couldn't get past them to keep up with the other men in his company.

It was slow going the rest of the way down, and Jimmy knew he could die waiting his turn to get out.

When he finally reached the lobby, the members of his company were not there. He worried that they had pulled off on a floor to wait for him and he had bypassed them without noticing. Then he considered that maybe they had kept on going and were already on the street.

"Now I'm conflicted as to what I should do. If I should look for them in the building. If I should get out of the building and try and find them."

He decided to follow the line of people out of the stairwell, and around to the other side of the lobby on the concourse level. The lobby was different now. When he'd arrived, the lobby was full of people. Now it was empty except for the stragglers he was with. There was thick dust everywhere, blood mixed with water on the floor, the windows were blown out, and Jimmy crunched glass shards under his boots on his way to safety.

"I didn't have time to process it," said Jimmy, "I was focused on keeping moving."

Jimmy went to the north side of the north tower, and toward the door leading to the plaza level and 6 World Trade, one of the smaller black buildings in the seven building complex. At the doorway, he was stopped by a heavyset black man in a uniform. It didn't register what agency he was from, but he remembers a gold oak leaf, which in the fire department would mean a battalion chief. In the police department it would be a deputy inspector.

He grabbed Jimmy and a few other firefighters and cops and told them there were more civilians coming out and they had to form a human line outside the building to take survivors around 6 World Trade out onto Vesey Street, which ran along the north part of the World Trade Center complex.

"So me being a good probie, I said, 'Okay, no problem.'"

Jimmy ran to 6 World Trade, which had an overhang that afforded some protection from falling debris or bodies. He was the first person that people ran to, and he shooed them on to the next person. They formed a human line out to Vesey Street.

He stood there and watched people look upward first so they wouldn't get hit by falling bodies, and then they ran across to him. He could hear bodies crashing down. He could hear a whistle as they fell to their deaths.

Eventually, the two Port Authority cops carrying the obese man came out the door and dragged him to where Jimmy was standing, and Jimmy pointed them on. And that's when he decided "that's it, I'm done."

He took a couple of steps in the direction of Vesey Street. He was maybe a hundred feet from the north tower on the concourse level—when the top floors of the north tower began to collapse, pancaking on top of each other.

"The sound started out faintly and picked up speed like a train and got closer. Because of all the air being pushed out of the building," said Jimmy. "I felt this huge blast of wind."

He could see beams and debris on the ground, but didn't know they were from the south tower, and there was so much dust billowing toward him, he couldn't even tell that the north tower was thundering down.

He turned toward 6 World Trade, his back to the crumbling north tower. On his right was one of the beams that supported the upper floors of 6 World Trade, and it protected his right side. His air tank protected his back. Nothing protected his left.

He knelt down and curled into a ball.

That's when the pulverized cement and glass and ground up office equipment hit ground level, and the debris cascaded towards him in a churning toxic cloud.

"I was getting hit with debris, and I was like, Holy shit, that hurt. And the next chunk that hit me was a little bigger, and it hurt a little more, and it was getting progressively worse. I was getting buried, and resigned myself to the fact that this was the day I was gonna die."

He reached for his face piece attached by a hose to his air tank to try to get some air, but it was down by his ankles, already buried.

The debris piled up over his knees and then over his waist. Very soon he would be completely buried.

"They say when you're dying, your whole life passes before your eyes. It wasn't like that for me. I thought about my wife. I thought about leaving her a widow, and we hadn't had any kids yet. I thought about how I told her it was safer in the fire department.

"And I thought about how they were gonna find me when they dug me out, curled up in the fetal position, and for some reason that bothered the hell out of me. I said to myself, I can't let them find me like this."

That's what prompted Jimmy to push off the debris burying him and stand up, and when he did, "I expected to get sliced in half by a beam."

He realized then that the windows in 6 World Trade were busted out. "I figured that inside had to be better, because where I'm at I'm definitely dead." And he dived headfirst into the building.

Then it occurred to him that there were several sub-basement levels, and he didn't know if there was a floor inside the building he was diving into. "The floor mighta gotten knocked down, and, for all I know, I'm falling six stories."

He landed on his back, face up, on the floor just underneath the windowsill. His helmet was gone, and the debris surging over him filled his mouth, nose and eyes with dust.

Several seconds later, everything stopped. It was quiet. No wind, no voices. He couldn't even hear the sound of his heart beating.

"It was like every sense was turned off. You couldn't see anything because it was pitch black. You couldn't hear anything because the fine particles of dust in the air blanketed the sound. You couldn't hear yourself talk. You couldn't breathe."

Jimmy got up on his hands and knees and sat on the windowsill. He took off his gloves, shoved a hand in his mouth and tried to scrape the muck out of his mouth with his fingernails.

"I couldn't get up any spit. The dust was so fine, it soaked up the moisture in your mouth. I tried breathing, and every time I took in a deep breath, it seared my lungs. So I tried to take short, shallow breaths."

He dug around for his face piece, shook it out, put it on, and turned on the tank's air regulator. But even though he thought he'd cleaned out the mask, the forced air blasted fine dust down into his lungs, and he ripped it off his face and choked.

Jimmy couldn't see anything, not even the glow from small fires surrounding him. It was so dark and silent, he didn't know if he was inside or outside. Once the dust settled, he could see hazy beams of sunlight coming through the blown out windows. Then he realized he was outside. He didn't know how he got there.

"I thought I was the only one left."

Then he saw a pale splash of light from a flashlight, and heard a faint sound of voices. He realized others had survived, too.

"One of the guys said, 'Vesey Street is out this way.' And we made our way in that direction. But you didn't have footing. Debris was piled everywhere, and you felt like you were walking on a garbage dump."

By the time Jimmy got near Vesey, the other men were gone. They seemed to have vanished into the sheets of dust hanging in the air, and he was alone.

"I felt like I was in a movie, '*The End of the World.*' You looked around, and everything was covered in gray dust. The leaves on the trees were gone. Nobody was there. I saw cop cars that were crushed by huge chunks of concrete, fire trucks burning.

"And I said to myself, 'What the fuck happened?' 'Cause I had no idea of the magnitude... I thought that just pieces of the building had come down. I didn't know anything about the south tower. And to see all of this, it was more than I had expected."

He kept walking. He went down a staircase from the concourse level to street level, without thinking about where he was going.

He went east on Vesey toward Church Street. "And as I'm walking, I'm trying to take everything in, but it's impossible. I pass this discount department store called Century 21 on Church Street at Cortlandt across from the Trade Center complex. It's badly damaged. My wife loves that store, and I'm thinking, *She's not gonna be shopping there for awhile.*"

He kept walking until he came to Broadway. "I see a church, St. Paul Chapel, and look at the barren trees amongst the headstones in the cemetery, and I don't see a living soul."

At the corner of Broadway and Vesey, in front of St. Paul's, he saw people, and realized he was not alone. Several fire department chiefs had set up a command center using a folding magnetic table to plot the tasks, assignments and locations of the companies. When Jimmy passed them, they were sliding square magnets with the company numbers on them around the board.

He drifted by the chiefs. They didn't look at him. They didn't talk to him. They didn't acknowledge his existence.

"I'm a walking zombie, covered from head to toe in gray dust. So I start thinking, Maybe I'm dead. Who the hell knows what happens when you die? Maybe I'm walking around as a ghost."

He passed them, and then came upon a police chief, who handed him a bottle of water. "At least I knew I was alive."

He wandered around trying to find members of his company. He thought they had all died.

He saw new firemen coming down the street. He knew they had just come on duty because they didn't have dust on their clothes.

He met up with a couple of firemen from his company who had been off, and returned on the recall notice. One of them was a lieutenant who asked who he was working with, where did he see them last, trying to find out if they had survived.

"I told him everybody I was working with in the engine and the last time I saw them. He asked me who was working in the truck, and I couldn't think of one person. I drew a blank."

"Alright, just go to the Woolworth Building, and get checked out," he said to Jimmy.

He must have realized that Jimmy was too stunned after all he'd been through to make much sense, and needed help. The department had set up a triage in the Woolworth Building on Broadway at Barclay Street, a couple of blocks from the destruction.

But the doctors and nurses at the triage didn't find anything wrong with Jimmy. He had bumps and bruises on his left side, the part that was exposed to the storm of debris that enveloped him. He said that his head was pounding. They gave him oxygen, and sent him back out to the street.

He was looking for a phone to call his wife. He used a couple of strangers' cell phones, but there was no signal. He tried pay phones. They were out, too. He went back to the Woolworth Building, and in an office in the basement he got a line out.

He called her again at work and told her he was okay. "She was distraught, relieved, but she was convinced I was missing something, an arm or a leg, that I couldn't have gotten out of this unharmed."

Later that afternoon outside the Woolworth Building, he bumped into a firefighter he'd gone to probie school with. Jimmy told him what had happened, but by then he was acting confused.

"Where's your helmet?" the probie asked.

"I don't know," said Jimmy.

"Did you get hit in the head?"

"I don't know. Maybe."

The firefighter grabbed a nurse who was doing triage, and told her Jimmy may have gotten hit in the head. She asked Jimmy a few questions, and seconds later he was in the back of an ambulance on its way uptown to a hospital.

"I didn't want to leave, but I had no fight left in me."

Jimmy was rushed to Weill Cornell Medical College on the upper east side. "A gauntlet of doctors and nurses took me out of the ambulance, and threw me in a wheelchair. I told them, 'No, I'm fine. I can walk.' They pushed me back down in the wheelchair, and they wheeled me in.

"And then I lost it. I was tearing up. Because I felt like a piece of shit. I left all the guys down at the Trade Center. Physically, I'm fine. I should be back down there, I shouldn't have come up here at all."

They put him on a gurney, stripped him down and checked him for injuries. They ran tests, and eventually gave him a phone to call his wife. He told her he was at the hospital.

"She was like, 'Oh, my God. I'll be there.' I told her I don't want you to come into the city. She came anyway."

His wife arrived in the early evening with a change of clothes. He stuffed his bunker gear and uniform into two clear garbage bags, and they took the train ride back home.

Jimmy felt that everybody on the train was looking at him. They could see his firefighter's gear, and he was covered in dust. *What must these people be thinking?* he wondered. "'Cause I still didn't know the full extent of what had happened. I didn't know if the other guys had survived. That's a shit feeling, man. It's the worst feeling in the world that you are the only one out of a group."

After he got home from the hospital on the night of 9/11, Jimmy sat in front of the television set for hours and watched CNN. "Even though I was exhausted, I had to find out what had happened as best they knew. Because I was in the center of it."

Jimmy learned that terrorists had hijacked four commercial jetliners, crashed two of them into the twin towers, one into the Pentagon, and another had crashed in a field in southwest Pennsylvania, about 150 miles northwest of Washington, D.C. Authorities believed it was on its way to destroy the White House when the passengers attacked the hijackers.[3]

The next day, Jimmy was going to go back in and help out. He tried calling the firehouse, but the phone line would not connect. "My firehouse was right there at the foot of the World Trade Center, and I was convinced it had gotten wiped out."

He called headquarters to find out where he should report. Civilians were manning the phones, and they told him to go to his firehouse. "I'm like... it ain't there anymore, where am I supposed to go?" He finally hung up and decided to deal with it another day.

The following morning, Jimmy got up to go in. "I got in the shower, and started thinking about what the area looked like, and I got so overwhelmed my knees gave out. I fell and almost busted my head open in the shower. I called my captain on my cell phone, and he said, 'Don't worry about it. Try to come in tomorrow.'"

If anybody was likely to develop Posttraumatic Stress Disorder, it was Jimmy. He had experienced a traumatic incident with mass casualties, hundreds of firefighters, police officers and civilians killed, enormous destruction, and he almost lost his life.

He had reacted with fear, helplessness and horror. To make it worst, the destruction was caused not by natural forces like a hurricane or earthquake, but by human beings that had a choice about whether or not to murder innocent human beings. That fact could intensify the trauma. All the criteria were stacked against Jimmy coming out of this with his mental health intact.

Nevertheless, he did not acquire PTSD, and here's why...

The next day, he phoned a peer support group he had volunteered for when he was a cop. The group is called Peer Organization Providing Peer Assistance or POPPA. He wanted to see if everybody there was okay. They told him they were setting up a debriefing center at the Federal Reserve building in lower Manhattan to help overwhelmed police officers and firefighters working on the pile.

Jimmy asked if he could help out, and arranged to get a ride in with one of the peer support people the following day.

"Drivin' through Brooklyn Battery Tunnel was like goin' from one world into another." The tunnel is the longest continuous underwater vehicular tunnel in North America, stretching for 9,117 feet, nearly two miles. On the Brooklyn side were neighborhoods of beautiful brownstones, shops, restaurants, the port and industrial areas. On the Manhattan end of the tunnel was Wall Street, City Hall, and, only a few days before, the magnificent World Trade Center.[4] Now it was gone, replaced by gray layers of twisted steel beams, shattered glass, smashed cars, and fragments of debris so small they could not be identified.

Jimmy was not prepared for the contrast, and devastation, and by the time he got to the Federal Reserve to join the other peer support officers (PSOs), "I was sittin' there in the car, and I was a wreck."

The director of the peer support program, Bill Genêt, was not happy to see Jimmy. Bill told him that he was in no condition to help anybody, because he was the one needing help. He'd just suffered a huge trauma. And Bill had Jimmy sit down with one of the clinicians for an *intervention* designed to address his feelings and thoughts and to get him back on the job. When tumultuous feelings are addressed early enough, there's a good chance PTSD won't set in. This intervention was one of the keys to Jimmy's good mental health and surviving the ordeal.

Afterwards, the PSO walked with Jimmy over to the firehouse. "On the way, he kept stopping and saying, 'Are you okay?' And I'm thinking, I just wanna get over there to see if there's anything left," said Jimmy.

Jimmy finally arrived at the firehouse and saw it was still standing. More than that, he saw men from his engine crew that he'd worked with the day of the attack, and he was thankful they were alive. It turned out that when they got to the concourse level, they headed in the opposite direction from Jimmy. Everyone had survived, except for the lieutenant who had climbed to the 40th floor and had waited for them. He was never seen again, and was presumed dead. Nobody knew much more about who else made it out.

His captain told him that they were working 24 hours on, 24 off, and all they were doing was maintaining the firehouse. They had no rigs, they were crushed, destroyed. They had no streets or buildings to service. The streets were impassable, and all seven buildings in the World Trade Center complex were uninhabitable and as good as gone. As a company, they had no response area. The captain told him to come back the next day and they'd figure out what to do from there.

Later on that day, Jimmy called a cop he'd gone to the police academy with. The man was shocked to hear Jimmy's voice—because Jimmy was on the *Dead List*, the makeshift record of those who didn't get out of the buildings in time.

Jimmy did not develop PTSD, but for the first while, he reacted to the overwhelming stress. He said that some of the symptoms came right away and disappeared, others came later. With the thought of going into Manhattan, he broke into a cold seat. He got lightheaded when he was outside walking the dog or doing anything if planes were flying over.

"I never noticed that the friggin' planes fly over my house. And now all of a sudden, I think they're flying lower than normal, and I feel compelled to watch and make sure the plane isn't coming down."

Loud noises startled him. He had frequent nightmares, and smells affected him. Construction sites, even to this day, smell to Jimmy like the Trade Center after it collapsed.

He became obsessed with finding out who had survived. Jimmy used the computer at work to search for others he had known. "We lost six guys from our probie class that never graduated. After I got to about thirty guys that I knew, I stopped counting. I never envisioned that I would know that many guys that died."

Eventually, it was determined that 343 New York City Fire Department firefighters and two paramedics were killed. Twenty-three New York City Police Department officers, 37 Port Authority Police Department officers, and 8 private ambulance personnel died as a result of the attack and collapse of the buildings.

It's estimated that almost 16,000 people below the impact zones in the World Trade Center complex at the time of the attacks were evacuated and survived, but approximately 2,750 civilians, including the people on the doomed jets, were killed. At least 200 human beings jumped to their deaths from the burning twin towers. At the Pentagon, including the passengers on the plane, another 184 died. In Shanksville, 40 people on United 93 died. These figures do not include the hijackers, nor the thousands who were injured both physically and mentally.[5]

Years before 9/11, Jimmy was a smoker and had quit, but he started up again. "When we went back to work, I felt like I was in a different body. I didn't feel like me at all. The cigarettes tasted like crap, and I would light one up, I would smoke it, and I remember being totally disgusted with myself and saying, 'Why the hell did I do that?' And as I'm thinking that I'm lighting up another one."

He said that at the firehouse, he couldn't get away from what had happened. "Because while you are down there, even though you are in the firehouse, and you close the door, there's no way you can get away from the smell and the noise. You could smell it, feel it, taste it, touch it, and you are there for 24 hours. For 24 hours, you feel like every sense is being assaulted."

On his break, he went up to the bunkroom and lay down for a couple of hours. But every time a crane moved outside, the building shook. He would wake up startled and frightened. He decided that the next time he came to work, he'd sneak in a 6-pack of beer, "just to take the edge off so I can get some rest." He drank one beer, and nothing happened. So he drank two, and then the entire half dozen, but he didn't even get a buzz.

Next time, he brought in a suitcase full of beer and stuck it in his locker. He decided that he would drink them all if that's what it took "to shut my head off." But they didn't help, and for a few tours he drank continually, got no rest, and was wide awake.

Besides the rumble of cranes and the shaking of the building, there was also the air horn. Many of the buildings at the site were damaged structurally. Anytime a building shifted, the air horn went off, and everyone was required to evacuate.

"The problem was they didn't tell you which building had shifted. I remember running one day with another guy from the firehouse, and I was thinking, We don't even know if we're running in the right direction. We might be running toward the building they're worried about."

The first real day back at work, Jimmy couldn't face the pile, that two-story mountain of debris and human remains. He stayed behind the firehouse to "try to insulate and shield myself from it." But there was no escaping the laboring engines, rumble of vehicles, and sounds of digging.

Two tours later, he set out for the pile in a 4-wheel drive golf cart. It was the only way around the site without walking, and he had the job of delivering messages and items people needed.

Before long, he went out on the pile to see what he could do to help. "And I'm being told, 'Ya gotta watch where you're stepping, you gotta make sure there are no voids,' and every time a crane moves, the entire pile shakes. So you start thinking, Well if there's voids and nothing's secure and the crane moves, and drops something, am I gonna get sucked into this friggin' thing? I still hadn't recovered from what I went through on 9/11, and now I'm dealing with this?"

Jimmy felt like he was on a downward spiral. "Between smoking and drinking and all the symptoms... I felt like a boxer that was getting combinations landed on him, and I had no time to breathe. Because of my training with POPPA, I realized I'm heading down a path I really do not want to go down. Because it's gonna start getting very, very dark."

He didn't feel comfortable talking to the other firefighters about his feelings. "At the firehouse, it was a lot of camaraderie, a lot of togetherness, where you're allowed to admit things you're having trouble with. You voice it, and let it go and move on from there, but if you bring it up again, it's like, 'Whoa... What's sa matter with you?'"

He decided to contact the fire department's counseling unit. He felt that the fire department did not have the same stigma as the police department. He was sure he would remain on full duty, and he didn't have to worry about his career.

He told the fire department's therapist that he needed to get out of lower Manhattan temporarily, for as little as thirty days, to get away from the source of his anxiety.

"I just need to get back into a regular firehouse routine where I'm responding to fires. I can't be going down to the Trade Center everyday. I'm not getting any relief," he told the therapist.

The answer he got from the therapist was, "Sorry, we can't help ya."

"That really pissed me off. I told the therapist, 'Your sole function in this thing is to either keep me from full duty or get me back to full duty. I'm telling you exactly what you need to do to attain that, and you're telling me you can't fucking help me?'"

At this point, Jimmy was still a probie and on probation for a year. He hadn't completed his academy training. He hadn't even graduated. So he could be fired at any moment for any reason.

Jimmy told the counselor that he wouldn't go back to work under these conditions, and the counselor said he had to. "I'll be back to work when I feel like I'm ready," he told the counselor.

"I knew that I needed to get my head straight, and there was no way I could keep going down to the Trade Center everyday and be able to take that step forward to recover."

Then Jimmy called a Peer Support Officer at POPPA, and asked who he could see to deal with his trauma. He was sent to therapist Gary Goldberg, who had an office in Brooklyn. Dr. Goldberg diagnosed Jimmy with Acute Stress Disorder (ASD), which has most of the same symptoms as Posttraumatic Stress Disorder, but the symptoms usually do not last longer than thirty days after a traumatic event. If they do last longer, then the therapist may determine that the condition had progressed and become PTSD.

To inform the department that he had a legitimate problem, Jimmy asked Dr. Goldberg to write the fire department a letter about his condition, and Jimmy told his captain that he would be back at work as soon as he was ready and able.

"I'm convinced that the main reason why I addressed the stuff as early as I did was because of the training I received from POPPA. Otherwise, I wouldn't have been open to acknowledging what I was going through. I would have buried it, like a lot of the guys I was working with."

Jimmy's turmoil was caught early, and the time off work and with the therapist "allowed me that breathing room to get back on the right track." He saw the therapist for about two months, and then felt he could now cope on his own.

As a result of his swift action and taking control over his own recovery, Jimmy never developed PTSD. "The bad seed was planted on 9/11, and through therapy, I was able to get it out before it grew deep roots."

Jimmy discovered that "you can go through something so terribly horrific, but if you catch it right away, and you look after yourself and don't try to bury it, you can prevent the worst from happening."

After his recovery, he resumed his involvement with POPPA, and volunteered on the police telephone hotline on a regular rotation to help police officers in trouble. What further helped him heal, however, was talking about the terrible event and its effect on him to audiences of police officers at various commands in the police department.

"I found that the first couple of times I talked about what happened, it was hard, a little emotional, and I could feel the goose bumps on my arms, but the more I did it, the easier it got. So I realized, I gotta keep talking about this."

Jimmy's work with POPPA was only with police officers. The fire department didn't have anything comparable, and when Jimmy explored trying to set something up, he says he was met with too much resistance.

"I felt like I was beating my head against a brick wall. The fire department doesn't have anything non-departmental like POPPA, which is totally independent. You can pick up a phone as a cop, whatever problem you've got, and talk to somebody, and not have to worry about it being in your record at work. No repercussions from the job. The fire department doesn't have that, but it needs it."

As it turned out, Jimmy did not have to finish his fire training. "The department felt that 9/11 trained us," he said. Nevertheless, the department did finally put together a quick graduation class, and Jimmy formally became a firefighter for the city of New York.

After the graduation ceremony, he was asked where he wanted to go. He was a squad leader, having been in the military, and was given preference for his deployment. He chose Brooklyn. That would put him close to home, he knew the area well, and "there were no tall buildings."

After that, "things got a little easier."

Jimmy continued to help out at POPPA, and found other avenues to help firefighters and police officers. He was asked to participate in a series of television public service announcements (PSAs) for the National Institute of Mental Health about men's depression.

His parents were divorced and his father was an alcoholic who also suffered from depression. As a result, Jimmy had experienced "little bouts of depression" during his childhood and early adult life. He didn't mind talking about depression, and felt that the PSAs were an extension of what he was already doing with POPPA, and agreed to appear. The television spots were sent out to stations across the country, and were accompanied by radio ads. When they started to air, he was a little embarrassed.

One day, a firefighter from a neighboring company was detailed to his firehouse. He said to Jimmy, "Listen, I gotta talk to ya. I saw this thing..."

"I knew he meant the ad," said Jimmy, and started to apologize, but then the man "threw me for a loop."

He said, "Well, you know things weren't right with me for awhile, and after I saw you on the thing, I spoke to my family doctor, and he sent me to see a psychologist and I got diagnosed with depression. After awhile, with the therapy and the drugs they put me on, everything's fine now."

When Jimmy did the public service announcements, he thought, *If I help one person, that's all that matters.* "No matter how much I got my balls broke at work. I didn't expect to even find out if I'd helped somebody. That was pretty good."

In 2006, Jimmy was injured in a store fire, and needed surgery on his shoulder. The operation didn't take, and he was told that either he had to have another surgery, or he couldn't work anymore. He'd had surgery on his other shoulder when he was a cop, and a heart problem after 9/11.

He said that somebody from POPPA put everything in perspective for him.

"Maybe it's time you read the writing on the wall," said the POPPA peer support cop.

"What do you mean?" said Jimmy.

"Well, when you were a cop, you had surgery on your shoulder, and you went back to work," said the officer. "9/11 happened, you went back to work. Something happened with your heart, you went back to work.

"So now you hurt your other shoulder. So what are you going to do? You going to go back to work, idiot? Somebody's trying to tell ya to retire."

As well as his injuries, Jimmy was also concerned about what he had inhaled after the collapse of the towers, and later while working down at the Trade Center site.

"I have no idea what toll that will take on me. I've read so many different reports about what was in that stuff, and you see guys dropping like flies. That was actually a thought I had when I was sitting in the Woolworth store getting triage. I thought, I survived 110 stories coming down on my head, so now I'm gonna friggin' wonder what kind of death am I gonna die like five, ten, twenty years from now?"

Jimmy had reason to be concerned. In May, 2008, the names of eight police officers who died after 9/11 as a result of illnesses such as lung disease that they developed from working on the pile were added to the NYPD's Wall of Heroes Memorial.[6]

"So I let them put me out to pasture," said Jimmy. He retired in October 2006 on a physical disability pension, nothing to do with the trauma he experienced on 9/11.

"I try to enjoy whatever time I've got left. Hopefully, it's a lot."

Two weeks after his retirement, Jimmy's first child was born. As far as enjoying life, it doesn't get much better than that.

Chapter 4

9/11
Months or Years Later...

*"I can't eat, I can't sleep, I can't think,
I feel sick. I can't do this anymore."*

Can you develop PTSD months or even years after a traumatic event like 9/11? Without showing any previous symptoms?

The answer is *yes*... and *no*. It depends on who you speak to and which study you read.

The therapist's diagnostic bible known as the DSM-IV-TR says that in "delayed onset PTSD," symptoms first appear at least six months *after* the traumatic event.

And that's where the trouble begins. Delayed onset PTSD is the most controversial type of PTSD.

> ➤ A study of some World War II veterans contends that they did not show symptoms of PTSD until thirty years after the war.[1]
> ➤ Another study describes victims of motor vehicle accidents that showed no symptoms of PTSD until two years after their accidents.[2]
> ➤ In yet another study, at least 10 percent of Israeli soldiers selected for examination who fought in the 1982 Lebanon War had no symptoms of PTSD until six months to five years later.[3]

There are dozens more studies that support similar findings. Yet some medical researchers question whether delayed onset PTSD even exists, arguing that the individual must have had symptoms early on, but didn't recognize them. They also suggest that the PTSD sufferer delayed getting help for months or years, not that the PTSD itself was delayed.

Even though these interpretations have validity, many police officers with no *obvious* previous symptoms do develop PTSD months or years after a traumatic event. The percentage or number of officers who experience this rare type of PTSD is unknown, as this is an area that is underreported, and not well understood.

As an example of delayed onset PTSD, here is the story of a police officer that developed the disorder *five years* after 9/11...

*   *   *

On the morning of September 11th, 2001, thirty-one-year old K9 officer Jonathan Figueroa, was sitting in the unit's Brooklyn office of the New York Police Department having breakfast: a cup of coffee, a bagel. He remembers what he was eating and where he was, as so many of us do on that momentous day seconds before our world changed.

He and his partner were watching the news. A bulletin came on that a plane had crashed into a building, they weren't sure where. They were watching as spectators, not paying a lot of attention.

About fifteen minutes later, his partner said, "Wait a minute. Another plane hit. What's goin' on?"

"The bosses rushed in," says Jonathan, and said "Suit up, this is a major event, we gotta get down there."

They didn't have specialized gear then. Suiting up meant putting on your uniform, riot gear, and helmet. They jumped into their cars and headed toward Manhattan. As they were crossing the Brooklyn Bridge, Jonathan saw people covered in gray dust walking and running over the bridge toward them. In the distance, they saw smoke.

On the way to the World Trade Center, his cell phone rang. It was his wife, and she said that his sister had called, and his brother-in-law, Mario Santoro, an EMT, was already there. She wanted Jonathan to find him and make sure he was okay.

They reached city hall, about three blocks from the Trade Center, and "it was just a cloud of dust. You couldn't see anything. It looked like a major snow storm, a blizzard."

They didn't know that the south tower had crumbled to the ground.

"Then we heard this large boom. It was earth-shaking, and metal twisting. You don't forget that sound because you never heard it before." He was listening to the north tower in the process of collapsing.

The officers got out of their cars, they couldn't go any farther, and started helping people. They came across a fireman having difficulty breathing, and Jonathan was assigned to take him to a hospital.

After Jonathan returned, he went to the Woolworth Building where triage was underway to join the police officers he'd come with. Jonathan asked about his brother-in-law, Mario, but nobody knew anything.

For a few days, his squad was held in reserve. An 11 year veteran, seven of those years in Patrol, and four in the K9 Unit, Jonathan was used to working, not waiting for something to do. "We couldn't even go on the pile. And that's what was so frustrating. You had people from out of state, out of town on the pile. They were on the bucket brigade, looking and searching. We were told to sit tight."

Then he was finally allowed to work the pile. "My whole motivation for going down there was to see if I could find my brother-in-law." Though unlikely, he might still be alive.

"I did the bucket brigade for awhile. You get a line of guys throwing stuff in a bucket, trying to clear debris, trying to dig down. We didn't have enough shovels, and we dug by hand, trying to recover something, somebody.

"On the first day, I found a skull. No flesh, no skin, like right out of a biology science class. I brought it over to a supervisor, and he said, 'We're looking for living people right now, put that down.' And I did.

"Afterwards, I thought, *I just left it there.* We could have given that to somebody and they could have got some DNA from it. I could have put some family member, some husband, some wife, a son, a daughter, a parent, out of their misery and they could have got some closure. To know what happened to their loved one."

When Jonathan started work on the pile, he wore regular clothes, boots, gloves, sometimes knee pads, and masks, but he didn't wear the mask all the time.

"You know, the air is good, the air is no good... Everyday there was a new story."

A month after 9/11, he still had no word about what had happened to his brother-in-law, and his family assumed Mario went down in one of the towers. It was difficult to grieve without a body, without knowing, and this weighed heavily on his mind.

Then, two months almost to the day after 9/11, on November 12, 2001, another unthinkable event occurred. At 9:17 AM, a jetliner with 260 people aboard, exploded just after takeoff, and pieces of the plane and bodies fell into the Queens neighborhoods of Belle Harbor and Rockaway Beach, part of Long Island, fifteen miles from Manhattan.[4]

It was not the result of terrorism, but the effect was just as bad. Everyone on board the plane was killed, as well as five people on the ground. What's more, the Rockaway community was home to many families of New York City firefighters and police officers killed in the twin towers collapse. For the grieving families, it seemed like yet another assault on those who serve and protect.

Jonathan was back at the office when he heard the news, and he was among the first responders to the crash.

"We were recovering the bodies... mothers holding their babies, charred, stuffed in the airplane seats," he said. "You can't block that out. That I definitely never told my wife because at the time we were in the process of adopting a baby boy. We already had a two-year-old daughter. And then I see this. At least at the pile, you weren't really seeing anything."

A few days after the plane crash, a friend of his on a midnight phoned him at home, and told him they had found his brother-in-law in the rubble. His friend was part of the procession that led the body from the pile. At least his family had a body, unlike so many other families. "In an odd way, when you think about all those families that never found a trace of their loved one, this was a blessing." Now they could bury him and mourn.

The pile burned for more than three months, a total of 99 days.[5] One moment, it was clear, and then the next, smoke would billow from several spots at the same time. "This thing was erupting. It was something that I'll take with me to the grave. Never forget something like that."

Jonathan didn't think about what working on the pile was doing to him emotionally and psychologically. "You don't think about it. You just do, and you keep going. You don't stop to think because if you stop to think, you won't be able to do it."

On the pile, Jonathan's main job was as a *spotter*. He would go out with a K9 team consisting of an officer and his dog. His responsibility was to make sure they didn't fall into a void or get hurt. "I was another set of eyes and ears, and hands to help them if they fell." Fortunately, on his watch, nobody got hurt.

But the stress from retrieving body parts day-after-day, the loss of his brother-in-law, and the pain his family was experiencing, built up in him. He didn't realize how frustrated and angry he was becoming.

One morning, he was on his way back to the site, and he was speeding. A state trooper pulled him over, and he showed him his ID and shield.

"Oh buddy, you didn't see me there?" said the trooper.

"No I didn't," said Jonathan, as his anger began to rise to the surface. "You know what I'm doing right now, man?"

"What, you goin' into work?"

"Yeah, I'm going into work. I'm going back to that godforsaken pile."

And the trooper said, "We were all there, buddy."

"Oh, yeah, but are you there right now? I'm still going back."

Jonathan was ready to take out his rage on the state trooper. "I look back now and think, *Wow... Thank God he knew to walk away.* He went back to his car and that was it. Because there's no doubt in my mind that it would have escalated to something terrible. I didn't realize what was going on inside myself."

Jonathan knows now that he was suppressing his emotions about what had gone on. "People at work, we'd sit around, we didn't talk about it. No way. That's icky. Talking about our feelings, our emotions? You're a wuss if you do because we're macho men, we're police officers, we can handle anything, nothing affects us. You stuff your emotions."

But is stuffing your emotions a symptom of PTSD? He was not yet experiencing the classic symptoms of PTSD such as dissociation, nightmares and flashbacks. Were the anger, rage, frustration and suppressing of emotions the first signs that PTSD was growing in him like some monstrous cancer? At this stage, it is unlikely that he would have been diagnosed with PTSD as he did not have sufficient symptoms.

While Jonathan was at the pile, his frustration built. "We weren't recovering anything, we felt like we weren't doing anything. Where are all these people that they're talking about? Day in and day out, I'm asking myself, What the hell am I coming here for? I worked twelve, thirteen, fourteen hours a day, I had to get back to a regular life, you know, pay the bills, have dinner, try to be like everything's normal. And it wasn't."

During this time, his sister and her daughter were staying at his home. "She had lost her husband. I was trying to comfort her, trying to maintain the family. I'm on the pile, I had the plane crash. There's a lot going on but I was doing it. I don't know how I did it.

"Then we were allowed to adopt our boy, but he wasn't sleeping through the night yet. Here I'm up all these hours working and worrying, he's not sleeping either. So even if I wanted to get some sleep, I couldn't. Everything converged at the same time."

Jonathan was on the pile from September 11th to December 17th, 98 hellish days. Then he left the pile, and returned to his normal routine at work, and he wondered, *How do you go back to business as usual? Without dealing with it?* "Fortunately, I was an active guy, I was into working out, running. That was helpful, that was therapeutic to me."

Jonathan kept himself together for years, but eventually, with no counseling or peer support, the symptoms of Posttraumatic Stress Disorder began to emerge.

Five years after 9/11, on January 16th, 2007, he went into work and his sergeant told him that his friend Ronnie, another K9 officer, was hit by a car during his midnight shift. They weren't sure how bad he was, and they were going to see him at the hospital.

"You know, I've seen many cops bandaged, bruised, beat up, in the hospital. So it was just another day to go see how

Ronnie's doing. So we get to the hospital, and he's on a stretcher, and his mother and father come in, his pregnant wife comes in. I saw the emotion with the mom and the dad and the wife, and I got anxious, and that's when it bubbled over. I felt very weird, like Whoa... What's going on here?"

He was at the hospital for a couple of hours, and his wife called about 8 o'clock in the morning. He worried that maybe one of his babies was sick, that something was wrong. She told him that her cousin's wife was killed in a car accident.

"I started feeling shaky and nervous, and right on that day, I spiraled down, and everything from the past came out: 9/11, the plane crash, my brother-in-law, the first homicide I ever saw as a rookie."

That began his night sweats, night terrors, anxiety, panic attacks, dry mouth, aches and pains, heart palpitations, nightmares and flashbacks of horrific images—except he became the victim.

"I was that first homicide on the street. I was my brother-in-law underneath the rubble. I was in the plane crash, strapped to a seat holding a charred baby. My dreams, my nightmares were putting me in all these situations. Every funeral I went to, I was the person in that coffin. I couldn't control it anymore."

For the next three months, Jonathan couldn't sleep, had difficulty eating, and lost weight.

"And I became obsessive-compulsive about death because it seemed like that's all I ever saw. Death on TV, death in my job, death in the newspaper. I couldn't read the paper anymore, I couldn't watch television. I couldn't even listen to music on my way to work because it would make me sad and I'd flashback about any death."

Jonathan began taking days off work. He didn't tell anybody about the turmoil inside him. "Because I didn't know what the heck was wrong with me. Do I have a brain tumor?

"I didn't think depression or anxiety, no way. I figured it would pass. You know, let me get a good night's sleep. I was trying to rationalize it all. Okay, I haven't been sleeping good, I was always tired. So I thought it was lack of sleep because of these nightmares. I didn't know anything about PTSD, that's for sure.

"This came on really fast because I had so much stuff inside of me that I never dealt with in a constructive or in a positive way. A couple of times you go out to the bar with the guys after work, have a couple of beers, but that's not therapy, my friend. We think it is, but that's not therapy."

On a few occasions, Jonathan rushed himself to the hospital in the middle of the night thinking he was having a heart attack. He couldn't breathe, had cold sweats, he was dizzy and hyperventilating. He had CAT scans that showed nothing. The doctor asked him, "You been having any stress? Or anxiety?"

"I said, 'No stress, life is great, life is good.'" The doctor prescribed Xanax, a drug used to treat anxiety and panic disorders. He said, 'Chill out, take a break.' And I was like, What are you talking about?"

After five days with no sleep, Jonathan started acting strange. "I was psychotic. I had no control over the thoughts in my head. This obsessiveness with death, this fear... I was walking around like a zombie, shaking, cotton mouthed, stuttering, I couldn't talk right. I really don't know how people didn't notice. They probably did, but didn't want to say anything.

"I said to myself, I can't take this anymore. I felt physically ill. I had lost 17 pounds, and had diarrhea, stomach cramps, the shakiness. I couldn't lay in bed, I couldn't close my eyes, I was afraid that I wasn't gonna wake up. Even though I did need sleep, I was afraid to go to sleep because I was gonna get these nightmares again.

"I finally decided, I'm gonna get some sleep on my own terms. I'm gonna drag myself into work, I'm gonna go right to my locker, open it up, get my gun—I don't take my gun home—I was gonna put the gun to my head, and pull the trigger. Because I was in so much emotional pain.

"So I got myself into work, I signed in. My focus was blurred, I couldn't read, couldn't concentrate, so I don't know how I did it. I opened my locker..."

On the back of the locker were pictures of his wife and kids. He had just had a baby, and now had four children, including his adopted son. "That's what stopped me. They're gonna think it's their fault. Daddy killed himself, and they'll always have that doubt in their minds. You know, was it because of something I did? I said, I can't do this to them.

"So I slammed my locker shut, and thought, *I need help.*"

He went to his sergeant, and said, "Listen, something's wrong with me, I don't know what it is, I can't eat, I can't sleep, I can't think, I feel sick. I can't do this anymore. Is there someplace I can go, is there something I can do, people I can talk to?"

His sergeant told him about a peer support organization called Police Organization Providing Peer Assistance (POPPA), and told Jonathan to go home and get some rest, he would call POPPA and set something up. "This is my immediate supervisor, my sergeant. A great man, I love him."

The sergeant called Jonathan and gave him the phone number, and "I took the first step, which was really hard. Did I think they were gonna be able to help me? Absolutely not. But I said I have to give it a try, for my wife, for my children."

Jonathan phoned POPPA, and was assigned to a Peer Support Officer (PSO). "This is someone who talks to you, and evaluates you, another police officer. They reassure you it's gonna be okay, I've been through that, this is what we do, we're gonna help you out. Let's get together. They want to meet you, they want to see how you're doin'. And then they ask you if you've had any thoughts of suicide.

"I was honest and upfront and said, 'Absolutely, yeah, yeah. That's why I'm here because that was the last straw for me.' So then they get me over to a psychologist who sits down and talks with me, and he said, 'You got PTSD, without a doubt.'"

The department took Jonathan out of work immediately and put him on sick leave. "They took my gun, and they started me on the path to Wellville."

He went down to the POPPA offices and met the support staff, and discussed the program. He signed a contract that he would take the prescribed medication, not drink, and go to meetings every Thursday, and call every Monday. "I knew that whatever they asked me, I had to do."

In any case, drinking was never an issue. "I was so physically ill, I couldn't even have a glass of wine. I couldn't eat. I couldn't drink. My throat was so dry, my mouth was so dry, I couldn't even swallow food."

To add to his anxiety and obsessive thoughts about death, he had become concerned about dying as a result of working on the pile, and breathing in the noxious air. "There was a retired police officer in the news who was dying from lung cancer that he claimed was because of 9/11, breathing in the dust down there. And he died soon after the interview. So all that was in my head too, thinking, Oh Boy, people are comin' up with lung cancer. I was down there longer than him. I'm definitely gonna die."

At POPPA, he was taught how to deal with his thoughts and feelings. "They gave me the tools to get through life, to get through any situation. They taught me that whatever I'm feeling, I have to communicate, I have to express myself.

"Another great tool I use is journaling. Whenever something triggers a reaction, I write in my journal. I get the obsessive-compulsive thoughts out of my head, and put them down on paper. I deal with the thoughts in the moment.

"After they're on paper, they just don't seem as big as I thought. Writing them out helps to validate my feelings. To say, Okay, this is what I'm thinking, this is what I'm going through. I can get through this. It's there on paper, it's out of my head. Now I'm not obsessing over it all day long. I'm not worried about it. A lot of my stuff was worry, worry, worry, all day long.

"I used to think that if I worried about something, that meant I cared. For me, worry was care. No it's not. I care about things, doesn't mean I have to worry about them. I was able to differentiate. Which I couldn't do before. I know the difference now."

It is not unusual for someone with PTSD to have obsessive-compulsive thinking. "Someone with PTSD is at risk for developing other mental health disorders such as panic disorder, phobias, major depressive disorder, and obsessive-compulsive disorder."[6]

Jonathan still had thoughts about his own death, but was no longer frightened by it. "In fact, it helped my wife and I discuss plans for when I do pass away. I got life insurance policies, she knows what I want done when I do pass away, and that's something no one could even mention to me, I would start shaking, and would freak out.

"But all of that stuff is okay now because I'm not running away from it. I have some control. Talk therapy does work, and group therapy with my peers helps, because there are other people just like me. I thought I was all alone in this situation, but it was happening to others, too, and we're not alone, and we can get through it together. I can't believe what I've been through because I'm feeling so darn good now."

After Jonathan talked to the peer support people at POPPA, he told his wife what he had done, and she was very supportive. "I told her that I had PTSD, and obsessive-compulsive thinking about death. She was understanding, it made sense to her, too. She said, 'Now what do we gotta do about this?'

"They prescribed medication to alleviate the symptoms. Which is the panic attacks, the anxiety and to help me get some sleep—that's what I really needed, to get some sleep, so I can deal with this rationally with a clear head. And I established lines of communication with my wife and with the peer support people."

Today, Jonathan is back to full duty in the K9 Unit. He used to do security, but is now a dog handler. He works with his very own bloodhound and is training a bloodhound puppy. A couple of years after 9/11, he became involved in searching for missing persons, and is on the road with his dogs a lot.

"People say, 'If I can just get back to where I was,' and I think, _No, no... You don't want to go back, you want to get here._ I'm better now, aware, I have some enlightenment. When you come out of this, you come out so much better, so much clearer."

Jonathan still sees a therapist, and is on a low dose of antidepressant. "I'm taking it to get through the winter. Winter is always a bad time for everybody, everybody's down and out.

"Now that I'm back to work, I see the same problems in so many officers. The short tempers, the anger... Everybody's angry at the world. I'm so laid back and enjoying everything. But I can see where a couple of people are gonna crash, and if I can help someone realize that there's help out there, that they're not alone, that they're not the only one going through this, I can save a life. Every life is precious."

The job is important to Jonathan, but he lives for his wife, Dawn, and his kids. Daughter Taylor is nine; Jonathan, the boy he was trying to adopt during 9/11, is six; Justin is five; and baby James is sixteen months.

Let's not forget his bloodhound Kojak, and the blood-hound puppy-in-training, Bella.

"I'm enjoying the job, enjoying life. I really am."

*   *   *

Now we go back to the question posed at the beginning of this chapter. Did Jonathan have delayed onset PTSD five years after 9/11, or did he show enough symptoms early on to imply that he was developing PTSD?

A ground-breaking study conducted by the University of London in 2007 on delayed onset PTSD in the military throws some light on the subject. The study reveals that delayed onsets accounted for almost 40 percent of PTSD in combat troops.

Most importantly, it claims that delayed onset PTSD *rarely* came out of the blue, and that there were usually some prior symptoms, if only we could recognize them.[7]

In Jonathan's case, nobody recognized the symptoms.

As far as police officers are concerned, whether PTSD develops within one month or not for months or years, why does it matter?

If police officers want to make a delayed onset PTSD disability claim, it matters a lot. It may be tough to prove that their PTSD is as a result of a specific incident that happened a long time ago, and that they had no previous symptoms.

Some jurisdictions have a two-year limit on reporting a claim to Workers' Compensation. The problem is in calculating when exactly the clock should start. Usually, the administrators will start from when the "injury" occurred. You will likely want to start from the moment you became *aware* of the PTSD. The end result may be a court case and a lot of anguish.

For instance, consider the delayed onset PTSD claims made by a police dispatcher working for the Wildwood Crest Police Department and by a police officer in the Lower Township Police Department. I can't reveal their names as this is considered confidential information in some states. The dispatcher was on duty when an officer on her watch died of a heart attack. In another incident, a police officer witnessed the death of his partner.

In both New Jersey cases, their claims of delayed onset PTSD to Workers' Compensation four and six years after the traumatic events occurred were denied. Workers Comp said they filed their claims too late.

The dispatcher and officer sued, but lost. Then they filed an appeal, and both received the results on February 21, 2002. The appeals judge determined that because they displayed some symptoms of PTSD shortly after the critical incidents, they did not have delayed onset PTSD.

In other words, the judge started the clock running from a point right after the incidents when the dispatcher and police officer knew or should have known they had PTSD. And because they had filed after the two-year limit allowed by law, they lost their cases and their benefits on a technicality.

As you can see, a claim of delayed onset PTSD can work against you. You may have to prove that you had no symptoms prior to the moment you were diagnosed with delayed onset. The judge said that if they had filed on time, their claims would have been honored.[8]

What this means for police officers is if you have symptoms, don't ignore them. Deal with them at the time. If you repress your feelings, and wait until you can't stand the pain anymore, it may be too late to file for a delayed onset PTSD disability.

Chapter 5

Drugs

"The psychos like to work midnights."

"I was sittin' in my unit smoking cocaine thinkin' if I get caught I'm gonna go to prison, and then looking at the coke thinking, 'Long as I got this, I don't need anything else.' My life revolved around getting and usin' cocaine. Bottom line is nothing else mattered.

"I lost weight. I'd wear the same clothes days in a row. I'd gone from Mister Health Nut to somebody smoking cigars. I had Bic thumb, my thumb and fingers rubbed raw and had cuts in them from flicking the Bic lighter and burned fingertips and fingernails.

"The worse for me was I was driving down the street in my car smoking cocaine and I blacked out. The car was drifting down the side of the road. I wake up and my shirt's on fire. I pull off to the side of the road. I had a beer, because I always drank when I smoked coke, and I put the fire out on my shirt with it, shook my head and thought, 'That was a great high,' and lit the pipe right back up again."

When I pulled into John Jenks' tree-lined driveway in the small California town of Ojai, I knew what to expect. Detective Bill Martin, with John's approval, had briefed me on the officer's history—his drug addiction, alcoholism and propensity for violence. I worried about meeting a bear of a man with wild eyes and rebellious hair, dressed in jeans and steel-nosed cowboy boots. I expected to shake a crushing hand and be scrutinized by a cynical gaze.

Instead, I was greeted at the door by a boyish-looking man with peaceful eyes, a warm smile and a friendly handshake. We went into his home office where he was on the phone. He apologized for the delay, asking me to sit. I wasn't listening to his subdued conversation, but I couldn't help observing the tone of his voice, the concern and nurturing it expressed. He spoke like a mentor, a guru, dispensing compassion and wisdom, a teddy bear providing solace. Indeed, he was all those things. Since his dismissal from the police department, he had become a counselor, dedicating himself to helping other fallen cops.

I've always been curious about what makes somebody violent, how somebody could actually strike another human being in anger or as a function of duty. Since the Rodney King trials, newspapers and books have expounded upon this issue in great depth. Now here in front of me on the phone comforting others was a former cop who had unjustly beaten people and admitted it. Here was a cop who had engaged in violence, drugs, alcohol and sex to relieve the pain from *something*.

From where did the violence come? What drove him? Detective Bill Martin told me that John had developed Posttraumatic Stress Disorder from suppressing his feelings about multiple traumatic events he experienced during his police career. Yet surely there was something, some incident, some confrontation that pushed him toward using violence to solve problems. Or was he primed for disaster before he became a cop?

If he had worked in a high-crime city like Los Angeles or New York, I could readily understand how extreme traumas might push him toward alcoholism and violence. Except John was a small-town cop. Where he worked didn't generate the volume of grisly crimes like the big city. Psychologists say all it takes is one bad incident to ruin an officer's life, one terrible event to kickstart the stressful reactions that induce PTSD. Whether a small town or big city doesn't matter.[1]

John hung up the phone and apologized again. He had a client who needed attention in a couple of hours, so we got right down to the first of what was to be many talks.

"What led to your developing Posttraumatic Stress Disorder?" I asked. "And how did drugs, alcohol and violence become part of it?"

He exhaled, pushed back in his chair and became thoughtful. His peaceful, blue-green eyes darkened with melancholy. "This is a long story," he said. He explained that his spiral toward self-destructive behaviors started right from the beginning in 1975 when, at twenty, he joined the Ojai police force. He wasn't ready to face the misery, the dead and the dying.

"Let's start with alcohol," I said.

"When I got out of academy, I did a lot of partying with the boys," he said, "and if you didn't drink with the guys, you weren't one of the guys. We called them wolf parties or choir practices. That's what real men, real cops did. And the drunker and crazier you got, the more accepted you were."[2]

John told me that choir practice is a well-honored and celebrated occasion in police circles, a popular coping tool. After work, officers hyped up from the day, gather at a bar to let off steam telling war stories. Alcohol relieves anxiety briefly, but rather than easing the buildup of stress, it can eventually increase it, sometimes leading to alcoholism.

He told me, "We used to stand around in bars laughing, 'Someday we're gonna be alcoholic.' I'd go out drinkin' all night, get a couple of hours sleep and then go to work."

John said that since the age of fifteen he drank a lot. Once he became a cop he drank obsessively. "If it was a good day, we drank. If it was a bad day, we drank."

"How much would you drink?" I asked.

"I was a big Long Island ice tea drinker, a mixed drink of vodka and rum. In the course of an evening, it was nothing for me to drink ten or twelve ice teas or a couple six packs of beer."

Apart from peer pressure, I wanted to know why John drank and how drinking related to PTSD. What was he trying to bury or forget? To explain, he presented me with a long list of traumatic incidents that he often relives in nightmares. When he was a cop, he tried to suppress his feelings about them and that's what made him drink and do a lot of things he's not proud of. These horrible incidents are what being a cop is all about, he said, and "why policing is damned debilitating."

The first traumatic scene occurred the Christmas of 1975. A drunk truck driver smashed into a tree. Fresh out of school and a rookie, John broke out the passenger window with his baton to render first aid. Surrounded by crushed gifts, the passenger was almost decapitated, the head attached by a flap of skin, and blood was everywhere.

Shortly after that, John came upon a motorcycle accident where a biker went off the road. The force of the crash almost tore his head off. Facing two similar grisly and hopeless situations in a short period of time shook John up. He began asking himself whether being a cop was such a great idea. John was an optimistic, high-energy person, with a strong desire to help people. Policing was not working out the way he had hoped.

Soon a confrontation became the pivotal point of his career, and it answered my question about whether some incident had pushed him toward using violence as a problem-solving tool.

He had stopped a drunk driver recently released from the county jail. John was now on the streets a year and a half. At a mere 5 foot 10, 145 pounds, he believed himself indestructible. He told me, "I had the blue uniform, the badge and bullets bounced off my chest."

The drunk ex-con, buffed up and muscled from pumping iron in the prison weight room, took one look at John's meager frame and said, "You're not taking me back to jail."

"Yes, I am," replied John. He reached around for his handcuffs, taking his eyes off the suspect for a second. The criminal slugged him, breaking his jaw.

A couple of sheriff's deputies arrived as backup at the moment John went down. They jumped the assailant and cuffed him.

One deputy, a twelve-year veteran, took out a sap, a flat, lead-filled leather sheath. He was going to work the man over.

"Hey, King's X," said John, calling for a time out. "You don't hit somebody who's handcuffed."

"Listen Rookie..." said the seasoned cop. "You'll learn."

"The guy's done wrong, he'll be punished," insisted John.

John was wrong. His attacker got probation. And John quickly came to the realization that if this was how the justice system worked, he was not going to let anyone hurt him again. "From now on," he said, "I'm gonna hurt them before they hurt me."

I think it's rare in anybody's life to remember the beginning of a process, and say, _This is when my desire to help people changed. This is when I started to become cynical._ But John recognized the process the moment it started, even though he couldn't stop its progress. He told me this was the moment he decided to turn against the world, against you, me, everyone.

To accomplish his new goal—hurting them before he got hurt—John went into body building, going from 145 pounds to 185 pounds in a couple of years. He redefined the slogan, _to serve and to protect,_ to mean, "I'm here to take assholes to jail and make society safe."

With today's violent crime, perhaps that perspective doesn't sound too bad. Except who decides who the "assholes" are and who makes up society? Aren't we supposed to be equal under the law? Ultimately, John evolved into a cop whom people feared. He told me, "I became big and bad, irritable, angry, very judgmental."

The few years John spent in the relatively quiet community of Ojai was a period of growing pessimism and distrust. Going from one traumatic incident to another, from shock to shock, he determined he couldn't really help anybody, and no one wanted his help anyway.

In 1979, he transferred to another California small town of under 20,000 people, Port Hueneme, a rough and tumble working-class town of warehouses, factories and vegetable fields, known for prostitution, drugs, muggings and shootings. "In Ojai, you drove around in a patrol car and people waved to you," he said. "In Hueneme, people flipped you off."

Stressed all the time, John continued to suppress his reactions to traumatic events. He was on the streets of Port Hueneme a few months when he was called to a crime scene that's forever burned into his memory. Today when he shuts his eyes, he can see every detail. Sometimes he doesn't have to shut his eyes. The scene is just _there_ in front of his face, running like a movie, and he can't turn it off.

A man had reported hearing screams from an apartment in his building. John arrived and pushed open the door to the presumed source of the noise. A blood trail crossed the living room floor, and he followed it to the balcony doorway. A woman lay there face down.

He carefully turned her over. "She had bullet holes everywhere." Doing what he could to stop the flow, his uniform was soon soaked with blood.

"What's your name?" he asked.

"Rose," she managed to choke out.

"You're gonna be okay, Rose."

Rose[3] was not going to be okay, and he knew it. After the paramedics arrived and took her away, John "had a feeling of total helplessness."

The night's job was only beginning. The Detective Sergeant in charge sent John to the hospital to secure evidence. The assignment was a feather in the cap of a streetcop wanting to make detective someday. John was told to get bullets, clothing, hair and skin from under the victim's fingernails. The task was a piece of cake.

It was. And it wasn't.

Upon entering the Emergency Room, he saw Rose stretched out on a polished silver table. She was naked, washed and scraped like a piece of raw meat. After all the blood, he marveled that "she didn't look bad." He shivered, but it wasn't cold in the room.

Her eyes were open, wandering, as if watching her own life drift away. John was told she had been shot repeatedly with a .357 Magnum. He thought rounds from that monster weapon would make enormous holes. To his surprise, the entry wounds were small. And there were only three. In the stomach, the head, and the heart. The last two looked fatal.

John collected the evidence, left the ER and called the Detective Sergeant.

"I've got the stuff. They're about to operate," he said.

"Good. Now, you have to get a dying declaration."

"Sure," said John, never having done the task before.

"What she says is hearsay in court," said the supervisor, "unless she identifies the guy that shot her—knowing she's gonna die."

"Sarge, I can't tell her she's gonna die." John was barely out of his teenage years, only twenty-four years old. "Can't you send a detective up?"

"You caught the case," his boss said.

"Man, I don't wanna take away her will to live."

"Don't let me down, John."

"This sucks."

John returned to the ER and pulled the doctor aside. "Doc, I gotta get a statement, but I'm afraid I'll put her over the edge."

"I don't think what you say will make any difference," said the doctor.

Biting his lower lip, John drew near the table. "Rose? I'm a police officer. Do you realize that?"

"Yes."

"You've been shot... Do you understand you are going to die?"

"Yes."

John noticed her face was impassive, showing no pain, no fear, no future. He leaned into her ear and whispered.

"Tell me who did this to you, and I'll nail the son-of-a-bitch."

With what seemed a last breath, she told him her assailant's name. Then attendants wheeled her into surgery. She was as good as dead. Nevertheless, the dying declaration was a success.

John went to a cop bar with the guys that night. That's what "real cops" did when things got tough. He didn't talk about how Rose affected him. He couldn't, not in front of other cops, not in front of anybody. Yet in the back of his mind he thought about her every minute.

Afterwards at home, he felt like his stomach was stuffed with sand. He couldn't eat. His throat stayed dry no matter what he drank. When he tried to sleep, he had nightmares. He saw her wandering blue eyes. He saw the dark holes and the dark blood. He feared he had helped kill an innocent person.

Rose lived, however, and in a story in the newspaper a few days later, said she was furious with the cop who told her she was going to die.

Despite arresting the attacker, John felt like a jerk. He had tried to save her. When he thought there was no hope, he had grieved for her. Now he felt guilty for doing what he was told, doing something he knew in his heart was morally wrong. *How could she have lived?* he wondered. There was so much blood.

When can we say PTSD took a hold on John? Was it now? Probably not. We recognize the growing evidence like nightmares and insomnia. These are possible signs of PTSD. His feeling of intense helplessness also falls within PTSD's guidelines.

Inability to eat, excessive drinking and growing cynicism may precede the condition and promote its progress. They may even appear after PTSD's onset as a reaction to it. But they are not considered symptoms of PTSD, only associated features of the disorder.

We know John was traumatized by the shooting. He was still feeling the effects of previous traumatic experiences such as the bloody vehicle accidents he had witnessed. Despite that, his reactions at this point would not have satisfied the criteria for PTSD. With time, John's distress might have eased if it were not for his exposure to more traumatic events and his tendency toward burying his feelings about them.

After trying to help Rose, John was soon up to his elbows in blood again. He was called to more fatal car accidents and suicides. And every time he realized there was nothing he could do, they took pieces out of him.

Like the suicide of an Asian woman with cancer who had hung herself in the garage. When John arrived, her husband, an ex-military man, was watching her hang from the rope, making no effort to cut her down. John admired how he kept his composure. In examining the body, John thought, *This is like TV, realistic. She looks like a mannequin.*

John told me he was distancing himself, gradually losing the ability to identify with victims, a sign of compassion fatigue or perhaps PTSD. Like many police officers, detaching emotionally was the only way John thought he could subdue traumatic images.

A defense mechanism, detaching is achieved by changing the "perception of reality."[4] It occurs when the police officer separates "an idea or object" from its emotional meaning. Then, when he gets home from work, he can't seem to turn his feelings back on. To his family, friends and neighbors, he appears aloof, unresponsive and unloving.

Looking back at his years as a police officer, John says he became a cop who was indifferent to everybody. Despite that, in 1980, after five years in policing, John married. He recalls his wife's affirmation about his job. She said, "I love you enough I'm willing to be second in your life behind your career."

She unintentionally gave him license to do whatever he wanted, to destroy their relationship, to destroy himself.

John was already drinking obsessively. As the body count increased, his actions were becoming more self-destructive. The same year he got married, he started taking anabolic steroids, a controlled substance, to increase the size of his build and, he believed, to give himself more energy. He got them at his gym where members dealt them on the black market.

"Did people at work know you took steroids?" I asked John.

"People knew. There'd be jokes around the DA's office. My Lieutenant said, 'Jenks, you're not stupid enough to take steroids, are you?'

" 'No, Lieutenant,' I said. 'Not me.' "

John told me anabolic steroids gave him an intense feeling of well being. He was soon psychologically dependent on them.

Anabolic steroids are synthetic derivatives of testosterone, a male hormone. Body builders use them to get "big and strong," though much of the weight gain is due to fluid retention. The drugs do increase lean muscle mass. They do not, however, enhance athletic ability, as many athletes swear, nor do they increase energy.[5]

From research, I learned that the anabolic steroids John was using are nothing to fool with. Improperly used, they can kill. They may cause liver failure and can dramatically increase the risk of coronary artery disease. Among many other problems, users may develop insomnia, depression, nausea, diarrhea and bleeding, and some conditions are irreversible.[6]

I asked John whether anabolic steroids affected him negatively. He told me he handled them cautiously at first. He cycled on for six weeks, then off for six to allow his internal organs to detoxify. In spite of that, he developed acne and suffered from occasional impotence. He said that the most toxic anabolic steroids were the ones that gave him the best results. His weight expanded to an imposing 235 pounds, and he became strong enough to bench press 350 pounds many times without getting tired.

When citizens encounter police officers abusing 'roids, as anabolic steroids are popularly called, the situation can turn ugly. Men and women on 'roids, especially those who exceed recommended dosages like John, sometimes become unexpectedly angry, aggressive and violent.

The violence may come from 'roid rage, an impulsive, uncontrollable fury that overcomes the drug user, although researchers are debating the likelihood of this reaction. In John's experience, 'roid rage is real enough. Consequently, before a police officer on steroids realizes what he's done, he may brutally beat or kill someone.

I asked John about his behavior on steroids. He said that sometimes his moods swung from manic invincibility to states of anxiousness and depression. He became angry for no reason and frequently got into off-duty bar fights. On-duty, he was often spoiling for a fight.

"I went to the worst areas to take assholes to jail," he told me, "where the parolees were, the pimps, the hookers. I wore sap gloves. The gloves had soft lead in the knuckles so I could really nail somebody, backhand them and injure them. I was into wearing short sleeve shirts and black sap gloves at night. You know, the macho image. And all the guys that I associated with, my work patrol, were the same.

"I also carried a flat sap and a big, heavy, metal flashlight I cracked heads with. Sometimes I used mace when I was pissed off at people."

"Did the effects of anabolic steroids cause you to become violent?" I asked.

"A combination of steroids and alcohol," he said. "My attitude was if somebody wants to fight a cop, it might as well be me, 'cause I like to do it, and I can take care of myself. So I was in a lot of fights and a lot of them I egged people into."

John told me that one year a serial rapist in the south end of town was attacking older women. John wanted the arrest in a big way.

"I was working midnight shift to midnight shift and it was nuts. All the crazy cops work midnights. The ass kickers, the rookies and the psychos. The psychos by choice. They like to work it because they can get away with murder.

"We caught the rapist during a foot pursuit and I started to beat the shit out of him. One of the cops grabbed me and said, 'It ain't worth it, man. It ain't worth it.' Well, I lost it on that guy. I would have beat him to death if given an opportunity."

On another occasion, John, then a ten-year veteran, was out on patrol with a rookie. They picked up a suspect for drunk and disorderly. As John was shoving his handcuffed prisoner into the back of the car, the drunk kicked him.

John dove in on top of him and beat him. "Help me, help me," screamed the man. "Somebody help me!" Nobody did.

"Why did you let yourself go like that?" I asked.

"I just went off," said John. "The rookie had this startled look on his face. And after I got done beatin' on the guy, the rookie got in the car and we drove back. We took him into booking and I told the rookie, 'You know, a real cop can beat somebody and then get him to thank him for it later. Watch the way I get this guy to thank me for not hurting him worse than I did.'"

As John predicted, the man thanked him.

"It kinda made me think I was doin' the right thing. I went off more than a couple of times doin' that."

John had a few unsubstantiated complaints for excessive use of force during his career. Internal Affairs never had enough to charge him with although the allegations, John said, "were true."

I do not condone John's use of violence. Looking back on it, he, too, shudders when he thinks about his behavior. I was not interviewing him to judge his past actions. I was there to try to understand what motivated him.

This is where the story gets confusing. I believe that alcohol and anabolic steroids drove John to commit acts of violence. So does he. Yet that presumption is too convenient and simple. There are other factors, deeper conditions that made John do what he did. There are causes behind the drinking and drugging. John told me that what also motivated him to act aggressively was fear. Fear of being thought weak, powerless or out of control.

It's known that "denial or suppression of fear can lead to over aggressiveness."[7] John was a master at suppressing his feelings, fear in particular.

Another factor that seriously affected John was hypervigilance. The concept of hypervigilance needs some explanation here since the condition is found in varying intensities in most police officers. Hypervigilance is a heightened state of awareness that can arise from having to be super-alert, super-vigilant, as a result of being "bombarded with constant frustration, negativity and unappreciativeness."[8]

There's a saying that "police work gets in the blood" and it's true physiologically. The extremely hypervigilant police officer's brain constantly orders adrenaline discharged into the blood. Adrenaline gushes through the body. The heart thrashes against the chest. Blood pressure soars. The officer wants to run, fight or freeze. It's the stress response at work.

He wants to see something, do something, beat the hell out of something. This is how John felt. Hypervigilance is part of the cycle of PTSD symptoms. Some research psychologists define PTSD *primarily* as a state of constant hypervigilance, arousal or excitement.[9]

The hypervigilant police officer loses the "capacity to discriminate which citizens are genuinely threatening to (his/her) safety and which are not." This causes the officer to "lump all non-police types into the same untrustworthy category."[10] Like John, many police officers begin to see everyone, criminal or good citizen, as threatening, as "them versus us." Consequently, it's not hard to imagine that a cop might overreact to a situation as John did and beat people sometimes for no reason.

Hypervigilance, fear, drinking, drugging, detachment, suppression of intense reactions to traumatic incidents—all of these factors can combine to contribute to a personality that might commit violence. They can promote the development of Posttraumatic Stress Disorder. But there's still more to the picture.

I don't know everything that's behind John's anger, fear and frustration. For this I must go back to his life before his police career and look at his upbringing to see if it offers clues to the police officer he would become. I must answer the question posed earlier, _Was he primed for disaster before he became a cop?_

John Jenks grew up the youngest of three children in an Irish Catholic family where expressing strong emotions, anger or happiness, was forbidden.

On the surface, the Jenks family behaved like other upper-middle-class families, but John hid a terrible secret. His father was an alcoholic. As a child of one, John told me he felt compelled to develop behaviors and attitudes that would maintain order in his life. He needed to control; he had low self-esteem, accepting failure more than success; he was willing to maintain peace at any cost; he tried hard to please others no matter how much they hurt him. A perfectionist, he carried all these self-destructive qualities into police work where he could never live up to his impossible standards.

When John's father, Patrick,[11] came home from work, he was usually intoxicated. He would sit in a chair and withdraw into himself. John said his father kept all his feelings pent-up inside, and John thought that was how you were supposed to handle emotions.

John also learned from his father that drinking excessively was normal and acceptable. That doubles the odds that John, too, would become an alcoholic.[12] John is convinced he inherited a biological and psychological predisposition from his father to getting hooked on self-medicating drugs.

When it comes to John's mother, John has mixed feelings about what she did or didn't do. His father's passivity forced Mary Jenks[13] into both parenting roles, making her a stern disciplinarian. The only way John could get approval from his father was by engaging in action, doing things like sports. He couldn't get loved solely because he was his son. Like her husband, Mary offered John conditional love. If he did things her way, only then she would show she loved him.

Mary was a devout believer in the Church. Because his mother wanted him to, John believed in God. During his twelve years as a police officer, however, he lost his faith. "I lost complete contact with Him because God didn't exist in a world this horrible."

When John Jenks joined the police department, he wanted to belong, needed to belong. In the exclusive subculture of policing, he found the comfort and acceptance he never got at home.

"Why did policing work for you?" I asked.

"At the academy, they drill into you, 'Take control.' Growing up in a family where I felt totally out of control, what a great line of work to go into where they tell you, 'You're in control.'

"What a great profession for a child from a dysfunctional family where you were not able to have emotions. You couldn't be angry, you couldn't be happy. And then you're told, 'Don't show emotions. Hold in your emotions.' What a great place to practice what I grew up with.

"Being in law enforcement gave me unconditional love and acceptance by other men which I didn't get from my dad."

This was a glimpse into John's childhood and adolescence, and I can now add to the picture I've been developing. Having low self-esteem, feeling unloved, a perfectionist who could never achieve his goals, schooled in suppressing feelings and drinking excessively, John entered the police force. To him it was a perfect union, but he was destined to fail.

John did everything, he thought, to be a better cop. To function properly, he drank to lessen the pain from suppressing his feelings. He took steroids to make himself into a big, strong cop. He said he didn't realize what he was doing to himself.

As with alcohol, he had become not merely psychologically addicted to anabolic steroids, but physically as well. When he cycled off steroids, he became depressed and lost his feeling of invincibility. His joints ached and he became smaller. Other people hardly noticed any change. John noticed. Weight and muscle loss, no matter how insignificant, frightened him.

Withdrawal also led to anxiety, so he would increase his standard anxiety reducer, alcohol. Soon, he was dependent on alcohol, needing more and more for less and less effect. And then the alcohol stopped working, instead producing insomnia, more depression and the condition he was trying to halt, anxiety.

John became an undercover narcotics' officer in 1983. A year or two later, he couldn't endure the withdrawal symptoms from steroids any longer. He gradually cycled off them for shorter and shorter periods until he remained on them most of the year, ignoring what reason told him was hazardous to his health. The combination of year round anabolic steroids and alcohol became a deadly mood bomb ready to detonate at any moment. He was already self-destructive in his substance abuse. Now he became reckless, dangerous to others as well as to himself.

"How were you reckless?" I asked.

"When you buy dope, you do it in a systematic way. You have backups set up. You're wired with a transmitter. People know what's goin' on and we've got a game plan if somethin' goes wrong. We were a family unit and we depended on each other for our lives."

Then John told me the story of a drug buy episode that nearly got him killed. One night a dope dealer paged him in a bar where he was drinking with officers from another department. She told him she was "holding." She had drugs for sale. Feeling bulletproof, he asked his drinking buddies to back him up.

On the way, John stuck a palm-sized tape recorder in the front of his pants and a small AMT .380 automatic in his back pocket. When they arrived at an apart-ment complex, an electronic security gate barred their way.

John rang the apartment and the dealer buzzed him in—alone. He knew it was a bad move, but alcohol and steroids made him think he could do anything, no matter how dumb, and get away with it.

This is not smart, thought John. _Backup can't get in quickly. I'm not wired. How will they know if I'm in trouble?_

As he wandered through the courtyard, someone called his name. "You J.J.?" John turned to face a big Samoan with hands like a sumo wrestler.

"Yeah, I'm J.J."

"Come on in."

John was expecting to buy dope from a woman he didn't consider a threat, not from an unknown man the size of a house. But he went into the apartment anyway.

"This old biker chick is sittin' there cuttin' up speed at the table," he told me.

"Sit down," she said. The Samoan was somewhere behind him. John wondered if he had a gun.

"Whaddaya want?" she asked.

"An eight-ball, nothin' big." He put his money down. The dealer chopped up some of the amphetamine.

"Here, have a line," she said.

The police administration did not allow undercover to use drugs or pretend to use them.

"No thanks. I'm trying to cut down."

"Do a line," she said, suspiciously.

"I don't want one."

"I think you're a cop."

"Look, I'm on parole," bluffed John. "If I use and test dirty, I'm goin' back. This is for business."

"See if he's got a gun or a badge," she said to the towering Samoan.

John told me he didn't know what to do. He thought if he went for the gun in his back pocket, the Samoan would shoot him dead. On pure nerve, he stood up, eyed the giant behind him and said, "Fuck you."

He turned back to the dealer. "And fuck you too!"

He snatched up his money. "This is bullshit."

As he crossed to the door, she said, "No, no. Ya gotta be careful, ya know."

John trembled as he bought the dope and left. When he got to the car, he told the officers waiting, "I was gonna die for an eight-ball," one-eighth ounce, worth then maybe $225.

John and the officers returned to the bar and got very drunk. John berated himself for being stupid, as he did after most operations no matter how they turned out. "As a perfectionist, I would constantly analyze how I performed and downgrade myself for when I didn't respond appropriately." The more he criticized, the more fear he aroused in himself. The more fearful he grew, the more extreme his acts became.

The mismanaged drug buy was a red flag. Although a high producer and a respected cop, achieving many good arrests on the dope detail and being awarded Officer of the Year four times, John's personality and work habits became erratic. He exhibited little restraint. "I was getting un-controllable, surly, rebellious."

Concerned about his behavioral changes, his superiors withdrew him from drug enforcement and temporarily demoted him to patrol as a field training officer (FTO). While in this assignment, John began to realize his actions were jeopardizing his life.

At three one morning, he and his partner responded to a 5150, code for a mentally ill subject.

Approaching a small, rundown house on the southside of town, the two cops heard "terror-filled screams." They took up positions on either side of the door. John knocked.

A woman in her seventies opened the door. "My son... He's lost his mind," said the woman.

John stepped inside the doorway. He could see a haggard man about fifty years old in the kitchen. His back was to the officer and he was screaming at the walls.

"Get outta here!"

He glanced over his shoulder at John. He had hollow, goofy eyes, John said, and was white as a ghost. Sweat ran down his face.

"It's okay," John said. "We'll take care of it."

Warning bells went off in the officer's brain, except as usual he ignored them. He ignored what training and instinct told him was perilous and advanced slowly.

When he was halfway across the kitchen, the man spun around, leveling a rifle on John. On the move, John drew his 9mm Smith & Wesson.

"I'm gonna kill you! Get 'em outta here!" the man said.

"We're the police," John said gently. "We're gonna get rid of the bad guy."

The man lowered the gun a fraction. The officer knew his partner was behind him but didn't know where. John figured he'd dropped back to cover, which is what he should have done.

I outta blow this guy away, he thought. *But I can't kill him in front of his mother.*

Talking quietly, John took a few small steps closer and jumped him. He ripped the rifle out of his hands and cuffed him.

The Peace Officers' Association of Ventura County awarded John and his partner the Medal of Valor. At the awards ceremony, Judge Fredrick A. Jones brought his two sons up to meet John. They wanted a hero's autograph on their programs.

"I got my medal for not killin' someone," John told me, "and I took shit from my supervisor because procedure said I shoulda blown the asshole away." Depending on whom you talked to, John was either courageous or foolhardy.

As John advanced in his career, his actions grew bolder and more careless. He willfully put himself in harm's way. This is not an uncommon method for a police officer to attempt suicide, dying a hero in-the-line of duty. And from all appearances, John wanted to kill himself.

Why? Possibly from feelings of hopelessness, helplessness and depression. When risk-takers like John suffer from depression, they may become self-destructive.[14]

"I had periods of serious depression," he said. "Not finding any pleasure in life. If it wasn't exciting, it was no emotion. There's no doubt in my mind now a lot of it was from the things I was encountering and not dealing with as a cop. Suppressing and self-medicating, that was just its surface. Underlying was a lot of pain."

One morning, John could not get out of bed. "My back blew out." Two discs had ruptured, the result of getting hurt during years of fights and pursuits. After surgery, unable to perform aggressive acts, the department dropped him into the detective division on light duty.

The detective assignment provided John with some quiet time for assessing his behavior, an introspective period that he didn't want or use. He longed for the excitement of heroin raids. "I loved kicking in doors. It was exciting and a big honor."

After his back healed sufficiently, he returned full-time to the narcotics' unit, and an incident quickly made it clear that his behavior had not improved. If anything, it had worsened.

John was the first person through the door in a suspected drug den. While he rushed through the apartment, he came upon several men watching television in the living room. One jumped up and ran down the hallway toward the bathroom. John charged after him, grabbing him as he flushed heroin down the toilet. He hooked him up and marched him back.

In the living room a man was lying on the floor. He was cuffed and a cop was holding a .45 he had taken from the man's belt. When John's drug team broke into the apartment, John had run past this man, not noticing his pistol. The patrol officer behind John saw it and coldcocked the gunman before the suspect could pull it. Realizing his error, John was dumbfounded at his own negligence, at how he had endangered everyone's life.

"I was getting sloppy. I was at the point where I was living on the edge."

In the context of PTSD, John was indulging in self-destructive and suicidal acts, flagrant indicators of the progress of the disorder. But self-destructive and suicidal behaviors do not cause PTSD. They may be reactions to the condition or to an unrelated event in a person's life. At this point, we cannot say, even with all his other symptoms, that John definitely had PTSD.

Shortly after the heroin raid, John experienced a trauma that finally pushed him off the delicate precipice on which he was balancing into more pronounced symptoms of Posttraumatic Stress Disorder. It was another in the long list of traumatic episodes that piled up over time, except this incident was different than the others. John was no longer able to bury his feelings, and they erupted like a firestorm. This pivotal moment marked the beginning of the end.

His supervisor pulled him out of the dope detail to work robbery/homicide. Called in the middle of the night to investigate a shooting, he arrived at the crime scene, the drive-through booth of a USA gas station. John was tired and hung over from drinking. He saw blood and brains splattered on the windows, the counter and the cash register. He was feeling shaky and didn't want to do the crime scene. But what choice did he have?

Paramedics had transported the victim, a gas station attendant, to St. John's hospital. Somebody had shot him with a 12-gauge shotgun, twice in the upper torso, once in the head. Remarkably, the attendant was alive, and once again the Sergeant ordered John to the hospital to get a dying declaration.

Suddenly, John interrupted the interview. "Would you mind turning the tape recorder off?"

I did as he asked.

John shut his eyes and stopped talking. After a moment of what I thought was silence, he told me his heart was pounding, his stomach was upset, and he was having flashbacks of other crime scenes. He had trouble, he said, whenever he thought about this incident. After a glass of water and some antacids, John wanted to go on. There was no point in delaying the telling, so he resumed his story.

At the hospital, John was led to a gurney outside the operating room. Part of the attendant's face was blown away by the shotgun blast, but what really got to John was the man's age, around thirty-three, his whole life ahead of him.

"What's with the guy?" John asked a nurse.

"He's alive, more or less."

"What's his name?"

The nurse looked at John like, *Does it really matter?* "Keith,"[15] she said.

"How can I talk to him? He has no mouth."

"We've communicated by getting him to blink his eyes, once for '*yes*,' two for '*no*.'"

John leaned over the gurney, sucked in his breath and began. "Keith, do you realize you are gonna die? Blink your eyes."

The eyes blinked once. He knew he was dying.

"Do you know who shot you?"

They blinked twice.

"Is it a man?"

They blinked once.

"Can you describe him?"

They blinked, *yes.*

"Is he bigger than you?"

Yes.

"About my size?"

No response. His eyelids had turned to stone. John watched the nurse wheel him through the swinging doors of the operating room. Within an hour, the young man was dead.

John learned the victim was a college student working part-time at the gas station. John took Keith's clothes, covered in blood and brain matter, outside where he tried to bag them. He threw up several times and cried.

Although the police captured the killer, no amount of justice would set officer John Jenks right again. The insane murder sent him into a free fall. He told me, "I don't think the human psyche has the ability to deal with some things."

This was the breaking point for John, the point at which I believe he demonstrated symptoms that could be considered full-blown Posttraumatic Stress Disorder. Nightmares about the man with the face blasted away began that night. They led to a succession of other bad dreams about the drunk trucker who was almost decapitated, the motorcyclist who smashed into a tree, the woman shot with a .357, the Asian woman hanging.

John's bed was soaked with sweat in the morning, and he never really slept well again. He became overwhelmed with fear, helplessness and grief. When he was awake, images of traumatic moments from his police career played out before his eyes. They flashed like scenes in a video. He tried to pretend they didn't happen, loading himself with alcohol to trick his mind. But he knew they happened.

He became ill. He couldn't keep his food down, and he experienced severe heart burn and stomach cramps. He developed colitis, had frequent bouts of diarrhea and got chest pains so bad he thought his heart would burst. In a sense, it already had.

His heart was racing from frequent adrenaline rushes and his blood pressure was up. Adrenaline rushes came when he felt in danger, which was now most of the time.

"When one of my young kids vomited," he told me, "the smell took me right back to bagging the man's clothes. I could drive down the street where the crime occurred and it flashed. If I saw ketchup, I flashed back on the blood and brains. All my senses were acute. I would jump at loud noises, firecrackers, backfires, screaming. I was hyper-vigilant."

Throughout his career John had been in a persistent state of hypervigilance. When he would get home from work, he would be exhausted as nobody can sustain a prolonged adrenaline rush. At the same time, an overly hypervigilant officer like John often finds the family dull compared to his job and gets depressed. To recreate the 'high' from work, sometimes officers will indulge in abusive drinking and promiscuity.[16]

Shortly after the USA gas attendant died, John started having a relationship with another woman. His pregnant wife found out and left with their three-year-old daughter. He felt guilty, ripped open. He couldn't reconcile the conflict within himself. "I was in pain because I was raised an Irish Catholic. I was taught you don't mess around on your wife, you don't get a divorce. I was pretty much excommunicated from my family when my wife and I separated."

To make matters worse, he was in constant physical pain from his back injury. And police work, his first love, had lost its joy. He believed the city's administrators and its insurance company were trying to cheat him out of medical benefits when they refused to pay for his disc surgery. He sued and won, but the whole matter left him bitter and disillusioned.

Feeling abandoned by everyone—his family, the department—he did what he never imagined he would do. He snorted a gram of cocaine. Then he went out drinking with his new girlfriend. They ended up arguing, and John left. He went to a run-down motel where he chopped up lines and snorted cocaine the rest of the night.

In the morning, depressed and ashamed of what he'd done, he finally admitted his suicidal tendencies. He drew his gun, pressed the muzzle against his throat and told himself, *I can do it.*

Something stopped him. He said his loyalty got in the way. A drug-induced suicide would embarrass the department and that was a no-no. Instead, he went to the police station. He opened a file cabinet drawer and when nobody was looking stole a quarter pound of cocaine from a drug bust. He returned to his car and coked up.

Four months into his habit, John escalated his cocaine use by freebasing—a process that turned powder cocaine into a highly addictive form of crack. By then his wife, child and new baby had returned. Even that didn't stop him from getting loaded.

"I'd call work and tell my Sergeant I'd be at home, I was takin' a day off. I'd tell my wife I was going to work and I'd go use dope. I was lying to everyone.

"I'd park on the side of the road and smoke cocaine in my car for sometimes two days or I'd check into a cheap motel room and smoke coke. Sometimes I would go to the station at night, the detective office, push a file cabinet in front of the door and rock up cocaine at my desk."

To rock up, John told me he performed an elaborate ceremony. First he lit a cigar to disguise the smell. Then he poured powder cocaine into the glass tube the cigar came in, adding baking soda and water. He pressed his thumb over the hole and shook them up until the cocaine dissolved into an amber colored fluid.

He rocked up by applying a flame to the bottom of the cigar tube, which turned the fluid into a hot oil. Then adding cold water, he shook it up again, and the remaining hot liquid solidified into what looked like a rock.

"It's like foreplay watching the rock be formed and made," he told me. "It was part of the ritual of getting high."

Powder cocaine and crack are fraught with danger, capable of damaging the liver's ability to detoxify blood. Among other things they can cause nausea, diarrhea, strokes, respiratory failure, convulsions and heart attack.

Chronic cocaine or crack use induces paranoid thoughts, panic attacks, delusions, anger, aggression, anxiety, weight loss, hypervigilance, impaired judgment and depression.[17] John was infused with steroids, liquor and cocaine, each producing similar side effects. It was anyone's guess which drug or combination of drugs was heightening his depression, anxiety and fear. Alcohol, drugs, aggression and other self-destructive acts often mask the effects of PTSD, making it hard to diagnosis.

On crack, John deteriorated rapidly. He said, "I lost 40 to 50 pounds. My hygiene was pathetic. I wore the same clothes days in a row. I was in a total fog and days ran together. I coughed up black phlegm and blood, and I was near death. Subconsciously, I was tryin' to kill myself.

"I couldn't turn anywhere. I was President of the Narcotics Officers Association. All my friends were cops. I couldn't go to them because of the shame."

As John's drug use progressed, his wife noticed the changes in him. One night she confronted him, and he broke down in tears. She demanded he give her his drugs. She threw them away and went to bed. John dug the drugs out of the trash, locked himself in the garage and rocked up.

The next day, Pam Jenks called hospitals all over the state, asking what to do. They told her to "tell him you love him and want to be in his life, but free of drugs." They encouraged her to enlist the help of John's best friend, and together they convinced John, after several days of prodding, to voluntarily enter a treatment center.

During the third week of his four week drug and alcohol recovery program, the District Attorney's office called John to produce some impounded drugs for evidence in a trial. He couldn't. He'd smoked them. "I was one of the experts used by the DA's office on drug cases. Everybody trusted me."

John had to face the consequences of his actions. He pled guilty to grand theft and destruction of evidence in stealing $35,000 worth of cocaine. On May 12, 1988, after twelve years in policing, he stood before the hardest sentencing judge on the Ventura County Superior Court—Judge Fredrick A. Jones.

John was humiliated. When John had received the Medal of Valor two years before, Judge Jones praised him at the awards ceremony for heroism.

The enormity of the irony was not lost on John as he waited for sentencing. He told me what ran through his mind at that moment. "A couple of years ago I was honored and now I'm goin' to prison. This is not the way I figured my life is gonna turn out. I'm one of the winners of life."

Amid protests from the prosecutor, the judge gave John probation. The judge believed he could be rehabilitated. John was not going to let him down.

After all the years of denial, John finally admitted he was an alcoholic and drug addict. He completed a thirty-day intensive residential program and attended counseling. After he returned to his family, he and his wife received joint counseling in an aftercare program once a week for six months. In spite of the therapy, he still didn't know he suffered from Posttraumatic Stress Disorder.

Dismissed from the police force, John sold cars for a year. "I was a terrible car salesman. But it taught me how to live on no money, on credit cards."

He moved on to construction work, banging nails into boards, putting up drywall. "I was gonna do whatever it took to support my family. My career wasn't gonna be my life again. My family was more important to me."

By 1988, John had started helping other people who were hooked on cocaine and alcohol, and that showed him a way to support his family and give something back to life instead of taking from it.

Before long, he was counseling clients from all walks of life. He was invited to teach a class to new sergeants. In the history of the Los Angeles Police Department, he was the first ex-cop, felon, alcoholic and cocaine addict to address students at the police academy.

As word of mouth spread, attorneys hired John to review cases for possible defenses. He wrote positive pretrial reports for probation, performed private investigation work and got involved in dope-related homicides.

Although he had turned his life around, something was not right. Why was he still having flashbacks, nightmares, episodes of hypervigilance, depression, insomnia, constant indigestion and diarrhea? He got his answer sooner than he expected.

A client whom John counseled for several months was due to go to trial for drug possession and sales. "Mike was a macho outlaw biker. I was once a macho cop." A lot alike, they became friends.

After being clean for four months, Mike started drinking and became depressed. He refused John's pleas for him to go into treatment. On the day of the trial, Mike didn't show, and the judge issued a warrant for his arrest.

Mike called his attorney and left a message—"Get John Jenks to call his answering machine."

The message on John's machine was chilling. "John, this is Mike. I've decided to go out back and end it all. The back door will be unlocked when you get here. There'll be notes telling you what to do. Thanks a lot, buddy."

John sped over, hoping he would catch Mike before he killed himself. John found him in the backyard lying in a pool of blood, a gun in his hand, flies buzzing around his face. John flashed on the image of the dying USA gas station attendant, setting off a sequence of flashbacks.

The sheriff's deputies questioned John as if the crime scene was a homicide, and he was the suspect. John despaired. He was in recovery for four years, four months without a drink. Now he wanted one badly. He thought, *I can't deal with this.*

Concerned, John's attorney sent him to a therapist, and the therapist was able to elicit emotions from John he had not felt before.

"This was the first time I allowed myself to feel for a victim and I cried and it was painful and I didn't want to do it, but it helped me see how far I'd come because I'd never felt that before. And I didn't want to go back to drinking or using. I was in a real fragile, vulnerable place."

About a year after John's first therapy session, just before I interviewed him, he was finally diagnosed with Posttraumatic Stress Disorder. Why did it take so long to diagnose him? There are acute and delayed types of PTSD. John's was delayed in its onset, meaning it didn't start to show itself for years. Acute types, on the otherhand, often give clear signs early on.[18]

Through therapy, John was able to begin the process of drawing out and grappling with feelings he had suppressed for years. His family life has improved since he went into treatment. "My relationship with my wife is better than ever because I've accepted responsibility for my behavior."

"Why did your wife stay?" I asked.

"There's no logical reason. She says she saw the good in me. I know she felt angry and betrayed. I'm lucky to have her still."

"What might have happened if you hadn't gone into treatment?"

"My family, my wife and kids... I'd have lost them. I'd be a practicing alcoholic and probably would have gone through two or three wives lookin' for the perfect relationship, things outside myself to make me happy."

"And now..."

"And now I'm able to help other people learn from my mistakes. I've seen so many crippled cops. They're afraid to deal with what's going on in their lives. It's not manly. For the guys who open up, that shows a lot of courage."

After the interview, I drove through the small town of Ojai. Its quiet streets belied the crime and drugs going on behind the scenes. Even here, cops like John were succumbing to overwhelming stress, and John was only one small-town cop of hundreds of thousands in America.

John was impaired during much of his police career, by alcohol, anabolic steroids, cocaine and PTSD. His impairment does not release him from responsibility for his actions. He told me he is accountable for what he did as a cop. Acceptance is the only way he can go on with life and heal. Drinking, poor parenting and other issues and influences are no excuses for his behavior. He endangered not only his own life but our lives, too.

I was told that some cops don't believe John Jenks' story. They think he's exaggerating parts of it, particularly about drug use. As an expert in alcohol and drug addiction, Detective Martin interviewed John at length on several occasions. He believes John's story and has used him to teach at the police academy. I believe John too. His wife prodded him into telling more than he really wanted to reveal, and his goals were never self-serving. All he wanted to do was help other officers avoid the traps into which he had fallen.

The central issue for cops challenging John's story is his use of illegal drugs. Alcohol is an accepted addiction. Cocaine is not. Cops abhor the thought of a law enforcement officer taking an illegal substance, because it means if a cop who started off good could fall into illicit drug use, then every cop is susceptible.

The central issue for me is not the unlawful use of drugs but what's behind their use. I think it is important that officers focus not on whether the addictions are legal or illegal, but on their causes. Whichever way you look at it, addiction is a cry of suffering. It is a plea for help.

Sadly, John Jenks' story is not atypical. Many officers share his psychological problems and addictions. A third of all cops may have PTSD symptoms. Peer supporters tell me that half the cops they talk to have either attempted suicide at work or thought about doing it.

More than a quarter of peace officers are alcoholic, compared to 10 percent of the general population. Drug abuse by cops is over 10 percent and may be higher as cops rarely admit to drug use because it jeopardizes their jobs and pensions. Unlike alcoholism, drug use is often a firing offense. An FBI report suggests that illegal drug use, specifically steroids and cocaine, is second in a list of factors that lead to police brutality.[19]

Statistics, although convincing, can be mind-numbing. It's hard to generalize for every cop in every department in every major city and small town in the nation. One fact is clear, however. Police officers are not coming to grips with the realities of their job. The dark side of the rescue personality causes them to act out their frustrations in self-destructive ways. And small-town departments like those John worked for do not usually provide support resources to help officers suffering from PTSD symptoms.

I called John a few days after I first interviewed him. He told me he hadn't slept in three days. The interview had triggered nightmares and flashbacks, and he was not in very good shape.

I felt bad for causing his distress, but he reassured me.

"It was worth it. Maybe people will appreciate us more when they realize how hard we try, how sometimes our own humanness gets us."

One of the reasons John wanted to tell his story was to honor the judge who had faith in him. "Judge Jones could easily have sent me to prison," John said. "But because of his mercy and kindness, I was able to become the person I wanted to be."

Judge Fredrick A. Jones has passed away. For giving John a chance to make something of his life, John dedicates this chapter to his memory.

Chapter 6

Shootings

"Take the mutt down. Drop him."

When the head of the New York Police Department's peer counseling unit asked Detective Ian Shaw[1] to meet me for an interview at my hotel room, he refused. Hence, my surprise when I opened the door to a knock and there he was.

"What changed your mind?" I asked.

After twenty-five years on the force, he said, he retired to a good job running security for a big company. "The past was the past. Why dredge it up?"

But then he thought this was a good opportunity to try to reconcile his role in the blood bath in which he took part. He decided he wanted to tell me everything, and he had never told anyone in all those years *absolutely* everything.

Ian had a round face, gray hair and fifty-one years on his back. Distinguished and polite, he reminded me of a magazine photograph in *Forbes* or *Fortune* showing a portly president of a big company with his arms folded across his chest, a closed-minded individual, firm, hard-line. Not some-one you could pull anything over on or make say what he didn't want to say. Ian appeared older than his age, maybe ten years. I learned he did not smile easily, but when he did, he lit up the room with good humor.

Ian stared down the barrel of the microphone. When I turned on the tape machine, he sighed and curled his mouth upwards in what I think was exasperation. We covered his first four years as a patrol officer in the Bronx, and then his move at age twenty-six to the armed robbery Stakeout Unit. Here he experienced multiple traumas in gunfights in which he was forced to shoot to kill. I asked Ian why the Stakeout Unit was formed.

"In the early 1970s, shopkeepers were being murdered," he said. "The robbers would get the money and then take them in the back room and make them watch as they raped their wives. Then they forced them to kneel down, and they'd shoot them."

"What was the unit supposed to do?" I asked.

"We were supposed to stop it. We were a small, highly trained unit, twenty to twenty-five guys. And we were placed inside the stores, waiting for the next time. Our primary goals were to make sure no civilians got hurt and to place these bad guys under arrest. But if there was any indication they were going to take the shopkeeper's life or our lives, we were to use deadly force."

"I was told the unit was controversial from the beginning. Why was that?" I asked.

"These were racially troubled times. We were requested by black shopkeepers in all-black areas, and the people we shot were mainly blacks. We were white and they were black. Many people saw us as an armed occupational army that would do nothing but shoot 'em down when they came in."

"So you knew it would be controversial?"

"Yes."

"Then why did you join the unit?"

"It seemed like a pretty noble thing to do. Plus I knew it was an avenue to promotion, a detective's gold shield. And not everybody got picked. The commissioner made sure we were screened meticulously on whether we would panic during a situation. He wanted people who were solid."

For one of his first assignments, Ian and his partner set up in the back room of an A&P grocery store in a run-down area of Brooklyn. Ian told me his regular partner was on a day off and a man he didn't know replaced him. Ian had no idea what his new partner, Charlie,[2] would do if events turned nasty. Would he run or would he fight?

After a few days of waiting for something to happen, Ian noticed three men enter the store and go to the back. Behind a two-way mirror, he watched them take out guns and pull on hats. One of the armed men entered a phone booth and pretended to be on the telephone. Ian assumed he was the backup.

As the other holdup men moved to the front and forced the manager and cashiers to open the money drawers, Ian carefully pushed the back door open and crept into the store. He glanced at the phone booth and whispered to his partner, "Take that mutt out. The third guy."

"Don't worry," said his partner.

Ian was worried. Charlie seemed too relaxed. "I mean it, take the mutt down. Drop him."

His partner moved out toward the phone booth. Ian inched to the end of the aisle near the checkout counters, shouldering an M1 Carbine. Never having shot anyone before, he didn't know if he could do it.

One of the gunmen spotted Ian and fired. Ian told me he didn't hear the blast from the gun. He saw an orange flash and a burst of gray smoke.

In response, Ian fired three quick shots. His bullets penetrated the gunman in front, striking the man behind, who then staggered toward the door and pushed through a wall of shoppers. The front man fell to the floor, his gun still pointing at Ian. Ian turned his rifle toward him.

"I was going to kill him," Ian told me, "and I couldn't. I said to him, 'Drop the gun, pal' and I kicked the gun across the floor."

Suddenly a shotgun blast shattered the phone booth. Wood and glass scattered across the floor. The man who was in the phone booth raced for the front door.

"I probably could have hit him," said Ian. "I decided it was over. I was alive. Fuck it."

The suspect on the floor sat himself up on a milk crate. He was raining blood into a widening dark puddle. "This pool of blood was like a vicious artery was cut," said Ian, "and I wanted to help him, but he was a pretty hard fuck. He was sweating. He was in shock and he said, 'Give me an ambulance.'"

"I said, 'No fucking ambulance 'til you tell me the names of them guys.' The man said, 'I wasn't one of them. I was shopping. Come on, man.' I told him, 'You ain't getting no ambulance.'"

Ian didn't tell him the ambulance was on its way. He wanted the names.

Paramedics soon stretchered the would-be robber out. "He never told me them names," said Ian.

Ian's partner wandered up to the front of the store. Ian asked him, "How'd you miss the guy in the phone booth?"

"He moved."

"The joke of the day in the precinct," said Ian, "was, 'Ian shoots two stickup men. Charlie shoots a Castro convertible sofa in a furniture store across the street.'"

Ian's first shooting was over. He praised himself for doing his job. Nobody innocent got hurt, and he lived through it. His knees weak, he sat down on a stool. His heart was pounding. He had a slight tremor in his hands and was out of breath, exhausted. He wanted to go home to lie down, but there was no way he could. He said he would have settled for a stiff drink. He'd have to wait because he still had work to do. In the 1970s, cops were obliged to finish their tours no matter how they felt.

"Nobody babied you," Ian said. "There was no stress debriefing or visits to the medical unit. There was no such thing as post-shooting trauma. Cops were expected to process the arrest, complete all paperwork, give interviews to superiors and finally draw up the complaint in the DA's office before they were allowed to do anything else. You had to be satisfied you were doing a man's job."

After a brief rest, Ian strolled through the grocery store itemizing the damage and crime scene evidence in his notebook—broken glass, splintered wood, shell casings, blood, discarded clothes, handbags. By now, the store was full of patrol officers. They acted like visitors to a zoo following the animal feeder. *What're they all doing here?* Ian wondered. He observed they weren't paying much attention to the damage and signs of struggle. They were looking at him.

Nobody asked Ian how he felt. When his bosses arrived, they didn't inquire. The other cops in the Stakeout Unit didn't mention it. And Ian didn't say anything. Nobody thought it was important, although the concept of post-traumatic stress (stress that appears moments or months after a traumatic event) had been around since the 1940s. Posttraumatic stress was applied to shellshocked soldiers and citizen victims of crime. It was not often applied to cops, although from our perspective in time it's hard to fathom why not.

The complex clusters of symptoms called Posttraumatic Stress Disorder hadn't been invented yet. The Vietnam War was still raging when Ian was in Stakeout. It would be several years before those emotionally damaged veterans, both men and women, were poked, prodded and analyzed and an all-encompassing diagnosis was formulated that would explain their plight.[3]

After finishing up at the station, Ian headed out to a bar. In the car, he was troubled about what he had done to survive. He asked himself, *Should I have used more compassion?* He had no answer. When he asked, *Why was everybody looking at me?* he grew even more bewildered.

Staring at someone who was engaged in a gun battle is an expected response from other police officers. But it reinforces the idea that "everyone is watching," what some psychologists call *The Mark of Cain.*[4]

While driving, Ian thought about the gawkers and how he was feeling. He couldn't ignore his perception that others were condemning him for the shooting.[5] He wanted to talk to somebody, but his work situation did not provide much support. Ian was in a special police unit—essentially, a family within a family. He didn't talk to officers in his unit about things like feelings.

As far as police officers outside his unit, talking to them about anything was forbidden. Under a gag order, he wasn't even allowed to talk to outside superior officers about his work. He was feeling separate and isolated before he shot someone. But now the gawking stares made him feel different than other cops. "The other cops acted as if I knew something they didn't," he said.

After a couple of drinks at the bar, he realized why he felt different. He was different.

He said, "I felt like I wasn't as innocent as I used to be. From that point on, an element of fear entered my body that wasn't there before. And I never had the same peace of mind that I had enjoyed up to that moment again. Never. I also knew it was easy to kill."

By choice, he sat alone at the bar and withdrew into his drink, thinking. He played the gunfight over and over again, a common traumatic reaction after a shooting.

"I kept wondering if them guys were dying or dead," he said. "You know, I always associated a big, dramatic organ-playing moment with shooting somebody. It's not like that. I just did what I had to do. I was very efficient. I'll tell you one thing, though. I was glad I was alive because for moments I thought I was gonna die."

Ian asked himself if he was doing the right thing. *What the fuck kind of a job is this? Maybe I ain't the person I think I am.* Round and round his thoughts went. *These guys were violent. They would have killed the manager. I did the right thing, didn't I?*

And then he did what most cops do. Unable to resolve his feelings, he shut them off and ordered another glass.

Although the Stakeout Unit was formed by the top brass, Ian wasn't told the bosses were becoming increasingly uneasy about the shootings. Up until this time the NYPD's policy on shootings was very liberal when it came to cops.[6] If a cop shot somebody, he must have had good reason to shoot. That was the approach. The political climate, however, was shifting.

Among other abuses, the black population complained about black men being cut down by white cops. With the advocacy of tolerance and black rights, the imagery of white killing black was embarrassing to the police command.

Another major change was in the attitude toward criminals. Ian was taught that violent felons were hardened and hopeless, worthy only for disposal in prison or a grave. Now Ian was told that even killers were capable of rehabilitation. Instead of being bad people, criminals were as victimized as their victims and needed counseling to make them better members of society. Tough cops like Ian balked at this new vision. To him, a killer was a killer, unredeemable.

Ian believed he had a job to do. Stop the robbing, rape and murder—although by now he thought it a dubious assignment. He was feeling isolated, withdrawn, wondering if what he was doing was right, unaware his bosses were planning a double-cross.

Within days after Ian's first shooting, he was on another stakeout. A Household Finance office (HFC) across from Gimbel's Department Store was getting hit frequently. It always had an abundance of cash on hand for garment workers who liked their loans in greenbacks instead of checks.

The HFC branch was on the second floor of an office building. Ian fitted a two-way mirror to a storage room door, which looked into the lobby where people exited an elevator. To get to the HFC entrance, they proceeded down a short corridor, made a turn into another corridor not visible to Ian and walked in.

To see into the office, Ian and his regular partner, Eric,[7] cut a rectangular hole in the storage closet wall and put in another two-way mirror. The girls in the office used it to tease their hair and dab on makeup, much to the police officers' amusement.

One day, Ian and his partner were in the HFC office. The manager's wife had had a baby, and he was handing out cigars. He asked Ian if the officer knew how to work a washing machine. The manager's wife was in the hospital, and he'd run out of clean underwear. This situation would soon prove embarrassing.

A half hour later, Ian was on point watching the elevator doors. The doors opened and a head stuck out and looked both ways. The doors closed. *Wrong stop*, thought Ian. A few minutes later, the doors opened again. Same man. He stepped out and plopped a wooden block against the door to keep the elevator on that floor. The elevator door banged against the block.

"Watch out," Ian said to his partner. "A guy's comin' in."

The well-dressed black man in his thirties straightened up. As he threw away a newspaper from under his arm, his jacket opened.

"He's got a gun!" said Ian. "It's a hit. It's a hit."

"What kind of fucking gun?" asked Eric.

"I don't know. I can't see."

"What is it?"

"What difference does it make?"

"I don't want to get shot with a fucking Magnum."

Eric was concerned whether his vest would stop a bullet from that powerful handgun. They stood motionless watching the holdup go down.

"Stick 'um up, motherfucker," yelled the bandit at the room full of employees and customers. "I'll blow your fucking heads off. You move, I'll fucking kill ya!"

Ian told me, "No one ever says, 'Please, don't move. Please be calm.'"

Then the bandit shouted, "Drop your pants, motherfuckers."

The manager's neck turned red. Obeying the order at gun point, he dropped his pants. He was naked. Despite the gravity of the situation, a couple of the women laughed.

The laughter ceased when the stickup man grabbed a woman by the hair, marched her around calling her "bitch" and repeatedly hit her on the head with his gun butt. He ordered the seven or eight people to lie down on the floor and kicked each of them in the ribs. Ian thought it was to assure they wouldn't come to the woman's defense or try to stop him from stealing their money.

Now Ian wanted to know. "Eric, what kinda gun's he got?"

"Looks like a Magnum."

This time Ian had a shotgun loaded with slugs for close quarters combat. A slug was capable of cracking an engine block. When he picked up the weapon, he said to himself, *What the fuck am I doing?*

"As I unlocked the door, I was real nervous, saying my prayers." He pushed open the door to the lobby. He was "going to do him" when he reached the elevators.

Eric watched through the window, reporting on the robber's actions.

"He's got the money...

"He's stuffing money in every pocket...

"He's still got the girl by the head...

"He's pickin' up the pants...

"He's comin' to you."

Ian stepped into the lobby. He told me, "If he come round with the girl, we were letting him go."

"He's comin' to you, alone!" shouted Eric.

But there was no guy. *There was no guy!* He was in the bathroom going through wallets in the pants he took.

Then all of a sudden, the man turned the corner into the hallway. His gun was out.

"Police!" barked Ian.

From a few feet away, the man fired his Magnum. Ian felt something hot hit his forehead. On reflex, he jerked the trigger of the shotgun.

The slug tore into the bandit's chest. The man stood there, puzzled. He didn't fall down. Then he tried to back toward the elevator, his gun still pointed at Ian.

"I shot him again," Ian told me. "And he kept looking at me, trying to get to the elevator. And I shot him again. And then I heard over my shoulder, *BANG*, and then he went down."

Over Ian's shoulder, Eric had fired his shotgun into the bandit.

"I stepped on his wrist," said Ian, "and took the gun off of him. And he immediately got like apologetic and he said, 'Oh shit, I'm hurt.' And he told me, 'Take my shoes off, man. I can't feel my feet.' And I thought, *He's dyin,' I've severed his spine.* And he tried to give me his jewelry. I said, 'Relax, guy, relax. We got an ambulance coming.'"

Ian said, "There was a lot of noise. Screamin' from the office. There was fucking gunsmoke all over the place and he was yelling and screaming. A lot of blood."

"You got something on your face," said Eric.

Ian touched his forehead and his fingertips came away black. He was so close to the robber's gun when he fired, it peppered his skin with lead shavings.

In minutes, the lobby filled with cops. Like before, they wanted to see the shooters, the cops who fired their guns and survived. Ian noticed "they had that look." Soon Ian's boss arrived at the crime scene.

"Look, Ian, how you doin'?" he said.

"All right, everything's all right."

"You okay to talk?"

"Fuck, I wanna get a drink and forget about this."

"Let's get the money off the mutt," said his boss, "and go in the office and count it, okay?"

They searched the gunman's pockets as he lay on the floor "like a mangled rag doll." They counted the money, most of it covered in blood, not talking much about the shooting, not talking at all about Ian's anguish over it.

In the bathroom where the perp had emptied the wallets, Ian scrubbed the blood off his hands. Then he went to the precinct. He had paperwork to do. At least he could be alone to sip a coffee.

After writing up the shooting report and noting the late hour, Ian signed out. He went to a bar, alone, and then he went home.

"I went home and stood in one spot in my kitchen," he said. "My wife was still up and we talked about the children, shopping, anything but what happened. I didn't tell her. My wife said, 'Ian, you're going to wear a hole in the rug. I think you're drinking too much.'"

Ian wanted to deny it but he couldn't. A drinker since a teenager, he drank more and more after joining the Stakeout.

He went to bed. It was now a few hours after he shot the HFC bandit. Unable to sleep, he lay in bed thinking about right and wrong.

"I was brought up a practicing Catholic," he told me. "And I had these ideas that God set out certain rules, and I didn't know if I violated these rules and was guilty of the biggest sin. Like should I have sacrificed myself more before firing the gun? I was always thinkin' like that when I had a few drinks."

He finally dozed off and dreamed. He dreamed in slow motion...

> *The bandit sailed around the corner.*
> *"Police" yelled Ian.*
> *A gun flashed.*
> *Ian pulled the trigger of his shotgun and out the end of the barrel a slug waltzed lazily a few feet and tumbled to the floor.*
> *"What's wrong with the bullet?" mumbled Ian.*
> *He fired again.*
> *Rotating to the end of the barrel, the bullet fell out of the gun...*

From repressing his feelings of vulnerability and fear, Ian could not untangle his many conflicts. In a sweat, he awoke from his nightmare with a distressing question on his lips. *Is it right to further your career in a detail that engages in violence?* He had no solution, and his nightmares continued for many months of nights.[8]

The HFC incident was a turning point in Ian's life in the Stakeout Unit. He told me, "I never really come to terms with it. I started questioning every little thing regarding that area of my life."

Before long, Ian's inner turmoil announced itself in a way he couldn't ignore or control. "I was driving over the George Washington Bridge on the way to work and I couldn't breathe no more," he said. "I was choking, and I felt like I was going to pass out, like I was going to die. I was way up in the air. I couldn't pull to the side. When I got to the other side, it didn't subside. I was sweating. Heart racing. I thought I was going to faint."

Ian's panic attacks occurred frequently throughout his third and final year in Stakeout. And they didn't only occur on the bridge. Sometimes when he was out for a walk, he would suddenly be overwhelmed. He'd become dizzy, nauseated and his heart would pound like it was in his throat. Feeling like he was smothering, he got chills or trembled for no apparent reason. And always, he believed he was going to die.[9]

"Did you see a doctor about it?" I asked.

"I didn't want people to call me a whiner or say, 'Well, what is he, nuts or something?' " Ian didn't consult a doctor or tell anyone about his stress reactions.

"What did you do?"

"I lived with it. I rationalized. I kept saying, 'Wait a minute, you didn't die last time. You're not gonna die this time.' The only way I wouldn't get the attacks is if I had a few drinks."

Ian experienced panic attacks and exhibited posttraumatic stress reactions common to combat soldiers and victims of violent crime. He said, "I had difficulty falling asleep. Difficulty staying asleep. Had night sweats. I got irritable and angry, but I got quiet. I didn't want to break my wife's chops because she didn't deserve it. My blood pressure went up. I had adrenaline rushes. If I drank, I had those little sad times and cried."

Ian told me he experienced depression and tried to deny feelings of guilt and remorse for the shootings. Sometimes images from shooting scenes unexpectedly invaded his thoughts. He tried to avoid thinking about the shootings or driving by places in which they happened.

At times his feelings fluctuated between wanting to scream to withdrawing into himself. Ian lost interest in doing things and stopped exercising. He became mistrustful of others. His sense of smell became quite keen, especially if something was dead nearby, and he could detect even the smallest trace of gunpowder in the air. Ian sought to medicate his symptoms by drinking too much.[10]

Aware of Ian's excessive drinking, his boss gave him an offer he knew he shouldn't refuse. "You wanna get out of here? What do you say?"

Ian knew it was time. "Yeah, I want out."

"I'm gonna give you a good recommendation. You'll get your detective's gold shield."

Recommendation in hand, Ian applied to the newly forming Organized Crime Control Bureau (OCCB). The department was planning a move on narcotics, prostitution and gambling. "It was a new concept," Ian told me, and "they were recruiting the cream of the crop."

Ian had an unblemished record and no citizen complaints. He had earned commendations and awards. Even birth was on his side. The Irish ran the police department. Coming from an elite unit, he was trained, tested under fire, a stable, respected, well-liked guy. Ian and his boss thought it was a shoo-in.

On the day of the interview, Ian sat on a hard bench outside the OCCB hearing room. He sat all day, from eight in the morning until late in the afternoon. Finally, they called him in, the last applicant. Ian told me, "I knew something was amiss." It wasn't so much *what* the three-man board members asked as *how* they asked it, with an edge of hostility. A supervisor's distaste for Ian became apparent.

"I want to ask you a question before you leave," said the supervisor. "What makes a person like you join an outfit like that?"

"Exactly what do you mean, Inspector?" Ian asked.

"What makes a decent guy like yourself join an outfit like that Stakeout Unit?"

Ian said his mouth was dry. He licked his lips and chose words he thought might get through to the man.

"People were being murdered," said Ian. "The police commissioner got people he felt were solid. Do you know how many lives we saved? How many times did we panic and hurt a civilian, sir? Not once. How many of our guys were shot? A few. We put ourselves out there. I guess they needed guys like me."

Another supervisor spoke up in Ian's defense. "The officer has a good record. What did you ask a question like that for? It doesn't have any relevance."

It didn't matter. Ian knew he was done. He got up, shook their hands and thought to himself, *You fucks.* "The brass had shitcanned many of the other guys in the Stakeout Unit for no good reason," Ian told me. "They were standup guys, Vietnam vets, jungle fighters and gunboat guys." Ian didn't think they would do it to him.

In a bar that night, Ian sat alone drinking Scotch, thinking about his day. The supervisors made him feel like he had done something wrong, something illegal. "We were branded, unwanted people like we were capable of what these bad guys were capable of." But he was under orders. He saved lives. *I did the right thing, didn't I?* Where he had doubts before about his own motives, now those doubts seemed like certainties.

"I began to think I wasn't the good person I thought I was," he told me. For the department he had risked his life and violated the fundamental principles he believed in. *Exodus 20:13—Thou shalt not kill.* Most of all, he felt shame. *How,* he wondered, *can I ever hold my head up again?*

A few days later he ran into his boss from the Stakeout Unit. He had already heard how Ian was treated and was ashamed to face him.

"Why?" asked Ian.

"It's political," said his boss. The newspapers had savaged the police department, and said there were too many shootings, the cops overreacted. "The brass threw us to the wolves."

"Where can I go?" said Ian.

"Nowhere," said his boss. "Nobody's moving from the outfit. Nobody will touch you."

There would be no gold shield. No move to the detective division. The Stakeout Unit was to be disbanded.

Ian was overwhelmed by the blatant message—he was expendable, as expendable as the soldiers fighting in Vietnam.

"How did you feel after this?" I asked Ian.

"Like a dark cloud was over my head. I just always felt hurt by that. There was a lot of anger that I turned inside. But you could never say nothing. Then you become a malcontent in the police department. You get labeled and you've done yourself a double whammy."

Ian was led to believe the stakeout job was ordained, sanctified. He believed the police commissioner, the mayor, the chief of police, all the top officials were behind him. He counted them among his friends in the police administration. His friends included supervisors like sergeants, lieutenants, captains. His pals were the patrol officers.

Perceiving that everybody at work now looked the other way when he walked by, he felt isolated, utterly alone. And the stress caused from being a scorned outsider, Ian said, was unbearable.

In numerous studies, psychologists have pointed the finger not at the danger on the streets, but at the police organization—administrators and supervisors—as the major source of stress for officers.[11]

"The bookworms avoided you. The up and coming that weren't interested in cleanin' up the streets. They were more interested in who they were seen with, and they didn't want to be seen with you. It was the change in the guard. My superiors were clamoring for recognition, and it was watch how quick I can fuck this cop.

"You were proud to have belonged to that Stakeout Unit, but they made it so bad you didn't want to be seen two of yous talking together."

While the brass were ostracizing Ian, officers Ian knew, and he believed respected him, continued to treat him as a disgraced police officer.

"The patrol guys I knew, they looked at me differently like was I still the same guy? Did I value human life? They wondered if I had a conscience. When somebody hears I shot people, they say 'He must be one real hard guy.' People form opinions on you. 'You murderer. You piece of shit.' The bottom line is I'm just like you."

The rejection by Ian's bosses intimated that what he'd done in Stakeout was morally wrong. Ian's assumption that even his buddies in patrol were rejecting him, forced him to conclude they believed it too. If they could not accept the shootings as justified, how could he? His internal conflict caused the panic attacks to increase in frequency and harshness. Still, he told no one. Whom could he trust to listen?

"Do you think the rejection blurred your perception about the Stakeout Unit?" I asked.

"Sure. I didn't see things clearly, but I saw them clearly after three drinks. I'd make my plans who I was gonna tell off someday. Then do nothing. The Stakeout Unit was just a sad part of my life. If I could, I'd like to wipe it out. I never found any goodness in it."

Ian was not allowed to move from his position. He could, however, move within his division of NYPD nowhere men. So he transferred to the Emergency Services Division, (ESD), today's equivalent of S.W.A.T. Ian thought he had seen everything in the Stakeout Unit. In ESD, the slaughter was astounding.

He said, "The South Bronx was the asshole of the world. More murders than in Saigon." The calls were a hurricane of heavy weapons, retrieving dead bodies, warrants, murders, barricaded criminals, jumpers from bridges and airplane crashes.

During his first airplane crash, he wandered through the rubble in shock. "I thought you were killed by impact," he told me. "I didn't realize how many people were killed by lacerations from the torn metal, severing limbs, throats, creating deep, gouging wounds. People bled to death. Children too. You wonder, why didn't God give 'em a break?"

"There was nothing you could do," I said.

"There was nothing I could do for them physically so I said a quiet prayer. If what they taught me in school is true, maybe some poor soul got into heaven."

Despite the horror, the work had saving graces for Ian. The assignment was exciting, and ESD received a lot of praise for its work. Unaccountably, Ian's panic attacks seemed to peak over the next two years, then lessened and disappeared. Ian believes the importance of the job increased his self-esteem, reducing depression and fear. As long as he was busy in something he liked, he didn't dwell on the past.

Nevertheless, he had changed, and resentments festered in his heart for years. The shootings hurt him psychologically and spiritually. The groundless criticism by his superiors created a secondary injury that intensified his posttraumatic symptoms.[12] He still had bad dreams from Stakeout. Sometimes when he tried to relax at home, sickening crime scenes preoccupied his thoughts.

"Did your wife say anything about your preoccupation?" I said.

"My wife knew I was damaged. I never gave in to it. She pointed out to me that my personality changed and she was right."

"Did the changes affect how you treated your children?" I asked.

"It was a cycle of getting angry, apologizing, getting angry, apologizing."

Then his status at work changed again. The NYPD began a series of layoffs. ESD was cut in half and Ian was moved back to patrol. Although four years had passed since the Stakeout Unit, he still had not dealt with his feelings from that period. And now he had stored many more traumatic images of death and depravity in his brain.

Returning to patrol was like a demotion. He began to feel bad about himself again. The bad feelings allowed the traumatic memories he had repressed for years to express themselves through dangerous or self-destructive behavior.

Ian revealed his self-destructive inclination during a hot day on patrol. He answered a call to a drug area in Washington Heights. In moments he was running after two men who had gunned down a group of drug dealers.

The first shooter turned around on Ian after Ian had made a tactical error of stopping parallel to him without any cover. From a few feet away the man fired at Ian eight times, missing him. Ian did not return fire. His partner shot the man. Ian took off after the second man. A similar situation occurred. Ian caught the man who then attempted to fire a pen gun into his face. Rather than shooting, Ian slugged it out with him, forcing the weapon from the perpetrator's hand.

"Why didn't you shoot?" I asked.

"I didn't shoot him... I think the Stakeout Unit changed me. For some reason, I became unsure of myself."

Even though Ian received the Medal of Valor for risking his life in apprehending the felons, his heart wasn't in being a cop any longer. Never shirking his duty, he continued to make numerous collars, but he became, at times, apathetic and despondent.

"My attitude was, 'If I do this, the result is not going to be right for me anyway.' I was disappointed my career wasn't going the way I thought it should."

In his sixteenth year on the force, Ian was finally promoted to detective. There in the robbery detail, he made "good arrests." He earned back the respect he thought he had lost. Yet, he never came to grips with his role in the Stakeout Unit and the things he had done. He always felt he couldn't talk about it to anybody. He felt somehow he had disgraced himself in the eyes of the department, his family, and in the eyes of God.

A few months from his twenty-fifth year in the NYPD, Ian decided to retire. He could no longer contain his memories or hide his anxiety.

"Why did you decide to leave?" I asked him.

"I felt I was drinking too much," Ian said.

For a man who had denied for many years that he had a drinking problem, a man who refused to tell anyone including his wife about the upheaval inside him, this was an immense step forward.

"I wanted to leave clean," he went on. "So I went down to the peer counseling unit, and I met with one of the guys there. I told him..." Ian's voice cracked. "I told him I wasn't comfortable with myself..."

Tears slid down Ian's face, and all at once he said, "I told him I'm not comfortable with myself and I'm drinkin' too much and I'd like to put an end to it and start off my retirement on the right foot."

Ian wiped away tears with the palm of his hand. "The counselor said, 'I want you to go to the hospital. I want you to go through detox for alcoholism.' I told him I don't need that. He said, 'You got to do it.' So I said, 'Okay.' I went to a treatment center for three weeks, and it took a year to make me better."

Ian allowed his tears to flow. He told me he felt humiliated for going to detox. Tough guys can hold their liquor. I told him I didn't think anybody was that tough except in movies.

I asked him, "Have you told many people about going to detox?"

"A few."

"There are a lot of cops," I said, "who don't even take the first step, who won't go to see a counselor."

"I know. I know guys that've killed themselves," he said. "I know what they were thinking. But that was never for me. Never for me."

After Ian retired in 1991, he saw a therapist for awhile about his unresolved issues. The doctor confirmed his panic attacks were stress-related. They evolved from suppressing feelings about the shoot-outs. Control, he was told, was at the base of his fear. At the shootings, he had no control. When he drove over the bridge, he was high in the air and couldn't pull to the side or turn around. The bridge took his control away, and he panicked.

The psychologist told Ian he had a very structured personality and liked to live by rules. Growing up in a strict Irish Catholic house, Ian obeyed rules and expected others to follow them too. Shoot-outs have no rules except for one tenet—kill or be killed. And once he realized how easy it was to kill, he came in conflict with his upbringing. The rejection by his superiors reinforced the conflict, rubbing his face in his sorrow.

Even though Ian displayed many of the symptoms for Posttraumatic Stress Disorder, the psychologist told him he did not have it. A key symptom of PTSD is flashbacks and Ian did not suffer from them persistently. He also did not experience other symptoms.[13] He did, however, suffer from posttraumatic stress.

A person with posttraumatic stress may experience a variety of reactions from panic attacks to depression to eating disorders. Not everyone will react in the same way. On the other hand, PTSD is an official diagnosis with specific symptoms (See chapter 2). If not managed by stress controlling techniques, posttraumatic stress may develop into PTSD.

As important as knowing what PTSD is, it is also necessary to know when the criteria for PTSD are not met. A therapist may determine a diagnosis of PTSD if the subject displays a minimum number of symptoms from different categories as defined in the American Psychiatric Association's diagnostic manual.[14] Ian did not satisfy the minimum.

For police officers, shooting someone is a terrifying, debilitating event. Studies say most will never forgive themselves no matter how justified they were. The shock is so great, many officers involved in a shooting leave law enforcement.[15] For those who stick it out, the job may become a source of fear, guilt and regret.

Fighting his personal convictions, Ian became overwrought when he had to shoot someone. Eventually, he came to terms with his religious belief that demands you don't kill people. He found that sometimes killing is justified, that at times God requires someone's life as punishment for a crime. Ian learned that there is a difference between killing and murder. Murder begins with evil intentions.[16] And Ian was never evil.

Ian said, "You know, it's only recently that people... It's a rah, rah thing. Now it's a badge of honor to have belonged to the Stakeout Unit. It's the last outfit that stood for anything in the job."

I turned off the tape recorder. We shook hands, and I followed Ian to the door. He turned to me and said, "This is something I'd like to give my children to read someday and say this is about me, and now you'll understand cops."

Chapter 7

Family

"I tried to keep my pain in
to allow him to get his stuff out."

It's rare that a cop's spouse or significant other knows how to cope when the police officer in their life is attacked. And they may develop inexplicable fears and anxiety that can lead to posttraumatic stress and even PTSD symptoms, as this story reveals.

It was January 29th, 1993. NYPD Patrol Officer Ed Brown was cruising with his partner in their RMP on 91st Street in Manhattan when a woman with long brown hair and glasses flagged him down on the street.

"What's the matter, ma'am?"

"The bank," she cried, pointing to the Chemical Bank on the corner of 91st and Broadway. "It's being robbed right now."

Ed wasn't sure if she was a crackpot or what, but his partner radioed it in.

Brown, 32, was on the job about nine months with the NYPD city police and still in FTU, field training unit. He had worked as a Transit Officer for four years before that in northern Manhattan so he was familiar with the area patrolled by the 24th precinct, sector Charlie Frank. New York City has three kinds of police: transit, housing and city. It was only Ed's second time in a city sector car.

He reached for his hat. The department was very clear about the rules. "Leave the freaking thing there." said his partner.

They got out of the car, and because of Ed's inexperience on the street, he said, "I'll follow your play." As they approached the bank, they drew their guns.

The bank had two doors. His partner peered in a window near the far door while Ed waited near the ATM machine door about 40 feet away.

"Take cover," shouted his partner.

Ed positioned himself against the stone wall of the bank. A man strode quickly out the far north door. His partner ordered him to stop. The man kept on moving. "That's one of them," he yelled.

"Police, don't move," Ed screamed at the suspect, and pointed his gun at him. The man lurched, then sprinted north up the street, Ed's partner in pursuit.

Ed knew Rule One—*You never leave your partner.* He started after him, and as he passed the bank window, he stopped. Call it an inner voice or a shout from heaven that said, *Look...*

He peered into the bank. Before his eyes could adjust to the dim light, a short, barrel-chested man in a ski mask popped out of the ATM door, "like a jack-in-the-box."

All Ed saw were big, bulging eyes and a huge black semiautomatic 9mm.

"Freeze!" Ed cried, leveling his revolver.

BAM! The man fired at Ed point-blank from about eight feet. All at once, a rush of conflicting thoughts roared through his mind—

I'm shot...

I didn't feel an impact...

The gun's not real...

But I saw the flash...

I saw smoke...

The gun's real.

Ed fired three rapid shots at the gunman who was running and almost on top of him. As if the bullets were annoying gnats instead of deadly projectiles, the gunman darted around the discharging gun, and headed west toward the other side of Broadway.

Ed calmly aimed his gun at the bank robber's back and tightened his finger on the trigger. However, frantic bystanders crisscrossed behind and in front of the fleeing suspect, and Ed could not fire safely.

Upon hearing Ed's shots, his partner ceased chasing the other man, and ran to Ed to check on him. Ed said he was okay, and then his partner took off after the man Ed had exchanged shots with.

Ed followed his partner for a few blocks to 93rd Street where the gunman snatched Bonnie Vargas, a forty-one-year old teacher, from the front doorway of her apartment building, put her in a headlock, and held her in front of him like a shield. By now 25 to 30 cops were on the scene surrounding the gunman. Ed was about 150 feet away, the only one between the suspect and escape in his direction.

Ed flipped the cylinder of his gun open, dumped out the rounds and spent cartridges, rammed in a speed loader and turned it, preparing to shoot again.

The gunman fired several shots at the cops, who were using parked cars and doorways for cover, taunting them, baiting them.

"Go ahead, shoot. Come on, shoot. I have her."

None of the cops returned fire. A couple of cops were hit, one in the foot, another in the abdomen from an earlier confrontation with the gunman, but his bulletproof vest saved him.

Suddenly, the woman seemed to push away from the gunman, creating a space. Many of the cops opened fire— shooting as many as 46 rounds.[1] But Ed did not have a clear shot, and held off.

Wounded during the onslaught, the hostage dropped to the ground.

The gunman sank to his knees, still firing. Soon out of bullets, bleeding out, the man, later identified as Sidney Fisher, a career criminal responsible for more than ten other bank robberies, fell over, dead.

Ed ran up to see what happened. "I was fuming. I wanted a piece of this guy. I was only married six weeks and he almost made my wife a widow."

As he stood over the suspect's dead body, Ed felt wobbly. His legs began to go out from under him. Later on, other officers told Ed he kept repeating, "This guy took a shot at me. He almost killed me. I can't believe I'm here." He has no recollection of ever saying that.

Fearing he was shot, his buddies loaded him into an RMP sector car and rushed him to St. Luke's hospital. Ed had no idea if he was hit. A week or two earlier, a Housing Officer was shot and didn't even know it. When the adrenaline pumps, sometimes you don't feel pain.

Ed wore a vest, except a vest is bullet *resistant*, not bulletproof. A bullet could still break ribs, tear tissue, rupture an artery, cause internal bleeding and even death from blunt trauma. For instance, before the final shootout, the officer shot in the abdomen took a 9mm round right above the spleen on the left side. The vest prevented the bullet from penetrating, but he suffered from a blunt trauma wound. No bones were broken, but he was badly bruised. Ed told me that "he picked the bullet out of the vest like a piece of lint and showed everyone."

As attendants wheeled Ed's hospital gurney into Emergency, the nurses wasted no time. Looking for a bullet wound, they tore off his jacket, vest and yanked up his shirt. It suddenly donned on him what they were doing. They were disrobing him in a hallway swarming with cops, bosses and curious people visiting other patients. *Holy shit*, he thought. *They think I'm shot.*

"Are you crazy?" he shouted, turning red with embarrassment.

They rolled him into a room, got him up and stripped him to his long johns and dressed him in a white hospital gown. "I'm okay, I'm okay," he reassured them, and himself. He lied back down on the gurney and the nurses draped him with a sheet. He wasn't hit, but he wasn't okay either.

Anxious, restless, and traumatized, he was becoming more agitated. His heart pounded, yet his pulse was weak. He was sweating, breathing rapidly, his skin was pale and he felt cold to the touch—possibly symptoms of emotional shock or an acute stress reaction.[2]

He wanted to tell his story because he'd seen the action in such detail. He was told to wait for a Patrolmen's Benevolent Association (PBA) representative. Frustrated, he began to reflect on the ordeal and the part he played in it.

He thought, *If only I could have stopped this bastard at the door. I could have fired more than three rounds, but that would have left me open because I only had a six-shooter.*

Ed's fear was he might run out of bullets and the gunman would kill him with his superior weapon. So he held back three rounds for self-protection. He wished he still had the gun issued to him as a Transit Officer, a Glock 19 9mm, an accurate gun in which he was proficient. Lighter, more balanced, its magazine held 15 cartridges, with a sixteenth in the chamber, a veritable arsenal compared to his Ruger Police Service Six .38 revolver. A few months later, 9mms were offered to every city cop in the department. Too late to make a difference in this case.

An array of people came in to see Ed, he can barely remember who. He told me that he was up and he was down, one moment depressed, the next worked-up, excited.

He couldn't stop talking. To let off steam, he told jokes, and couldn't stop himself from laughing. He was venting, rambling, trying to unburden himself of the despair he felt.

"I started feeling guilty about the woman being shot," he said.

Despite his agitated state, Ed was able to focus outside himself. He sought every piece of information he could get about the wounded police officers, and he was very concerned about his wife.

He knew reports of the shootout would be on radio and television and he wanted her to know he was okay. He asked one of the PBA delegates to call her and get a car out to pick her up.

Insurance underwriter Ann Marie Brown, 31, was sitting at her office desk on Long Island, 33 miles from St. Luke's Hospital in Manhattan, working on a policy when the phone rang at 11:15 Friday morning.

"Mrs. Brown," the voice said. "Your husband's been involved in a shooting. We're arranging for an officer to pick you up and take you to the hospital."

"Is he going to be okay?"

"We'd appreciate it if you didn't tell anyone about the incident right now. Keep your line clear for the officer to call you."

"Please, my husband..."

"Don't worry. We'll talk more when we see you."

Somehow, as the message passed from person to person, it got scrambled, and the delegate who ultimately called Ann Marie wasn't told if Ed was shot or not.

She hung up and thought, *Oh, my God. We haven't even got the proofs back from our wedding and I'm going to be a widow.* She shuddered and started to cry.

"What's wrong?" A co-worker was at her door. Before long, everyone in the office piled into her room to comfort her.

The phone rang again. The Highway Patrol in Queens was sending a car to pick her up.

"Can you please tell me how my husband is," she pleaded.

"No, I can't. I'm sorry. The police officer will be there in a half hour," said the dispatcher and hung up.

"Nobody will tell me a thing. What am I gonna do?" Ann Marie didn't want to call her parents, brothers or mother-in-law. She wasn't going to put them through agony, especially since she didn't know what to tell them.

As the minutes ticked by, she became increasingly more frightened. She was still suffering from the effects of a bad car accident right after her honeymoon when a truck broadsided her car. She had disk problems, nerve damage and now her neck was throbbing.

Fifteen minutes passed, then a half hour, then an hour...

The highway patrol officer finally showed up. He had gotten lost, but they took off and he raced them to the hospital at speeds sometimes exceeding 90 miles an hour, siren wailing and lights flashing. They screamed through red lights, toll booths and bulldozed over sidewalks.

"You'll have to forgive me," Ann Marie said to the officer as the car bucked and swayed into a curve. "I was in a car accident recently..."

The officer assured her he was trained to drive like this.

"Look, I'm not questioning your ability. I'm scared."

"Don't worry. We'll be fine," he promised.

This guy has a real attitude, she thought. *And I'm gonna get killed and never find out what happened.*

She asked him about her husband's condition and the shootout. He didn't know anything about them.

In her heart, she never thought anything like this would happen. Many of her friends whose husbands or children were police officers had never confronted the possibility of their loved one getting shot. Yet, "we always said, no matter what, before either of us ever left the house and when we came home, we would always wake the other up to say hello or goodbye and I love you. It could be the last time we ever see each other."

At the hospital, Ed was moved into Patrick White's room, the officer who was shot in the foot. A ceaseless traffic jam of bosses, inspectors and streetcops shuttled through wanting to know how they were and what happened, including the new police commissioner.

"Everyone did their job," Ed told him. Smiles ignited around the room.

Moments before Ed's wife arrived, a PBA rep told him the woman grabbed in the shootout had died, and they weren't sure if the gunman had killed her or a stray police bullet. Ed's heart ached. When the hospital chaplain came in, they said a prayer for her and her family.

Ann Marie arrived at the hospital in Manhattan from East Meadow, Long Island, normally a 45-minute drive on a good day with no traffic, in almost 20 minutes.

"You better prepare yourself for the press," said the highway patrol officer.

"You gotta be kidding me?" she said. "I don't know what's going on." Ann Marie didn't even know there was a bank robbery.

The second she stepped from the car, she was swarmed by photographers flashing pictures and reporters screaming, "Whose wife is this? Whose wife is this?"

A phalanx of police officers cut through the mob and whisked her, arm-in-arm, inside the hospital.

Later, the press inadvertently provided the only light moment in the entire affair. *New York Newsday* published a picture of Ann Marie rushing into the hospital, but identified her as the wife of Patrick White, the officer who got shot in the foot.

After Ed's release from the hospital, he called Patrick to see how he was, and the first thing Patrick said was—

"How's my wife?"

"She's fine, but she's cheating on you," Ed replied.

"Be sure to kiss my wife hello for me," said Patrick.

In the hospital corridor, Ann Marie was met by a sea of blue uniforms. The crowd and the smell of urine and vomit overpowered her. She wanted to run, to get away from the noise and press of bodies. Except her husband needed her, and she needed him, "please God, don't let him be hurt, not today, not ever."

Ann Marie was led through the throng of police officers and brass jamming the hallway to her husband's room. The room was filled with people. You could hardly move. A PBA delegate was interviewing Ed as he lay on a gurney under a blanket.

Seeing him, she started to weep uncontrollably. She wasn't allowed to go to him yet. She had to wait near the door until the interview was over. Her eyes scanned him for sign of injury. Face, arms and upper chest looked fine. The blanket hid the rest of him from her. Maybe he was hit in the leg or the stomach and they had to get his statement before surgery. She conjured up all kinds of horrors.

The waiting was intolerable. Right when she thought she might barge through the crowd if they didn't let her see her husband immediately, they were finished, and she was in his arms, crying, hugging and kissing.

"Are you all right," she asked, caressing his face. He said the best words she'd ever heard. "Yeah, I'm okay."

He grabbed her and they held each other for a long moment.

After awhile, Ed got out of bed. His pulse was back to normal and he wasn't nauseous anymore. Ann Marie accompanied him back to the precinct where the supervisors took his gun, along with everybody else's who was there during the shootout, and sent the weapons to ballistics. They wanted to get a signature from each gun to compare them to the bullets that killed the hostage.

Then Ed and Ann Marie headed home.

"I should've taken out the guy in front of the bank," he said in the car. "I should've."

Guilt is a natural response from an officer when he's disappointed in the outcome of an operation or feeling responsible for something he did or didn't do. Should Ed have disregarded his training, fired more bullets and risked being killed? Nobody has the answer.

What is the probability Ed would have hit his target in any case? According to NYPD statistics, not great. Less than 25 percent of rounds fired by police in gunfights actually hit their intended mark. Among other factors, the stress of a situation, fear, and the resulting surge of adrenaline from the automatic stress-response interfere with accuracy. Adrenaline makes you tremble. This probably accounts for why the gunman and Ed, although they fired at close range, missed each other completely.[3]

Once they were home, Ann Marie asked Ed to tell her everything that had happened, and he did. Not every loved one wants to know.

"I have a girlfriend, and her husband's a cop in Brooklyn," said Ann Marie, "one of the worst neighborhoods where you could be a police officer. Ed and I know more about what her husband's been through than she does. She doesn't want to know. That's her way of dealing with his work. I would rather know the details, because this is what we deal with everyday and I don't want to be shocked if this happens again."

Ed and Ann Marie were too upset to have dinner that night. They talked about the events and cried a little. Ed watched television to try to drive everything from his mind. He was worn out. For the first time in his life, his back hurt. Unusual for him, he drank three beers and fell asleep on the couch. Ann Marie woke him up and they went to bed.

"She was very worried about me. She didn't know how I'd react to this," he said.

Neither of them slept very well. Ed was experiencing post-shooting trauma symptoms. His sleep was frequently interrupted over a period of two to three weeks by nightmares and flashbacks of the episode.

"This was a videotape loop, over and over and a lot was in slow motion. The scene I remember most is the smoke coming from the gun when he shot at me. You could see him and the puff of smoke frozen right there."

Ed dreamed about it at night. He flashed on it during the day when something resembled smoke like car exhaust, a beam of sunlight catching dust, a swirl of leaves.

"Ann Marie told me I was talking in my sleep. She said I was fighting. I yelled, 'Get him! Grab him!' I took Tylenol to help me sleep and it worked, but the back pain... I think I buried all the tension inside me."

Ed thought about the woman who died. And he had frequent flashbacks of seeing her dead or dying on the sidewalk.

"If the woman was my wife, I mean, I would say, 'I don't care what the circumstances are. I don't care who else gets shot. Set up a way that she can get away.' If we could have saved her, we would have."

Ann Marie was afraid to wake Ed from his nightmares. But she didn't tell him about her own bad dreams, the ones about him dying. The more afraid she became about the incident, the more she avoided telling him about her own increasing distress.

Seeing Ed at breakfast the next day, Saturday, was hard for her because it brought the shootout back to reality. She couldn't confront the fear that she could lose Ed and her life with him in an instant.

Ann Marie tried to alleviate her stress by calling friends and relatives. She needed someone to talk to.

"Everybody said, 'Well, he's okay. Don't worry.' Everyone I associate with, my friends and family, nobody could relate to how I was feeling. Nobody understood. Everyone would ask about him and very few people asked me, 'How are you doing?' I was holding everything in. I felt shut off because I had nobody to talk to."

After breakfast, Ann Marie went to see her mother at work and then to see her father. She went in and out of stores in a daze.

"I realized anything can happen. I didn't want to make him feel any worse by bawling my eyes out, releasing my own emotions, because he had enough to worry about. I tried to keep my pain in to allow him to get his stuff out."

Ed was aware of her anxiety and tried to distract her by being funny. "I joked with my wife. I said, 'I almost made you a rich woman, honey. You could have bought the storybook house you wanted with the insurance money.'"

Ann Marie didn't think this was funny. She was too scared and anxious—as a result of a lot of things... Her fear came from more than the shootout. In the past two years, she had experienced several losses that consumed her with apprehension and grief.

She'd lost her grandmother and her uncle recently. Her grandmother was like a best friend, and, although her death was expected, Ann Marie took it very hard. Her uncle was fifty-years-old when he died unexpectedly. An unexpected death, especially of someone relatively young, can have more emotional impact than an anticipated one. She was still in shock from both of these deaths when her brother was assaulted and nearly died.

To add to her stress, so much had changed in her life and was new to her. Although she and Ed dated for two years before marrying, getting married, moving to a new apartment, living together and adjusting to each other's habits contributed to her nervousness. Cop life—working all hours of the day and night, weekends, holidays, spending days off in court, canceling plans at the last minute— increased her anxiety.

Just when things seemed like they couldn't make her more unsettled, she had the car accident, and sustained a physical injury that reminded her of how fragile life is. She'd reached the point where she didn't think she could take much more when the phone rang about Ed being involved in a shootout.

Now the idyllic picture of her life in the future felt threatened. She and Ed expected to have a family of two or three children. Where are her children if Ed is killed?

"I'm normally a very independent person," said Ann Marie. "But I found myself not wanting to leave him, you know, even to go to the store."

When you add up all the tragedies and losses that occurred in Ann Marie's life over a short period of time, you can see, now with the prospect of Ed's life being in danger, that she was on the verge of being totally overwhelmed. Her "stress bucket" had overflowed.[4]

After a week at home, Ed returned to work. Although he was off the street for the duration of the investigation and spent most of his time answering phones and watching TV, Ann Marie obsessed about him.

"The first day he went back to work, I was petrified even though I knew he was going to be on an inside detail. I didn't have anything to be fearful of. It's the idea he's back to work."

About a month after the shooting, while Ed was still on light duty, her usually punctual husband was two hours late getting home one night, and she didn't know where he was.

"My body was shaking and I was crying and thinking to myself, I'm acting really stupid. But I couldn't help it."

When Ed came in the door, Ann Marie was "bouncing off the walls," trembling and weeping. He explained that he was in court and couldn't get to a phone.

"You should call me before you get on the train to come home," she said, "because here I am reliving this all over again. For all I know, you were dead on the street in a pool of blood."

Ann Marie felt that danger was waiting for her husband around every corner. "I felt like when he went back to the streets, this will be the end, something else was going to happen. I was settling into my life as a wife and all of a sudden my life was up in the air. I didn't know what to expect. I was afraid to be without him. It's hard to put everything else in perspective when somebody you love is almost taken from you."

Surprisingly, the trauma that Ed experienced did not affect him in the long term as much as it did Ann Marie. After spending four years as a Transit Officer, he was used to stressful and dangerous situations.

In the subway, he knew he was open to attack at anytime. He usually patrolled alone at night, and often his radio wouldn't work underground. He was on his own if a confrontation went bad, and he learned to depend on himself and his training.

He was a street smart guy who grew up in the Bronx, and to keep his fear in control, he used his wits to survive. He came into contact with homeless people living in the tunnels and trains, the mentally ill, people with lice, tuberculosis and other diseases, crack addicts, panhandlers, turnstile jumpers, vandals, thieves, pickpockets, and killers.

Although he had reacted to the shootout with emotional shock, he was conditioned to expect a certain level of danger. And because he was able to share the experience with caring people, not keeping anything inside, and he had a loving wife who doted on him, he was able to recover swiftly.

But Ann Marie was not prepared for the dangers of his job. Feeling rebuffed by her friends, she no longer turned to them for help, and started to see less of them. When the news reports of the shooting began, she felt singled out, isolated. Her husband took the newspaper stories badly, finding the community unsympathetic and "downright anti-police." She empathized with his hurt and felt like the whole world was closing in around them.

"After living through this experience, I never realized how one-sided the press could be, how unfair. I read every article on the incident and not one of them held the truth. Everybody, of course, blamed these guys for the woman's death and they were only trying to do their job."

Ann Marie focused her attention on Ed. She wanted him to know he was loved and appreciated. "My wife helped me through this," he said. "A lot of support and tender, loving care. The woman catered to me, anything I wanted, I had. She made special meals for me, she checked on me to make sure I was okay. She really tried to discuss what happened because she thought it'd be good for me."

But Ann Marie couldn't escape from herself. She found that the pain from fear was impairing her ability to function. She couldn't concentrate at work, wasn't sleeping, was exhausted all the time, and tearing herself apart if Ed was a minute late getting home. She believed the people dearest to her couldn't relate, and she "felt shut off" from those she cared about.

She called a retired police officer from the New York Police Self-Support Group, and he comforted her, but as the days went by, she became more and more anxious. About a month and a half after the shootout, she turned to her office's Employee Assistance Program, which provided a counselor. "I really needed to know I wasn't losing my mind."

Ann Marie's symptoms were attributed to posttraumatic stress. She exhibited a number of disturbances: sleeplessness, denial, arousal, anxiety, fear, uncontrollable crying fits, loss of control, grief, poor concentration, obsessive thinking, headaches, hypervigilance, withdrawal, emotional ups and downs and a sense of impending misfortune.

More damaging, she was suppressing her feelings, and the longer she kept them hidden, the more likely her posttraumatic stress could develop into something more long-term like Posttraumatic Stress Disorder (PTSD).

However, after her first therapy session, she "felt like a ten ton truck was lifted off" her. Talking with a professional alleviated many of her fears and let the air out of her out of control feelings.

To help her further in the therapy process, Ann Marie turned to her family priest, a man who understood her worry as he had two nephews who were police officers. He provided her with another outlet to express her emotions.

As a practicing Catholic, she was also able to derive comfort from prayer. Ann Marie attended church every Sunday; Ed was usually working all weekend. However, the Sunday after the shootout, Ed was home, and they were able to attend Mass together.

"Devastating events like the shootout make you put your life in perspective," said Ann Marie. "We get so carried away with the everyday grind and materialistic things, we forget why people are in our lives. After this, I felt an even stronger bond between us. We were grateful we had each other."

After Ann Marie's second counseling session, she felt she had her feelings sufficiently under control to function in her work and personal life. To help further, she realized what she really needed was a support group of police officer spouses. None existed for the families of NYPD officers at that time unless a loved one was killed in-the-line-of-duty.

"Maybe I would have felt differently if there were a group that could talk about their fears and what it was like for them. I mean, if I hadn't experienced this, I would never in a million years relate to it.

"Everybody should know they're not alone, that what they're feeling is normal, that somebody else knows what you went through and can help you go through it. Otherwise, the next devastating thing that happens to you, all those fears are going to come rushing back."

As well as seriously affecting Ed and Ann Marie, the shooting had a ripple effect on their friends. "One of Ann Marie's friends, her husband is a police officer who works in Queens," said Ed, "and this incident showed his wife how susceptible he is to getting killed. Now they're all worried about their husbands. You know, 'If this could happen to Ed, what could happen to my husband?' It opens a lot of peoples' eyes."

A couple of months after the shooting, Ed testified at a grand jury hearing. It became clear that a police bullet had killed the hostage, but unclear whose gun had fired it. Unlike the officers who fired their guns in the final moments, Ed had not, and didn't have to anguish over whether his bullet killed her. He couldn't imagine how awful the other officers felt, not knowing who was the one who fired the fatal shot.

Nevertheless, he was traumatized. The acts of firing his gun, being shot at, seeing an innocent woman get hit, witnessing the whole deadly situation from beginning to end, affected him deeply.

"Always have respect for life because it can leave you in a flash. And I'm lucky I'm here right now."

After the grand jury hearing, Ed involved himself in police work on the street once again, and most of his stress-related symptoms disappeared. His back hurt on occasion when he got irritated, something he never had before. During the crisis, he received a lot of support from colleagues, his wife and family. His profound belief in God gave him comfort and his sense of humor helped him get through the tough times.

While the attention was on Ed, his wife became an inadvertent casualty of his job.

"We each lived our own kind of hell," said Ann Marie, "and neither of us will ever understand the other's hell, no matter how much we'd want to. I'm not a police officer. I don't go out everyday with fear that somebody may try to kill me. But I have the fear somebody may try to kill my husband. And I can't control that and I have nobody really to speak to.

"You know, the officers get counseling and physicals before they can return to work. The families don't, but they're expected to go on like nothing ever happened."

Chapter 8

Soldiers

*"I knew that if I drank enough
I would not hear the sound of rotor blades."*

The military is a natural place for police departments to recruit. Soldiers are accustomed to following orders without question. From a police administration's standpoint, they make perfect cops.

For thousands of troops returning from combat, the police department is a good place to apply for work. Because of their experience, they get preferential treatment and are one step ahead of the rookies who have never seen the horror that can be done to the human body.[1]

Soldiers who handle psychological trauma well are assets to police departments. They keep cool under the most frightening and disgusting circumstances such as shootouts, hostage-taking, child abuse and dismembered bodies.

But many do not handle trauma well. Almost a million Vietnam veterans still suffer from PTSD. After years of silence, World War II veterans are now coming forward with stories of nightmares and flashbacks. And PTSD is showing up in Gulf War veterans.[2] So when soldiers arrive at the precinct door, many are already suffering. Police work only intensifies their torment.

This chapter sketches the lives of three Vietnam veterans who became police officers. As a group, Vietnam vets are the most picked on, picked apart, vilified and praised armed force in history. Remember, it is in Vietnam veterans that Posttraumatic Stress Disorder was originally diagnosed and treated.

The first story is about former infantryman Bob Mc-Clellan. At forty-six, Bob is just over 6 feet, 210 pounds, with brown hair and a smile like a bent tire iron. His dark brown eyes have a way of piercing your thoughts, striking you with terror and amusement in the same blow. After I asked him if Vietnam influenced his police work, he described an incident that happened when he was only six weeks overseas.

As a grunt with the 1st Cavalry Division (Airmobile), called the 1st Cav, he was wandering through thick vegetation one day in Phuoc Vinh province on a search-and-destroy mission. He was carrying a ninety pound pack on his back. It was 115 degrees and 100 percent humidity. Sweat streamed down his face. Insects crawled through his hair and clothes.

"As if that isn't uncomfortable enough," he said, "we were walking along for several hours on a mission that was meaningless to us. You're walking through the jungle and worrying about snipers and trip wires. All this creates an aura of unbelievable stress. It's putting one foot in front of the other and then *BANG*."

A sniper opened up on his squad. The soldiers hit the ground and swept the area with small arms and automatic weapons fire. But the sniper was gone. Later, they tracked the sniper to a village and observed people running behind one of the hootches.

"Somebody started firing and we all did," said Bob. "And when the smoke had cleared, we went in and checked. There were three kills. The Sergeant rolled over one of the bodies that he attributed to me. She had a gun, but it was a girl, maybe about fourteen. I wasn't prepared for that.

"And I was even less prepared for... He took out a knife, cut her ear off and slapped it in my hand. That was my souvenir."

"What did you do?" I said.

"At nineteen years old from Brooklyn, I had no idea what to do because I didn't know if it was right or wrong. That night, I made a little grave and buried it."

About a decade later, distanced in time and geography from Vietnam, Bob was a New York cop working youth gangs one hot summer day. A light rain was falling. Steam rippled up from the pavement. His shirt stuck to his back in salty splotches and sweat trickled down his neck. The air tasted wet like in Vietnam.

Bob told me that gang members went to the home of a rival gang lord and rang the bell. When they saw an eye appear in the door's peephole, they fired a shotgun blast through the door, striking the gang lord's sister, a Hispanic girl about fifteen years old. When Bob arrived, detectives and crime scene techs were examining the body.

"It was as if I stepped in between two dimensions," said Bob. "When I saw her facedown on the floor—she had long black hair and it was all around her—I saw the girl I shot in Vietnam. This Hispanic girl was wearing black jeans and a dark blouse, which was made darker by all the blood. The girl in Vietnam was wearing black pajamas. Suddenly, I could smell the jungle, that corrosive rot of the jungle. I could smell cordite, which was probably still in the air from the shotgun blast. And I blanked out."

The next thing Bob remembered was sitting in the unmarked police car. He was sweating when his partner got in.

"What the fuck is wrong with you?" asked his partner.

"What're you talkin' about?" said Bob.

"Why did you say that upstairs?"

"What?"

"You turned to one of the homicide detectives and said, 'Who's gonna cut off her ear?' And then you turned around and walked out."

Bob does not recall saying anything. "But I went home that night and drank because I was embarrassed and scared. I really wasn't sure what was wrong. From that point on, things changed drastically."

Bob was married about a year when his frightened wife called one of his partners, also a Vietnam vet, to the house. She said, "He's up in the attic crawling around looking for Viet Cong." When his partner peered into the attic, he saw Bob's outline. Bob was sitting in the crawl space, cradling an AR-15 assault rifle. It was August, the hottest part of the summer.

"What're you doing?" his partner asked.

"I'm relaxing. This is where I relax."

Bob sat in the dark and heat for hours. "I guess it was reminiscent of sitting in the jungle on ambushes," he said. "I'd sit up there and feel the sweat pool under my eyes and drip off. And drink. And go into crying jags and have conversations with the guys who died, long-dead grunts and door-gunners."

Bob's partner could not persuade him to leave the attic nor to talk about his sorrow. Bob says he carried a lot of guilt and shame about Vietnam. Guilt about surviving when most of his buddies didn't, shame about what he did.

Not all Vietnam veterans returned from war as tormented as Bob. Many were able to come to terms with the horror of their ordeal. They accepted it as part of their lives and moved on without punishing themselves. For hundreds of thousands of psychologically scarred soldiers, many physically wounded, it was not possible. Bob is one of those who did not escape the harsh consequences of trying to justify unforgivable actions.

Let's go back in time for a moment to his freshfaced youth to see why it took ten years for him to climb the stairs to the attic.

Bob says his father believed in "obligation to country." And that belief made Bob feel guilty for not going to war. After all, his brother had gone. To please his father, Bob volunteered.

"In my family, success meant you had to finish high school, complete your military obligation and get a civil service job," said Bob. "I was discouraged from going to college. My father actually went to my high school and told a teacher, 'Stop pressuring him into college. It's only for queers, Communists and liberals.'"

Bob's view of the world was colored by his father's working class attitude. Men were men. They worked for the city and fought and sometimes died for their country. They didn't send their children to college.

Bob's life at eighteen was filled with stories of what the Irish and Italian Catholic men in his parish did to prove themselves. He often watched from the windows of his school the big events across the street at the funeral parlor. Many a flag-draped coffin with the remains of somebody he knew drifted by.

"Their ghosts inspired me, and we sat in the Night Owl Bar and would say, 'We're gonna go into the military and be Green Berets, and we're gonna avenge Jimmy and this one and that one.'

"I had a friend who'd been shot at Hamburger Hill and he was crippled. He'd say, 'It's up to you guys now to go over there.'"

Bob said his neighborhood was pro-military in 1970. The bar had a board on the wall honoring the names of those who went to Vietnam. If you were wounded, a silver star was pinned next to you. If you were killed, a gold star. His brother's name was up there for serving two tours without getting hurt. In a nightly ritual, everyone toasted the men on the board.

"I wanted my name to be up there," said Bob. "I had all the fear and fascination with this ultimately manly thing—combat. When I returned home from basic training, I was sitting in the bar next to my crippled friend, Mike. All of a sudden he started crying."

"What's the big deal? I'm goin' off to war," said Bob.

"You have no fucking idea what you're getting into," said Mike.

"Come on. How bad can it be?"

He soon found out how bad it can be. Not long after Bob shot the girl who inhabits his dreams, his squad walked into an ambush. Several of his friends were killed, and he was shot in the chest.

"I was lying there in shock and these little gnats were flying in my mouth and in my eyes and I thought, *I don't wanna die like this.*"

The bullet fragmented when it went in. A piece went through his shoulder blade, another piece perforated a lung. Other shards traveled down along his spine where they remain today. Even though the wounds were life-threatening, he was not allowed to go home.

After a month and a half recuperating, Bob returned to the 1st Cav front lines and became a helicopter door-gunner, flying hunter/killer. With two other crew members in a Loach, a small egg-shaped chopper with bubble Plexiglas, he flew at treetop level to attract fire. Like a worm on a hook, he was bait. When someone shot at the chopper, a circling Cobra gunship would dive on the hostiles and spray the area with rocket and machine-gun fire.[3]

I asked Bob if this was an insane thing to do. It struck me as suicidal. He said it was a standard procedure that proved to be a very effective, if costly, tactic.

To neutralize the tension from daily dancing with death, Bob and his buddies drank. Some smoked pot and took heroin "to chase away the terrors."

"There were times the body counts were so great," he said, "when we would lose so many people, that the stress would permeate the entire unit. At one period we were losing a ship a week."

After a few months playing chicken with a heavily armed enemy, Bob was shot down. Everyone walked away, but he felt his "time was coming." Completing his tour of duty, he went home. A week later, his ship was shot down and his replacement and two buddies were killed. He says he felt somehow responsible for their deaths.

"It's like it was bad karma for me to leave," he said. "We had been through so much, even getting shot down. My leaving broke the magic spell."

Not telling his parents he was returning, Bob thought he would surprise his father at work. His father was a cop. Four rows of medals across the chest of his uniform, Bob strutted into his dad's precinct.

Before he could say anything, a young cop rebuked all GIs for "coming to town on leave to get drunk and make pests of themselves."

"He didn't know who I was, but he treated me and my uniform with disdain," Bob said. "This was the same way people treated me at the airport, and I had had enough. My father was out on patrol, and I didn't even wait for him."

Bob set out for the Night Owl Bar.

"One of the things that got me through Vietnam was that I have looked death in the eyes and survived and have the scars and medals to prove it. I've earned my place on that wall, complete with star. I'm a true warrior, expecting a hero's welcome. This was a visit I'd dreamed about for months."

Bob went into the bar. It was early. Harry the bartender shook his hand and bought him a drink.

"What happened to the names on the wall?" Bob asked.

"They took 'em down," Harry said. "There's a different crowd here now. They're not really pro-military anymore. As a matter of fact, they're actually pretty anti-Vietnam War."

Then he added, "It's probably not a good idea for you to be in uniform here. I'm proud of ya, but things have changed."

"Well, fuck you. And fuck this," said Bob, who proceeded up Flatbush Avenue to drink in every bar until he couldn't stand.

A few days later, he went to see Mike, the crippled friend who warned him about what he was getting into. Bob told him, "I know what you're talking about now. I'll never be the same again. I'll never, ever view anything the same again."

"What was different?" I asked Bob.

"Reality. The loss of being immortal."

This is the response police officers often give after shooting someone, being shot or having been on the street a short while. Like combat soldiers, cops give up early their youthful fantasies.

After Bob's flashback of the Vietnamese girl he killed and many episodes of "relaxing" in the sweltering attic that basted him in sweat and memories, he rapidly went downhill. He left his wife and two young children and moved into a Brooklyn apartment near work.

"I was terrified of going to sleep at night," he said. "I was afraid of what might happen when I was alone. And the nightmares. I was afraid I wouldn't come back from Vietnam."

"What do you mean?" I asked.

"Before I'd fall sleep I would hear helicopters. And I would go to the windows and look for them. When I got shot and was lying there waiting for the Medevac, I remember the first time the chopper came in. They took some serious fire from the NVA who ambushed us, so the chopper turned around and left without me. I heard our medic yelling into the radio, 'If we don't get him outta here, he's gonna bleed to death. I can't stop the fucking bleeding.' And I knew he was talking about me.

"Through it all I wanted to go to sleep, but Doc said, 'If you go to sleep you'll die.' So then I became afraid to go to sleep. I thought, *If I sleep, I die.*"

As Bob's condition worsened, friends and family distanced themselves from him, and alone with his fears, he returned nightly to the jungle, his only weapon a bottle of alcohol.

"At night I opened the cylinder and handcuffed my gun to the radiator because I was afraid of what I might do," he said. "Then I lay down with my bottle and drank. And the nightmares... Every night I'd wake up scared with palpitating heart, sweating, throwing up. But I knew that if I drank enough I would not hear the sound of rotor blades."

To escape the nightmares, Bob thought relief might come from suicide.

"At work I would respond to *investigate prowler* runs, especially the rooftop jobs. And I would look over and say, 'This is how I'm gonna do it. I'm just gonna step off one of these roofs. I'll get an inspector's funeral. It'll be ruled accidental, but still a line-of-duty fatality. I'll be a hero. My family will be taken care of for life, and I'll be done with it. This is my out.'"

More than anything else, he thought he was losing control. Because he blanked out when he saw the murdered Hispanic girl, he believed it was only a matter of time before he overreacted in a situation. "I was afraid I might kill somebody or just go crazy."

Alone, reclusive, sleeping by day and drinking on the job, Bob was finally reported. He went to the peer support unit for help. After therapy for alcoholism, he moved on to the Veterans Administration hospital where he was treated for Posttraumatic Stress Disorder.

"I was finally able to grieve. I was able to cry and let myself go."

I asked Bob if he sees likenesses between warfare and police work.

"There are enormous parallels," he said. "Policing is a paramilitary operation, so you do everything without the chance to process emotions. You're in, you're out. You do your job and you're on to the next one, just like in war."

And Bob says there is another parallel, with a major difference.

"In some precincts, every day you are exposed to violent death. In Vietnam in one year, you were exposed on numerous occasions, but not everyday. And still 40 to 60 percent of us came home with emotional scars. A New York City police officer can be exposed to that for twenty years, or thirty or thirty-five. Depending on how lucky or unlucky he is, he could spend his entire career in a shithouse."[4]

*   *   *

"Don't give up.
Try and get some help.
We're all gonna die, but why die early?"

A cop who returned from war with emotional scars was NYPD Sergeant Joseph Kroon. Stepping, as if through a curtain, from the rice patties of Vietnam onto the concrete and asphalt streets of America, he saw little difference between the countries. War was war.

Although shot at and shelled by mortars, Joe's job as a marine in Vietnam was not search and destroy. It was air dropping of equipment. He said his worst mission was a trip to the so-called demilitarized zone, the DMZ.

"The C-130 is a big cargo plane," he told me. "As soon as the guys touched down, they reversed props and if things weren't tied down good...

"We got out and found out what we had to do—fill the plane up with dead bodies. They were covered with ponchos, no body bags. The prop blast already'd blown off the ponchos. And you see people decapitated, parts missing. As we put the stretchers up, the body fluids... I froze. I stood there holding the stretcher and this gunnery Sergeant kept yelling at me, 'Joe, Joe, get 'em on the plane.'

"He got me outta the trance I was in and we loaded the plane. At Da Nang, we unloaded the plane, and we all took off our uniforms and threw 'em away. Sometimes I wake up dreamin' of that."

I met Joe Kroon more than a quarter century later. The image of the ponchos blowing away still lingered fresh in his mind. From his poker face and collected manner, you wouldn't say the incident affected him greatly. But the pain blazing from his green eyes gave him away.

If you had met Joe, you'd probably have thought to yourself, *What a nice guy.* That was Joe's trademark, a manner both engaging and sweet-tempered. When he arrived for the interview, I didn't see a cop. I saw a small-boned, elegant statesman. A Puerto Rican with long bushy side-burns, an aquiline nose, a skinny mustache and receding hairline.

I didn't know what an achievement it was for him to smile and open his mouth. Soon after Vietnam, Joe joined the police department, and eleven years later he was shot in our urban war zone.

He was in a building observing drug sales across the street. Somebody was always getting shot on the corner as drug dealers battled for territory.

"I try to get a look at the seller," he said, "and I pick up my head too high. We try to stand away from the window. And I hear someone yell, 'Five-0, third floor.'[5] And I look and everybody starts running. So I said to my partner, 'I think we got made.' Everything goes dead on the street."

Minutes later, Joe heard footsteps running up the stairs. He went to the door and knelt down to listen. Then as he looked around the door, he heard a blast.

"First thing I remember was seeing the blood gushing outta my face. I was hit right up to the side of my nose. The bullet traveled downward, shattered my jaw and lodged in my neck on the right side.

"I thought, *What the fuck happens if I die? What's to happen to my family?*"

At the hospital, he asked the cops who brought him in to call his family.

"My wife and kids were very much into me being a cop. I used to go home and tell them stories," Joe said. "I used to tell my wife, 'Look, if you see a cop come here, someone you know, to take you to see me, I'm alive. If he comes here with a chaplain, I'm dead.'

"I'm sitting there and someone comes over and puts a hand on my wrist. I turn around, it's a chaplain. I go, 'Fuck, I'm dying.'"

Much to Joe's relief, the chaplain happened to be in the neighborhood and was not there to give last rites.

"When they got my family, and the doctor at the hospital said, 'Joe's been shot in the face,' my daughter fainted. She was seven. And she told me later on, in her mind she thought I was dead. And my wife she went into shock. She saw the front seat of the police car covered with my blood.

"At the hospital, my wife broke down crying when she saw the side of my face all swollen. My daughter was white as a ghost. But we had to wait because they had to find somebody to do an angiogram. They didn't know if I was bleeding internally or if it hit my carotid artery.

"My main worry was my son. He was always very supportive of me. He wanted to become a cop also. He was at the time I think fifteen. When he got home, the next-door neighbor brought him to the hospital, and once he got there I started to calm down."

The doctors feared that the bullet in Joe's neck might have split and entered his brain. But the angiogram showed that the bullet was intact.

"And ever since then, I've said, 'I'm glad I'm alive.'"

Joe made a pendant of the bullet removed from his jaw and wore it like a good luck charm. But the talisman didn't hurry his recovery. For over two months, his jaw was wired shut.

"My first frustration was when they take the wires outta my mouth. Here it is almost ten weeks without eating solid food and everybody's promising me twelve inch steaks and my jaw won't open.

"So I go home and say, 'Shit, I was planning to eat something solid today.' So I go through the cupboards and find a can of tuna. I shoved this tuna with my finger and I ate half a that can. It tasted like lobster."

Although told he would recover fully, the side of his face where he was shot remained sore.

"Three months down the line, I saw the specialist and he tells me, 'Oh, you gotta learn to live with that.' And I says, 'You didn't tell me that. You told me I'd be back to normal and I thought all this pain would go away.' That was my first real anger at all the medical work. And the way I found not to feel the pain was to drink."

When Joe was able to insert a finger into his mouth, the police department insisted he return to full duty, despite hardly being able to talk. Even though the surgeon interceded to keep him at home, Joe became disillusioned with the insensitivity shown by the administration.

"They're a bunch of pencil pushers," he said. "That makes people very angry. There's no morale on this job from the higher ups."[6]

Joe was not the only one who suffered from the shooting. His family did too. Having nightmares, his daughter was sent to a psychologist. Although one of the street-corner drug traffickers was shot and killed, at least two were at large, and the child thought they would come to her house and kill her family.

"The person who was brought down a lot was my wife. I thought by me always tellin' her about the job she'd be well prepared, and I guess when something like that happens, you're never prepared. I used to hear her sobbing at night. I'd say, 'Whatsamatter?' She goes, 'You almost died on me.' That would happen to her quite often."

This was not the first incident in which Joe was shot at. But it triggered nightmares, not only of being shot, but of other traumatic incidents in his life. Foremost, was the dream about picking up bodies in Vietnam.

"I've never slept as well as I did before," he said. "You have an unease. Even though I slept five hours, it seemed like one hour."

Joe brooded about what happened, and like many officers involved in shootings, blamed himself.

"I used to feel I fucked up when I got shot," he said. "It's the *what ifs*. If I waited two more seconds before I came to the door... If I had challenged them... Should I have yelled, 'Police'? Maybe they would have runned away and the shooting wouldn't of happened."

He worried about what might happen if he was shot again. Nervous once he returned to work, he requested that Psychological Services examine him.

"I didn't feel at ease with myself. I didn't feel at ease with the public," he said.

The department put him on ninety days restricted duty while he went to therapy once a week. Afterwards, deciding that working the drug unit was too dangerous, he returned to patrol. Although lessened, his anxiety persisted. At home, he became irritable.

"I started to get on the family's nerves," he said. "My kids, who were very supportive when I first came home, they were staying in their room all the time. Almost any little thing would annoy me. As I was sitting in front of the boob tube, I started to drink more and more. I'm saying to myself, 'I've been doing everything right so far, why is everybody acting this way? Why are they getting so uptight?' I didn't realize it was me.

"My biggest regret is in the beginning I reached out to Psych Services, and then I didn't. It led me to... I became an alcoholic."

Joe eventually called the peer support unit and said, "I've had it with drinking. I got to go away."

After a four-week stay in a rehabilitation center, he was ready to face issues he hadn't confronted before. One of the psychiatrists told him he was holding in his feelings about Vietnam, that he suffered from PTSD from both Vietnam and police work. So Joe began therapy to deal with many years of accumulated trauma.

He also joined the Police Self-Support Group, to learn from others who were physically and psychologically damaged, and to give something back. As one of the prime motivators of the group, he visited wounded officers, shared insights and brought them comfort. He would tell them, "Don't give up. Try and get some help. We're all gonna die, but why die early?"

Throughout his career, Joe empathized with citizens, particularly those who were poor or underprivileged. When he worked Harlem, his greatest pleasure, he told me, was helping people.

"When you went to some job, you couldn't believe you were still in this country, how people were living. To me, this used to bother me a lot. I used to go home and hug my kids more."

Joe had a distinguished career. He held three citations for bravery, five for meritorious duty and eight for excellent police work. Wounded in-the-line-of-duty, he received the Police Combat Cross.

Early in 1996, after twenty-two years on the police force, Joe was considering retirement. He was forty-nine. But something changed for him. Did the demons of Vietnam return to haunt him? Did traumatic images that accumulated from his police years, especially the shock of being shot, finally reach out for him? Did alcoholism tighten its grip? Could he not bear the thought of retiring from a job in which he had invested his life? We'll never know.

Without leaving a note or saying good-bye, he shot himself.

On the urban battlefield, the enemy is not always the bank robber or drug dealer. The enemy can live within. Police officers have told me that suicide, to them, is not an unspeakable act. They see it so often in civilians that it has become an ordinary event, a way to solve monumental problems.[7]

This explains partly why police officers kill themselves at least twice as often as civilians. The suicide rate differs from city to city, state to state, and cannot be generalized or accurate since fellow officers often cover up suicides to avoid embarrassing the department or to allow families to collect insurance benefits.[8]

Soldiers who have seen combat carry an extra burden when they join the police force. They join already conditioned to accepting carnage and misery as normal. The idea of suicide is not a big leap.

No one can say for sure what made Joe's life unbearable. Perhaps it was a combination of experiences. As a soldier, he saw combat. As a cop, he was wounded, did not receive timely psychological care and became disillusioned with the department. Although he was eventually treated for alcoholism and PTSD, counseling, long after traumatic events, does not solve everyone's problems. Like the stubborn humidity in Vietnam, they can hang on.

Why did Bob McClellan, who also found life unendurable, not commit suicide as he had fantasized, but Joe did? Bob doesn't know, and Joe will never tell us.

Like many officers who have committed suicide before and since, Joe Kroon, that elegant, gentle man, has left family, neighbors and fellow officers grieving and asking, "Why?"

Sergeant Joseph Kroon, NYPD
March 5, 1947—March 27, 1996

"you mattered"

* * *

"You've got more warfare goin' on here
than you had over there."

Not everyone who enlisted to fight the war in Vietnam did so out of a sense of duty. Hector Rodriguez[9] joined because he believed he would be murdered if he didn't.

Attending high school in a mostly black area in South Central Los Angeles, he was frequently beaten and robbed. On his first day at the notorious Manual Arts High School, he watched a student get stabbed and thrown down the stairs. He attended classes that students, on occasion, forcibly took over.

Having learned never to show weakness, Hector eventually carried a .22 revolver and a knife to defend himself. "Everything I did was to survive," he said. Once word got around he was armed, bullies rarely challenged him.

To ease his anxiety from the stress of playing a street tough, he drank heavily and knocked back barbiturates like Red Devils. The mixing of drink and drugs made him feel invincible. One day he and his friends surrounded a boy who had beaten Hector up. Hector was prepared to exact revenge with a bicycle chain and switchblade. Then he made a decision that changed his life. He walked away.

"I'd always been taught by my parents to be compassionate, that fighting was wrong. I put myself in this guy's shoes."

But he also walked away for another reason—he wanted a future.

"You could see the way the street was going," he said. "People were getting more violent. Robbings, shootings. I knew I had to do something with my life. I looked ahead and saw zero. I saw I was gonna die. So I went to Vietnam."

Hector trained as a military police officer. Although his job in the 18th Brigade was to investigate GIs who had "screwed up," he still saw battle. While escorting convoys, he was sometimes fired upon by snipers.

In the only incident in which he is certain he shot someone, sappers with satchel bombs tried to cut through barbed wire at his barracks in Bien Hoa. He and his comrades mowed them down with hundreds of rounds of machine-gun fire. Having witnessed the mutilated bodies of

American soldiers, he said, "You don't want to say things like this, but it was payback time."

For Hector, the war was an exchange of paybacks. He felt a Viet Cong payback was going to kill him one night when he was asleep. The Quonset hut barracks were made of aluminum. Flimsy and full of holes, they inhaled swarms of mosquitoes, intense heat and humidity. Hector told me, "It's the only place in the world where you can take a cold shower and still sweat."

In the darkness, a rocket attack hopscotched across the camp. As rockets burst near Hector's hut, he and another soldier scrambled under beds, trying to get as close to the wall as they could. Then one landed beside the hut.

"The hut blew in and blew us clear across the room and slammed us against the walls," he said. "We thought that was it, we were gonna die. Think of it like running into a concrete wall, bouncing off and trying to shake that off. That was the hardest we've been hit, maybe a hundred rockets over an hour. But only five people died.

"You felt real helpless because there's nothing you can do. So we broke out a bottle of Jack Daniels and passed it around."

Hector made it through Vietnam unscathed—physically. With ten months still to serve, he upset a colonel by arresting one of the colonel's officers for drunk driving. "You don't know who you fucked with," said the enraged colonel. He punished Hector by having him shipped from Vietnam to an east coast American base. Hard to imagine anywhere as bad as Vietnam, but Hector says it was here on this base that he experienced overwhelming abuse.

"The commanding officers were deadbeats, lifers who hated the people they supervised, and enjoyed inflicting misery on younger people. My morale was the worst that it ever got, worse than Vietnam. I was getting more pissed off, more angry, more frustrated. We would go out and get drunk and come back in a rage and throw things out the window of our third floor day room. We stuffed chairs through the windows. We even stuffed a guy out a window."

One night Hector had enough of being harassed by superiors. He lay down on his bunk with an M16 across his chest.

"I felt a tremendous pressure on my head," he said. "Two hours later the captain and a sergeant came in the door. They knew I had the weapon. We talked, and the captain asked if I would give him the M16. I did. He then put me in charge of the gym to get away from everyone and asked if I'd see a psychiatrist."

The psychiatrist examined Hector "for a tendency for violence because of maybe something that happened in Vietnam." This was before anyone had codified the condition we now call PTSD. The examination was inconclusive, but Hector was concerned. Wanting to join a police department when he finished service, he feared the doctor's report might jeopardize his prospects.

"Are you sure you want to do this? Go into police work?" said the psychiatrist.

"Yes," said Hector. "Police work is different."

Different?—In years to come, when he thought about his comment, he would laugh at his own naiveté. He discovered that all that was different was the uniform.

He told the psychiatrist, "I hope what you write up doesn't hurt my chances to get on the police department."

Hector need not have worried. The Los Angeles Police Department in 1975 was looking for people like him.

"When I joined the department, they were recruiting guys that had been in the service, especially those from Vietnam. They wanted someone who didn't have a problem shooting someone, to who it wasn't going to be a shock. In my interview I had ten questions that had to do with having to shoot. They asked me, 'If your mother was pointing a weapon, would you shoot her to save another person's life?'"

"What did you say?" I asked.

"I said what they wanted me to say, and that was, 'Yeah.'"

"How did you do in the interview?"

"I came out with one of the highest scores of anybody in my academy class."

It helped that the LAPD gave him ten extra points in the interview for military service.

I met Hector on a blistering Los Angeles day. He seemed comfortable in the heat, like wearing old clothes that fit well. Visiting him in his home, I met his girlfriend, had lunch and dinner with them and talked for many hours.

This became the first of three day-long interviews. Everyone I talked to before had difficulty recalling details of traumatic incidents. Not Hector. He was impressive in his ability to recall even the most inconsequential aspects of a traumatic event.

Trauma survivors often cannot remember details of the most hurtful moments. Trauma can affect short-term and long-term memories.[10] The event becomes a smog, like the brown muck on hot summer days in L.A. But there are rare exceptions when trauma, rather than muddying memory, seems to sharpen it. Hector is that rarity.

Hector is engaging to look at. Built like a wrestler, about 5 and a half feet tall, what he lacks in height he makes up for in girth. Over 200 pounds, he's not fat, just a big boned, muscled forty-two year old. A black belt in karate, he works out regularly. He has a flat nose, a wide face and toothbrush eyebrows that join in the middle like fur. I can imagine a lawbreaker might consider other options before going up against him.

Hector developed a reputation as a tough cop, an elephant hunter who made good felony arrests. He was someone every cop wanted to work with. His outside persona was the cool, competent guy.

Inside was a different story. He was experiencing unbearable posttraumatic stress symptoms. Although he had suffered only a few migraine headaches, stomach problems plagued him all his life, a common physical response to stress. Sometimes he would become angry at his wife and two children for no reason. He ignored his family, preferring to go drinking after work with his police buddies. When he came home from work, he locked himself in the bedroom and would not come out.

Hector would rarely sleep through a night. Like in Vietnam, he slept lightly and woke frequently. In the barracks, he always slept with his hand on a gun and continued this habit through his police years.[11]

Hector believed his behavior and physical problems were "normal" until he read a magazine article about how severe stress on the job can change a police officer. Rather than Posttraumatic Stress Disorder, the article called it *combat fatigue.*

"It was like lookin' in a doggone mirror," he told me. "I noticed all kinds of symptoms. Like heavy drinking... When our friends that we grew up with would come over, I wouldn't come out of the room. I'd snap at people, snap at the kids and my wife. There were times I'd get so angry, all I could do was scream.

"I'm lookin' at that article and saying, 'That's it, I'm crazy.' I'm hypervigilant. I'm frustrated. My wife would yell at me because she couldn't get me to talk or communicate. I thought I was communicating. But she says, 'It's like you're empty inside. Like you're a robot going through the motions.'"

With his newfound knowledge, Hector did nothing. He buried his fears. Before long he became disenchanted with the department, and his arrests and encounters with suspects became brutal. One day he lost control.

He was sent to investigate a domestic disturbance at an apartment building. As he and his partner were walking through a courtyard under the apartment to which they were called, he heard glass shattering and then sharp pieces rained down on them. His partner's face was cut and bleeding. Though unhurt, Hector was incensed.

"I kicked the door in and this guy tries to take a punch at me, but I nailed him right in the forehead with my flashlight. And we started fighting, and I knocked him down. I must of hit this guy in the head ten or more times with my light. They pulled me off him and there was blood all over the place. And then I grabbed the front of his sweater and started punching him in the face.

"I prided myself in always being under control and for the first time I lost control."

"Why do you think you lost it?" I asked.

He said, "There's a real anger and frustration that builds up inside of you because of police work, a rage that happens from seeing people treating each other the worst possible way you could treat someone, and I think you are more prone to do crazy things. When you see the extremes of this society, it makes you extreme because you have to cope with it."

"What happened to the suspect?"

"When they pulled me off, one of the guys took me aside and said, 'Man, you fucked this guy bad. We'll get the ambulance, but get outta here.'"

"What did you do?"

"I walked up and down Devonshire and had my flashlight in my hand and this guy's blood all over me. I walked like I was in a daze. I didn't even feel happy about beatin' this guy. I went to the station and they called and said they think the guy's not gonna make it. I thought, *Fuck, I'm gonna go to prison.* But I don't feel anything. I mean, I wanted to at least feel sorry for what I did. I wanted to feel that I could cry or something, but I felt nothing."

"What happened?"

"The guy lived because he was so drunk he didn't go into shock from loss of blood. Then he skipped back to Mexico. That's when I realized that I'm getting dangerous. I'm out of control. I was getting to like the idea of violence. I was finding myself feeling like the bullies I hated when I was growing up."

From then on, Hector's attitude worsened. He got into conflicts with his superiors. He argued incessantly with his wife. He took the graveyard shift, "when the vampires come out," because he knew he could hide from everyone at night. He stopped caring about his appearance. And his buddies, like the psychiatrist in the military, covered for him.

"I wasn't handling things too well," he said. "I had no passion for the job anymore, a job I used to love. At roll call, I didn't say a single word. Then I would go get my coffee and sit on the hood of the car, lean back against the driver's windshield and look up at the stars."

One clear night, Hector was on his way to a coffee shop so he could enjoy the peaceful ritual looking at the stars when his life was almost taken from him.

He spotted a man breaking into a car. While his partner walked toward the suspect, Hector, not wanting to be bothered, stayed by the cruiser.

"Normally both of us walk toward a suspect, but I didn't. Then something clicked. *Something's wrong. This guy is sharp, like an ex-con.*

"My partner tells him to put his hands behind his head and grabs his left arm to force it back. The guy looks at me and I knew, *He's settin' us up.*

"I yell, 'Motherfucker,' and get my stick out and run toward him. With some martial arts move, he breaks my partner's grip with his left hand, takes off and we chase after him between the cars.

"We catch the guy in a little walkway. We're fighting and I've nailed him about six times in the groin with kicks and hit him in the head about the same number. He's built like a bull. And nothing is phasing him.

"My partner maces him and all the guy does is push him away. I hit the guy in the back of the head and on the side of the neck and he goes down.

"And I'm thinking, *Here we are locked in this fight, and I don't wanna do this.* When he's down on the ground and I crouch right over his head, I'm wishing, *Don't get up, man. Stay down. I don't wanna hurt you.*

"All of a sudden the guy does a one-hand pushup and comes up with a .25 automatic.

"As I see the gun coming up, I throw the stick down and at the same time do a back roll like I was taught. I hit the button on my clamshell holster and take my gun out."

The suspect fired twice. Hector rocked forward with his leg straight out and opened fire, their barrels about three feet from each other.

"I see the orange flame from the guns. I hear the popping sound and then my ears go numb from the ringing.

"Every time I shoot him, it lights his face up. And every time he shoots, I think, *He's not hitting me.* And as soon as I say that, I get hit twice.

"I shoot at this guy until my gun goes empty. It's only a six-shot Smith an' Wesson. I click the gun twice as he's moving away from me and I try to open up the cylinder. My hand's like rubber, like it's not there anymore. The guy starts to bring the gun back towards me and my partner opens up on him. The guy takes off running, and I know I hit him at least five of six shots."

While Hector dumped empty cartridges from his gun, his partner went after the suspect. Hector's right hand was unusable. With his other hand, he positioned a speed loader of bullets over the cylinder, but they wouldn't slip in.

"I could hear my partner yellin', 'Freeze, Freeze.'

"And I'm thinking, *We're past 'Freeze.' This guy is gonna kill you.*

"And I know I have to help my partner. I get up and as I move, the bullets fall in and I slam the cylinder shut."

Hector ran down the street and caught up to them. "I said to my partner, 'Take the outside of the cars, use that for cover. I'll get him by the building and we'll get the guy into a position to take him into custody.' Only I'm not thinking custody."

Hector spotted the suspect about half a block away and fired twice with his left hand, but missed. The man ran behind a building.

"I yell, 'Police officers! Throw the gun out and come out with your hands up.'

"I know he isn't gonna do it, but I say it because I want him to hear my voice over here, and then I move somewhere else."

Hector positioned himself over the hood of a car to brace his shooting arm, waiting for the man to show himself.

"He comes up with his gun and I fire twice. Then I roll off the car and crawl across the street and get underneath a car.

"The guy falls over, but I wonder if he's faking. I can hear my partner's footsteps running. I hear dogs barking in the neighborhood. I look at this guy. I have my gun pointed at him from under the car, waiting for him to move.

"I say, 'I ought to shoot you right now, you motherfucker.' I say it aloud. But there's no feeling in it. I don't feel anger towards this guy. What goes through my mind is all the cop funerals I've gone to. *For what? It ain't worth it no more.* I hear the sirens coming and then I pass out."

Hector woke up in the emergency room. His wrist was bandaged to stop the bleeding. "It feels like my hand is on fire." To check another wound, the nurses cut away his uniform pants to get to his backside.

"Funny the things you think about. I remembered all the times my mom told me to wear clean underwear. Then when they started cutting my shorts off, there was a nurse there I knew and I thought, *Gee, I hope I'm big enough.*"

Hector was told later that the suspect was hit eight times. "He took at least five or six rounds at close range and it didn't knock him back, didn't even put an expression on his face. To me his face was blank."

Although badly wounded, the suspect, an ex-con high on the drug PCP, survived.

The damage to Hector's arm was severe. The bullet entered his wrist and went straight up to his elbow. He sustained permanent nerve damage and still has difficulty making a fist. The other bullet was not removed. It lies near his pelvic bone, causing him to limp on occasion.

"Some people said they would pray for the healing of my hand. I said, 'No. I think this is God's way of being merciful to me and letting me end my career. I don't want to do this anymore. I don't like what I've turned into.

"'There has got to be more to life than knowing how to kill someone. There's got to be more to life than getting off on hurting someone real bad.'"

Hector wasn't going to get out of policing that easy. His greatest hardships were yet to begin. About a month after being shot, he underwent a seven-hour operation to remove the bullet from his wrist and to repair severed and fused nerves. But the pain that persisted after the surgery was so excruciating he would bite the pillow to muffle his screams.

Hector took the prescription pain-killers Percodan, Codeine and Demerol. Addicted after a couple of months, he had to go cold turkey to shake the habit.

His psychological problems deepened. He couldn't stand the phone ringing or his kids making noise. The sounds would irritate his damaged nerves. Because he was unable to show affection for his family, his wife talked of divorce. Often losing his temper, he threatened to harm his wife and children. She reported to a doctor that he once grabbed her and threw her down. He was having tight band-like sensations around the head, headaches, shortness of breath, heart palpitations and flashbacks of the shooting.[12]

"I could be talkin' to you right now and all of a sudden I could see the orange flashes goin' back and forth illuminating this guy's face. And I'm thinking, _How come he ain't goin' down?_"

He had crying episodes one or two times a day. Nights were very bad.

"I knew there was something wrong when you're not talking to people, when you lock yourself in a room, when you go into rages. There's something wrong when you sit up at night when everyone's asleep and you look out an open window and you wind up crying, but you don't know why."

When his grip strength partially returned after nine months off, the department ordered Hector back to work or he would lose pay. According to psychiatric reports, "he had no self-worth and was ashamed to be around other police officers."

He went back to light duty training recruits at the police academy. He says he went to work each day and stared at the walls.

"It wasn't in me to train anybody. I was sitting there and I started crying," he said. "I felt like a prisoner, hopeless. I knew something's happened in me and I'm falling apart. And I got to really hate the department. I hated everybody and everything."

Hector went to see a psychologist who diagnosed him with depression and chronic Posttraumatic Stress Disorder. The PTSD was attributed to the shooting, not to Vietnam nor his teenage years, although Hector had never dealt with trauma from those times.

After seeing the psychologist for awhile, Hector felt his symptoms were getting worse. In a bank one day, he started to draw his gun on someone he thought was "hard core." On another occasion, he almost shot an undercover police officer. Full of fears, he drove to work with his gun on his lap. Weary of the constant tension, he became suicidal. On one or two occasions, he put a gun to his head, but didn't pull the trigger because he "knew it was wrong."[13]

After seeing another doctor, Hector voluntarily committed himself to the mental ward of a hospital. It didn't help. Although on strong antianxiety and antidepressant medication, he believed his roommate was spying on him from Internal Affairs. He refused to attend therapy or even work out in the gym, and he stopped eating.[14]

After three weeks, Hector left. A few days later, he called his old precinct and told one of the officers he wanted to kill himself. The police picked him up and returned him to the hospital.

"This was the rock bottom of my life," he told me. "The whole night I stayed up in that bed crouched against the wall, my fist balled up, thinking, *The first person who comes at me, I'm gonna take them out.*"

That night he had a nightmare.

"I saw every dead body I've ever seen in my life, like a gallery of photos, one after another. Like one would come and I'd look at it. I'd see the face and that one would disappear and then the next would appear. And I was completely soaked in sweat and scared. After I woke up, I went up to the nurses and told them what I'd seen and how clear the pictures were. I could even name some of the bodies I saw.

"The second night, another nightmare. This one was... I was in bed and this huge black widow spider, I could see its legs comin' up the bed and I couldn't move. I could feel it literally sucking the life right outta me.

"Then it hit me. I said, 'God, this isn't me. I'm the guy that was always in control. What's happened to me?' I told the nurses I'm so drugged out I can't think clearly anymore. And then I decided to get off the drugs."

The next day, the doctor agreed with Hector's decision. Unlike his last hospital stay, he attended all his group and one-on-one therapy sessions. He participated in psychodrama, in which he acted out parts of his life, allowing himself to feel.

"I decided I was gonna fight my way outta this," he said. "My dad always taught us to survive the worst circumstances. And it was survival, but it wasn't a physical survival. It was a mental survival and the survival of the spirit. And I refused to quit. I went to every session and worked as hard as I could and got a lot of stuff out that I needed to get out."

After a month of therapy and healing, Hector looked at life differently.

"On the last days there, I made friends with people and started hangin' out and laughin' again. I felt things again. For the first time, I felt clean inside. The best confession anybody's ever went to. I got issues out that felt like tons of pressure on me. And that time in the hospital set the tone for the rest of my life."

Once again at home, Hector faced the reality that his marriage was unworkable. He also accepted that his career was over.

Hector told me he's happy he's no longer a police officer. "Finally, my war is over," he said. But he worries about the welfare of other police officers.

"Hell, in Vietnam, you know what's gonna happen," he said. "You know you may have to kill someone. You may get killed. But here, these are cities we grew up in and you've got more warfare goin' on here than you had over there.

"Here you don't have an expectation of war. And yet for a lot of police officers, that's what it is for them."

The effect Hector's Vietnam experiences had on his psychological problems is unclear. The psychiatric reports do not mention the war. But Hector believes he fought not one war, but three—the wars in his childhood, in the military and in police work—and has accumulated traumatic incidents from all of them.

He admits he had a habituation to violence. Violence was part of his lifestyle, a tool for survival before joining the police department and during his years as an officer. The police culture in which he was submerged tended to encourage it to solve problems. He said that the LAPD hired him *because* he was acclimatized to violence.

Despite claiming he disliked violence, throughout his life he witnessed and practiced it. Hector Rodriguez was a likely candidate for developing PTSD.

Chapter 9

Flashbacks

"The smell of blood was sweet and smothering."

Many sufferers feel that PTSD's most frightening feature is flashbacks. A flashback is more than a dream. It's a total break with reality, like going crazy. Bob McClellan described how he flashed back on Vietnam when he saw the dead Hispanic girl. He lost all sense of where he was, believing he was in a country thousands of miles away, ten years earlier.

Bob's flashbacks grew out of military operations. The first time I heard about flashbacks directly related to police work, they were described by Los Angeles Police Detective William H. Martin.

After I phoned him, Bill invited me down to Parker Center, the LAPD fortress. Considering current events, visiting the knights' castle was maybe not a good idea. The first of the Rodney King trials charging four police officers with beating King was underway, and the cops were expecting trouble.

A decade earlier in New York, bombs exploded outside police buildings, maiming officers for a lot less reason than thrashing a civilian who resisted arrest. Here in L.A.'s copland, about a dozen wary officers funneled visitors toward a hand search. I saw fingers toying with nightsticks, hands resting on gun butts.

The lobby had an air of unpredictability. Anything could happen. Was the man behind me carrying a bomb? Did the woman at the door have an Uzi submachine gun in her shopping bag? Was my imagination running wild or was I thinking like a cop, anticipating the most absurd scenarios? Absurd, until something happens.

The cop checking my tape recorder eyeballed me. "What you gonna do with this thing?" he said. Since the Rodney King mess, recording devices were not appreciated. After checking with Bill, the officer waved me through the search.

On the eighth floor, I shook hands with Detective Martin, head of the LAPD's Drug and Alcohol Rehabilitation Program, the police officer with whom I had spent an hour on the phone a week before. He told me later he hadn't planned on spending so much time on the phone with me. He was going to blow me off after a few minutes and hang up, but something caught his curiosity. He said for the first time he was talking to a civilian who was willing to listen.

He led me to a tiny interrogation room in which I set up my tape recorder and microphone. Bill seemed to cast a large shadow over me. Six feet, a beefy 200 or so pounds, clumsy hands like paddles. A rugged, regal face, probing blue eyes. I felt unnerved in such close quarters by this cop's appearance.

What comforted me was what he wore on his wrist, a delicate silver bracelet with the name of a Vietnam soldier missing in action. Though Bill did not serve in Vietnam, he told me wearing the bracelet was a sign of respect for those who had died and hope for those who could possibly be alive.

Belying his size and apparent toughness, Bill spoke in a quiet voice and disclosed episodes in his life that are personal and embarrassing.

He described his father as a violent alcoholic who beat Bill ruthlessly when he was a small child. He told me how traumatic events in his life contributed to developing PTSD, how flashbacks, in particular, took control.

To illustrate an "attack" of flashbacks, he told me a story of what happened on a day he was called to a crime scene. It was September 21st, 1980, a Sunday, a day whose anniversary reminds him there is no bottom to despair. He'd been a detective for eight years, most of it in death investigations.

Bill told me it was a routine call, "another dead baby run." Hating those K-car calls, he groaned himself into the seat, threw the car in gear and braked.

What's the hurry, he thought. *The kid's not goin' anywhere.* Bill hadn't slept well the night before or for many nights before that. He was always in a cold sweat and wasn't eating a lot these days. He snapped open the lock on the glove compartment, pulled out a flask and drank deeply.

"Ah, man..." He popped half a dozen antacids for the slow stomach burn he couldn't control and rolled out onto Los Angeles Street. He did two to three bodies a day, maybe a thousand during his career. Stinkers, floaters, accidentals, industrials, overdoses, suicides, naturals. A lot of bodies. "A lot of meat," he said.

Bill had gone to his boss at Detective Headquarters and implored him to change his assignment. "I've had too many dead bodies and too many crying and grieving relatives," Bill told him.

His boss said experienced detectives were hard to find. He suggested Bill take a day off and then get back in the trenches. Bill needed more than a day off. He needed the rest of his life off.

To cope, Bill sneaked a quart of whisky every day. He relieved the pain across his chest by taking twenty-five milligrams every four to six hours of Thorazine, a powerful anti-psychotic drug that can have a sedating effect. He didn't link his drinking or drugging to the images of corpses swirling in and out of his brain.

"Even if I had made the connection, I would have denied it," he said.

Bill used the pills in the daytime so he wouldn't smell of alcohol around fellow officers and the normies (civilians) he met on crime scenes. Major bar time was after work—six to eight double martinis at a stretch. Then more at home where it was "cheaper and more plentiful."

Bill got loaded for a lot of reasons, any reason really. He especially hated the dead baby runs. After investigating, he would dream about them. All of them. And there were hundreds.

He drove up to the crime scene, a Spanish-style stucco on the east side. "Got a fresh one for me?" he deadpanned to the cop at the open door as he went in. Bill told me he loved to startle the uniform cops.

A stench of fouled clothes rode the air, filling his head with thoughts of stale cooking and unwashed bodies. He knew that smell well from when he was a kid. He'd bury himself under the dirty clothes to hide from his drunken father.

He told me, "I was a cop and sober for some time before I asked myself, 'Why do I feel apprehension when I walk into an unfit home?' There's no danger, but I feel impending doom because I'm smelling the dirty laundry. I knew I was safe, but I didn't feel safe."

Bill entered the living room. Despite the booze and pills dampening his system, his heart pounded. "Whadda we got?" he asked the uniform stationed there, as if Bill didn't know. The cop nodded toward the kitchen.

"Any brass here?"

"No."

"Good."

Bill told me he didn't like higher-ups "fucking up the crime scene." Too many times a boss stomped through a blood pool leaving blotchy footprints in every room of a house for which Bill had to account. Bill resented the interference of "the paper pushers." He often felt victimized by them. Not today. "It was my crime scene," he said.

As Bill headed for the kitchen, he could see the place was in disarray with things thrown on a sofa, heaped on tables, broken in corners. "But crime scenes always made sense," he said, "because I lived in one as a child. Chaos was normal for me." This scene was like the home he grew up in.

A tall, bony man was leaning against a wall in a corner of the kitchen, arms folded across his chest. He was staring off into the universe somewhere.

It was lying in the sink on top of a shattered wine bottle. Eighteen months old. Empty eyes. No matter where Bill went in the room, the eyes pierced the drunken aura protecting him.

"You the father? What happened?" Bill asked the man.

In a resentful grumble, the man said, "The baby was screamin.'"

Like that explains everything, Bill thought.

The uniform brought Bill a cold coffee. He drained it in a couple of gulps, then jotted a few notes in his pad.

> *The father picked the baby up by its heels, smashed its head on the sink two or three times. Its brains fell out. Splatter everywhere.*

Bill examined the body. "The smell of blood was sweet and smothering," he told me, "and almost every ounce from the body was coagulating in the sink." A safety pin was stuck through the diaper into the skin at the hip.

When stabbed with safety pins, babies scream...

"The father was another asshole drunk," Bill said, "and he'd really fucked over this kid. He abused this kid and I'm an abused kid. He was a drunk, and he smelled and looked like a drunk and my dad smelled and looked like a drunk. There's a thousand buttons that got pushed."

Then Bill added, "I wanted to hurt him. But I'm L.A.'s finest." He chuckled.

Bill's job as a death investigator was to inspect every death other than traffics and homicides. If he found a murder, he was to protect the crime scene until the homicide team arrived. "You better get here fast," he said on the phone. After the homicide detectives arrived, he took one last look at the baby with the empty eyes and "got the hell out of there."

"Fuck!" he shouted into the steering wheel. He sped onto the freeway doing seventy when suddenly his windshield went dark, and he couldn't see the traffic.

"It's like the windshield in front of me was a canvas, a painting," he said. "I couldn't see through it. And if I shook my head, it went with it."

This was commonly how Bill's flashbacks began. Without warning, a veil would obliterate whatever he was looking at.

"The canvas then became like a movie of a former crime scene," he said. "It was bloody and messy, almost like somebody threw a bucket of red paint on the windshield. It was extremely frightening because I lost all control. The only thing I could do was remember where I was aiming the car, pray no other cars were in the way and pull into the emergency lane."

To the person having a flashback, the scene is real. Although the actual event happened before, days or even years previously, now it is repeated, relived, as if this were the first time.

Bill pulled to the side of the road and turned the engine off. He took a deep breath and laid his head back, focusing on the car's cheap felt ceiling. Then he awaited his own internal horror show...

He visualized the velvety texture of a rusty screen door, a door he went up on five years earlier in a 415 family dispute. The flashbacks always started with this one.

It was a moonless night. No porch light. No lights on inside the house. He could taste the sourness of his sweat at the corners of his mouth. He stood to one side of the screen door, his partner to the other, "out of the line of fire."

As he tapped on the screen door, it chattered against the door jamb. He couldn't see the door behind the screen.

"Ring the fucking bell," whispered his partner.

"What bell?" said Bill, blinking into the gloom.

Bill couldn't tell that the inside door was open. And a black man was standing in the darkness.

Something moved. Light from a distant street lamp sparked the end of shiny metal tubes. Bill saw his life squeeze into two black holes less than a foot from his face. He said he heard two clicks. Hammers fell on primers. Primers dented. The double barreled 12-gauge shotgun didn't go off. "Or I'd have no head," Bill said.

Then everything got scrambled. His partner threw himself through the screen door and took the man down. Soon Bill was on top of him too. "You coulda killed me...!" he cried.

A half hour later in the car, Bill got the shakes. He heard his heart slapping against his chest.

"Wanna get a drink?" he asked. His partner's eyes were glazed, and Bill did not make another attempt to discuss what happened.

The flashback faded...

The windshield cleared, and Bill could see through it. He was at the side of the highway again.

A flashback is not a nightmare. A person is awake when it occurs. And it can be more frightening than the actual event because it presents itself out of context, out of time, out of place. The mind suddenly turns inside out and throws its memory on a wall, into midair, or even on a car's windshield.

Bill told me his flashbacks happened any time, usually when he was stressed-out, but sometimes when he was calm. "I could be having a normal conversation, talking police business or vacations when all of a sudden the show begins."

And it was not simply visual. He said if the flashbacks involved triggers like fetid clothes, blood, excrement, gun powder or burning brake linings from the black and whites, they caused all five senses to react like he was there all over again. "I could smell it, taste it, feel it, hear it, see it."

Bill took a swallow from the flask. The whiskey gave him a jolt in preparation for the next flashback. In it, a stocky caucasian man who lived in Venice Division sat down in a chair in the garage. Bill saw every detail unroll like a tapestry on which a story is woven. The man drank four beers of a six-pack, put the rifle butt of a .30-06 hunting rifle he'd rented from a sporting goods store on the floor and his forehead on the muzzle.

With his thumb, he pulled the trigger. "The bullet spiraled up the barrel," Bill said, "boring a hole into the skull. Before it exited out the back, the gas from the explosion that pushed the bullet entered the skull cavity and blew the cranial vault empty."

Try as he might, Bill could not remember the man's name and it was in every newspaper. Bill rarely remembered names. He shoved them away and slammed the door to his mind because to remember names, Bill believed, would put faces on the victims, giving them tickets to ride in his nightmares.

The victims stole into his thoughts anyway, nameless, demanding to be noticed, looking for justice he could not provide.

Bill said he saw light through the hole in the victim's forehead. *What was his name?* He remembered he was a telephone company executive who was transferring to a larger office. Kind of a demotion.

"Man, don't work for these big companies," Bill had said to his partner.

Bill looked deeply into the dead man's face. "From the eyebrows down, he was absolutely normal. His eyes were clear and fixed like he was watching his favorite television show. He even had a toothpick in his mouth. But, from the top of the eyebrows back to the base of the occipital lobe, the head was completely gone."

A greasiness was in the air. Fluid from the head was atomized into a fine spray—blood, mucous, cerebrospinal fluid. It permeated Bill's clothes and clung to his skin. It attached to the hairs in his nostrils.

Skull and brain had exploded all over the wall, ceiling and floor. Brain matter was dripping down boxes and shelves. Bill slipped and slid in it. "Kinda looked like yogurt to me," he said. While searching for parts of the head, he crunched and snapped skull fragments under his feet "like walking on Styrofoam bits."

Bill said, "When the brain was blown out of the skull, the heart still pumped. And all the blood was right there on the floor in a huge pool about four feet wide and five feet long. He was quite literally exsanguinated, drained dry."

The day was warm, and "the blood had the consistency of sticky maple syrup." Bill had it on the bottom of his shoes. When he went home, the crime scene went with him. "The scene contaminated my safe place, like seeing a ghost." His dog backed away from him until he threw the shoes in the trash.

Gathering physical evidence at the suicide, Bill inspected a hole in the roof. The lead round had punched through the man's head and continued with enough energy to burst through the roof of the garage. On the floor was *Weight Watchers Magazine*.

"There's one way to control your weight," Bill had told his partner.

Two weeks later the man's wife went into the garage and did the same thing in the same place. "What was remarkable," said Bill, "the bullet holes in the ceiling were less than an inch apart."

Bill chuckled. I didn't. I felt sick, not realizing that Bill felt the same way. "It was the coincidence, and we laughed about the proximity of the bullet holes," he said. "It seemed funny or odd."

That was how the flashback would end, with Bill looking up at the two bullet holes in the ceiling.

When Bill investigated the murdered-baby-in-the-sink crime scene, he had already experienced flashbacks for several years. Repulsive crime scenes always triggered flashbacks. Every time he had them, he would see the same flashback first and it, in turn, sparked another and then another. They came in the same order like cars thundering along on a runaway train.

I realized Bill wanted to give me the full effect of what it's like to suffer through a succession of flashbacks. He wanted me to comprehend why they are terrifying. To reinforce his descriptions, he showed me photographs of crime scenes. To this day, I can still visualize them—bodies melted into the ground, pieces of bodies, faces unrecognizable as faces.

As he snapped the pictures down like playing cards side-by-side on the table, I tried to shut myself off, to not see what was in front of me. But it was like watching a plane crash. Even if I wanted to, I couldn't turn away. Imagine seeing not photos, but real scenes like that every day. Bill saw them. Bill wanted me to have no doubt about how images get locked in the mind and can psychologically cripple. And so he told me about another flashback.

I warn the reader, however, that the flashback about to be depicted is gross and sickening. It is not thrown in here for shock value. Police officers witness atrocious scenes like this regularly. They go with the job...

After the suicide of the man with the hunting rifle, Bill relived the suicide of an obese woman in her seventies. She killed herself by drinking bleach. "She must not have liked herself very much," said Bill.

In her death throes, she vomited and knocked the gallon jug over. The bathroom had a linoleum floor that rolled to the edge of the room and then up the wall two inches. "What you had was a gigantic pan called a bathroom floor with a gallon of bleach and a person in it," he said.

Bill was called, assessed the situation and contacted the coroner's office. "Send a couple of people," he said. "I'm with the stiff in a second floor apartment. And bring a body bag, not a rubber sheet, and a can of air freshener. It's a stinker."

The coroner arrived alone, without a bag. "We tried anyway to get this fat person out of the bleach," Bill said. Since her nightie was too flimsy to hold onto, they grabbed her by the arms and legs. "Some of her skin shredded," he said. "Maggots crawled out from under it, and we had to put her down."

Maggots, which are worm-like fly larvae, were expected. "Often you saw bumps crawl around under the skin while handling the body. Those bad boys took merely a few hours to get going," Bill said. "One fly would lay hundreds of eggs in an open wound. In less than a day, a body was infested with maggots. Warmer was faster, colder was slower." Maggots were not the bad part of a crime scene, Bill told me. There was much worse.

Bacteria produce a foul smelling gas that bloats the body as it rots. The gas eventually forms what resemble big burn blisters or bubbles on the skin.[1]

"The blisters are generally half full of fluid," Bill said, "depending on how long the body was down, the condition of the body, the temperature and the humidity.

"When you're picking the body up, a blister sometimes bursts and fluid squirts as far as a couple of feet," he said. "And if you're in the right place at the right time, you get this crap all over you. It's happened to me. It feels greasy. It stinks. It's from other people's body parts."

They were going to attempt to pick the woman up again, but they wanted to avoid tearing her skin as they had before. That would not be easy. Apart from the caustic effect of the bleach on her skin, it shredded for another reason—skin slip.

Shortly after death, the muscles stiffen, a condition called rigor mortis. Two to four days later, the muscles relax and gas bloats the body. Around seven days after death, the skin loosens.[2] "It kind of slides along the body like a shirt sleeve," said Bill. "When you apply a tiny bit of force, the top layer of skin can come off in sheets."

She was also hard to move because she had been dead about three weeks. "A rigid body is easier to lift and drop on the sheet," said Bill. "When you've got a plus four rigor, you can pick a corpse up like a fence post and ease it out the door. But with her, after so long, rigor had set in and left and the result was a slimy mass of stuff that smelled like sour cheese. She was limp and hard to pick up."

Skin slip and limpness were not Bill's only concerns when he was required to lift a body that had been dead awhile. "We usually pick the thing up and you're grabbing it by its feet or by its arms and you flip it up on the stretcher. Sometimes a whole shoulder will come off like a drumstick coming off a boiled chicken."

They began to move the woman once again. Bill took the shoulders and the coroner took the feet, and they raised the body onto the gurney with no further mishaps. They wrapped the body in a rubber sheet and covered it with a blanket to hide it from curious eyes.

"When the police show up, people come out and look," said Bill. "When the coroner and detective get there, more people come out and look. So there was a lot of looky-looin' goin' on. There were people up on the second floor where we were and there were people down below. So we started down the stairs. This gets a little sick..."

Bill was at the bottom of the gurney, the coroner at the top when they heard a *shuffffffffff* sound. "The body came sliding out of the rubber sheet and blanket like a torpedo," said Bill. And Bill was in the way.

"I quick-stepped to one side like a toreador with a cape. The body hit the stairs head first, somersaulted and disassembled all the way down. The arms and legs split open. Flesh, body fluid, excrement—they went all the way down the steps. The looky-loos didn't do well. The people on the second floor threw up on the people on the first floor who threw up on the tulips.

"At that point, the coroner and I lost it, man. We laughed so hard we damn near wet our pants while we scooped up goo with our hands, trying to get this puddle of jam into the sheet. It was gory. It was gruesome. I stunk of bleach. I mean, it was a bastard to clean up. And we didn't do a very good job. There was still blood all over the place and slime. It looked like a giant snail had come down the stairs.

"I mean, it was so horrible, it was funny. And you do develop a sick sense of humor about this shit when that's all you see every day."

Bill seemed to be enjoying the telling of the story, as if describing a rowdy trip to the mall. I thought he was demonstrating a lack of compassion. He told me I had misunderstood his reactions. There is a fine line between humor and tragedy. Sometimes we cannot immediately distinguish the difference.

"If you don't laugh," he said, "sometimes you'll cry and never stop."

After the flashbacks ended, with images of the dead baby-in-the-sink still fresh in his mind, Bill turned his car back onto the freeway and went home. Instead of putting his .38 Police Special up on the shelf in the walk-in closet the way he usually did, he sat down on the closet floor. He shoved the muzzle of the four-inch revolver into his mouth. The front sight blade cut into the soft palate. Blood squirted down the barrel and spread over the cylinder.

I can't do this anymore, he thought. He lay down on the floor, curled into a ball and wept.

"I realized then I had become everything I swore I'd never be. I was overweight like my dad. I was abusive like my dad. I was a drunk like my dad."

Bill told me he knew what he had to do. Working suicides all the time made them part of everyday life. He knew a lot of cops who killed themselves.

"The logical solution to leaving the problem," he said, "was to blow my brains all over the wall. And I couldn't think of any reason not to do that. I'd lost the ability to see other options."

He sat up with his thumb on the hammer of the gun and pulled it back.

"Sitting there on the floor with the gun jammed in my mouth, the hammer all the way back, I flashed on a picture. It was a sign on the wall at an alcoholics' meeting, something about my life being unmanageable. And that was the first time in twenty-two years of drinking and drugging that that thought ever got into my head."

Bill put the gun down. "Then I did the first intelligent thing I'd ever done as an adult," he said. He called his doctor and told him he tried to commit suicide.

What followed were a few visits to a psychiatrist and unsuccessful attempts to stop drinking. Finally, desperate, Bill went into therapy at the Veterans Administration (VA). He sidestepped the police department's Psychological Services because he feared they would "take my gun away and put me out to pasture."[3]

For over a year, VA therapist Kathy Koepplin worked with Bill. In all that time, Bill did not tell her of his flashbacks. He wasn't trying to hide them. He thought they were so natural to everyone's life that they weren't worth mentioning. "I thought everybody had them," he said.

Once Kathy became aware of his flashbacks, she was able to identify Posttraumatic Stress Disorder as the cause of his problems. This was not a routine diagnosis. In 1985, PTSD's clusters of symptoms were not often applied to cops.

Kathy worked with Bill for months on his flashbacks, compelling him to describe the crime scenes again and again until they were no longer secrets he was trying to hide. They lost some of their luster and ultimately their power over him.[4]

"How did the therapist help?" I asked.

"When I had the flashbacks, I experienced the fright of what I was reliving—the sweaty hands, the tight throat, the upset stomach. When Kathy helped me realize the flashbacks weren't real, the feelings disappeared."

"And what happens now?"

"Now when it happens, I see a light show and it can be intrusive, but I don't get sweaty hands anymore," he said. "My throat doesn't get tied up in knots. If I'm driving, it doesn't cover the windshield like a can of paint. I can see through the movie. I don't feel the fear any more deep in my bowels."

The crime scenes do not represent all the events in Bill's life that the therapist explored. She discovered he also experienced trauma in his childhood and military career. Examining his life before police work will help us understand his eventual development of PTSD.

Bill grew up in Toronto, Canada. His father, Norman,[5] a traveling salesman for a flooring company, was 6 feet, 240 pounds. "To little Billy, he was a giant," said Bill. Never able to make enough money, Norman took his frustrations out on his son. When the boy was around one year old, his father began beating him.

"He used to kick me, used to throw me," said Bill. "He hit me with a closed fist or kicked me with sufficient force that I'd hit the wall. He hit me with a belt and really wailed on me. He smacked me in the face. He slammed me in the throat. That's why I have problems with my voice, getting enough volume.

"He used to smash me around the ears. And when I was a cop, shooting practice made my ears worse, so now I wear hearing aides. As a kid I had headaches and aches and pains from joint hyperextensions. It was life-threatening, felony child abuse."

"Why did he do it?"

"You never knew what set off the fuse. It was never anything consistent. I would get rewarded one day and beat the shit out of the next for the same behavior. So I was always waiting. That's what increased the anxiety."

"You had no warning?"

"I could always tell when a beating was heating up. I'd come home from school and there was that *look*. I'd boogie out of there and hide in the one place he never found me, the dirty clothes basket under the kitchen sink."

"When would it happen?" I said.

"A lot was at dinner, at the table. He'd say, 'You're making a goddamn mess,' and then he'd backhand me right off the chair. Now years later, I can't sit at the dining room table. It's very stressful, even threatening. I sit at the coffee table and watch TV to soften the anxiety. For me, food equals pain."

"Was there emotional abuse?" I asked.

"As bad as the physical abuse was, the emotional abuse hurt more. He did a lot of put-down stuff. He'd say, 'You're stupid. Nobody will like you.' So when I went to school, I already knew I was stupid, so why study? I already knew nobody liked me, so why make friends? I had an avoidance and denial system in place before I was ever in school."[6]

"Where was your mother during all this?"

"She was there. Today you would call her a silent perpetrator."

"Did he ever beat her?"

"He didn't touch her. Looking at it as an adult, I suspect he would have knocked her every way from sundown if she ever stepped in. Looking at it as a child, I noticed she did nothing. But she was all I had. After a beating, she would sit on the edge of my bed while I cried. 'What did I do wrong?' I'd ask her. She just stroked my head. I really felt abandoned by my mom. It's only recently I've been able to forgive her."

"How did you cope with the beatings?"

"I told myself the beatings never happened or I got off into fantasy a lot. Or I spent nights with my friends because I didn't want to be home."[7]

Bill said he pushed his feelings down inside himself so he wouldn't have to face what was actually happening. His feelings numbed at an early age, he believes he was well on the way to developing PTSD. Many of us tend to think young children are resilient because they don't seem to react strongly, if at all, to trauma. That's because, like Bill, they usually keep hurtful feelings bottled up inside.

From the beatings, Bill experienced some of the symptoms of PTSD and its associated reactions. Foremost, he feared for his life. In addition, he became expert at denying the beatings happened. He dissociated himself from them. He had nightmares but he did not have flashbacks, which is more an adult response. He didn't get those until he became a detective. Instead of flashbacks, young children usually engage in fantasy and daydreaming as Bill did.[8]

When Bill was around eight, he could no longer deny the abuse. He put together enough money to buy a .22 caliber pistol from another child. "I slept with that gun under my pillow."

"Why did you want the gun?" I asked.

"When he went for me during the day, I saw him coming. My fear at night was that he'd catch me off guard in bed. If that bastard came for me, I was gonna kill him. And I suspect I would've."[9]

Norman was too drunk at night to come for Bill. Despite being blameless for his father's outbursts, Bill felt tremendous guilt. Bill says he figured his father must have had some reason for beating him and blamed himself for causing the beatings.[10]

The inconsistency and distrust he learned as a member of an alcoholic family forced him to adopt dangerous ways of coping.[11] His usual coping tool was drinking. Like his father, he would later use drinking to contend with stress, anxiety and day-to-day problems in the adult world.

After years of enduring his father's abuse and alcoholism, Bill's mother finally had enough. She tricked Norman into moving to California where it was easy to get a divorce. She soon moved out, and ten years later he died of an alcohol-related heart attack.

Bill waited twenty-five years before he visited the grave for the first and only time. He took a few photographs of the headstone. He told me, "I wanted to be sure he was really dead."

As he stood at the grave, Bill swore he felt nothing. Not anger, not love. He said he'd trained himself to detach from his feelings since the age of two.

"Do you hate your father for what he did?" I asked.

"Yes," said Bill. "No," he corrected. "Sometimes. All the time."

His eyes moistened. "You know, once when I was seven," he said, "we were in the bedroom and he was beating me with a belt. I looked into his eyes and I could see he was waiting for me to cry. I wouldn't. I don't know why I'm crying now."

"Perhaps you're feeling pain," I said.

"Maybe. I remember the pain from back then. I remember the fear. But what I remember most was the only way I could get back at that son-of-a-bitch was not showing it hurt. So from a very young age, I learned to internalize, not show you anything. I would not risk. What I perceived at that time was I couldn't trust anybody. Everybody I trusted hurt me."

At thirteen, Bill was still having trouble adjusting to life. He told me he was shy and found it difficult to make friends. As an abused child, he lacked confidence. He performed poorly in school. He was withdrawn, moody, had low self-esteem and tended to criticize himself a lot. With other children, he became a social misfit. Before long, somebody took advantage of Bill's neediness. A man in his early twenties hung around the schoolyard, watching the teenagers play baseball and began paying attention to Bill.

"Nobody'd ever been nice to me. This guy was soft spoken. My dad had always roared. This guy was gentle. He didn't grab at me like my dad. He was safe, non-threatening.

"One day we were sitting in his car in front of the schoolyard watching the kids play baseball and talking like we always did. He somehow got me into the back, and the next thing I know, my pants are down and I'm on my face on the backseat, and he's poking me in the ass with his penis."

Bill got out of the car and ran. Ashamed of what happened, he didn't tell his mother or anyone.

"What hurt the most, he was one of the first people I'd tried to get close to. I had no idea he was a chicken hawk. I felt violated. I gave trust and what did it get me? Sodomized. That hurt longer than the physical rape."

"How did the rape affect you?" I said.

"I told myself nothing happened. I was still really good at denial."

"Did that work?"

"It did for awhile and then it didn't matter because I discovered alcohol. I was in high school, and the first time I drank, I had two cans of beer, and I experienced euphoria. The anxiety, the waiting for something bad to happen—all disappeared. I became social. I went to dances and enjoyed it and never looked back."

By the time Bill was in college for a year, he could easily drink a case of beer to get the same feeling he had had from two cans.

"My bladder got in the way," he said. "I couldn't pour enough beer down my throat and piss fast enough to get high. I had to switch to hard liquor."

After a couple years of college, Bill enlisted in the Coast Guard as a medic during the early part of the Vietnam War. He didn't go to the shooting war. Instead he saw every insult thrown at the human body right at home.

Stationed in remote Ketchikan, Alaska, he encountered hunting, logging, and fishing accidents, the bloody results of barroom fights and attempted suicides. If he couldn't help people, sometimes they died because they were hours from a hospital. On a Coast Guard's forty-footer, he delivered babies under emergency conditions. But he lost some of the mothers and their newborns and took it very hard.

To relieve anxiety from the suffering he saw, he used uppers (amphetamines like diet pills) and downers (booze and prescription tranquilizers). The alcohol was effective for a short time, but as his tolerance increased, he needed more and more of everything to cope.

"It was no accident I was a medic," Bill told me. "I had the key to the drug locker. I used the amphetamines during the work day and the booze and other depressants after. When I got out of the military at the tender age of twenty-four, I could drink straight ethanol."

When he left the military and joined the LAPD, Bill was a heavy drinker and prescription drug abuser. But he was welcomed into the fraternity. "Detectives are drunks by trade," a cop told him when he applied to the department. Bill was comfortable with that. "But no drugs." *That's okay*, thought Bill. He could do without drugs as long as he had his old friend to subdue his adrenaline highs.

When Bill took his police entrance exams, one of them was a psychiatric interview.

"Do you drink?" said the doctor.

"No," said Bill. He was sitting a chair width away from the doctor.

"Do you use drugs?"

"No, sir." And Bill was loaded on both alcohol and drugs.

Bill told me, "It wasn't that he was a bad doctor. I was a real good actor. The only part of the procedure that scared me was the medical. They were going to draw blood. My fear was if they put it next to an open flame, they'd have to call a HAZMAT team to put it out."

No one found Bill out. As a uniformed patrol officer walking the beat, he hid booze in strategic spots like street call boxes. When he graduated to a car, he concealed a pint of whiskey in a leather helmet bag in the trunk. To make room in the bag, he removed safety goggles and a box of ammunition.

Once he became a plainclothes cop, he kept a bottle in the glove box. He said that alcohol made him think he could do and get away with anything, no matter how self-destructive.

"I've done stupid things as a police officer that should have got me or somebody injured or killed."

"What kinds of things?" I said.

"In numerous, life-threatening situations, I went straight in like I'm marching into hell with an army. I did things like stop a carload of suspects and not ask for backup, piss somebody off instead of talk to him, force a pursuit."

"How did you force a pursuit?"

"One of the oldest tricks in the book is this... A car's coming toward you loaded with guys or whoever you're gonna fuck over for the night. As it passes, you look at them and you flip on the reds. They believe—foolish, foolish thinking—that they're gonna have a head start on you and they start haulin' ass. We got a radio and helicopters. There's no way in the world this poor fool's gonna win this thing.

"While you're whippin' a U-turn, they accelerate. The first intersection they cross, they leave their oil pan. And you get to play cop. Very exciting."

"And you were drunk during these pursuits?"

"I've chased guys when I was blasted, code 3, red light and siren wailing. All I saw was this big, yellow spot in front of my eyes. I had a blinding headache, and I couldn't see where I was going. I was chasing a car at sixty miles an hour, and I wasn't lookin' right and I wasn't lookin' left."

"Didn't you know you were drunk and impaired?"

"What I brought with me into the job, even before I was impaired with alcohol, was the ability to say, 'It's not that bad.' Deny it. And then when I became alcoholic, the insanity of the disease changes your perception. I'd say to myself, *I know I'm impaired, but so what?* Or I'd say, *I know I'm impaired, but I'll do it anyway.*"

"Were there other instances in which you were impaired? I asked.

"Many, many. When I was working homicide, I was once checking a door. Behind it was a known felony suspect who swore he'd never be taken alive. I was so smashed that when I went through the door, I couldn't hit my ass with both hands, let alone take down a suspect. Lucky my partner was there."

"What do you think of those acts now?" I asked.

"They were careless, reckless, putting my life and my partner's life on the line. Thank you, Lord, I didn't kill myself or somebody else. I was a pretend cop, loaded and bookable everyday."

"In this condition, how did you do as a cop?" I asked.

"I made outstanding arrests and got half a dozen commendations. I was what's called a functional alcoholic. My work was acceptable, but below what I was capable of and high on hazard. Because I just couldn't cope."

Bill made detective one month before his fifth year at the department. Having stopped the pills, he noticed it took a lot more liquor to get where he wanted to go. But the stress became too much. He began to combine pills and alcohol again.

He worked as a detective in death investigations for the next eight years. Investigating deaths like suicides was emotionally debilitating for Bill, causing feelings of frustration and failure.[12] Along with burying himself in alcohol and drugs, he sought to overcome the effects of flashbacks, depression and suicidal thoughts by engaging in wild sexual pursuits. At cop bars, he made it with female groupies who were attracted to his charm and recklessness.

"All I wanted to do was get screwed up and loaded," he told me. "When my dick was hard I didn't give a damn. I fucked anyone, anytime, any place and I gave no thought to sexually transmitted diseases, and I knew better."

During and after his first marriage, he had a long-term relationship with a prostitute. He said perhaps he wanted to get caught the night he took her to a dance at the police academy.

"The lights were down. The dance floor was crowded and the police bar flowed like an ocean. Otherwise, why go?" said Bill. "My girlfriend was wearing a short dress, no underpants. We sat at a table drinking. I had my suit coat off and my pistol swinging from a shoulder holster. She pulled me up to dance.

"She opened my collar and then stroked me and got me hard. She unzipped me, pulled out my penis and jumped on.

"She hung around my neck and I was carrying her and we were dancing. Her legs were in the air. She kinda bounced up and down to the music. She was fucking me and nobody noticed. On the dance floor at the *po*-lice academy? Surrounded by cops? Very risky behavior."

Bill acknowledges that it was more than risky behavior. His conduct was part of a deadly cycle. Driving while drunk, getting loaded with prescription drugs, trying to arrest dangerous suspects while impaired, forcing pursuits, flagrantly having sex in public, having sex with a prostitute who might be infected with a disease. All of these actions announce someone who is out of control, who cares nothing for himself or anybody else. Bill wanted to get caught because he needed somebody to put controls on him before he killed himself. He was the only one who could stop his self-destructive actions.

When Bill went to see the therapist at the Veterans Administration for their first meeting, she asked him to describe himself.

"I am not a good husband or a faithful husband. I am not a good father. I am not a good cop. I have a fuse a millimeter long. Anything sets me off. I am vindictive. I am an asshole."

After determining that Bill's flashbacks came from PTSD, the therapist sought good outcomes from traumatic incidents to offset the bad. For instance, she asked whether anything positive came out of the rape.

"I was a patrolman in a black and white, and I was interviewing a rape victim who was having trouble talking. The last person she wanted to talk to was a male. She would gladly have torn my heart out.

"I looked at her and said, 'I've never told anyone, but I was raped.' She was speechless. Then I talked to her about what I felt. Many rape victims feel disassociation. They're up on the ceiling looking down on this act. I felt that. I felt guilt. I felt anger and shame. We connected. She told me everything, and I was able to help her."

The therapist probed Bill's childhood, especially his relationship with his father, to see if any form of comfort evolved from that terrible period.

"The instant the therapist discovered angels in my childhood like my aunt, uncle and grandparents, memories came back about good things. The good things allowed me to heal and go back and look at more of the bad ones. The angels allowed me to change my perception of things and actually forgive my father. Not everything was bad."

"What are some of the good things?" I said.

"At my aunt and uncle's house in Canada, I was safe. They gave me cookies, hugs, warm blankets and nurturing. I didn't get punished for nothing. When they said let's do something, we did. They provided some consistency in my life. I could visualize myself back there, feeling their love and attention.

"They also gave me, although they weren't trying to, the sound of bagpipes. A Highland Regiment practiced nearby and I would go to sleep to the bagpipes weeping in the distance. They're a safe, warm, comforting sound to me.

"And they weren't the only angels. A train spur went by my grandmother's house back when we had steam engines. When I heard the train coming, I ran outside to meet it. The thing chugged and it steamed and whistled. The engineer didn't need to whistle here. I believe he did it for me.

"He was gray hair, smile, wrinkled face, black and gray striped cap, big hands and big gauntlet gloves.

"And when I ran out, his face lit up. He waved and backed off the engine. I ran as fast as I could. My heart pounded and he kept that sucker level with me. I always beat him to the intersection by a little bit.

"I can hear the steam. You know how steam engines breathe. I can hear the clickety-clack. I can close my eyes and smell it, taste it, hear it, feel it. One of the most loving memories of my childhood—this guy in the train with the big grin.

"He always let me win. Always."

Chapter 10

Not Shooting

"I'd rather be tried by twelve than carried by six."

The dream...

> *The man runs. In his hand a .45 caliber pistol. He turns a corner, the cop almost on him.*
>
> *A schoolyard. Children. A red brick wall. They face each other, guns pointed. "Drop it or I'll kill ya," screams the cop. The man smiles.*
>
> *An orange flash from the .45. A blast of metal spiraling through a barrel. Dark red erupts from the cop's leg. Burning pain. The cop shoots back. The man's smile fills with blood...*

The reality...

He wakes suddenly, his leg against his chest. He's dripping with sweat. It was a muscle spasm, that's all. An involuntary contraction. He was dreaming.

The cop had had the dream for many nights. The chase, the shooting, the throbbing in his leg. The chase had in reality happened but the shooting was not real. It didn't happen. And that's the source of the officer's nightmares. Not shooting was as harmful to him as if he had actually pulled the trigger.

Not shooting is more typical of what happens during thousands of police confrontations. A shooting is an uncommon event. Although pulling the trigger can have consequences psychologically, a decision not to use deadly force can throw a police officer into a paralyzing cycle of second-guessing.

I met police constable Terry Nunn in Toronto. Why Toronto? Because when it comes to the effects of trauma, cops react the same everywhere in the world. Toronto is also the city where I grew up and worked as a television journalist. I know the terrain. I had written stories about police officers, usually involving charges of brutality, but never heard one about a cop tortured by his decision *not* to shoot someone.

At the Toronto Police Service's Employee and Family Assistance Program (EFAP) office, I interviewed Terry in a boardroom across a polished oak table. He was not as tall as I expected. He told me he barely squeaked through the height restrictions of 5 foot 9 by pivoting on the balls of his feet. The table reflected his egg-shaped jaw, eyes slouched from reading too many reports, light brown hair and gladiator's nose. Quick to laugh, Terry turned his smile sober and narrowed his hazel eyes when he recalled the incident that happened over fifteen years ago that reversed his life.

This is what really took place during a sunny, spring day on the streets of Toronto...

"It came over as a hotshot," said Terry, "which is an assault in progress or a shooting, something serious. I was going in for lunch and figured somebody else can take it. Nobody did."

The dispatcher confirmed a jewelry store was robbed and the suspects had left moments before. A few blocks away, Terry rushed to the scene. He was alone in the car, without backup, and in 1981 Canadian officers did not wear bulletproof vests.

"I see a lady pointing down the street at a guy running. The guy looks back, and he's got this Clint Eastwood special in his hand. It was a big sucker, and he goes around the corner. I got back on the radio and said, 'I'm southbound on Yonge,' and that's all I said."

Terry jumped from the car and ran down the street after the suspect. He left the lights flashing, the door open, the engine idling. He snapped the flap covering his revolver and drew it, holding it down as he ran.

"When I turned the first corner, he could've stood right there and nailed me. I never even thought of it, the adrenaline was pumping so hard. My whole concentration was on this guy. Nothing else mattered."

Catching up to the gunman in a schoolyard at the Metropolitan Toronto School for the Deaf, Terry faced off with him.

"Drop it," yelled Terry, mouthing the requisite police warning.

Then he realized that behind the suspect was a classroom full of children. Terry could see them at their desks through the large windows. The gunman stood his ground and smiled. Terry thought, *If I fire and it goes through him, if I hit a fleshy part, and it hits a kid, I will never be able to live with myself.*

He knew he couldn't allow himself to shoot. Yet Terry was violating the first rule for staying alive on the streets—"If a guy points a gun at me, I'd rather be tried by twelve than carried by six."

A crowd of people, adults and school children, gathered around the scene. A cop with a gun out in "Toronto the Good" was a novelty.

"Get outta the way, get back!" he said to disperse them. And then he did what he's always been good at—talk.

"I'm as scared as you are," he told the robber. "I don't want to shoot you, but if I have to I will." Terry thought, *This is my last day. He's going to kill me.*

The suspect lowered the gun and pressed it into the hollow of his back, and brought his hands out in front of him.

"Turn around," said Terry.

As the gunman started to turn, he smiled again. Terry didn't get it. *Why the silly grins?* Then he saw a movement to the man's right. *What's this woman doing here?*

Stepping from behind the gunman, she plucked a pistol from her purse, and trained it on the officer.

"Put it down or I *will* shoot you," said Terry.

It was a standoff. Nobody moved or gave in. According to police rules of engagement, Terry had the right, some say the duty, to shoot them both. No questions asked. His life and the lives of others were endangered. He didn't shoot.

Finally the male accomplice gave up.

"Forget it. We're done," he told the woman. "Let it go."

She dropped the gun into her purse. Terry ordered them to turn around, kneel down, interlock their fingers at the back of their heads and cross their ankles. He felt a hand on his shoulder and a voice said, "Terry, I'll take the broad. You take the guy." It was his road sergeant.

Terry attempted to shove his revolver back in the holster, but it wouldn't go in all the way. He put it in the waist band of his pants. The officers cuffed the suspects and recovered the jewelry. After putting the robbers in the back of the car, they headed for booking and lock-up.

As they drove, the sergeant reminded Terry he had his gun in his pants. Terry took it out, realizing at once why it wouldn't fit in the holster. In the excitement of the moment, he forgot to uncock it. The slightest pressure might have set it off.

At the station house, Terry briefed a flabbergasted holdup squad and wrote up a report. He itemized every piece of jewelry. Delighted to identify his $57,000 worth of brooches, rings and necklaces, the store owner congratulated the constable.

On closer inspection, the lethal looking weapon the male gunman aimed at the police officer was a .45 caliber look-alike, a pellet gun, capable of wounding, but not usually killing. The woman's revolver was a starter's pistol.

When Terry put himself in front of the guns, he believed they were real. All that mattered was what he believed. "Perception is everything."[1] Terry lived the incident at a high peak of stress. He perceived he was going to die, and although he learned later he was not in great danger, his brain had suffered the terror of preparing for immediate combat. His mind was not going to let him forget he had had a near-death experience.

Terry went home. He doesn't remember going to his car. He doesn't remember driving. He opened the door to his apartment where a friend had come over to cook dinner.

"I shut the door and started crying," he said. "I knew something was wrong, but I didn't know what it was. I told my friend what happened and she gave me the look like *Big deal, you didn't get shot.* She said, 'You're just uptight. Don't worry about it.' She kept on cooking the dinner and put it on the table. I couldn't eat, so I phoned a buddy of mine, another copper, and we talked for hours. I was out of control."[2]

Terry was back at work on full duty the next day without a break. Then the newspapers called and kept calling for over a year. The reporters nicknamed the six-year police veteran "Officer Coolie" and "Coolie Joe" for his "cool restraint." In several articles they commented on his courage, composure and cool-headedness. He was named Policeman of the Month, Policeman of the Year and received a merit award for outstanding police work.

He was a hero, and the public loved him. Except he didn't feel like a hero. Other police officers didn't think he was either.

"One guy said, 'You got a death wish? A guy points a gun at me, I'm gonna kill him.' Another guy said, 'You're an idiot. You coulda shot both of them, and you were totally justified. You coulda got promoted for that.' Some of the guys shunned me. They didn't want to talk or work with me now because I didn't shoot somebody."

Why did other police officers not want to work with Terry? It has to do with trust. Other officers have to feel their partner can be trusted "to act decisively in any situation, because their lives may depend upon it."[3]

Perhaps Terry was ahead of his time, only he couldn't know it then. According to today's definition of community policing, he acted decisively and courageously. The easy route would have been to shoot. Instead, he analyzed the situation and did what author Joseph Wambaugh says policing is all about—talking. Terry defused a potentially lethal situation and everyone got to walk away.

But back then, unspoken rules dictated by police culture clearly marked the line a cop did not cross. Talking your way out of a gunfight was almost unheard of. In violation of his society's combat code, Terry suffered the consequences.

He told me he felt guilty for what he did *not* do, maybe should have done, and undeserving of the praise he received. "I didn't feel worthy of it," he said. Even though he tried to comfort himself with the knowledge that very few cops who draw their guns actually shoot someone, he said he felt less of a man.

"I wondered, *If I come up against another situation, will I do the same thing again?*"

Although Terry felt alone in confronting his reactions, many police officers who do not shoot experience the same doubts. In most major police departments, police officers who shoot someone are ordered to seek counseling. The post-shooting trauma repercussions are well known. The cops who don't shoot are usually ignored because few suspect they are suffering.

What do cops do who don't shoot? They live with their painful feelings until they cannot contain them any longer. But nobody can hide a feeling forever.[4] It will find its way out and express itself, often in a far more dramatic form than when the feeling was originally experienced.

During the first few months following the holdup, Terry underwent a disturbing transformation. He had nightmares, and in them he relived every moment, only his mind reinvented the details.

"I would see the flash from his gun. He would hit me in my leg and I would shoot him. Sound, color, everything. And I would wake up, covered in sweat, holding the top of my right leg, and look down to see the blood and there was nothing there."

No matter how much he dreamed, he could not change the facts nor accept what happened. He said he was stuck, incapable of "chalking it up to experience" and moving on. In the years to come, Terry suffered far more than the bandits he put in jail. The male gunman got four years, the female two. Terry felt his sentence was for a lifetime. He told me, "I'll never have an answer about why I didn't shoot."[5]

Nightmares were only the first signs of his self-inflicted punishment. He also lost weight. "A couple of people asked me why I was losing weight because in one year I went from 196 pounds down to 158 pounds. I told them I was on a diet. Meanwhile, I couldn't eat. I tried to eat and got sick. I'd either vomit or it'd come out the other end."

Feeling rundown by not eating, he would eat chocolate bars. "And then I got sick because I was only eating chocolate. So I would drink water. And then I'd drink booze.[6] It was booze and water, booze and water and smoke. In an hour I'd smoke six cigarettes. I went down from a thirty-four waist to a thirty waist... I can feel myself getting clammy talking about this..."

At the time of the robbery, Terry was separated from his wife and two small children. He thinks "the stress of the job" drew them apart. Now living alone, Terry dreaded going home. He said home was "unsafe."

"I couldn't deal with what I was thinking or feeling."

"What were you feeling?" I asked.

"I thought I was gonna get killed on the job. Because my luck had to run out. What I was thinking about was how inadequate I was."

Terry felt a sense of doom more common to officers who shoot people. To avoid spending time at home, Terry's schedule went like this. He would go home after work, have a shower and go to the Police Club for a few drinks and some companionship. He would drive home around eleven or midnight, go to bed, have a nightmare about the robbery and wake up in a cold sweat.

He would smoke some cigarettes, turn on the television and stand on the balcony watching cars. He said he needed the noise. He'd have a couple of drinks and then a couple more. He said he couldn't get back to sleep after that. He was averaging three hours a night. Around four o'clock in the morning, he'd shower, get ready for work and leave. Too early to start his 7 A.M. shift, he'd drink coffee and watch television at the station.

The sense of feeling unsafe entered his work too. Not having fired his gun, he feared it might not function at all. He didn't permit himself to focus on the operator of the gun, so he focused on the firearm.

"I had an obsession with the gun," he said. "It's a black, Smith & Wesson .38 revolver. I would take the bullets out and clean it every day. I would dry fire it, check it, make sure it would work. I painted my sights white and still do today. Because I felt if I got involved in a situation at night, the white would help me see the front sight. I had bonded with my gun. I got very possessive with it. My gun was my buddy."

Despite preparations for "the next time," Terry continued to ask himself whether he should have fired his gun that April day. Knowing he could never answer the question, he avoided anything reminding him of it. When he was on patrol in his car and received a call for the same street where he cornered the robbers, he wouldn't go.

"For two or three years I couldn't drive up or down that street or walk the beat," he said. "I didn't know why. A couple of times I've received calls and other coppers would intervene and say, 'I'm right there, I'll do it.' They would cover for me."

Despite his distress, Terry denied there was anything wrong. He couldn't express hurt because he felt it reflected weakness, a flaw to which cops don't like to admit.

Years later, when he became acquainted with the criteria for PTSD, he realized he satisfied more than half the conditions for the affliction—enough to make a diagnosis. Besides stress reactions like compulsive gun cleaning, depression, dissociation, an eating disorder and trying to bury his troubles in alcohol, caffeine and nicotine, he experienced specific PTSD symptoms such as flashbacks, nightmares, avoidance, concentration problems and emotional numbing.

"I felt like a body, but there was nothing there. Like I was going through the motions. Say if somebody's daughter was missing, I'd do my job, but I wouldn't have any feelings."

Sometimes Terry would feel something, but he dealt with upsetting emotions by hiding them. He learned this technique at the police academy. At one point, fed up by repeated displays of macho insensitivity, he thought of quitting, but his new police friends talked him out of it. The academy taught Terry to handle anger, rage and compass-ion by suppressing them.

"They told you to stay impersonal, and when I came on the job, they said you cannot get involved or it will eat at ya. You're a copper. You're there to do a job. Do your job and leave. People are there looking to you for help. You've gotta be able to help them. I agree, but there's only so much you can cope with."

On the surface, the idea of police officers maintaining an impersonal attitude is to our benefit. In a crisis, we need somebody to look after us and make cool-headed decisions. However, suppressing feelings has devastating long-term effects.[7]

For Terry, it seems, ignoring feelings was the only way he could cope with the violence he experienced while doing his job. His nose and hand were broken twice. He lost three teeth and had all his front teeth broken and replaced. Terry received six black eyes, was kicked in the groin at least five times and was run over by a car. He says he had a job to do and believed in never backing down from anyone.

"If there was a big fight like in a bar, I loved goin' to 'em because you learn a lot. You learn to play head games. Usually you get into a donnybrook. I won't start something, but I won't back down. Once a guy pushed my partner. We were in uniform, and I told him, 'If you ever do that again, I'll deck ya.' He then tried to push me through a window. I got him down and then took on two other guys."

Police culture and violence shaped Terry's attitudes before the jewelry store robbery. But one violent incident sticks out as puzzling. It was likely the most traumatic incident in his police career, yet, according to him, it was insignificant.

One night in 1979 Terry and his partner were patrolling an area known for house break-and-enters. They spotted a man sneaking from the back of some houses. He was wearing dark clothing and gloves and was peering up and down the street. When the officers asked him what he was doing, the man responded with obscenities and then bolted.

Terry's partner chased the man into the lobby of an apartment building where they scuffled. By the time Terry secured the car and followed his partner, the man had knocked his partner off his feet and taken the officer's gun. In the ensuing brawl, Terry pinned the man down on a couch.

"He pressed my partner's gun against my forehead and he's spitting on my face and yellin,' 'I'm gonna blow your fuckin' brains out!'

"I grabbed onto the gun, and I could feel him pulling on the trigger and the chamber turning. I closed my eyes waiting for the bang.

"At the same time, I held on to the chamber real hard so it didn't turn all the way and the trigger wouldn't pull right back. I kept hitting him and hitting him until he let go of the gun.

"It really bothered the other officer. He was very upset. He figured I saved his life. He even bought me breakfast. It didn't bother me at all."

"Why not?" I asked.

"I figured it was all part of the job and somebody upstairs was lookin' out after me. But I didn't feel anything."

It seems unreasonable that Terry would feel nothing about this terrifying situation, yet would nearly break down after the jewelry store robbery. Perhaps an explanation centers on what was going on in his life at the time of the robbery.

As mentioned earlier, Terry was living alone, having recently split up with his wife. She had the children and he grieved for their loss. Then, the media got to him. The publicity and praise, offset by cold shoulders he was getting at work, made him anxious. He didn't want the praise, but he got it anyway, and the more he got, the more tension he experienced on the job.

Lack of support at work is often the main reason that officers feel intense pressure and insecurity. Always one to get along with everybody, now Terry was regularly getting into arguments with superiors. He said, "I'd lost my two children and work was my savior. After the jewelry store robbery, I had nowhere to go."

Why did Terry seem to overreact to the aftermath of the robbery when he didn't react to a terrifying situation like a gun pressed to his head? He probably had enough. His stress bucket was too full and had overflowed.[8] Terry had had too many stressful incidents in his life and police career, and having dealt with none of them, negative feelings piled up. He surpassed his ability to cope. "You can respond to only so much stress."[9]

Of course, there's more to it. Apart from grief and hostility from people in many parts of his life, Terry experienced a philosophical upheaval. His world view of who he was and how things worked was shattered by contradiction.

He saw himself as a tough guy. He thought his job was to solve problems through violence. He believed whole-heartedly in the police macho code—if someone points a gun at you, shoot him. His life as a cop was based on never backing down, but he backed down from shooting two people who pointed guns at him. Now he was praised by the media and the public for violating his beliefs but berated by his fellow cops for the same act.

How could he live with the contradiction? He said he couldn't. Consequently, he decided to prove to his fellow officers, and to himself, that he was capable of making the ultimate decision.

"At one time I used to hope, pray, that I would be challenged again to see if in fact it was me or maybe you don't need to shoot. To justify it. When I met officers who had shot and killed somebody, I would wonder what it would be like to kill somebody. If a hotshot came over for a gun call, I'd fly to it. To put myself through the test again."

One summer day a few months after he received the Policeman of the Year Award, Terry saw his chance to be tested at the scene of a bank robbery.

"I went to go down the stairs with my gun out and a guy turned at the bottom to come up," he said. "He was wearing a trench coat on a warm day and had his hands in his pockets. I put a bead on him and said, 'Freeze.' He said, 'Pardon?' I said, 'Don't move. Take your hands out of your pockets slowly.' He turned out to be a customer.

"When I went back that night to the station, we went through pop the chamber. You popped the chamber of the gun and handed it in. You didn't take it home with you. When I popped it, it had no bullets. I was so obsessed with cleaning my gun, I forgot to reload it. I put it in my holster, and I'd gone out on the street all day with an empty gun."

"What did that mean to you?" I asked.

"It meant I had problems. I didn't have my stuff together."

On a friend's encouragement, shortly after the bank holdup incident, Terry took a step he feared might ruin his career. He attended a post-shooting trauma group, a support group sponsored by the police department. For a person like Terry, socialized into never revealing feelings, the group at first threatened who he thought he was—the tough guy. Tough guys didn't talk about feelings, and tough guys who did were not in control.[10]

Terry said initially he couldn't connect with the other officers who attended. He hadn't shot anyone. "I wasn't one of *those* guys," he said. Within a few meetings, however, he realized he was experiencing the same problems as those who had shot and killed people.

"I would sit in a room and hear guys say they shot this guy and they always questioned themselves whether they really had to. I didn't shoot anybody and I'm saying to myself, *Maybe I should of.*"

"What did you discuss?" I said.

"We'd talk about if you're eating properly, getting proper sleep, if you find things at work are gathering up on you. Like I would think people were ganging up on me. I'd get into an argument with a supervisor and realize afterwards I had made an ass of myself."

"Did the meetings help?"

"They helped me get myself back together. I told my doctor I was going through a divorce and what was happening at work and when he looked at my weight loss he said, 'Holy Christ.' He got me eating again."

Everything improved for Terry. He attended the trauma group regularly. He was sleeping better, having fewer nightmares and flashbacks and was able to concentrate. He wasn't afraid to spend time at home alone any more. Nevertheless, a full five years after he rightfully could have shot two people dead, his fears returned after he was called to a hostage-taking in a hospital.

"A mentally ill person cornered an orderly in the cafeteria and was gonna cut him up with a piece of plate glass. It was curved, like an Arabian sword the way it was broken. It was about eighteen inches long, and at one end he had it taped. He was gonna kill this orderly because he claimed the man killed his brother."

"What did you do?"

"I tried to get the orderly out, but he didn't speak English. And he wouldn't move. He was so petrified, he urinated in his pants. I got between the hostage and the suspect who was a few feet in front of me. I took my gun out, but I didn't fire. If he lunged at me, he would have gotten me. I took more of a chance than I should have. I should have shot him, and I was totally justified. He eventually dropped the glass, and I jumped him and cuffed him."

"What did you think after this?" I said.

"It set me right back again. I'd since gotten remarried and I was late getting home and my wife said, 'You look a bit funny. Is everything okay?' And I said, 'I come up against it again and I didn't shoot the guy.' She understood what I was feeling and she took our daughter out while I phoned a friend to talk this thing through.

"Even with the trauma group, I hadn't answered the question about shooting or not shooting. I hadn't put myself to the test. And I started second-guessing myself all over again."

Terry took his problems back to the support group. "I believed before that I was having abnormal feelings in a normal situation. The group made me see it's a normal reaction to an abnormal situation. And I thought to myself, _Whoa, I'm not the only one who's experienced this._"

After a time in the support group, a change came over Terry. For many years when he investigated gruesome murders, suicides or took missing persons reports, he hadn't felt anything inside. And even after he had had a gun pressed to his head, the suspect trying to pull the trigger, he felt nothing. Now when he saw something awful, he allowed himself to feel bad inside.

"I would see it and think, _Holy Shit, am I ever glad that's not me._ But I'm glad it still affects me because it shows that I've got feelings."

"How do you contend with the feelings?"

"I analyze myself, which I couldn't do before. I let the feelings come, not fight them. Not so much to control them but to let them come because they gotta come out. It's a pain or injury that you can't see. Same as somebody walking up to you and punching you in the face, only you see that guy who hit you. You feel the pain, you know where it is.

"The feelings you get, you can't touch. You have to learn to cope with that. The other thing I do that I didn't do before—when I leave work, I leave everything behind."

Chapter 11

Bomb Squad

*"It blew him back and blew me over
and we were on fire."*

Detective Tony Senft was late. I offered to go to his home in East Islip, New York, but Tony insisted on traveling into Manhattan. He wanted to go up in an elevator. He wanted to sit in an office. Perhaps those acts don't mean much to you and me. To Tony, they mean a lot.

After checking my watch half a dozen times, I phoned the reception desk. Nobody had entered the police union building asking for me. I vaulted the stairs to the waiting area and sat on a sofa.

The trip was difficult for Tony. Although someone was driving him in, he'd have to negotiate the hallways and elevator himself. His balance and eyesight were not great, and he had occasional memory lapses. I worried that he might have lost his way. I was having a hard time myself in the maze of unnumbered offices that looked the same.

You may recall that Tony was instrumental in helping transit officer Christine McIntyre who is described in Chapter 1. Tony is president of the New York Police Self-Support Group, a group that does not recruit or lack members.

Before long, a man in a dark suit appeared at the reception area's glass doors. He clinked one door and then the other against the floor bolts. The receptionist buzzed him in. As we shook hands, Tony laughed. He'd been up and down in the elevator, gotten off at wrong floors and tried to get through locked doors. He'd learned to deal with irritating situations by seeing the humor in them.

His blue eyes were full of mirth and his unruffled manner gave away nothing of his daily frustration with the products of civilization to which most of us are indifferent—elevators, doors and stairs.

After relaxing for awhile in the boardroom that served as an interview setting, Tony described how he had acquired Posttraumatic Stress Disorder as a result of an act of terrorism. In 1982, he was ten years on the New York police force. He'd worked patrol, plain clothes burglary, street crime and was now in the bomb squad. The idea of dismantling bombs mystifies me. Why would anybody want to do such a dangerous job? Tony told me he took the job because it was *safer* than other jobs.

"How's that possible?" I asked him.

"When I was a cop in street crime," he said, "I acted as a decoy. People would attack me. The bomb squad was less dangerous. Because how often do you take apart bombs?"

Tony had a point. The situations didn't arise that often. But when they did, what then?

On New Year's Eve, around half past nine Tony and his partner, Richie Pastorella, had just finished dinner in the precinct house. The phone rang. A bomb had gone off at 26 Federal Plaza, a towering office building that housed many U.S. agencies including the local headquarters of the FBI and the Justice Department.

They rushed to the site. Tony saw several stories of shattered glass on the sidewalk. Fire trucks and ambulances were everywhere. Fortunately, no one was injured. While looking for the seat of the bomb, they heard an explosion not too far away at 1 Police Plaza, police headquarters

Again, when they got there, they saw a mountain of glass and a bomb crater. But this time they found a wounded officer, his leg blown off. A few minutes later, another bomb exploded, ravaging the U.S. District Courthouse at Cadman Plaza in Brooklyn.

It was now only three-quarters of an hour since Tony had finished eating a sandwich. WCBS radio received a call from a man saying, "This is the FALN. We're responsible for the bombings in New York City tonight. Free Puerto Rico. Free all political prisoners and all prisoners of war."

Moments later, police officers discovered two small boxes at St. Andrew's Plaza beside the federal courthouse, just west of police headquarters. A bomb-sniffing dog checked them out and sat down, the signal for explosives. Tony and his partner threw blast-absorbing blankets over the bombs and began to clear the kill zone.

"A number of Chinese people were walking through the area," Tony said. "Once we started screaming 'Police!' they froze. So we had to physically go out and pick people up and move them. I picked up a woman and then a child and after I did that a couple of times, they realized what was happening and got out of the way. Meanwhile, we lost time."

The officers zipped themselves into their bulky bomb suits. The suits were made of thick kevlar, the material used in bulletproof vests, and were reinforced by steel plates covering the chest and groin. The officers did not wear helmets because the visors would fog up from their breathing and obscure their vision.[1]

Tony and Richie prepared to tackle the first bomb, which consisted of four sticks of dynamite. Wrapped in newspaper, the sticks were attached to a nine-volt battery and a pocket watch detonator and stuffed into a fast-food box.

Tony thought the device was so crudely constructed, it would be easy to dismantle. He opened a tool box behind Richie who bent over the bomb and lifted the blanket.

It blew up.

Richie took the brunt of the explosion. "It blew him back and blew me over and we were on fire," said Tony.

Richie lost both eyes, the fingers on his right hand and most of his hearing. Chunks of concrete punctured his body.

For ten days, Tony was delirious and blind. Every bone in his face was smashed. His hip was broken, and most of his body was bruised and torn.

Doctors rebuilt his face and barely a scar shows today. Tony's nose is straight, and he continues to be as good looking as the 5 foot 8, brown haired husband and father in his family photographs. Sight in his left eye was restored, but work on the right eye was unsuccessful. The doctors could not remove tiny bits of concrete, wire and bomb parts that riddled the rest of his body.

Despite having both eardrums replaced, Tony lost 60 percent of his hearing on the right side and 40 percent on the other. Both Tony and Richie spent over a month in hospital and endured multiple operations over a number of years. They will likely require more surgical procedures in the future.

Terrorism has become a familiar occurrence in many countries around the world. The bombings of the federal building in Oklahoma City, the Olympic Park and New York's World Trade Center, have destroyed America's innocence. Once rare, bomb blasts and other terrorist acts that wound and kill civilians and police officers have become commonplace in the United States. Reports by government agencies studying terrorism say we can expect more deliberate acts of murder and mayhem.[2]

Even with follow-up reports in the media, we often don't know what happens to police officers who survive a terrorist attack or how their families are affected. Injured officers seem to drop from sight, trying to cope with their wounds out of the public eye. We seldom get a glimpse of the long-term physical and psychological effects on them and what they do to heal.

"I have debris that comes out as time goes on. And this is more than ten years later," said Tony. "I got one coming out of my good eye, one behind the ear. I'll be washing myself and I'll go, 'What the heck is that?' And I'll pull a stone out. I had one piece of the pocketwatch in my ankle."

As well as permanent injuries, Tony has continuing medical problems as a result of the blast.

"If I'm talking to you, I cannot be talking to someone next to you. Because once I start moving my head back and forth, I get sick like I'm car sick. It's vertigo from the ear damage. If cold weather comes, my face pulsates constantly. My ears ring. I got bursitis in my hip from it being broken. I had fiber damage in my neck. If I go to sneeze, I have to grab my head because my neck goes out. And I have high blood pressure from the stress and the heavy medication.

"I used to be an athlete. I was a weightlifter. I was running six miles a day. I went from that to sitting on the couch. I was thirty-six years old feeling like I was ninety-six."

I asked Tony what life was like after he got home from the hospital.

"I went from being invulnerable to realizing you can get your ass kicked. You know, when I first got injured, I'd wake up five, six, seven times a night totally disoriented.

Didn't know if I was five years old. I didn't know if I was twenty-five years old, if I was married, or if I had children. My wife and children would sit with me for hours. And then all of a sudden, it would click back in, and I knew what was happening.

"Awhile after I was hurt, I'd go into a store with my wife and then completely forget what parking lot I put the car in. I'd pick up the phone and talk and I'd put the phone down and say, 'Who the hell was that?'

"We laugh about it now, but sometimes people came to the house. I'd invited them for dinner and forgot to tell my wife. It was really embarrassing. I've watched movies two or three times and said, 'Boy, this is a good movie.' And my wife would say, 'Don't you remember seeing this?' My short term memory was badly damaged."

"And how are you today?"

"It still happens. Not as long and not as frequent. I'll find myself getting disoriented and getting confused, but for very short periods of time. Like thirty or forty seconds."

Tony experienced many of the same psychological symptoms as officers injured in shootings and diagnosed with PTSD. He couldn't eat or sleep. He second-guessed himself, was depressed and had frequent flashbacks and nightmares.

"I dreamed of losing control," he said. "You know, turning a corner and losing control of the car. And even today, I dream of things I've never dreamed of before. Like a woman who jumped off a building in 1973. I was standing close to where she hit the ground, and I had her brains and tissue all over me.

"The boss said to me, 'I think you ought to go home.' I said, 'For what?' He said, 'To calm down.' I said, 'I have no problem.' I went into the precinct bathroom, took my gun belt off and my leather goods, got in the shower with the rest of my clothes on and let everything go right down the drain. I put new clothes on and went out on my post.

"No debriefing. No talking about it. You couldn't show any weakness. And now twenty years later, I'm dreaming of this woman jumping off the building. I hadn't dreamt about that woman until I got hurt. Now I dream of her every few weeks.

"My biggest recollection of the explosion is the noise and the biggest recollection of the woman jumping off the building is the noise when she hit. It was like a watermelon hitting the ground and everything just splattered all over."

Current traumas tend to dredge up memories of past traumas. If Tony had been counseled or debriefed after the woman's suicide, he might not suffer from recurring nightmares about her today. Because the suicide remains unresolved in Tony's mind, it's likely the images will continue to rerun themselves until he confronts and accepts the experience as part of his life.

"Do you have good dreams too?" I asked.

"Yeah, all kinds of dreams. I sometimes make a joke with my wife. I say, 'I wonder where I'm going tonight.' Like I dreamed I was back in my first radio car with my first partner. And I woke up and sat up in bed laughing.

"I dream about when I went to South Jamaica one time and delivered a baby. On the way to the hospital, the baby stopped breathing so I brought that baby back. I dream about a Jewish baby sometimes. The parents were arguing about what hospital to take it to. I determined that the child's life was in danger, wrapped it in a towel and took it to the nearest hospital, which was not a kosher hospital. They were quite angry with me, but they named the baby after me.

"But for the first few years after the explosion, the dreams were totally nightmares. At least three times a night."

"How did you feel about the terrorist group that set the bomb?"

"I didn't get personally angry at the FALN. I've never got caught up in that blaming thing. But I was angry because I can't do the things I could before. Like I can't drive myself without getting sick. I don't get on ladders. I don't do things around the house. You know, if I go into a shopping mall and I make a turn and I walk into somebody—that's happened to me... And they look at you like you're a degenerate."

"How did your children react?"

"You know, after the bomb, the kids came to see me. I have three boys. Then they were seventeen, fifteen and twelve. They held me and touched me. They wanted to see what I looked like under my clothes. My oldest guy is very mature. He asked me if there was anything I wanted to talk to him about.

"My young guy, the twelve-year-old, I've had some tough times with. He became the man of the house. He became the father. He was telling me, 'Wear the red shirt today. The pants don't go with that. Take that off.' And I'd listen and take that off. And when I started to recover, I didn't want to be controlled as much and that's where the conflict came in.

"He'd say, 'Listen, tie your shoes. Can't you bend over and tie your shoes? Oh, never mind, I'll get them.' And he'd bend over and tie my shoes for me. It was humiliating. You know, he was the maintenance person."

"How about your wife?"

"We've been married for twenty-seven years. And we have a good marriage. But it hasn't been easy. We've had some tough times along the road. Because of my frustration. Because the family goes on and I'm still sitting on the couch."

"Your life has changed radically."

"I was in charge. I handled my own affairs. And I don't do that anymore. I can't make decisions. I go over and over and over things. I'm not the same man. From playing ball with my kids to jogging to weightlifting to swimming. I can't do that. I avoid conflict where that was my business to take care of conflict.

"I lost a good part of my life and I'm angry for that. I became depressed. I sought counseling from day one and took antidepressants for awhile to get me through. But I have never contemplated suicide. I love myself and my family too much. But I tell you, I can understand somebody committing suicide, which I never could before. From the pain, the depression and the loneliness and not having a feeling of worth, you feel helpless."

"Did you receive emotional support?"

"It's what you feel inside. If you're strong minded and you have the right support from the job, from your family, from your peers, you get through it. If you don't, you get sucked down."

Love and support from those around him helped Tony cope with his extensive physical and psychological injuries. He also tried to heal himself by helping others. For instance, he persuaded the Lions Club to help him raise $40,000 for a quadriplegic boy in his community. He also spoke frequently to individuals and groups about what it's like to "have your ass kicked and come back to function somewhat and get around okay."

Several months after the bombing, Tony's injured partner decided to do something with his life. Richie acquired a list of injured police officers from the department. He and Tony called them all, inviting them to join a new organization called The New York Police Self-Support Group. Their goal was to offer emotional support to injured officers—days, months, years after nobody else would. Eventually, Richie passed the leadership to Tony.

"What do you and the other officers do in the group?" I asked.

"We help police officers that have had severe accidents in-the-line-of-duty," he said. "And we let them understand what Posttraumatic Stress Disorder is. We tell them it is okay to be nervous and scared and have some depression. And we let them know that there's people out there like them. And if you lost eyes, we will send somebody who lost eyes to visit you. If someone's lost a leg, we send someone who's lost a leg.

"We tell you, 'Hey man. I've been there.' And we will lean over and kiss 'em and hug 'em and tell them, 'I understand how it is to be worried.' And they will say, 'What am I going to do? Here I'm twenty-five years old. I can't walk anymore. I can't pick my babies up. I can't touch my wife.' We're showing them that you can go on."

"Do you visit right after an accident or injury?"

"We come right away and we come later when they're just sitting around. It's horrible to be left alone, you know. After all the medals and the balloons and hurrahs are gone, we're there for them. When the phone calls stop, and they don't get as many visitors, and they know they don't belong no more, we are there to make sure nobody's forgotten.

"We get people involved. At least if they can come to a monthly meeting and hang out with people as traumatically injured as they've been, then we've accomplished something. And they're not alone. They're not alone."

The Police Self-Support Group provides more than monthly meetings. It gets injured officers active again. As well as sending them to visit other afflicted officers to offer comfort, they have social gatherings like picnics during the year. Their enrollment is now 140 officers and their families. They started with eleven. Charging little for dues, they rely on benefactors to fund their various services, and they often go begging.

When Tony talks to injured officers who don't think they can make it, he tells them about his visit to the National Law Enforcement Officers Memorial in Washington, DC. The blue-gray marble walls hold the names of more than 18,000 police officers who have died in-the-line-of-duty. Tony says that citizens who visit the police memorial are often astonished at seeing so many names.

"What was it like for you to visit the memorial?"

"I was overwhelmed because I knew a lot of the New York officers. I knew their names and I knew the incidents. And it was depressing for me, you know? And I was saying to myself, 'Here I am alive and these guys are dead. These are the real heroes.' And I was whipped. I mean, I had to sit down.

"You know, I thought it was a beautiful thing, the tribute. But there's no city like the City of New York for police officers who have lost their lives. It was horrifying. It took me some time to get over it. It's something I would encourage everybody to see. It really brings you down to earth.[3]

"I told a young man in Good Samaritan Hospital about it. He was hurt in the Twin Towers explosion. He says, 'You want to know something? That was my birthday when I got hurt.' And I said, 'That was your lucky day, man, because you're here. You made it. You can talk and you can see. So make your life better. Don't get caught up in trivial things anymore.'"

I said to Tony, "It was your lucky day too."

"I've been very lucky in my life. I've seen three people killed in front of me. I never had to take a life. I was supposed to be with some friends who were killed in a boating accident. I fell three stories one time at a construction site down an elevator shaft, and I walked away. And on New Year's Eve, I coulda been killed in the bomb explosion."

"You're like a cat with nine lives," I said.

He laughed. "I don't think I have any left though, you know? I've had enough. Let the young guys take over."

As well as visiting injured officers, Tony talks to rookie cops at the police academy each time a class graduates. He wants them to be aware of the dangers of the job and the support his group provides.

"We tell them how we got injured," he said. "We advise them to keep healthy, physically and mentally, and to stay alert. We tell them to wear their vests. And we tell them we're there for them and that we will be seeing some of them, unfortunately. And it's very moving because we have people up there in wheelchairs and walking blind. We're not the speaking engagement they love to see or they enjoy. We're there to make a lasting impression."[4]

Tony believes for police officers to survive acts of violence, they need support, not only from their families and their own kind, but also from the public and the media. Too often the media focuses on the few bad cops, he says, and doesn't recognize the work and sacrifice made by the majority of well-meaning, hard-working police officers.

"I loved it. I loved policing. And it was taken away from me. That's why you're here. You love the job. The job is your life. If you don't love it, you don't belong here. When you become a police officer, you're there to do good. And if you don't want to be a good guy, get out. Most police officers don't have tolerance for bad cops. But we take it on the chin all the time because of the few bad cops.

"We have a certain percentage that are bad, like any occupation. But you take the majority of police officers and they're doing a bang-up job. They want to make a difference. You come on to help and serve the public. You're not there to beat people up or to shoot people. But that happens.

"We're the only occupation that's required, if you have to, to take a life. We don't want to do that. Everybody else like doctors, paramedics and firefighters can save lives. Nobody ever asks the doctor to take a life. All they do is save. But the police officer sometimes has to use violence to correct the situation. That's why they get PTSD. That's why you have guys and women cops getting banged up."

A couple of weeks after Tony nearly lost his life, President Ronald Reagan called him in his hospital room. It was just after Reagan was shot, and they spoke as survivors.

"How you feeling, Mr. President?" Tony asked him.

"I'm asking the questions," the President said. "How do you feel?"

"Well, I'm messed up pretty bad," he said.

"So am I," said Reagan.

Tony said that a common bond was felt with the President because he was suffering from trauma, too. "Everyone is insecure, everyone has depression, even the President. He told me that. He said I should fight it. And I was humbled because it was the President of the United States."

After talking to the President and recognizing what helps members of his own group, Tony is convinced that the most help comes from the self. That's why the group is called a "self" support group. But to develop strength within, survivors first need the help of those outside themselves— family, friends, coworkers, counselors, administrators, the public, the media, politicians and even the President.

The New York Police Self-Support Group no longer meets in tiny rooms. The members no longer sit on the floor. They now have an auditorium assigned to them for their monthly meetings. Tony and Richie helped start support groups in a number of other police departments, but few departments offer the vital assistance wounded officers need.

When Tony thinks about the support he has received, he is grateful. That support has helped him manage the symptoms of PTSD.

"I'm fortunate. I'm alive. I can see the grass grow, and I can see the sun come up."

Chapter 12

Police Dispatchers

*"I've been waiting to hear somebody die,
and this is it."*

"Was I stressed? Yeah, from day one.

"Like the first two years of this job when 9-1-1 rang, I'd go like, 'Oh, crap.' It was the unknown. Is it going to be a situation that's real easy to handle or is it going to be something completely out of your comfort zone, which it often was."

"A robbery is a robbery, that's scary enough, but is there a gun involved? Is there a bomb involved? Is one of my officers going to get hurt or worse? Am I gonna have to hear somebody scream? Am I gonna hear somebody kill somebody?"

These are the thoughts of Jan Myers. For five years, she was a hospital emergency room admitting clerk. For the next two years, she kept the records for police and fire, but, at the age of twenty-seven, she finally found what she really wanted to do.

She joined the Novato Police Department as a dispatcher. She worked there for a decade, and then joined the San Rafael Police Department in the same capacity. Both departments are small California agencies serving about 50,000 people. But small or large, doesn't matter. Civilians go nuts on a large scale everywhere.

She was at Novato in her ninth year when she got a call that still sticks in her mind.

"Honey, my husband has a gun to my head," an 85-year old woman named Ethel said calmly.

Jan thought, *Holy Cow.* "As I'm talking to her, he slams the gun down on the table next to her, so all I hear on my end is a loud pop. My heart falls to my gut."

"Ethel, what was that?" said Jan.

"He slammed the gun on the table," she said meekly. "He did not shoot me."

Ethel realized what Jan was thinking. He slammed the gun down next to the phone three more times, and Jan jumped every time.

The sergeant on duty was monitoring the radio, and ordered Jan to call out the SWAT team. The team then set up around the house while Jan stayed on the phone with Ethel. The woman was describing where her husband was walking and waving his gun.

"She was an amazing reporting party. At one point, she says, 'He's walking down the hall towards the back bedroom,' and I know that one of my officers is at a screen door watching her at the phone, and I'm working radio at the same time. This was back in the day when the Novato Police Department had you work the radio and the phone simultaneously," Jan told me.

"L3, do you have a visual on the X, on the female?" Jan asked the officer.

"Affirmative," he said.

"Is he still in the back bedroom?" she asked Ethel.

"Yes," she said.

"Can you see the officer at the door?"

"Yes."

"Don't hang up the phone, just lay it down," she said, "and run to the officer."

"Okay, Honey," she said, and waddled toward the door.

No one had given Jan permission to order the woman out of the house, but she had to get her out at the first opportunity.

Jan felt that it was the longest five seconds of her life. She was afraid the elderly man might kill her and the officer.

"I've got her, she's okay," said the officer.

But Jan's work was not done. Next she called the man's daughter who lived a few blocks away. The daughter talked him into putting down the gun, and he walked out of the house into the arms of the police. It turned out that the man had dementia, and didn't realize what he was doing.

"It was the most draining call I'd ever worked," said Jan. "Why this call bothered me so much was my physical response when the gun hit the table three friggin' times. I thought, *I've been waiting to hear somebody die, and this is it..*"

Jan took many calls throughout her career that were frightening and had the potential for being deadly, but the call from the elderly woman particularly disturbed her, likely due to the vivid description of the man with the gun's movements, and the caller's advanced age and vulnerability. Jan felt an obligation to save her. But there was another call that affected her even more.

Jan had recently moved to the San Rafael Police Department, and had gotten to know a female officer who was on duty one night. The officer was sitting at an off-ramp near a post office parking lot watching for people to blow the red light.

At 3:23 AM, the officer keyed the mic and said, "Radio, I think I'm being shot at."

Jan was working the 9-1-1 calls, and another dispatcher was working the primary radio. "We copy, where are you?"

They knew where the officer was, but wanted to make sure she hadn't suddenly moved her location. They could hear gunfire in the background.

The officer confirmed her location and said, "I'm taking live fire." She didn't know where the shots were coming from or where to hide.

Then a truck pulled through the intersection, stopped in front of a pizza parlor, and the officer could see the suspect shooting from the truck window. "Apparently, the guy got in a beef with his girlfriend, was drunk, and was looking for a fight, and by chance came upon my officer near the post office parking lot.

With only two dispatchers on that night, both were scrambling to contact officers. "I'm waking up the SWAT team leader, saying, 'I need you to sit up and listen to me.' Which made him go, 'Okay, Jan's not kidding...'"

About a block and a half away from the shooting scene, another officer was monitoring the radio traffic. He sped over to where the female officer was under attack, attached a night scope to his rifle, and shot the suspect.

Jan wasn't immediately advised that the suspect had been shot. It was still considered an active shooter situation until it could be confirmed the suspect was down, and Jan worried about the officers on the scene. She stayed on through the whole ordeal, and once the sun came up, she found out the guy was dead.

"Some people presumed it was suicide-by-cop. Now that I'm saying it out loud, that was always my biggest fear, and it happened. It was somebody who wants to end their life, and they're going to pull a uniform into it, which sucks. 'Cause no cop wants to do that, no dispatcher wants to hear it.

"Oh, Lord. That's the one that I had nightmares about. I dealt with a lot of calls, I was a dispatcher for twelve years, and I worked in the ER before that, but that one... that was a horrible one."

Jan was finally relieved after five nerve-racking hours. She then went to the restroom and broke down.

"For the first time since I joined Dispatch, I lost it. Crying, and shaking, and I said to myself, I'm sick of it. I'm tired of listening to evil. And then I did what every professional, caring dispatcher does. I walked over to the sink, threw water on my face, wiped my face, and headed back to work."

She was coming out of the bathroom when the officer who shot the suspect entered the police station and walked down the hall towards her. "When you work a call like that, you form a bond with the officers that you can't verbalize," Jan told me. "It's like they're part of you forever."

They saw each other, and she started yelling, "I'm tired of this shit. I'm tired of feeling like this, and waiting for the day that one of my officers is going to be killed."

"Let's go for a walk," said the officer, comforting her.

They walked around the block at the police department, and she said, "This job has a shelf life, and mine's expired. I gotta go."

Jan said that she knew at the nine year mark after the call with the elderly woman that she should have gotten out, but she stayed in for another three years. "It just wears and tears you in between the stress and the hours that you work."

After the shooting, she had stomach problems, insomnia, and nightmares. "I had nightmares where the officer that shot and killed the guy ran over his own two boys, his sons, with his patrol car, and then shot them. And then I had dreams that the officer and I were grocery shopping and a gunfight ensued in the grocery store, and I've got a gun and he's got a gun, and my bullets are hitting people and his bullets are dropping to the ground."

Jan didn't want to live like this anymore. For five months, she was sick with sinusitis and bronchitis. She appealed to her bosses, but they said her illness wasn't work related.

"I was stuck on graveyard, and I asked, 'Can I please get off graveyard for six months so I can allow my health to get back to normal?' They said, 'No, you're lowest in seniority.'"

Jan had ten years on the job in Novato, but because she had recently _lateraled_ over to San Rafael, she was "low on the totem pole, and they weren't going to make any special exceptions for me."

Jan's symptoms got worse, and she began flashing back on incidents she thought she'd forgotten about.

"I started remembering people hitting their children to the point where their retinas detached."

"I recalled a man who decided that he needed to be done with his ex-wife, and got tape and garbage bags to wrap her body in and cord to wrap her arms and legs and hands. He was wanted by the police, and he walked into her home, and he was wearing a leather jacket. He took it off, and when he laid the leather jacket down, she heard a thud. She knew it was a gun, and when he was outside smoking a cigarette, she picked up the phone and called 9-1-1.

"He came back in the house, and I was talking to her and acting like I was her girlfriend so he wouldn't realize that she was on the phone with the police. Whenever I asked a question, I'd ask it so she could answer Yes or No, and occasionally she'd throw in innuendos like she's talking to her girlfriend. He ended up fleeing the house without killing her, and we caught him later.

"I flashed back to the two men from El Salvador who were robbing churches, and they showed up at a church in Novato. Somebody called in and said he discovered a man lying in a puddle of blood over at the church, and he saw a vehicle leaving the scene. As I'm giving this information over the air, my officer passes the suspects' vehicle, turns around and pursues them."

Jan was the officer's lifeline as he transmitted his locations and the details of the pursuit. The car suddenly stopped, and the suspects jumped out and took off on foot.

He ran after them and kept updating her on where they were going, their clothing, weapons and so on.

"That sort of contact forms a bond with an officer, something you never forget."

The officer caught the men with the help of other cops. It turned out that the body in the church was the thirty-three-year-old pastor, and his wife was pregnant. The killers eventually got life in prison.

"Four months later we were working on Christmas Day, and we get a phone call that the pastor's wife had her baby that same day. We sat there with big smiles on our faces and gave each other a big hug, like Okay, there's some good that comes out of these things."

The burnout rate for police dispatchers is often two to three years before they can't take it anymore and have to get out. Jan had survived a dozen years, much longer than the average.

"I think most people that survive this job beyond the burnout rate are from dysfunctional families," she said. "So they thrive on the family atmosphere, they thrive on the chaos. I'm speaking for myself as well. I was raised in an alcoholic family, and it was nothing for me to talk on the phone with a drunk or somebody reporting a drunk driver or to listen to chaos in the background of a family argument. That was home for me. I understood that. It was like... I get paid for this? I grew up with this.

"And then after work, everybody hangs out and has hamburgers and beers and goes, 'Well, that sucks.' But we got through it. It was fun, it was a great adrenaline rush, and you got paid decent money for it."

But it wasn't fun or exciting anymore. And it became too stressful and filled with terror for Jan to cope with the fear and uncertainty.

"We're not given the tools to recognize what to do when an incident occurs and to prepare yourself for that incident. As with firefighters and police officers, dispatchers can't show that we're weak, that we need help, or that something scares us. We're supposed to keep it steady on the radio when the officer's screaming for help. So you suck it up. You act like it doesn't bother you. You build up your emotional wall so high, nobody can tell that it's hurting you.

"Nobody tells us when we're getting into the job that it's extremely normal to feel like crap after a bad call. It's totally normal to have nightmares after a bad call. It's normal to be irritated, to not sleep well. A lot of us are thinking, I'm screwed up, but I'm not going to act like I'm screwed up because I don't want anybody to know I'm screwed up... because everybody else looks great."

Jan thought that something must be wrong with her because she believed she was the only one affected by a bad call. However, almost everyone working a difficult or traumatic call is affected in some way. And as many as a third experience stress symptoms that persist longer than a month, and could develop into PTSD.

"So it's a vicious cycle. You look at dispatchers, and they have the thousand-yard stare. They are often grossly overweight. Because they just sit at that radio and they shove crap in their face. It's a standing joke in law enforcement. The first year, they gain 15 pounds, they don't take care of themselves, and they keep gaining. Because they're sitting at the radio console going from call to call to call."

Dispatch is the central location, and everybody visits and brings donuts, cakes, cookies, coffee, anything with fat, sugar, chocolate, salt and caffeine. "You sit there, and socialize, and shove food in your face and you wait for the next call."

As well as overeating, Jan told me that dispatchers suffer from several other issues due to the overwhelming stress of the job. "I've known or counseled dispatchers who were compulsive gamblers, sex addicts, compulsive shoppers, alcoholics, obsessive-compulsive, and addicted to prescribed medications."

In addition, dispatchers stew in their own stress hormones. "The officers get the chance to chase down the suspects. The firefighters put out a fire. They physically do something to alleviate that stress. Dispatchers don't."

Jan went to see her family doctor about her constant sinusitis and bronchitis, and after several visits, the doctor wondered if the cause of Jan's medical problems was more psychological and emotional than physical.

"How are you sleeping?"

"Not well."

"Well, how often do you sleep?"

"I'm working graveyard and I get an average of three to four hours sleep a day."

Which Jan realized was like walking around drunk.

The doctor continued to probe until Jan started crying. "I said that I've been sick for so long, and I'm dealing with all this stress, and feel so stupid. And the doctor said, 'Don't feel stupid. You do a difficult job, and it's raising havoc in your life.' And it was so nice to hear somebody objective say that to me."

The doctor said that Jan was exhibiting anxiety and depression. And suggested that she might have PTSD, and should consult a psychologist. She then saw a therapist who confirmed her family doctor's concerns. Jan had Posttraumatic Stress Disorder.

To deal with her PTSD symptoms, Jan decided to attend a five-day residential treatment program designed for first responders at the *On Site Academy* in Massachusetts. The clinicians there treated her for PTSD, and after the program, her nightmares stopped. She continued to see the therapist for a couple of months, but they both knew what she had to do to recover from the anxiety disorder—get out of the job.

"That was a kick in the gut. I had joined a critical incident stress management (CISM) team a few years before, and was teaching how to deal with stress and trauma to other dispatchers, but wasn't following my own advice.

"You see this a lot in people who join stress management teams. They're either incredibly stressed and looking for help, or they've already been through the hell and are there to help other people. I was looking for help and didn't realize it. I was walking the walk, but I wasn't talking the talk.

"What would have happened to me if I hadn't gotten help? I can guarantee you I wouldn't have a marriage. I probably would have gotten very sick or died after something else in my body had failed. It would have gone from bronchitis and sinusitis to something else."

Jan said that she grasped the consequences of her situation after she met a New Hampshire state trooper during treatment who was also attending the program. The trooper said that she had had sinusitis for months and couldn't get rid of it, and had such serious thyroid problems that her thyroid was surgically removed.

"When she told her story, I realized I am going down a really bad road, and I don't want to be a statistic. I don't want to be in my forties and not be able to do anything because I didn't take care of myself."

Jan was carrying unresolved trauma not only from calls she'd received as a dispatcher, but from a traumatic incident that occurred years earlier in 1993, when she'd been a dispatcher for only three years. An incident that made her feel intense fear, helpless and horror, the prerequisites for developing PTSD. A detective she knew who had been on the job for more than twenty years jumped off the Golden Gate Bridge, "and that shattered all of us. Something like that hits a small agency like ours very hard."

Jan told me that his suicide is the main reason why another treatment facility exclusively for cops, firefighters and other emergency responders was started on the west coast—the *West Coast Post-Trauma Retreat* (WCPR) in California.

Jan has a lot of experience with WCPR from a volunteer standpoint. She says that the overall goal is to get the person "out of the fog of depression" so they can see more clearly.

"People come in for all different reasons. Some are sent by their agency, some don't want their agency to know and they're paying cash. Some are taking vacation time to deal with an addiction or they're going to lose everything in life including their career, their marriage, and their family.

"We're not trying to say we're going to get everybody back to work. Because not everybody should go back to work. There are some people that are so burnt, and so hurt by the job that it's probably better that they not go back to work.

"Then there's the whole identification of being a first responder... I'm a cop, I'm a dispatcher. When you say that to people, people go 'Ahhhh... Oh, wow... You are a life saver.' Well, if you can't do it anymore, you ask, What else am I going to do?"

Jan says that WCPR tries to help people understand why they're under so much stress. They make them aware that they have options. They don't have to stay in this job, there are other things you can do because of their abilities as a cop, or as a dispatcher.

"It drives me nuts when dispatchers say, 'I can't do anything else, I'm *just* a dispatcher.' A dispatcher is a family therapist, a judge, a teacher, a mentor... I mean they wear fifty different hats in one shift. If they stepped back and wrote down all the tasks that you do, you could run circles around anybody in the private industry. But they don't recognize that.

"It's always *I'm just a dispatcher...* because you're not a cop, you're not a firefighter, you're this chick on the radio who presses a button and talks. Well, folks, it's time to wake up."

Jan says that the focus at WCPR is on education, healing and support. "We're there to educate them on why their minds and bodies responded to the stress, and that they're not freaks, and their feelings are completely normal. We let them come to the reality of what they did or didn't do. They couldn't save the person, they are not superhuman. Nothing else they would have done that day would have changed the situation.

"And they talk to support people that are volunteers, they are peers, people in the business who understand what you're going through. And it's not just for the dispatcher or the cop. We have a spouses and significant others retreat as well."

"I feel weird saying this, but WCPR is magical. You see people walk in on Sunday with the thousand-yard stare, with their heads down... I had a deputy from California walk in with his big jacket on, his baseball cap, and his head shrunken into his jacket. He looked like a turtle. Just defeated, petrified, thinking he's a failure.

"Five days later, on Friday, he was laughing, joking. He had a spark in his eye. He was immensely better, and it's because you talk to peers who understand. It's an intensive five days where we do the stress debriefing process drawn out over a three-day period, and you really get down to the nitty-gritty of what the hell is bothering you."

Jan says that not many dispatchers have gone through the program. Why not? "My opinion... they don't think they deserve it. I'm just a dispatcher. I'm not going to tell anybody I need help because I've got to have the officers' confidence that I can do my job. When in reality, three-quarters of the officers are probably feeling stressed out in the same way."

It's hard for a lot of people to accept that dispatchers can get PTSD. "Because when you say a dispatcher has PTSD, they get a critical look on their face like, 'What the hell, how does that happen?' When you have nothing but your imagination, you create that evil scene in your mind, and when you see crime scene photos of it later, you look at them and say, 'Oh my God, it's not nearly as bad as I pictured it.'"

After twelve years, Jan quit Dispatch, and went back to school where she earned her degree in Emergency Management Operations.

She is now working in Oregon as an academy class training coordinator, and teaches critical incident stress awareness and emotional survival for law enforcement to police academies. She no longer works for WCPR because of the distance, but is still on the board of directors.

*   *   *

Jan brings up important issues in her story. The stress factors that affect dispatchers the most are: [1]

- ➤ the inability to physically get rid of stress
- ➤ poor communication within the department
- ➤ lack of control over their work schedule and duties
- ➤ poor diets
- ➤ night shifts that interrupt proper sleep patterns
- ➤ lack of a life outside of the job
- ➤ striving for perfection
- ➤ lack of proper training
- ➤ false expectations and beliefs

Unaddressed, these issues can lead to burnout, including: [2]

- ➤ feelings of anger and resentment toward supervisors
- ➤ poor appetite or increase in eating
- ➤ insomnia
- ➤ stomachaches
- ➤ headaches

- ➢ constipation
- ➢ chest pain
- ➢ feelings of worthlessness
- ➢ cynicism
- ➢ depression
- ➢ an inability to concentrate
- ➢ a sense of being overwhelmed
- ➢ becoming forgetful
- ➢ thoughts of suicide
- ➢ recklessness and loss of control

Please note that burnout is not the same thing as PTSD, but if unaddressed, burnout could possibly lead to PTSD symptoms. That was the route that Jan unintentionally took.

Jan experienced almost every job problem and burnout issue that affects dispatchers. Dispatchers are often treated like second class citizens because they are not trained as cops, yet in her jurisdiction dispatchers attend only a basic three week training course within one year of being hired. "Most of the tough stuff is learned by doing the job," she said. Like so many other dispatchers, Jan was mostly trained on the job, and consequently, didn't always know what was the right or wrong thing to do.

She had no physical outlet for her stress; the departments she worked for provided the bare minimum of training, which was 24 hours every two years; she got little sleep; ate food full of fat, salt and sugar; strove for a perfection she could never reach, which led to frustration and a sense of feeling overwhelmed; and felt that everybody else was coping better than she was. When she realized that she needed help, the department was uncooperative or didn't understand the stress that dispatchers undergo. It's no wonder that her untreated anxiety and unresolved trauma eventually led to PTSD symptoms.

Departments can prevent burnout, the extreme drop-out rate and help dispatchers feel that they are part of a professional team by clearly defining the dispatchers' roles and responsibilities, as ambiguousness often leads to increased stress. To alleviate stress and reduce illness, the department needs to give dispatchers some control over their hours, job and life. In addition, they can open up lines of communication between dispatchers and officers so dispatchers feel they are part of a team. It is essential that dispatchers have access to peer support and critical incident management teams so they can defuse tense feelings before they get out of hand, especially after a critical incident has occurred.

Departments might also wish to have a look at the physical plant or environment in which the dispatchers work. Poor working conditions such as bad lighting, noise, not enough ventilation, recycling of unfiltered, bacteria-laden air, uncomfortable chairs are but a few of the things supervisors can address to prevent illness, to build morale, and to make it a better place to work.

But departments are not the only source for improving a dispatcher's life. Sometimes dispatchers are their own worst enemies, and need to empower themselves by taking control over their own welfare. To improve their situations, they need to seek out training opportunities, stop eating bad food, assess their sleep rhythms, exercise, determine if they can cope with night shifts, get a life outside the job so all they see or hear is not conflict, realize that there is no such thing as perfection, and, the main thing—be good to yourself. You are not *just* a dispatcher, but a capable, skilled, deserving human being who does an extremely complicated job under difficult conditions.

For dispatchers, there is one more thing they should consider before signing on to a communications center and picking up the phone from a frantic caller—experience *before* the job—as the next story demonstrates.

* * *

Corrine Mossman[3] was a crime scene photographer in a mid-western city for several years, but in 1998, at the age of twenty-nine, she transferred to Dispatch.

Like Jan Myers, she dealt with callers' issues from child abuse to bloody car accidents to suicide, but she did *not* develop PTSD. She did *not* have nightmares, flashbacks or compulsive thoughts, and with such a high burnout rate for dispatchers, perhaps there is a lesson here for both would-be dispatchers and those who hire them.

"I grew up in law enforcement in the early 80s as an Explorer with the Sheriff's Department," said Corrine. "I saw a lot of things that typical fifteen- and sixteen-year-olds don't see. Everything from people that live in absolute poverty to drugs and hookers, things that I never even knew existed in the city I lived in."

After volunteering as an Explorer, Corrine became a crime scene technician, took photos at crime scenes, fingerprinted dead people, and even photographed autopsies. When she became a dispatcher, she was already habituated to the horror she would experience. She didn't suddenly walk in off the street and become shocked by what she heard and experienced.

From an early age, she was gradually introduced to the bad things that can happen to people. She was given the chance to decide early on whether this was the career direction she wanted to take, whether she could withstand the pressure from the suffering and pain she witnessed without becoming overwhelmed. By the time she became a dispatcher, there was nothing much that surprised or traumatized her that could lead to developing PTSD.

She felt anger and frustration at times from unresolved calls, but she didn't take them personally, which allowed her to continue to do her job effectively.

"I'm very frustrated with people and their child custody disputes. People shouldn't be putting their children in the middle of things like that. And they just have no reasoning skills when you try to help them.

"Or, the woman you're trying to help because her husband beat her up *again*... You know, you can only talk to these people so much before you're like, *jimminy*... We hear them crying, we hear it's a horrible situation, yet people don't even want to help themselves. Those are the parts of my job that frustrate me the most.

"As far as how I deal with it, I think it's because of everything I saw before that I can cope. I see that it takes a toll on the younger generation or people that come into dispatching from the civilian world. The calls affect them more than they affect those of us who have had law enforcement experience.

"A dispatcher I work with gets very affected by a lot of calls. She worked in a retail shop before this. She loves her job, but she is a really sweet, naïve person who didn't realize that things like that went on. And she was an adult when she discovered this. I was fifteen. So that makes a huge difference.

"To me, dispatching is just a job and a phone call. So the incidents that have affected other dispatchers don't seem to have affected me."

One of the problems that dispatchers experience universally is the natural tendency to exaggerate what occurred during a call. Consequently, in many departments, crime scene photos are provided so the dispatchers don't fall into the trap of allowing their imaginations to run wild, and they end up embellishing stories with inaccurate details. Sometimes imagining is far worst than what happened.

However, Corrine has a different take on showing dispatchers crime scene photos from calls they were on. She doesn't think it's always a good idea.

"When we have a critical incident, I can see it in my head, I can picture what I think is probably going on out there, just because I've been at so many crime scenes. But my partners often can't visualize what's going on.

"If there's a homicide or a really bad accident, the dispatchers want the officers to bring them photos of the scenes they've just left. And I think that helps the dispatchers see what went on out there so they have a visual picture.

"But some of the pictures they ask the officers to bring, I've told them, 'You don't want to see that. You don't want to see that twelve-year-old that hung himself. You don't want to see the autopsy where the woman was eight months pregnant.'

"I don't think it helps to see photos like that. I think it ingrains the image in your brain forever. And people have said to me, 'That was gross. Oh, my God... I wish I had listened to you.'

"We had a guy jump off one of our bridges, and he didn't use a thick enough rope, and it severed his head. And the dispatchers wanted to see that photo. And I told them, 'You don't want to see this. Because then every time you cross over that bridge, you are going to see the image of what actually happened instead of just getting a phone call. If you just have the *Oh some guy just jumped off the bridge* memory, that's all you're going to remember. But now that you've seen a headless body, and this pale head sitting there, this is what you are going to remember."

Because of her background, Corrine was not affected to the same degree as other dispatchers when presented with a gruesome situation. At the same time, one call, in particular, has bothered her over the years.

It was early morning, and a person who had spent time in mental health facilities was on the line. From the way he talked, she realized he was a bona fide 5150 crazy person. The caller told Corrine that he'd driven by his ex-girlfriend's trailer, shot it up with a gun, and then went home.

Corrine kept the man talking and developed a rapport. "He was drunk, loaded, and going to kill himself. He felt bad and blah blah blah blah blah. We talked about his dog, its name was Whiskey. We talked about his parents, his girl-friend, and why he was in the predicament that he was in, things a dispatcher doesn't normally talk to people about."

Her department is the biggest regional dispatch agency in the county, yet she was given no training on how to deal with a suicidal person. To handle the call, she followed her instincts, and talked to him for almost five hours.

She could not transfer him to a suicide hotline because a crime had been committed. He was still armed, and SWAT was ordered out to his home. He mentioned a doctor he wanted to talk to, indicated he might come out, and she thought she was making headway.

Although she had no formal training concerning suicidal people, a hostage negotiator had once told her how crucial it was that "You don't ever transfer them off to somebody else without introducing who you're sending them to." She soon learned that could mean the difference between life and death.

Sometime after seven in the morning, the Sheriff's Office told her to drop off with the suspect and they would pick up with a throw phone.

"That's okay," she said, "but I need to know who I'm transferring him to. He said he doesn't want to talk to anybody else, and I have to tell him."

According to Corrine, the officer in charge of the incident refused to give her the name of the crisis negotiator, and he called her supervisor to complain.

"My supervisor told me, 'When they say hang up, you hang up.' I said, 'That's fine,' and hung up."

The impression she got was: "I'm just the dispatcher, and I'm not going to tell them what to do."

The Sheriff disconnected her line, but their throw phone didn't work. And the man shot himself, and died at the scene. "He was ready to come out and talk to them, and they wouldn't listen to me."

This is an example of poor communication between Dispatch and officers in the field. And, unfortunately, bad communication is a typical scenario that plays out across the country everyday. Dispatchers feel that they are being treated like lackeys, and not being heard, and officers feel that they are not getting the cooperation they require. What they need is training, for both dispatchers and officers, so they know what to expect from each other. The onus is on police departments to initiate effective training courses to solve the communication problems.

"I care about the people on the other side of that _radio_. And I care about the people on the other side of the _phone_. I think most dispatchers that are in it for several years—ones that get past that burnout period—we are a rare breed. Most of us are very dedicated and very loyal and we just love our jobs."

Corrine is still on the job taking calls and helping people and police officers. And our lives are better for it.

Chapter 13

What To Do About CopShock

*"A normal reaction
to an abnormal amount of stress."*

What can law enforcement officers do about trauma? How can they prevent Posttraumatic Stress Disorder? And if they have PTSD, how can they control the symptoms? To help answer these questions, this chapter prepares officers and their families to use the hundreds of resources in the following chapters.

Posttraumatic Stress and Post-Shooting Trauma

Posttraumatic stress (PTS) and post-shooting trauma (PST) reactions may occur immediately following a frightening or life-threatening event. A shooting, car accident or decomposing body may cause law enforcement officers to feel fear, guilt, disgust, hopelessness and terror. Some officers may have suicidal thoughts, sleep poorly and stop eating. But PTS and PST symptoms can be managed and, in most cases, eliminated.

The key ingredient for ending the reactions is communication. Talking, not only to fellow officers but to other support sources.

To begin the process of opening up, officers may ask themselves:

➤ Am I keeping my feelings hidden?
➤ Am I minimizing what happened?
➤ Do I know all the facts?
➤ What am I feeling?
➤ Do I have a support system in place?

Suppressed feelings have a way of exploding months or years after horrifying incidents, but facing these emotions immediately may prevent that from happening. It may also stop PTSD from developing later.

By establishing a support system before a critical incident occurs, peace officers empower themselves. Preparing for the inevitable puts officers in control during a period when control is sometimes taken away.

What Is A Support System?

A support system is a network of people whom officers in crisis can turn to. It's a game plan for reducing stress.

Who Is In A Support System?
➤ Fellow officers
➤ Family members
➤ Civilian friends
➤ Peer counselors and therapists
➤ Clergy
➤ Support groups

What Is A Game Plan?

A support system also features a stress management plan. A plan may include routines such as exercise and relaxation procedures like deep breathing and yoga. If officers use these resources regularly, suddenly employing them will not be a hardship when circumstances are already distressing.

Why should officers bother setting up a support system? A support system will help diminish stressful reactions and speed up the time it takes to recover. But officers should consult with people in their support networks before a traumatic event happens. Otherwise, supporters may not be available or know what is expected of them.

To locate civilian support groups, see Chapter 15 under *Finding Local Support Groups*. To find police trauma groups, call the peer support unit in your department. Stress management sources are featured in Chapter 16 under *Stress Management*.

Posttraumatic Stress Disorder (PTSD)

Police officers cannot manage PTSD on their own, but healing is possible.[1] As PTSD is difficult to identify, only a trained mental health professional should attempt a diagnosis. Therapy is essential and medication, at least for awhile, may be necessary. How to choose a therapist is discussed in detail later in this chapter.

In conjunction with therapy, police officers with PTSD can take an active role in controlling symptoms. They can attend support groups such as Trauma Anonymous or participate in post-trauma groups that many police departments offer.

To find a therapist, see Chapter 15 under *Counseling*. For local support groups, see Chapter 15 under *Finding Local Support Groups* and Chapter 16 under *PTSD Support Groups*. Stress management sources are featured in Chapter 16 under *Stress Management.*.

For many officers, PTSD can be prevented by going to inoculation training, learning Critical Incident Stress Management (CISM) techniques, attending support groups regularly and by relying on a support network of trusted people.

Have You Been Traumatized?

Sometimes we take for granted that police officers who have had a frightening experience are traumatized. But not everybody is traumatized by even the most terrifying event. So how do we know when someone has been traumatized?

Here are possible signs:[2]

Emotional Signs of Trauma

➢ Denial, fear, depression, grief, anxiety
➢ Feeling hopeless, helpless, overwhelmed or numb
➢ Anger, irritability, aggression, uncertainty
➢ Dwelling on details of the event
➢ Suicidal thoughts, loss of belief in a higher being

Physical Signs of Trauma

➢ Chest pain, trouble breathing, high blood pressure
➢ Stomach pains, indigestion, headaches
➢ Dizziness, vomiting, sweating, chills, diarrhea
➢ Muscle aches, trembling, rapid heart rate
➢ Sleep disturbance, dry mouth, fatigue

Cognitive Signs of Trauma
➤ Confusion, disorientation, trouble making decisions
➤ Hyperalert, memory and concentration problems
➤ Dreams, nightmares, flashbacks of the event
➤ Calculation problems, disruption in logical thinking
➤ Slowed thinking
➤ Blaming others

Behavioral Signs of Trauma
➤ Change in speech patterns
➤ Angry outbursts, arguments, acts of violence
➤ Withdrawal, suspicion, excessive silence
➤ Increase in consuming alcohol, tobacco, drugs, food
➤ Disruption in eating habits
➤ Gambling, buying sprees, promiscuity
➤ Changes in work habits and interaction with others
➤ Unexplained or prolonged crying spells

If you are experiencing one or more of these symptoms, you may be traumatized. What do these reactions have in common? They are normal responses to abnormal occurrences. No matter how accustomed officers are to witnessing or participating in horrific or dangerous events, a traumatic incident is not a normal circumstance.

Is Trauma Resolved?
If officers take no action to manage traumatic stress reactions, often the symptoms will appear to go away on their own after a few days or weeks. But is the trauma resolved?

Years ago I was driving up a mountain in Colorado in a sports car. Suddenly I was thrust back in my seat, the engine roaring out of control. After I pulled over to the emergency lane and shut the engine off, the roar stopped. Upon opening the hood, I discovered that the throttle was stuck open. I closed it, drove away and had no further problem. A few months later it stuck again. Fortunately, I didn't hit anything. But I got the message and took the car to a mechanic.

A traumatized person is like my sports car with the stuck throttle. Even if the problem seems to go away on its own, sometime later the throttle may jam again, making the engine roar out of control. Until you deal with what has happened, the incident may stick like a bad throttle and cause you harm.

How The Past Affects The Present

One traumatic incident is sufficient to set PTSD in motion. But sometimes a history of unresolved trauma will affect a police officer's perception of events.

After the baby-in-the-sink homicide, Bill Martin flashed back on his most horrific crime scenes. He went home and attempted suicide. Following years of shootouts, Ian Shaw froze when confronted by a drug dealer who fired a gun at him. Ian said he couldn't shoot back because his past had changed him. Seeing a dead girl in New York, Bob McClellan believed he was back in Vietnam. From that point on he spiraled out of control, sitting with an assault rifle in his house's attic looking for the Viet Cong enemy.

What might intensify reactions after a trauma and hinder recovery? For some, a past history of childhood abuse will cause a response. Alcohol, drug, caffeine and nicotine consumption, sleep problems and eating disorders may affect how you feel. Gambling, buying sprees, arguing with a spouse or life partner may contribute to feelings of guilt, shame, insecurity, fear and hopelessness. Bloody crime scenes from the past may disturb officers who experience new traumas.

Trying to cope with depression, low self-esteem, hostility at work, a sick child or injuries from a car accident may also magnify reactions following a trauma.

Ask yourself these questions that indicate you may be holding on to past events:

➢   Have I resolved stressful situations?
➢   Have I integrated them into my life?
➢   Am I fighting the unfairness of a previous event?
➢   Am I angry at people in my life?
➢   Am I able to forgive people?

Why do previous traumas affect how you respond to traumas today? Your *stress bucket* may be too full. For instance, after more than sixty, years, World War II veterans who had not confronted their feelings about the atrocities of that war, are coming forward with symptoms of PTSD. Along with memories of battle, many have accumulated a lifetime of unresolved feelings from stressful situations. During the Los Angeles riots, a number of police officers who served in Vietnam had to leave the scene because they were reexperiencing scenes from combat they had never dealt with before.

What you did not confront in the past may plague you in the future. In assessing your needs as police officers, you may wish to resolve past events before a new trauma occurs.

To resolve or transform your feelings about an event, you need to:

➢ Think about it
➢ Talk about it
➢ Write about it in a journal or in a letter to yourself
➢ See a therapist to get your feelings out

At the same time, exposing feelings is not for everybody. Some people do fine without ever addressing the issues because in some way they have found meaning in the traumatic event and integrated it into their lives. They have made sense of a senseless incident.

The questions to ask yourself are as follows:

➢ Do I still think about the events?
➢ Have I accepted them?
➢ Do I torment myself about what happened?
➢ What can I do today to resolve the events?

Despite some exceptions, officers can prepare themselves to cope with future incidents by resolving traumatic events from the past. Your objective is to empty the stress bucket before something else is poured into it.

What Is Self-Help?

Police officers can help themselves cope with trauma. It's something they do all the time. They are constantly saying to themselves, *If I do such-and-such, what will be the outcome?*

But what is self-help? What is it not? Self-help is not allowing emotions to automatically kick in to control a situation, even if this response has worked in the past. Self-help is not living with a bad situation, helplessness, hopelessness or cynicism.

Self-help is *believing* that you can handle trauma if you analyze the problem and take measures to solve it. It is discarding poor coping techniques and accepting new ways to survive. Self-help is focusing not only on shortcomings but primarily on strengths.

Some people prefer to work things out on paper. If you are comfortable with the idea, on a sheet of paper outline the following:

➤ Your strengths
➤ How to apply your strengths to coping with a traumatic situation

Self-help also means accepting that a traumatic event has happened and is now part of your life, but you can do something about how you are feeling. That may require asking others for help, joining support groups and being willing to look deeply inside yourself. Self-help does not mean doing it alone. It means doing whatever is necessary to orchestrate your recovery.

What To Do Before A Trauma Occurs

Planning for the day you will face a trauma gives you more control over future circumstances. Nothing will soften the initial blow, but planning will tell you what you need to do to help yourself. What can you do?

➤ Attend seminars on stress management.
➤ Attend courses on coping with stress like Calibre Press' Street Survival® Seminar.
➤ See videos like Massad Ayoob's *Post-Violent Event Trauma*. Many departments offer training material and videos that can prepare you for the worst.

➤ Ask your department if they are planning stress management workshops. If they aren't, ask if they would conduct them.

➤ Routinely talk to trusted family and friends about the police experience including your feelings.

➤ On a sheet of paper, write down who you feel you could confide in during a crisis. Who will be sympathetic? Who will listen and not offer advice you don't want? Who will ask questions if it's too hard for you to talk?

➤ Reduce or eliminate stimulants like caffeine, alcohol, sugar and tobacco.

➤ If you overeat or don't eat enough, try to maintain a nutritious, balanced diet.

➤ Research support groups—where they are, who is involved, what they discuss.

What To Do After A Trauma Occurs

The First Day

During the first day, you will go through excruciating pain. The scene will replay itself thousands of times in your head. You will deny it happened. You will get irritable and angry. You will despair. You may blame everybody, everything and even yourself. You may curse God for not intervening. Like John Jenks, your stomach will feel like it's stuffed with sand. You won't sleep. You may cry.

But not everybody responds the same way. You may be too numb to feel anything at first. You may sleep well and eat a hearty meal.

What should you do during the first twenty-four hours after a critical incident?

➤ Chances are you are upset and irritable. Try not to take your irritation or anger out on your family. What happened is not their fault.

➤ Don't blame yourself. You are responding normally to an abnormal situation.

➤ Don't make important decisions until you have some perspective on events.

➤ Rest, if you feel like it.

➤ Talk, if you feel like it.

➤ Pamper yourself. Have a hot bath, a nap, a good dinner if you feel like eating. Spend time with loved ones. Do not isolate yourself.

➤ Find out as much information as possible from colleagues and the department about what happened.

➤ Avoid newspapers and television news stories about the incident. They will upset you. Reporters rarely have time to investigate stories thoroughly. When I was in journalism school, the senior editor of a major newspaper told me that in every report you can expect at least five major errors of fact or interpretation.

➤ Take time off from the job to work through your feelings. If you wish, ask loved ones, friends or professionals to listen to your thoughts. But it may be too soon to analyze events or feelings.

➤ For many, attending a one-on-one intervention with a peer supporter or participating in a Critical Incident Stress Defusing or Debriefing will help begin the process of healing.

The Psychological Services Unit of your department may offer emergency counseling as well as access to peer supporters and debriefers. If you work at a small department, however, resources may not be offered.

In small departments with limited or no services, officers may need to set up support systems before a traumatic event unfolds.

What you require during the first twenty-four hours depends on you. There is no right or wrong. Many officers only want to rest. They don't want to talk to anybody or do anything for the first day or so. Family members and fellow officers should respect this wish. Some officers benefit more by talking about events right away. Which approach do you prefer?

After The First Day

After the first day or sometimes on the first day, officers may wish to employ stress management techniques. These include routines such as physical exercise, biofeedback, yoga, nutrition, meditation, hypnosis, humor, assertiveness training, deep breathing, massage and spiritual awakening.

The stress management section of this book offers sources for many different techniques. See Chapter 16.

Ask yourself:

➤ What can I do to lessen the impact of trauma days afterwards?
➤ What relaxes me? What helps me work out tension?
➤ Who will I talk to about the events?

Know ahead of time which techniques to employ. Make them a habit. For instance, if you work out three times a week, exercise after a trauma will already be part of your regular schedule and will not offer a hardship.

Now that you have more perspective on events, it is time for you to accept your role in the incident because the "what ifs" will drive you crazy. *What if I was a little faster? What if my aim was better? What if I didn't shoot? What if I was driving a little slower?* You are only human. You can't do or know everything. Forgive yourself.

What Family And Friends Can Do

When Terry Nunn returned home after confronting two jewelry store robbers, he was distressed. His friend said he wasn't shot so there was no reason to be upset. Then she ignored his reactions. No matter what family members might think of the events, they should never minimize what the officer has experienced. Perception is everything. If officers feel traumatized, then they are.

Family members and friends should accept that traumatized officers are in crisis. It's not always clear what to do for the officers, but here are some pointers.

➤ Officers need your attention. Listen.
➤ Encourage them to talk, but don't push.
➤ Do not say everything is okay. It isn't.
➤ Don't allow officers to cover up. You won't be doing anybody any favors. Instead, you'll be allowing them to suppress feelings that will one day come out in a way far worse than this day.

➤ No matter how many times officers' repeat the story, don't show impatience. It's difficult to remember everything about a traumatic event. Repeating the story helps restore missing details.

➤ This is a terrible time for officers and often they feel alone or abandoned. Stick with them. They need you.

➤ Officers very often express anger, guilt, grief and other unpleasant emotions. Sometimes expressing these feelings is the only way to get the story out to speed recovery. Recognize that the bond created will often bring family members and the officer closer. If possible, include children in this process. Officers' trauma will affect them too. Sheltering children from the details will make them feel outside the family.

➤ Be prepared that officers may choose to talk to fellow officers or a minister instead of spouses or life partners. Don't be offended. Officers will tap into their support systems. You are a part of that system, not the whole thing.

➤ Family members and friends should realize that things will never be the same. The critical incident cannot be undone. Don't try to put things back to normal. By helping officers accept the events, you will find a new normal.[3]

What Family Members Should Not Accept

What family members should not accept, however, is any form of abuse or inappropriate behavior. Officers need your companionship and attention but not your complicity. Family members should not enable officers to act out self-destructive behavior like drugging, excessive drinking, driving while drunk or committing violence.

To help prepare for the unavoidable day, family members may wish to take courses sometimes offered by the police department or police union in crisis management, in coping with a loved one's trauma or in what law enforcement officers do. For instance, Police Officers Providing Peer Assistance (POPPA) in New York City offers a program for families as do many departments. An explanation of what POPPA offers is in Chapter 16 under *Peer Support For Police Officers' Family*.

If Departments Do Not Offer Courses

Family members should check local community colleges or adult education for courses in stress management and crisis intervention. At the very least every family member should read Dr. Ellen Kirschman's book *I Love A Cop, What Police Families Need To Know* and *Developing A Law Enforcement Stress Program for Officers and Their Families*. See the *Publications* section of Chapter 16 for information.

Families And Friends Must Look After Themselves

As well as looking after a traumatized officer, family members and friends must also look after themselves. If they hold in their own problems in order to help, they may internalize many of the officers' emotional reactions. They should get help for themselves by talking to friends, seeing a counselor, attending a support group, or writing in a journal. Like the police officer in their lives, they should not keep their feelings locked inside.

How To Select A Therapist Or Counselor

If you need professional help, there is no disgrace in turning to outside sources. But not all therapists are equal. Since therapists inexperienced in helping traumatized people or people with PTSD can cause more harm, it is important to audition therapists. You will be spending a lot of time applying this person's coping techniques and, depending on your insurance plan, possibly a lot of money. You want to be sure you are getting what you need and are paying for. Pretend you are a casting director for a movie. Take time. Compare counselors. Ask questions.

I've talked with several police officers who told me they don't trust psychologists, psychiatrists, journalists or mechanics. It's difficult to believe a generalized statement. If the statement is even partly true, however, this is all the more reason why officers should not start the therapeutic process with somebody they haven't talked to at length. Ask for a free or reduced price first session to determine if the therapist is right for you. Most therapists will grant it.

What Makes A Therapist Right For You?

Ask yourself these questions:

➢ What type of person would make me comfortable? Aggressive, quiet, opinionated, a listener?
➢ In what surroundings would I feel safe? An office? The therapist's home?
➢ Is the office away from a precinct where somebody might recognize me?
➢ Do I prefer a man or a woman?
➢ Should the therapist be formal or informal?
➢ Do I care if the person writes down everything I say?
➢ Is confidentiality a big issue for me?
➢ Am I willing to try medication for depression or PTSD?
➢ What do I wish to accomplish by seeing a therapist?
➢ How many sessions will my insurance allow?
➢ Should I inform my insurance company that I want to see a therapist? Would that affect future insurance coverage if I leave the police force?
➢ What can I pay beyond the sessions the insurance company will pay for?

I have received counseling from several therapists, all of whom operated differently. During one period of my life, I sat across a desk from a very formal, low-key female psychiatrist. She wrote down a lot of what I would say. Often I talked to the top of her head because it was bent over a pad of paper. She rarely said a word until the end of the session at which time she poured out a massive amount of information I could not absorb.

Another psychiatrist was a man who frequently offered his opinion and gave me specific directions for what I should do. He also wrote a lot. He was well-meaning, but I found myself resisting his suggestions.

For four years, I saw a female psychologist. I came to her with one traumatic experience I wished to resolve—the death of my father. But this ultimately led to confronting my past to draw out other traumatic experiences I had never processed. She did not write anything down in my presence. She sat in a chair opposite me, listened intently, was sympathetic, asked me questions that led me to making decisions for myself.

With her informal technique, I made great progress. Others may prefer a more formal approach. The turning point for me was early on when she asked me to write a letter to my dead father. The therapist was not allowing me to sit back and do nothing. I became actively involved in my own recovery.

You cannot expect the therapist to do all the work. Treat therapy like an assignment. Map out goals, do your home-work and be active in your recovery. As I discovered, writing things down is a great therapy tool. It helps you get organized and see things clearly when they appear distorted.

At first I was opposed to taking medication for depression, but I trusted the therapist enough to try it. I stayed on medication for a couple of years while seeing her. Anti-depressant medication by itself without therapy is pointless, although I have read that, depending on the problem, many clients do as well with or without medication. Antidepressants are very effective in treating Posttraumatic Stress Disorder.

If after three or four sessions you feel you are not making progress, ask yourself if you are the problem. Sometimes you won't even realize you are resisting the therapist's suggestions. Bill Martin did not tell his therapist about his flashbacks for almost a year and a half. He said he didn't think they were important, but they were the key to his PTSD diagnosis.

The most important lessons I learned in therapy are that it takes time and it is hard work. It takes time to get everything out, and it's hard to adopt new coping techniques when you are used to the old ones, even if they don't work very well.

When I saw the psychologist, I began with what seemed to be a traumatic reaction to a recent event. But I was also bringing her forty-five years of suppressed reactions to traumatic stress. I couldn't expect her to help me undo in a few sessions what took me almost a half century to accumulate. Give therapy a chance, but acknowledge when the problem is you or your relationship with the therapist. If after several sessions you don't have confidence in the therapist, ask for a referral to somebody else.

How Do You Find A Good Therapist?

Like shopping for a mechanic start by asking a friend. You would also ask a therapist many of the following questions.

Ask:

➢ What was the experience like?
➢ How would you describe the therapist's process or technique in working with you?
➢ Did he or she help you?
➢ Are you still seeing the therapist?
➢ If you aren't still seeing the therapist, why not?
➢ Did you see the therapist for problems coping with trauma?
➢ Was the therapist supportive and compassionate?
➢ Did the therapist listen well?
➢ How did you find out about the therapist?
➢ What are the therapist's credentials?
➢ Does the therapist work with other police officers?
➢ Does the therapist maintain confidentiality?
➢ When you go to a session, is there a separate entrance and exit door? Do you sometimes see other clients?
➢ Did the phone ring during the session? Did the therapist answer it?
➢ How long were the sessions?
➢ Did the therapist set treatment goals?
➢ How much did you pay?
➢ Will the therapist cut rates once insurance runs out?
➢ What is the therapist's availability?
➢ Do you know somebody else I could call who saw the therapist?
➢ Would you go back? If not, why not?

If you don't know anyone who has seen a therapist or don't want anybody to know you are looking for one, consult the *Counseling* section of Chapter 15. This section provides online counselors and referral services that offer credentials and background information. Some therapists specialize in treating survivors of trauma and belong to organizations that provide training and examination. A call to these groups will often yield extensive information on the therapist's experience.

There are many different kinds of therapists from psychologists to social workers to substance abuse counselors. Much will depend on what you can afford and with whom you feel comfortable. But just because you don't have a lot of money doesn't mean you must accept anybody who comes along. Be choosy. Make sure the therapist is licensed or registered and is bound by professional ethics. Don't ignore chaplains and ministers, many of whom are trained in helping traumatized people.

Peer supporters in police departments are not intended to be therapists, but sometimes individuals are trained in trauma therapy. Their role is to comfort and to offer referrals to qualified therapists or treatment centers. But ask about their background and get to know them, preferably before you experience a crisis. See the sections called *Peer Support For Police Officers* and *Peer Support For Police Officers' Family* in Chapter 16.

For more information on choosing a therapist, see the section in Chapter 16 called *Counseling* or the section titled *PTSD/Trauma Research And Referral* for referral and training organizations. Consult Ellen Kirschman's book, *I Love A Cop, What Police Families Need To Know*. If you are online, read Dr. John Grohol's essay on how to choose a therapist at: http://www.grohol.com/therapst.htm.

How To Work With The Department's Resources

Psychological Services

Behavioral Science Sections, Health Services Sections or Psychological Services Units in police departments offer counseling to police officers. These units are often run by psychologists with years of experience in counseling police officers suffering from trauma. In view of the criticism in some of the chapters of this book, officers should be aware that these units operate differently throughout the country.

Dedicated and compassionate mental health professionals provide good service to police officers in crisis and often offer confidentiality. Before discounting the unit in your department, find out what its policies are. For instance, many of these units hire outside consultants to offer confidential therapy to officers. Ask if Psych Services is located away from the department.

Before committing to counseling, call first to discuss your needs. You do not have to identify yourself. For a rundown of what questions to ask therapists in Psychological Services Units, see the section titled *Behavioral Science Units* in Chapter 15.

Peer Support

Peer support units are made up of caring fellow officers trained to offer comfort, intervention, education and referrals to officers in crisis. Peer supporters help officers with many problems including post-shooting trauma, posttraumatic stress symptoms, PTSD, alcohol and drug problems, a death or illness in the family, friction with superiors and marriage and family conflicts.

Often the units are not on police department premises, making it easier for officers who fear being seen by other officers to attend sessions. Most peer support units honor confidentiality. So there is no misunderstanding, ask members of your unit if they offer confidentiality. Referrals are usually to experienced therapists outside the department. In addition to helping police officers, many units offer programs to law enforcement families. These programs often focus on trauma, what officers do and family support.

To contact a peer support unit, officers may wish to phone first. Until you are sure you wish to pursue the contact, you don't have to identify yourself. If the unit is on department premises, ask to meet on neutral territory away from the department. For more on the peer support role, see *Peer Support For Police Officers* in Chapter 16.

Inoculation Training

Many departments provide inoculation training for officers assigned to investigate, for instance, multiple murders or a disaster scene like an airplane crash. Officers are briefed on what to expect before they enter the scene. This preparation tends to lessen the shock from seeing body parts or dead children.

For example, before rescuers entered the blown-up building at the site of the 1995 Oklahoma City bombing, they were counseled in graphic detail about what to expect. When they came out, they were debriefed. The debriefing process is explained in the next section.

Critical Incident Stress Interventions

Many departments offer a program called Critical Incident Stress Management (CISM) to help officers who may become distressed over situations such as gruesome crime scenes, the death of fellow officers or major disasters like a train wreck. Some officers have expressed concern to me about what the process involves. One officer asked, "What are they gonna make me do this time?" Other officers are concerned about confidentiality. The following explanation should allay fears.

What is a critical incident? It is an event so strong in emotional power that it rapidly breaks through police officers' defenses. Against such force, officers' abilities to cope and respond are overwhelmed. The event may interfere with their functioning at a crime scene or even later at home.

What do officers experience during critical incidents? On the scene, police officers sometimes become highly anxious and agitated or go into shock and become stunned and lethargic. They may react with confusion, fear, anxiety, anger, frustration, racing heart, headaches, nausea, vomiting, fainting, sweating and irritability.

Many officers perceive that time has slowed down or speeded up. They are suddenly living in either slow motion or a Charlie Chaplin movie. On the other hand, they may exhibit no reaction. Observers sometimes notice stressed-out officers staring off into space, a symptom called the thousand-yard-stare.

Days, weeks or months later, officers could have trouble planning, become preoccupied with the incident, deny the incident happened or diminish its importance. As well as experiencing depression, grief, loss and guilt, many officers fear they are out of control and going crazy. They may express anger in inappropriate ways, have problems with superiors, lose or gain weight, have trouble sleeping, feel tired all the time, withdraw from social outings, become physically ill or engage in substance abuse.

Is there something wrong with an officer who does not experience these symptoms? No. Not everybody reacts in the same way to stressful situations. The reasons may include background, upbringing, training, experience, confidence from handling previous traumas and availability of support systems.

How does CISM prevent or minimize critical incident stress reactions? An intervention essentially plucks police officers out of stress-laden situations and places them with caring people who talk them through their emotions.

Here are how interventions work.[4]

➤ One-On-One Interventions. When police officers show signs of distress like crying, staring off into space or shouting, and are open to help, then peer counselors will take them away from the scene of the crisis for a brief talk. The counselors' main objective is to get the officers back on the job, not to remove them.

   In the One-On-One Intervention, counselors ask the officers what is happening to them, what the worst part is, what will help right now. Police officers in shock have an overwhelming sense of being alone, isolated and unique. Counselors give sympathetic support by listening and reassuring officers that what they feel is normal.

   Although officers should show signs of improvement within the fifteen minutes of the process, they should be allowed to rest for a half hour or more before returning to the scene that caused the distress in the first place. If officers are still disturbed after the One-On-One, sometimes they are removed from the scene to get more help.

   The One-On-One is the fastest kind of intervention. But sometimes the next level of help, the defusing, is needed.

➤ Defusings. A defusing is a group process in which people involved in the crisis attend. The key is immediate intervention after the event, from one to two hours later, but no longer than eight because people tend to rationalize away their fears. Although peer counselors can perform the process, sometimes psychologists or other mental health professionals are needed as well.

In contrast to the short One-On-One, a defusing takes up to an hour. First the group discusses what happened, then elaborates on the worst part. The counselor allows the participants to ventilate their feelings. Acknowledging the feelings and validating them, the counselor does not probe or dwell on them. It is much too early after the incident for dissecting feelings. To wrap up, the counselor tells the group about the signs of stress and what they can do about it.

➢ Debriefing. While similar to a defusing, a debriefing is a more involved process. Although the shorter, less costly defusing may eliminate the need for a debriefing, sometimes it does not. For three hours or longer, the debriefing can involve everyone touched by a crisis, sometimes an entire precinct, including dispatchers and office personnel. It will often require a CISM team of peer counselors and mental health professionals.

There are many reasons why a debriefing is necessary. The debriefing team may want to relieve strong reactions to the death of an officer, a mass casualty incident or the accidental death of a civilian by an officer.

As in the One-On-One and the Defusing, a debriefing is not a critique of operations, what someone did or did not do, and no notes are taken. The press is not allowed, nor are superiors who could affect a police officer's career.

Participants are asked never to disclose anything said during the debriefing. Confidentiality is sacred. Otherwise, cops would not tell how they feel.

The debriefing team does not sit in judgment. No one is accused of anything. There are no repercussions for participants saying what's in their hearts or for breaking down. Although not psychotherapy or treatment, rather a process for stress prevention, debriefing provides an opportunity for catharsis—a purging, a cleansing of the emotions and the soul.

The debriefing process provides several phases that allow people to express feelings, to reconstruct and to integrate the trauma into their lives. The phases have titles such as the Fact Phase, Thought Phase, Reaction Phase, Symptom Phase, Teaching Phase, and Re-entry Phase.

For more information about the CISM process, see Chapter 15 under the section *Critical Incidents And Intervention.*

Officers whose departments do not offer support programs may wish to see an outside therapist or attend support groups made up of officers or civilians. Sometimes officers without resources can attend CISM sessions at their local fire department, hospital or other city agency involved in the same crisis.

Non-departmental Support Groups

There are no typical support groups. Some have leaders, some do not. Some provide mental health professionals, most do not. Usually free of charge, they allow members to compare experiences and benefit from hearing different methods of coping. The process of talking with others who share similar problems and feelings begins the healing process.

Police officers usually like to stay with their own kind, but they may find joining a civilian group beneficial. Often officers do not have to identify their occupation or even give their names. They can remain relatively anonymous and not worry about how they might appear in front of fellow officers.

Officers who are war veterans may wish to attend support groups designed specifically for those who have experienced battle or witnessed atrocities. A major source for support groups may be the local Veterans Administration office.

Thousands of support groups exist, many concentrating on survivors of crime, violence, abuse and other traumatic experiences. In Chapter 15, see the section titled *Finding Local Support Groups.* The section offers sources for support groups in cities and towns all over the world. See also the section on *Assault* in Chapter 15 and *PTSD Support Groups* in Chapter 16.

How To Use The Support Sources Chapters

Chapters 15 and 16 offer descriptions of over 200 support sources as well as discussion of many issues related to the police experience. The references cover so much ground that they may at first appear overwhelming. I suggest the following approach.

➢ Flip through the pages, noting subject and resource headings to get a sense of what is offered.
➢ Read the discussions offered in most sections to become familiar with the issues.
➢ Choose the subjects that interest you the most right now. Other subjects may interest you later, but by approaching the material in this manner you will be aware of what is available.

But first, read Chapter 14 about Resiliency and your ability to bounce back from bad situations.

Chapter 14

Resiliency

*"The ability to bounce back
from adversity can be learned."*

When you read books like *CopShock*, some of you may get the impression that there is no other recourse but to go immediately to a peer support counselor or therapist. For some of you, that may be true. You may feel that there is something wrong with you. However, in most cases, there is nothing wrong with you. You are experiencing a normal reaction to abnormal circumstances.

Posttraumatic stress, post-shooting trauma, panic attacks, even PTSD—these are normal reactions to an extraordinary amount of stress that is overwhelming your inner resources. By all means, please check out the many support sources I describe, and make enquiries.

But there is something else you may wish to consider. Every one of us has a natural ability to cope with adverse situations. Depending on your family history, the way you've handled stress and trauma in the past, even perhaps your genetics, you may be able to cope with a bad situation just fine.

Why is it that two cops can see the same scene, one will react emotionally and may not be able to carry on, whereas the other officer does not appear to react at all, and may actually seem to thrive on the traumatic incident? It has to do with *resiliency*.

At the same time, when situations are enormous in their impact, like 9/11, or situations pile on top of situations in a short period of time, you may find yourself overwhelmed, staring off into space, what's called "the thousand yard stare." It's as if all your systems have shut down. Then you need help to get back on track emotionally. Not necessarily therapy, but somebody to help trigger your natural ability to cope and survive, such as in a critical incident stress one-on-one intervention.

Consider the following points in the paper called *The Corrections and Law Enforcement Family Support Solicitation for the Implementation of the Corrections Field Test*:[1]

➢ Most people who experience chronic stress or critical incident stress are able to cope without significant problems.

➢ Not all the effects of stress are negative. For instance, some people under stress experience a reinforcement of their ability to cope with adversity. They appreciate the value of life more, and have a sense of accomplishment for the job they did, even if their efforts were futile. Many people experience positive feelings, along with the negative ones, during periods of chronic or critical incident stress. If you are one of the police officers who does not react negatively during a terrible situation, there is nothing wrong with you. You are normal. You just have a great resiliency, and don't have to feel pressured or guilty if you don't want to seek counseling for problems you are not experiencing.

➢ It can, in fact, be detrimental to you if you focus only on the negative effects of stress. For instance, if you pay excessive attention to the negative consequences of stress, you may actually victimize or revictimize yourself by focusing *exclusively* on the need for therapy when none is needed. If you ignore the beneficial effects of even undesirable stress and concentrate only on the negative effects of stress, you may undermine your restorative capabilities.

In view of these findings, you have a lot to think about. When do you know when you've had enough? When do you know when to see a peer support person? It's best to play it safe, and talk to a PSO, counselor, friend or loved one. But it doesn't mean that you are suddenly incapable, or overwhelmed, or even in need of counseling or therapy.

If you find that you are not talking about the event, that you are isolating yourself, that you are not sleeping well, and having nightmares or flashbacks, or having suicidal thoughts, that you are depressed and medicating yourself with drugs or alcohol or both, then it's time to see a PSO or therapist. But if you see both the negative and positive aspects of the critical incident you have experienced, and have learned from it, and feel capable and content, then you may not need help. Only you can judge.

I've reviewed many websites about resiliency, trying to find the best explanation of resiliency most appropriate for law enforcement officers. And I've found an excellent description on the website for the American Psychological Association. They have allowed me to reproduce their guidebook here in its entirety.[2]

After you finish reading it, you may wish to go to the APA website and fill out their _Post Traumatic Growth Inventory_ that will help you assess your resilience and survival abilities. It is extremely well done.

* * *

The Road To Resilience

Reprinted with permission from the American Psychological Association at www.apahelpcenter.org/featuredtopics

Introduction

How do people deal with difficult events that change their lives? The death of a loved one, loss of a job, serious illness, terrorist attacks and other traumatic events: these are all examples of very challenging life experiences. Many people react to such circumstances with a flood of strong emotions and a sense of uncertainty.

Yet people generally adapt well over time to life-changing situations and stressful conditions. What enables them to do so? It involves resilience, an ongoing process that requires time and effort and engages people in taking a number of steps.

This brochure is intended to help readers with taking their own road to resilience. The information within describes resilience and some factors that affect how people deal with hardship. Much of the brochure focuses on developing and using a personal strategy for enhancing resilience.

What Is Resilience?

Resilience is the process of adapting well in the face of adversity, trauma, tragedy, threats, or even significant sources of stress—such as family and relationship problems, serious health problems, or workplace and financial stressors. It means "bouncing back" from difficult experiences.

Research has shown that resilience is ordinary, not extraordinary. People commonly demonstrate resilience. One example is the response of many Americans to the September 11, 2001 terrorist attacks and individuals' efforts to rebuild their lives.

Being resilient does not mean that a person doesn't experience difficulty or distress. Emotional pain and sadness are common in people who have suffered major adversity or trauma in their lives. In fact, the road to resilience is likely to involve considerable emotional distress.

Resilience is not a trait that people either have or do not have. It involves behaviors, thoughts, and actions that can be learned and developed in anyone.

Resilience Factors & Strategies
Factors in Resilience

A combination of factors contributes to resilience. Many studies show that the primary factor in resilience is having caring and supportive relationships within and outside the family. Relationships that create love and trust, provide role models, and offer encouragement and reassurance help bolster a person's resilience.

Several additional factors are associated with resilience, including:
> ➢ The capacity to make realistic plans and take steps to carry them out
> ➢ A positive view of yourself and confidence in your strengths and abilities
> ➢ Skills in communication and problem solving
> ➢ The capacity to manage strong feelings and impulses

All of these are factors that people can develop in themselves.

Strategies For Building Resilience

Developing resilience is a personal journey. People do not all react the same to traumatic and stressful life events. An approach to building resilience that works for one person might not work for another. People use varying strategies. Some variation may reflect cultural differences. A person's culture might have an impact on how he or she communicates feelings and deals with adversity—for example, whether and how a person connects with significant others, including extended family members and community resources. With growing cultural diversity, the public has greater access to a number of different approaches to building resilience.

Some or many of the ways to build resilience in the following pages may be appropriate to consider in developing your personal strategy.

10 Ways to Build Resilience

Make connections. Good relationships with close family members, friends, or others are important. Accepting help and support from those who care about you and will listen to you strengthens resilience. Some people find that being active in civic groups, faith-based organizations, or other local groups provides social support and can help with reclaiming hope. Assisting others in their time of need also can benefit the helper.

Avoid seeing crises as insurmountable problems. You can't change the fact that highly stressful events happen, but you can change how you interpret and respond to these events. Try looking beyond the present to how future circumstances may be a little better. Note any subtle ways in which you might already feel somewhat better as you deal with difficult situations.

Accept that change is a part of living. Certain goals may no longer be attainable as a result of adverse situations. Accepting circumstances that cannot be changed can help you focus on circumstances that you can alter.

Move toward your goals. Develop some realistic goals. Do something regularly—even if it seems like a small accomplishment—that enables you to move toward your goals. Instead of focusing on tasks that seem unachievable, ask yourself, "What's one thing I know I can accomplish today that helps me move in the direction I want to go?"

Take decisive actions. Act on adverse situations as much as you can. Take decisive actions, rather than detaching completely from problems and stresses and wishing they would just go away.

Look for opportunities for self-discovery. People often learn something about themselves and may find that they have grown in some respect as a result of their struggle with loss. Many people who have experienced tragedies and hardship have reported better relationships, greater sense of strength even while feeling vulnerable, increased sense of self-worth, a more developed spirituality, and heightened appreciation for life.

Nurture a positive view of yourself. Developing confidence in your ability to solve problems and trusting your instincts helps build resilience.

Keep things in perspective. Even when facing very painful events, try to consider the stressful situation in a broader context and keep a long-term perspective. Avoid blowing the event out of proportion.

Maintain a hopeful outlook. An optimistic outlook enables you to expect that good things will happen in your life. Try visualizing what you want, rather than worrying about what you fear.

Take care of yourself. Pay attention to your own needs and feelings. Engage in activities that you enjoy and find relaxing. Exercise regularly. Taking care of yourself helps to keep your mind and body primed to deal with situations that require resilience.

Additional ways of strengthening resilience may be helpful. For example, some people write about their deepest thoughts and feelings related to trauma or other stressful events in their life. Meditation and spiritual practices help some people build connections and restore hope.

The key is to identify ways that are likely to work well for you as part of your own personal strategy for fostering resilience.

Learning From Your Past

Some Questions to Ask Yourself

Focusing on past experiences and sources of personal strength can help you learn about what strategies for building resilience might work for you. By exploring answers to the following questions about yourself and your reactions to challenging life events, you may discover how you can respond effectively to difficult situations in your life.

Consider the following :

> ➤ What kinds of events have been most stressful for me?
> ➤ How have those events typically affected me?
> ➤ Have I found it helpful to think of important people in my life when I am distressed?
> ➤ To whom have I reached out for support in working through a traumatic or stressful experience?
> ➤ What have I learned about myself and my interactions with others during difficult times?
> ➤ Has it been helpful for me to assist someone else going through a similar experience?
> ➤ Have I been able to overcome obstacles, and if so, how?
> ➤ What has helped make me feel more hopeful about the future?

Staying Flexible

Resilience involves maintaining flexibility and balance in your life as you deal with stressful circumstances and traumatic events. This happens in several ways, including:

> ➤ Letting yourself experience strong emotions, and also realizing when you may need to avoid experiencing them at times in order to continue functioning
> ➤ Stepping forward and taking action to deal with your problems and meet the demands of daily living, and also stepping back to rest and reenergize yourself
> ➤ Spending time with loved ones to gain support and encouragement, and also nurturing yourself
> ➤ Relying on others, and also relying on yourself

Places To Look For Help

Getting help when you need it is crucial in building your resilience. Beyond caring family members and friends, people often find it helpful to turn to:

> ➤ **Self-help and support groups**. Such community groups can aid people struggling with hardships such as the death of a loved one. By sharing information, ideas, and emotions, group participants can assist one another and find comfort in knowing that they are not alone in experiencing difficulty.

> ➤ **Books and other publications** by people who have successfully managed adverse situations such as surviving cancer. These stories can motivate readers to find a strategy that might work for them personally.

> ➤ **Online resources**. Information on the web can be a helpful source of ideas, though the quality of information varies among sources.

For many people, using their own resources and the kinds of help listed above may be sufficient for building resilience. At times, however, an individual might get stuck or have difficulty making progress on the road to resilience.

> ➤ **A licensed mental health professional** such as a psychologist can assist people in developing an appropriate strategy for moving forward. It is important to get professional help if you feel like you are unable to function or perform basic activities of daily living as a result of a traumatic or other stressful life experience.

Different people tend to be comfortable with somewhat different styles of interaction. A person should feel at ease and have good rapport in working with a mental health professional or participating in a support group.

Continuing On Your Journey

To help summarize several of the main points in this brochure, think of resilience as similar to taking a raft trip down a river.

On a river, you may encounter rapids, turns, slow water, and shallows. As in life, the changes you experience affect you differently along the way.

In traveling the river, it helps to have knowledge about it and past experience in dealing with it. Your journey should be guided by a plan, a strategy that you consider likely to work well for you.

Perseverance and trust in your ability to work your way around boulders and other obstacles are important. You can gain courage and insight by successfully navigating your way through white water. Trusted companions who accompany you on the journey can be especially helpful for dealing with rapids, upstream currents, and other difficult stretches of the river.

You can climb out to rest alongside the river. But to get to the end of your journey, you need to get back in the raft and continue.

* * *

After you have finished reading this APA guidebook, you may wish to go to the APA website and fill out their _Post Traumatic Growth Inventory_ at: http://locator.apa.org/ptgi to give you a sense of your resilience and ability to survive severe traumatic critical incidents.

You may also wish to fill out the self-tests contained in this book on resiliency, anxiety, depression, stress, panic disorder and PTSD. Please check the Appendices.

Chapter 15

Support Sources
Issues and Commentaries

The support sources described here are more than just a listing of randomly chosen resources. They are pre-screened organizations and information. In addition, I have written commentaries about the issues they represent that affect law enforcement officers, their families, partners and departments. Rather than just being an add-on or minor part of the book, the support sources are an essential expansion of the stories you have read.

Please note that the organizations and people described here have not solicited me and do not pay for their listing. Instead, I researched, evaluated, and selected them for their usefulness and importance to law enforcement officers, their families, police departments, peer support units, law enforcement programs, police media journalists, and the civilian press.

How can cops survive the pressures of the job? They need support—support from fellow officers, family members, administrators, union representatives, counselors, community leaders, the clergy and the public. The necessity for support is a byproduct of the job, as natural as putting on the uniform or checking equipment.

Support appears in many forms. It may be a group that meets regularly or a one-on-one talk. It could occur on the phone or in an online chat group. It may happen at a family picnic, a union meeting or through a piece of legislation.

Chapters 15 and 16 describe many kinds of support and where to find that support. In most instances, I offer physical addresses and telephone numbers as well as addresses for Internet websites. Websites provide an extraordinary amount of information for those with access to a computer and an Internet server.

Because of the personal and confidential nature of your Internet searches, it's best to use your personal home computer, Internet cafés or a public library.

Websites from around the world showing the effects of trauma, stress, PTSD, alcohol use, panic attacks and other conditions are abundant. Counseling services, treatment plans, referrals to qualified therapists and advice are also offered. As a bonus, many sites feature links to other valuable police and psychology sites.

Provided here are highlights of numerous support sources that address issues raised in *CopShock*. Once searching, readers will likely find many other resources not mentioned.

Take note, however, that the following educational information should NOT be used as a substitute for seeking care from a trained trauma or recovery professional. Information on the Internet, even from major medical centers, is sometimes outdated or wrong. Readers should decide the value of a resource only after careful investigation.

A to M

* * *

Alcohol Use

Alcohol is frequently used to self-medicate, to soften the pain from trauma. Heavy drinking does not always mean alcoholism but it may. Sources listed here provide support for both alcohol and, in some cases, drug-dependent people.

Adult Children of Alcoholics,
World Service Organization (ACA WSO)

ACA is a twelve-step, twelve-tradition program of men and women who grew up in alcoholic or otherwise dysfunctional homes. In the safe environment of their support meetings, ACAs discover how their childhoods affected them in the past and influence them in the present. They take positive action to find freedom from the past and improve their lives today.

Go to: http://adultchildren.org. Write: ACA WSO, P.O. Box 3216, Torrance, CA 90510. Phone: 310-534-1815.

Al-Anon/Alateen

This worldwide organization offers a self-help recovery program for families and friends of alcoholics whether or not the alcoholic seeks help or even recognizes the drinking problem. Based on the twelve steps of Alcoholics Anonymous, the program has no dues or fees for membership. In twelve languages, the website focuses on adults whose lives have been affected by someone else's drinking and on teenagers growing up in alcoholic families.

Go to: http://www.al-anon-alateen.org. Write: Al-Anon World Service Office, 1600 Corporate Landing Parkway, Virginia Beach, VA 23454-5617. For meetings in the USA and Canada, call toll-free: 888-425-2666. In the US, phone (757) 563-1600.; in Canada, phone (613) 723-8484. For meetings in over thirty-eight other countries, see the Al-Anon website.

Alcoholics Anonymous (AA)
AA is the foremost organization for sufferers of alcoholism and heavy drinking with many groups worldwide. Presented in English, Spanish and French, AA's website provides a self-test for alcoholism and a description of what AA offers such as anonymity and a twelve-step program. Check the telephone book for the nearest group.

Go to: http://www.alcoholics-anonymous.org. For the U.S. and Canada, write: General Service Office of AA, P.O. Box 459, Grand Central Station, New York, NY 10163. Phone: 212-870-3400. For over forty other countries, see the site's International Section.

Center for Alcohol and Addiction Studies (CAAS)
CAAS conducts research and provides publications, education and training. Its website offers information and resources for people who may be addicted to alcohol or drugs.

Go to: http://www.caas.brown.edu. Write: CAAS, Box G-S121-5, Brown University, Providence, RI 02912. Phone: 401-863-6600.

Focused Treatment Systems (FTS)
FTS provides information about alcohol and drug abuse treatment. It offers for sale the *Alcohol Withdrawal Treatment Manual*, a clinically proven method for alcohol withdrawal syndrome (AWS) treatment. This is a practical book for clinicians.

Go to: http://www.sagetalk.com/. Write: P.O. Box 530, Glen Echo, MD 20812-0530. Call toll-free: 800-728-6799. Phone: 301-320-0529.

Internet Alcohol Recovery Center
This website offers extensive information and support for people who feel they drink too much. For those uncertain about the extent of the problem, a self-test is provided. Featured also are alcohol and recovery news stories, a library and a description of clinics, organizations and support groups.

Go to: http://www.uphs.upenn.edu/recovery. Write: Joseph R. Volpicelli, MD, Ph.D., Treatment Research Center, 3900 Chestnut Street, Philadelphia, PA 19104-6178. Phone: 215-248-6025.

National Association for Children of Alcoholics (NACoA)
NACoA is a national membership organization that educates the public about the harm caused to children growing up in alcoholic families and about the steps needed to support and protect these children. It publishes a newsletter and offers videos, booklets and

other educational materials to assist those who can intervene and support children. Officers who grew up with an alcoholic parent or families and friends of alcoholic officers may find this service invaluable.

Go to: http://www.nacoa.org. Write: NACoA, 11426 Rockville Pike, Suite 301, Rockville, MD 20852. Call toll-free: 888-554-2627. Phone: 301-468-0985.

Secular Organizations for Sobriety (SOS)
An alternative to AA's deference to a higher power, this international secular (not atheist) group believes that "we all have the power within ourselves to get and stay clean and sober..." The site offers sources for nearby groups as well as literature, videos and audiotapes.

Go to: http://www.secularsobriety.org or www.sossobriety.org. Write: Save Our Selves (SOS), 4773 Hollywood Blvd., Hollywood, CA 90027. Phone: 323-666-4295.

For meetings outside the United States, please check for a directory on the website for more than 20 countries.

See also: _Drug Use_
For more alcohol-related sources.

* * *

Anabolic Steroids
Misused, anabolic steroids can make people ill or even kill them. Some Internet websites praise the so-called "virtues" of anabolic steroids and encourage athletes to use them. But other sites condemn the dangerous practice of taking a controlled substance. If in doubt, please examine the following web pages that start with http://

➢ www.aafp.org/afp. Search _anabolic steroids_

➢ www.ctclearinghouse.org. Search _anabolic steroids._

➢ www.drugfreesport.com

➢ www.health.nih.gov. Search _anabolic steroids._

➢ www.mayoclinic.com. Search _anabolic steroids._

➢ www.mesomorphosis.com

➢   www.steroidabuse.org

➢   www.steroidlaw.com

➢   www.thebody.com

*   *   *

Assault

Support services generally focus on citizens, not individuals who place themselves in harm's way as part of their job. But aren't assaulted peace officers survivors of crime? Shouldn't they receive support from the same sources as citizens? The saying that police agencies look after their own is not always true.

And what should the families of assaulted police officers do for their loved ones? How do wives, husbands, children and parents of officers cope with the aftermath? Many police websites offer comfort to officers and their families, but civilian sites also offer effective support, despite referring to survivors as "victims." The first place to look for help is in the telephone book under Victim Services.

National Center for Victims of Crime (NCVC)
One of the most comprehensive websites for help and resources.

Go to: http://www.ncvc.org/. Write: Victim Services, NCVC, 2000 "M" Street, NW, Suite 480, Washington, DC 20036. For referral to local resources, call toll-free: 800-394-2255.

National Crime Victim Hotline Numbers
This website provides telephone numbers for most U.S. states that offer crime victim compensation for such things as medical expenses, lost wages, funeral costs, psychological counseling and childcare.

Go to: http://www.ojp.usdoj.gov/ovc/help/numb.htm *and* http://ovc.ncjrs.gov/findvictimservices.

National Crime Victim's Research and Treatment Center (NCVRTC)
The NCVRTC provides scientific research, treatment, professional education and consultation. Its clinical services offer care to adult and child victims of violent crime and their families.

Go to: http://colleges.musc.edu/ncvc/. Write: NCVRTC, Department of Psychiatry and Behavioral Sciences, Medical University of South Carolina, 165 Cannon Street, PO Box 250852, Charleston, SC 29425. Phone: 843-792-2945.

National Organization for Victim Assistance (NOVA)

NOVA provides services for survivors of crime and disaster. Its crisis resources provide many hotlines for information, comfort and aid concerning domestic violence, survivors of crime, child abuse, rape and violence against women.

Go to: http://www.trynova.org. Write: NOVA, 510 King Street, Suite 424, Alexandria, VA 22314. Phone: 703-535-232-6682. Crisis Hotline: 800-879-6682.

Victim Services (VS)—Safe Horizon

Although focused on New York, this large site provides articles about assault and other crimes as well as information on services that may be available in other communities. Its many valuable links cover such areas as crime victim issues, stranger assault, child abuse, domestic violence and families of homicide victims.

Go to: http://www.victimservices.org and www.safe horizon.org. Write: Victim Services, 2 Lafayette Street, New York, NY 10007. Phone: 212-577-7700. NY Crime Victims Hotline: 212-577-7777. NY Domestic Violence Hot-line: 800-621-4673.

See also: *Rape, Child Abuse*

For more assault related sources.

* * *

Behavioral Science Units

Not all Behavioral Science Units (BSUs) are insensitive to police officers' needs and report everything officers say to administrators. Under most circumstances, BSUs are supportive. It would be a shame if officers ignored resources in their own backyard.

There are many good BSU programs across the country. For example, a model program is conducted by the San Francisco Police Department, featuring both in-house and external programs. The in-house program offers an Employee Assistance Program, a Peer Support Program, a Critical Incident Response Team (CIRT), a Stress Unit, Catastrophic Illness Program, and the Chaplain's program For outside support, the department employs police psychologists.

Why does the SFPD BSU work well for police officers? Perhaps because it is not a tool of the police administration. The peer support program, for example, is owned and run by police officers. Since a steering committee of cops runs the unit, cops and not administrators make the decisions. And in the peer support unit confidentiality is maintained except under rare circumstances.

The purpose of the SFPD BSU is to support law enforcement officers through rough times. For instance, at the SFPD illegal drug use is considered a medical problem first to allow officers to pursue treatment before the habit becomes a disciplinary or legal issue.

For further information about this model BSU program, contact the San Francisco Police Department Behavioral Science Unit, 850 Bryant Street, San Francisco, CA 94103-4603. Phone: 415-837-0875.

In assessing the value of their own Behavioral Science Unit, officers should ask counselors:

➤ Under what circumstances do you report what I say to the administration?
➤ Do you offer therapy?
➤ If I receive therapy from you, how will this affect my career advancement?
➤ What is your background in counseling trauma survivors and clients with PTSD?
➤ Can you recommend outside sources that offer confidential therapy?
➤ How many therapy sessions will my insurance cover with you or an outside therapist?

Psychologists who offer therapy and are obligated to report details of their sessions to police administrators find themselves in a professional and moral dilemma. How can a client receive effective therapy when a bond of trust is violated?[1]

* * *

Child Abuse

Some police officers come from troubled backgrounds, including child maltreatment and sexual abuse. Issues about trust may eventually resolve themselves but not always. Officers who were or are abusers need help as much as those abused.

Child Abuse Prevention Network

Although targeted for professionals, this site has special pages about survivor issues including PTSD.

Go to: http://child.cornell.edu.

How to Report Suspected Abuse—Childhelp

The purpose of the organization called Childhelp is to meet the physical, educational, emotional and spiritual needs of abused, neglected at at-risk children. The Child Abuse hotline is staffed 24/7 by professional crisis counselors throughout the U.S. and Canada. Through interpreters, they can respond in 140 languages, and offer crisis intervention, information, literature, and referrals to thousands of emergency, social service, and support sources. All calls are anonymous and confidential. The website outlines many more programs including treatment sources.

Go to: http://www.childhelp.org. Call the National Child Abuse Hotline toll-free at: 800-422-4453. For Childhelp National Head-quarters, write to: 15757 N. 78th Street, Scottsdale, AZ 85260. Phone: (480) 922-8212.

International Child Abuse Network (ICAN)

Online, ICAN defines child maltreatment and provides articles on a variety of related subjects. It offers a chat room, bulletin board, statistics, book references and links.

Go to: http://www.yesican.org. Write: International Child Abuse Network, (YesICAN), 7657 Winnetka Avenue, PMB 155, Canoga Park, CA 91306-2677. Call toll-free: 888-224-4226.

National Center for Fathering (NCF)

A resource for men, NCF seeks to strengthen fathering skills. The site provides access to other fathers, a nationwide radio program, research, live seminars, books and tapes.

Go to: http://www.fathers.com. Write: NCF, P.O. Box 413888, Kansas City, MO 64141. Call toll-free: 800-593-3237.

Parents Anonymous (PA)

Founded in 1970, Parents Anonymous, Inc., is the oldest and largest child abuse prevention organization in the United States dedicated to strengthening families through mutual support and parent leadership. The organization leads a diverse network of 2,300 PA community-based groups that meet weekly. Co-led by parents and professionally trained facilitators, the groups are free of charge to participants. Parenting tips are provided online as well as a list of Parents Anonymous groups and hotlines in many states and other countries.

Go to: http://www.parentsanonymous.org. Write: Parents Anonymous, The National Organization, 675 W. Foothill Boulevard, Suite 220, Claremont, CA 91711-3475. Phone: 909-621-6184.

Parents Without Partners (PWP)

With about 200 chapters in the U.S. and Canada, PWP is the largest international organization devoted to the interests of single parents and their children. The website offers parenting links, bulletin boards, pen pals and leadership training. The organization provides educational and family activities, adult social and recreational activities, advocacy, scholarships and conventions.

Go to: http://www.parentswithoutpartners.org. Write: PWP, 1650 S. Dixie Highway, Suite 510, Boca Raton, FL 33432. Call toll-free: 800-637-7974. Phone: 561-391-8833.

Prevent Child Abuse America

Made up of friends, professionals, volunteers, donors and parents, this organization has been foremost in building awareness, providing education and inspiring hope to everyone involved in the effort to prevent the abuse and neglect of our nation's children. Through state and local chapters and many local programs, they endeavor to strengthen families.

Go to: http://www.preventchildabuse.org. Write to: PCA America National Office, 500 North Michigan Avenue, Suite 200, Chicago, IL 60611. Phone: 312-663-3520.

Stepfamily Foundation (SF)

More than half of all Americans are involved in step relationships. The website provides phone counseling, free articles and resources.

Go to: http://www.stepfamily.org. Write: SF, 333 West End Avenue, New York, NY 10023. 24-hour information line: 212-799-7837. Phone: 212-877-3244.

See also: *Assault, Rape, Domestic Abuse*

For more child abuse help sources.

* * *

Citizen Involvement

What can citizens do about PTSD in police officers? Involvement with officers helps reduce the cynicism that can contribute to PTSD symptoms.

Citizen Patrol and Volunteers

Trained civilians are handling many patrol and volunteer responsibilities in departments throughout the U.S. and Canada. These duties range from wearing uniforms and driving around in marked cars to preparing paperwork and running communications at the station. Mostly, citizens use their own vehicles, wear plain clothes and rarely, if ever, carry firearms or confront perpetrators of crime. The citizens' purpose is observation and many use video recorders.

Departments that want to start patrol or volunteer programs may wish to search the Internet for model programs.

Citizen Police Academy

Hundreds of police departments are running citizen police academies. Why should citizens attend? Here's my experience with the Santa Barbara Police Department's school.

In the SBPD's fifty-two hour course, I learned about use of force, car stops, hot calls, building searches and drug use. I was schooled in fingerprinting, investigation of homicides, patrol procedures, hostage negotiation, animal control and the paperwork cops are required to complete.

During a ridealong, I witnessed verbal abuse from street toughs and drunks. The impact of repeated verbal abuse on police officers should not be minimized. Like physical violence, verbal violence wears officers down, contributing to cynicism and feelings of discouragement and hopelessness.

I left the course understanding the strain cops are under and why they keep their feelings inside after encountering violence.

One exchange in particular between the police officers teaching the course and the students still sticks out in my mind. We were asked why we were attending the academy. A man stood up and said in a quavering voice that he was from a third-world country where the police had tortured him. He wanted to know if police officers in America were different. At the end of the first class, he was talking amicably with the officers. And by the end of the course, he declared that he knew what police in America were about: helping people. One can only imagine how he had been harmed previously, but the academy became a healing experience for him.

For departments not offering a course but who wish to start one, search the Internet for one that follows criteria you favor.

Victim Witness Assistance Program

The Victim Witness Assistance Program not only acts to ensure that victims of crime are treated with fairness, respect, and dignity while dealing with the justice system, but also helps law enforcement officers.

Civilian volunteers trained in crisis intervention are often called out by police departments to help with victims. Police officers don't usually have the time to stay with victims to assess their needs and comfort them. Instead, the Victim Witness volunteers stay with victims, do death notifications, go to scenes of break-ins, home invasions, robberies, rapes and murders, and help the victims and survivors deal with the aftermath.

For example, I worked as a volunteer with the Pima County Attorney's Office Victim Witness program in Tucson, Arizona. With a staff of 25 paid and 125 volunteers, we were on call 24 hours a day, seven days a week, to assist police and help victims. In Tucson, Victim Witness makes 16,000 victim contacts each year, and helps more than 5,000 people at crisis scenes.

This is a very worthwhile program that frees up police officers so they can go to more calls, and often saves officers from suffering compassion overload or fatigue from dealing with so much misery in the course of the job.

Please check the Internet and local telephone listings for a Victim Witness program near you.

For reference, you may wish to look at the following websites: Pima County Arizona Victim Witness Program: http://www. pcao.pima.gov/vicwit.htm.
Victim Witness Assistance Center, San Jose, CA: http://www. victim.org.
New Jersey Office of Victim Witness Advocacy: http://www.nj.gov/ oag/dcj/victimwitness.

* * *

Counseling

An uncomfortable relationship has always existed between police officers and therapists. I've been told that many officers believe no one besides other cops can under-stand how they feel. Cops fear that healthcare professionals will take away their jobs. But therapists' goals are to get officers functioning and back to work. Concerns about confidentiality should be reconciled before therapy begins.

Not every kind of counseling is right for every person, nor are all therapists equal in what they provide. Officers or family members should question therapists about the therapists' experience with traumatized people. Many counselors can help, but those who know little about psychological trauma may cause additional damage.

For a candid description of "How to Choose a Therapist," check out Dr. John Grohol's Mental Health Page called Psych Central: http://www.grohol.com/pageone.htm. Also offering advice are the American Psychiatric Association at http://www.psych.org/ (go to site map and click on "Psychiatry FAQ") and the American Psychological Association at http://apa.org (enter "How to choose a therapist" on the website's search engine).

At Health

At Health provides information about psychological disorders and referral to qualified therapists. Online, it defines PTSD, answers frequently asked questions and provides resources and a list of treatment centers. If hesitant about contacting mental health professionals in its database, call toll-free: 888-284-3258.

Go to: http://www.athealth.com. (Click on "Disorders and Conditions." Write: At Health, Inc., 14241 NE Woodinville-Duvall Road, #104, Woodinville, WA 98072-8564. Phone: 360-668-3808.

Concerned Counseling (CC)/HealthyPlace.com

HealthyPlace.com (also known as Concerned Counseling) is the largest consumer mental health site, providing comprehensive information on psychological disorders and psychiatric medications from both a consumer and expert point of view. The website provides active chatrooms, hosted support groups, people who keep online journals/diaries, psychological tests, breaking mental health news, mental health videos, online documentary films, a mental health radio show and more.

The website also provides a "PTSD Self-Test" that you can access by typing "PTSD" in the site's search engine. Or have a look at the self-test for PTSD provided in Appendix 5 of this book.

Go to: http://www.concernedcounseling.com/ or go to http://www.Healthy Place.com.

NetWellness

NetWellness offers the world's largest base of medical experts who provide online consumer health information. The "Ask An Expert" section features pharmacists, nurses, physicians and other health professionals who provide answers to health questions.

Go to: http://www.netwellness.org/. Write: NetWellness, 231 Albert Sabin Way, PO Box 670574, University of Cincinnati Cincinnati, OH 45267-0574. Phone: 513-558-8766.

Stressline

A resident of Middleboro, MA, Hal Brown wore a badge as a reserve officer for twenty years. Now as a clinical social worker, he examines an array of subjects on his Stressline website including causes of police officer stress, critical incidents, and conflicts between police officers and therapists.

Go to: http://stressline.com. At bottom of opening page, click on "police stressline." Phone: 508-947-5601.

See also: **Eating Disorders, Panic Attacks, Stress Management and PTSD/Trauma Research And Referral**
For more counseling services.

* * *

Critical Incidents and Intervention

A critical incident is an event so strong in emotional power that it rapidly breaks through police officers' defenses. Against such force, their abilities to cope and respond are overwhelmed. The incident, like the murder of a child, could interfere with their functioning at a crime scene or even later at home. The event may make them feel numb, shocked and helpless. Officers may react with anxiety, inability to sleep, difficulty concentrating, fear, confusion, anger and depression.

Although these are normal reactions to abnormal situations, officers experiencing them may require an intervention, a way of telling what happened to a sympathetic listener trained in understanding the issues. An intervention is not therapy. It's designed to assure the affected officers that what they feel is normal and that they will recover.

An intervention is not appropriate for every person. Officers with strong support systems in place may not need one. Interventions using health professionals may be met with mistrust, resistance and even anger. Police officers often, but not always, wish to be addressed by fellow officers.

Since intervention methods and techniques continue to evolve, perhaps the most practical way for police departments to assess stress intervention programs is to find out what works in other peer counseling units.

International Critical Incident Stress Foundation (ICISF)

The ICISF has developed a comprehensive, systematic and multi-component approach to managing emergency services stress including that of police officers. The program is called Critical Incident Stress Management (CISM). CISM emphasizes pre-incident stress education, but also highlights peer support programs during operations as well as after their completion.

CISM also provides defusings and Critical Incident Stress Debriefings (CISD) after incidents. One-on-one support services and family interventions are part of the CISM program.

The CISM program is used in many law enforcement agencies in many countries around the world. CISM seeks to prevent stress when possible, to intervene when stress overwhelms and to guide people toward recovery whenever stress produces damage.

Go to: http://www.icisf.org. Write: ICISF, 3290 Pine Orchard Lane, Suite 106, Ellicott City, MD 21042. For emergencies, call: 410-313-2473. Phone: 410-750-9600.

* * *

Death In-The-Line-Of-Duty

According to the National Law Enforcement Officers Memorial Fund (NLEOMF), about 160 U.S. law enforcement officers on average are killed on the job each year. The year 2007 was particularly deadly, with 181 officers losing their lives. Of those, more than one-third were shot and killed, a substantial increase from previous years. Word on the street is that criminals, with more deadly weapons than ever before, are going out of their way to kill police officers. The year 2008 is turning into a better year for officers, however, and is down about 40 percent in police officer deaths. The danger has not decreased, but training and better equipment have helped more officers stay safe.

Nevertheless, one death is far too many, and we must never forget those who gave their lives. After the initial shock of a police officer's death, departments do not offer ongoing support to family members, coworkers and friends. Continuing contact with the department would help survivors heal.[2] The following organizations offer support and information for the families and friends of those who died.

100 Club

Supported by the donations of its members and the community, the 100 Club provides financial assistance to families of public safety officers and firefighters who are seriously injured or killed in the line-of-duty, and also provides resources to enhance their safety and welfare. A benevolent non-profit organization, the 100 Club operates in many US states. To find out which states, please go to http://www.100clubChicago.org and click on the club directory.

No amount of money can bring back somebody's loved one, but the 100 Club tries to ease some of the financial burden during a time of severe crisis and loss. The amount of financial aid varies from club to club and state to state.

For basic information, please go to the 100 Club of Arizona website. Then click on Resources and Links to reach other states. Go to: http://www.100club.org. Write: 100 Club, 5033 N. 19th Avenue, Suite 123, Phoenix, AZ 85015. Phone: 602-485-0100.

Concerns of Police Survivors (COPS)

Concerns of Police Survivors provides programs and services for devastated families, coworkers and friends of law enforcement officers killed in-the-line-of-duty. The organization offers seminars, scholarships, peer support, child counseling, summer camp and retreats for survivors as well as training to police agencies on how to respond to an officer's death.

Go to: http://www.nationalcops.org/. Write: Suzie Sawyer, Executive Director, COPS National Office, P.O. Box 3199, S. Highway 5, Camdenton, MO 65020. Phone: 573-346-4911.

National Law Enforcement Officers Memorial

The National Law Enforcement Officers Memorial in Washington, DC, honors all of America's federal, state and local law enforcers killed in-the-line-of-duty. It has catalogued information on more than 18,000 law enforcement deaths, and it built and maintains a Memorial where all those names can be seen and visited by friends and loved ones. In addition, the NLEOMF's website contains a complete listing.

A memorial is a sacred responsibility. It allows loved ones and friends to reclaim a moment with the person who died. It lets them honor their memory.

When you see name after name, you realize that they are not just statistics. They are somebody's child, someone's husband, or wife, mother or father, somebody's friend. A memorial means they are not forgotten, that they have not been left behind.

Many of us derive a lot of comfort from visiting a memorial such as this. Those who have died live on in our hearts. The Memorial sits on three acres of federal park land called Judiciary Square, located on the 400 block of E Street, NW. A glance around the space finds plush carpets of grass, nearly 60,000 plants and 128 trees decorating the Memorial grounds. Each year, around the first of April, some 14,000 orange and yellow daffodils make the Memorial one of Washington's most spectacular attractions.

If you can visit Washington, please go to the Memorial and honor _our_ law enforcement dead.

For information online, please go to http://www.nleomf. org. Click on Visitor Information, and then on the Walking Tour for points of interest. A separate click will get you a map of the memorial. You can also schedule a guided tour of the memorial on this website.

Scholarships
Many police departments offer college scholarship programs to spouses and children of slain or incapacitated public safety officers. Consult departments, legislators, or the Internet for details in your jurisdiction.

See also: _Publications_
Sharon Knutson-Felix, Executive Director of the 100 Club of Arizona, tells about losing her police officer husband in her book, _Gifts My Father Gave Me, Finding Joy After Tragedy._ The book includes a _Grieving and Healing Guide._

*   *   *

Depression
Trauma frequently causes depression, and depression is often associated with drinking, drug use and suicide. Depression is not officially listed by the American Psychiatric Association as a PTSD symptom, but it may precede PTSD, or occur at the same time as PTSD. Sometimes a person trying to cope with PTSD symptoms becomes depressed because it is difficult to stop the flashbacks, nightmares and fear. Seriously depressed people feel hopeless, bitter, irritable, restless and pessimistic. They don't function well at work or in a social setting. They are withdrawn, and find little joy in life. They may have trouble sleeping, have no appetite and lose weight. Depressed people are often filled with guilt, shame and self-hatred, and often think about suicide.

Depression.com
This website, supported by pharmaceutical company Glaxo-SmithKline, states that "depression is not something you can just snap out of." The site provides information on the causes and

treatment for depression. It describes the different types of depression, and how to live with a depressed person.

Go to: http://www.depression.com.

Depression and Bipolar Support Alliance (DBSA)

DBSA is the leading patient-directed national organization focusing on the most prevalent mental illnesses. The organization fosters an environment of understanding about the impact and management of these life-threatening illnesses by providing up-to-date, scientifically-based tools and information written in language the general public can understand. DBSA supports research to promote more timely diagnosis, and develop more effective and tolerable treatments.

DBSA's prestigious 65-member Scientific Advisory Board is comprised of the leading researchers and clinicians in the field of mood disorders. DBSA has a grassroots network of nearly 1,000 patient-run support groups across the country.

Go to: http://www.dbsalliance.org. Write: Depression and Bipolar Support Alliance (DBSA), 730 N. Franklin Street, Suite 501, Chicago, Illinois 60610-7224. Toll free: (800) 826 -3632. If you are in crisis, call 1-800-273-8255.

Depression Chat—Online Support

DepressionChat.com provides a way for people suffering from depression to speak to others with the same problems. You can share experiences, treatment that has worked for you, and read the latest information and news about dealing with depression.

Go to: http://www.depressionchat.com

Emotions Anonymous (EA)

Emotions Anonymous is a twelve-step organization, similar to Alcoholics Anonymous, and is composed of people who come together in weekly meetings for the purpose of working toward recovery from emotional difficulties such as depression, anger, grief, anxiety and so on.

Today there are over 1000 EA chapters in 35 countries, including the United States.

Go to: http://www.emotionsanonymous.org. Write: EA International, P.O. Box 4245, St. Paul, MN 55104-0245. Phone: 651-647-9712.

* * *

Domestic Abuse

Although statistics vary from study to study, some form of domestic abuse and violence occur in 14 percent to nearly 60 percent of police marriages. Military families experience a similar incidence of abuse.[3] These reactions may be attributed to the stress of the job, unreasonable expectations, and exposure to trauma. Although family violence is not addressed in the chapters of this book, the subject deserves attention as one of the least talked about secrets concerning the effects of police work.

Blain Nelson's Abuse Pages

Blain is a recovering spouse abuser. The website tells his story, provides a lot of information, and offers a list of Frequently Asked Questions that determine spousal abuse.

Go to: http://blainn.com/abuse.

Domestic Violence Hotlines & Resources

Offering phone numbers and addresses for organizations that combat family violence throughout the U.S., this site also provides Internet resources and shelter information.

Go to: http://www.feminist.org/911/crisis.html. Call the National Domestic Violence Hotline toll-free: 800-799-7233. 800-787-3224 TDD.

National Center for Women & Policing (NCWP)

The NCWP provides resources for victims of police family abuse as well as information about work place harassment and discrimination. In particular, check out a fact sheet on the website about police officer domestic violence at www.womenandpolicing.org/publications.asp.

Go to: http://www.womenandpolicing.org. Write: The National Center for Women and Policing, 433 S. Beverly Drive, Beverly Hills, CA 90212. Phone: 310-556-2526.

See also: _Assault, Child Abuse, Rape_

For more resources on domestic abuse and violence.

* * *

Drug Use

Drugs are often addictive and, like alcohol and other sub-stances, may mask other problems. Drug abuse can represent an inability to express intense pain or feeling. It is a cry for help.

Illegal drug use is almost always a firing offense for a law enforcement officer, so getting the department to pay for treat-ment is not easy, but it is possible. Peer counseling units frequently send alcohol abusers to confidential treatment facilities that provide drug treatment. Peer counselors treating drug problems do not usually report to police administrators.

Officers needing drug treatment may wish to ask peer and treatment center counselors about confidentiality. No matter the response, drug abusers *must* seek treatment. Without help, their lives and the lives of those they care about are endangered.

Some of the following sources apply equally to drug and alcohol abuse.

Co-Anon Family Groups

Co-Anon Family Groups are a fellowship of men and women who are husbands, wives, parents, relatives or close friends of someone who is chemically dependent. The website features information regarding the problem and the solution via the twelve-step program, as well as an online e-mail meeting for members all over the world. While most of the members come from the U.S., Co-Anon is reaching Europe, North, Central and South America, and countries on all other continents. The Meeting Directory currently lists face-to-face meetings spread across the U.S. and Canada.

Go to: http://www.co-anon.org. Write: Co-Anon Family Groups, World Services, P.O. Box 12722, Tucson, AZ 85732-2722. Phone: 800-898-9985.

Cocaine Anonymous World Service Organization (CAWSO)

Using a twelve-step program, Cocaine Anonymous (CA) is open to anyone with the desire to stop using cocaine, crack and all other mind-altering substances. The website provides a self-test for cocaine addiction and listings and websites for CA groups in the U.S. and other countries.

Go to: http://www.ca.org. Write: CAWSO, P.O. Box 492000, Los Angeles, CA 90049-8000 USA. Call the National Referral Line toll-free: 800-347-8998. Phone: 310-559-5833.

Nar-Anon Family Group

For friends and family of drug addicts, this recovery group provides a forum for expressing the pain of watching someone they love suffer with addiction.

Go to: http://nar-anon.org. To reach groups in the U.S. and other countries, consult the telephone book or call their headquarters at 800-477-6291. Write: Nar-Anon F. G. Headquarters, Inc., 22527 Crenshaw Blvd., #200B, Torrence, CA 90505.

Narcotics Anonymous (NA)

NA is an international association of recovering drug addicts who share personal experiences and solutions. Holding meetings in seventy countries, it follows a twelve-step program that focuses on "spiritual awakening." NA's website provides much information about groups in every state and many countries.

Go to: http://www.na.org. Write: NA, World Service Office, P.O. Box 9999, Van Nuys, CA 91409. Call: 818-773-9999.

For groups in Europe, write: NA, WSO, 48 Rue de l'Éte/ Zomerstraat, B-1050 Brussels, Belgium. Phone: 32-2-646-6012. Fax: 32-2-649-92239.

National Council On Alcoholism And Drug Dependence (NCADD)

With more than one hundred councils in the U.S., NCADD provides education, help and hope in the fight against chronic alcoholism and drug addiction. Online, the group provides health information, an intervention network, prevention programs, resources and a referral guide.

Go to: http://www.ncadd.org. Write: NCADD, 244 E. 58th Street, 4th Floor, New York, NY 10022. Call: 212-269-7797. Toll-free 24-hour referral Hope Line: 800-622-2255.

Web of Addictions

Website creators Andrew L. Homer, Ph.D., and Dick Dillon, are very concerned about "the appalling extent of misinformation about abused drugs on the Internet, particularly on some Usenet Newsgroups."

Their fact sheets cover alcohol abuse and many drugs including amphetamines, barbiturates, caffeine, cocaine, hallucinogens, heroin, LSD, marijuana, nicotine, opiates, steroids and tranquilizers.

Go to: http://www.well.com/user/woa.

See also: _Alcohol Abuse_

For more resources about drug abuse.

* * *

Eating Disorders

When experiencing the aftermath of psychological trauma, police officers sometimes stop eating, overeat or binge eat and then purge. They are like alcoholics trying to deaden the pain in order to cope with life. More than 8 million Americans have eating disorders: 7,000,000 women and 1,000,000 men. Here are a few of the many sources on the web that offer explanation and help.

Eating-Disorder.com

This website defines eating disorders, but primarily offers ways to find treatment centers. To find treatment centers in the United States, call: 866-575-8179.

Go to: http://www.eating-disorder.com.

Internet Mental Health Net (IMHN)

IMHN describes eating disorders as well as many other disorders in detail, but a most interesting feature is that it allows for a confidential self-diagnosis. For information on eating disorders, use the site's search engine by typing in key words such as "anorexia," "bulimia," and so on.

Go to: http://mentalhealth.com.

Mirror Mirror

This site provides information on signs and symptoms of eating disorders, relapse warnings and prevention, getting help and choosing a therapist. It features resources, a survivor's wall and letters of hope as well as discusses what family members can do and how they can cope with their own feelings about the problem.

Go to: http://www.mirror-mirror.org.

National Eating Disorders Association (NEDA)

NEDA is dedicated to increasing the awareness and prevention of eating disorders. Among other things, the site describes how to help a friend with an eating disorder, allows you to ask questions from Ask An Expert, and includes videos, resources, a parent, family and friends network, and information about their annual conference.

Go to: http://www.nationaleatingdisorders.org. Write: NEDA, 603 Stewart Street, Suite 803, Seattle, WA 98101. Phone: 206-382-3587.

Something Fishy Website on Eating Disorders

One of the oldest and largest sites on eating disorders, "something fishy" includes treatment locations, online support, signs and symptoms, physical dangers, vitamin deficiencies and managing stress. It helps you find a therapist and even accommodates online therapy. In English, Spanish, or French, the site offers many Internet and off-web listings of eating disorder organizations in the United States and other countries.

Go to: http://www.something-fishy.com.

* * *

Families and Officers Support

The police community is often referred to as a family. And the prime source of support for officers who are experiencing PTSD symptoms or having any crisis difficulty is the family—their spouses, friends, and fellow police officers.

Beside the Badge (BTB)

A low-cost, bimonthly newsletter, BTB encourages support and fellowship among officers, their families and friends. It's packed full of stories, columns, counseling information and even material for young readers. This newsletter is hardcopy only and not a website.

Write: Beside The Badge Newsletter, P.O. Box 304, Tecumseh, MI 49286-0304. Call toll-free: 888-536-3267.

Canadian Police Wives (CPW)

CPW is a dedicated online law enforcement support group for spouses. It's open to Canadian police wives who are either married or living with a Canadian police officer. Its purpose is to meet others who share the same problems and lifestyle.

Go to: http://groups.msn.com/canadianpolicewives.

Loveacop

Police spouses often feel they don't belong in either civilian or police societies. Isolated and alone, they need somewhere to share their feelings. Lovacop provides a forum for spouses of current, former and retired law enforcement officers to share secrets of coping and to develop new friendships.

Go to: http://www.loveacop.org.

Peace Officers' Wives Clubs Affiliated (POWCA)

POWCA is committed to enhancing the positive image of law enforcement, promoting the education of law enforcement issues, and supporting the law enforcement family. The organization cultivates relationships between families of peace officers within departments, statewide, and across the nation.

Go to: http://www.powca.org. Write: POWCA, P.O. Box 4471, Whittier, CA 90607.

Police Families

The purpose of the Police Families website is to provide information and referral for spouses, children and parents of police officers. The site features chatrooms, guest psychologists, games and activities for children, and material for departments wishing to extend services to police families.

Dr. Ellen Kirschman, author of *I Love A Cop, What Police Families Need To Know*, and Dr. Lorraine Greene, Manager of Police Counseling for the Nashville/Davidson County Metropolitan Police Department, created the website in coordination with a national advisory group of police families, law enforcement organizations and police psychologists.

Go to: http://www.policefamilies.com.

Police Wives

PoliceWives.org is an online forum that offers support and encouragement to the spouses of police officers.

Go to: http://www.policewives.org.

PoliceWivesOnline.com (PWO)

This organization is available to everyone in law enforcement— wives, husbands, family members, and significant others. PWO provides support, resources, and friendship to those who support law enforcement officers every day. And they are dedicated to helping those who love cops to face the daily struggles of being in a law enforcement relationship. Among other things, the website provides forums, articles and a gift shop.

Go to: www.policewivesonline.com. Write: PWO, PO Box 361, Chatham, IL 62629.

Wives Behind the Badge (WBTB)

WBTB is a national organization dedicated to offering support and resources to law enforcement wives, families and significant others such as fiancés and life partners, as well as directly to police officers and their departments. Their website offers forums, a gift shop, and a program to send condolence cards to the wives of fallen officers.

Go to: www.wivesbehindthebadge.org. Write: WBTB, PO Box 5472, Orange, CA 92863.

* * *

Finding Local Support Groups

Information on local support or self-help groups can be found in several ways. Local libraries and hospitals usually provide handbooks of community resources. Major groups are frequently listed in the telephone book under social service agencies. National groups can provide information about local support groups. Self-help does not mean you try to cope alone. It means you seek help from others.

American Self-Help Clearinghouse (ASHC)

This organization provides a searchable online database of over 1,100 mutual aid support groups, and offers materials and assistance in starting new types of groups. Support groups include those for crime victims, car accident survivors, abuse victims, alcoholism, abusive parents and many others.

The website also lists local self-help group clearinghouses in the U.S. with toll-free 800 numbers, as well as worldwide groups that provide similar services.

Go to: http://www.selfhelpgroups.org.

National Self-Help Clearinghouse (NSHC)

Among many other things, NSHC serves as an information and referral service to self-help support groups and regional self-help clearinghouses or listings of self-help organizations.

Go to: http://www.selfhelpweb.org.

* * *

Firefighters

CopShock is a book about police officers, but it is hard not to recognize firefighters as brothers and sisters in harm's way. They experience PTSD just as much as police officers, and need the same consideration and support. Many firefighters have read the first edition of this book and derived a lot from the stories and resources. In this second edition, the chapter about police officer turned firefighter Jimmy Brown and his experiences during 9/11 and its aftermath, shows us the sacrifices that firefighters make for our society, and how they suffer silently from trauma.

North American Fire Fighter Veteran Network (NAFFVN)

The NAFFVN addresses the needs and concerns of firefighters who run into burning buildings when everybody else is running from them. Firefighters experience PTSD at the same rate as police officers, which can be as high as one-third. Some say firefighters exhibit more PTSD than cops. But firefighters do not have many resources, and, like police, they have a culture that frowns on revealing feelings or saying they need help. This website intends to change that perspective.

Prepared by Senior Chief Shannon H. Pennington, this website aims to provide a much needed resource so firefighters and their families can learn about PTSD and its effects. It describes firefighter "self-care," and the steps a firefighter (or anyone) can take to make sure they don't develop PTSD.

Go to: http://firefighterveteran.com. Phone: 250-812-3737.

* * *

Free E-Mail Addresses

E-mail addresses that are separate from the department provide a degree of privacy and confidentiality. You don't want other people reading your e-mail messages to support group members, friends or counselors.

It is advisable that you do not use the department's computer for contacting sources you feel are personal. And you don't even need to own a computer. You can access e-mail from sources like a public library, a friend's computer or a cybercafe.

Free e-mail accounts are available from a number of sources. The only drawback is that the hundreds of free e-mail providers flog advertising in order to pay themselves for offering the service. What the heck, it's still free.

Take note, however, that some "free" e-mail providers have hidden fees for extra features and some of the smaller companies tend to go out of business. Check out the provider thoroughly before subscribing. In particular, have a look at law enforcement websites such as www.officer.com that provide a free e-mail service.

For a list of free e-mail providers, go to: http://www.email addresses.com.

* * *

Grief And Bereavement

After witnessing a horrific crime scene, many officers believe they don't dare show how they feel, not even to loved ones. But holding grief inside can become overwhelming. Talking to friends, family, clergy, counselors or participating in support groups can help heal officers and their families.

Grief is not limited to what officers experience on the job. They experience the death of loved ones, illness, job loss and many other forms of loss. Sometimes the stress of the job intensifies other sorrows. Few of us seem to know what grief is and how to handle this natural process.

Crisis, Grief & Healing

An internationally known psychotherapist, author and speaker on healing and loss, Tom Golden offers many resources on this website. He provides stories from over 450 people who have written of their grief and healing, as well as articles, a discussions page and workshop information.

Go to: http://www.webhealing.com. Write: Tom Golden, 149 Little Quarry Mews, Gaithersburg, MD 20878. Phone: 301-670-1027.

Grief Recovery Institute (GRI)

GRI provides a series of articles with commonly asked questions on grief recovery and reaction to loss. It offers books, audiotapes, workshops and a certification program for professionals.

Go to: http://www.grief-recovery.com. Call toll-free in the U.S.: 818-907-9600. In Canada, call: 519-586-8825.

Grief Talk

This website provides links to counseling, support groups, stress management and more to help deal with loss and grief.

Go to: http://www.grieftalk.com

Grief Work

Barbara Rubel, MA, BCETS, CBS, is a Certified Bereavement Specialist. Her father, a retired New York City police officer, took his own life, and she has sought ways to cope and help others ever since. A nationally acclaimed speaker on stress management, burnout, compassion fatigue, loss and resiliency, Barbara has drawn on her experience as a suicide survivor and has written several books on grief and loss, in particular, *Death, Dying and Bereavement*. She is a consultant for the Department of Justice and Office for Victims of Crime. Among other things, her website discusses how to cope with vicarious trauma.

Go to: http://www.griefworkcenter.com. Write: P.O. Box 5177, Kendall Park, NJ 08824. Phone: 732-422-0400.

Living With Loss Magazine

This magazine offers "Hope and Healing for the Body, Mind, and Spirit." It is a support group in print offering articles, stories, poems, and resources for the bereaved by grief educators and presenters, facilitators and caregivers, authors and writers, and most important the bereaved themselves. It often offers articles about traditional and alternative perspectives, coping techniques and resources that address physical and mental health issues, the psychology of mourning, ecumenical faith and cross-cultural perspectives, the grief of children and seniors, grief in the workplace and even appropriate humor.

Go to: www.bereavementmag.com. Write: Bereavement Publications, Inc., PO Box 101, Eckert, CO 81418. Phone toll-free: 888-604-4673.

Sympathy Sharing Site

This website allows you to share your feelings if you are unable to visit someone who is ill or dying or prefer not to attend funeral services. It is a worldwide compendium where written greetings and tributes can be conveyed. It also provides a free open forum.

Go to: http://www.bereavement.com.

The Compassionate Friends

This organization helps families cope with grief following the death of a child and to provide information to help others be supportive. It is a national self-help support organization that offers friendship, understanding, and hope to bereaved parents, grandparents and siblings. There is no religious affiliation and no membership fees. It has chapters throughout the country.

Go to: www.compassionatefriends.org. Write: The Compassionate Friends, Inc., P.O. Box 3696, Oak Brook, IL 60522. Call toll-free: 877-969-0010. Phone: 630-990-0010.

Webster's Death, Dying and Grief Guide

On this large site, Kathi Webster, BSN, RN, discusses the meaning of grief and healing, depression, anxiety, suicide and surviving. She describes eulogies, funerals, memorials, aging, and the effect of death on children. She also offers comfort to those who lose pets, an important subject for K9 officers.

Go to: http://www.katsden.com/death.

WidowNet

WidowNet is an information and self-help resource for and by widows and widowers. Articles and news include topics like grief, bereavement and recovery for people who have suffered the death of a spouse or life partner. The site offers chat rooms, public forums, books about grief, and it describes where to find support groups.

Go to: http://www.widownet.org.

See also: *Publications*

Sharon Knutson-Felix, Executive Director of the 100 Club of Arizona, tells about losing her police officer husband in her book, *Gifts My Father Gave Me, Finding Joy After Tragedy*. The book includes a *Grieving and Healing Guide*.

* * *

Healing Opportunities

For many sufferers of PTSD, visiting memorials helps heal psychic wounds. A study on Vietnam veterans who visited the Vietnam War Memorial in Washington, DC, and participated in Memorial Day programs is inconclusive. In some veterans, PTSD symptoms diminished while in others they increased.[4]

Many police officers and their families who have participated in Police Week and have visited the National Law Enforcement Officers Memorial in the U.S. capital say the experience was beneficial. As well as having an opportunity to express feelings, officers were able to renew friendships and receive comfort and support from family, friends and fellow officers.

American Police Hall of Fame and Museum (APHF)

The APHF contains a memorial listing of officers killed on duty, exhibits, and crime prevention information. Before Police Week, the administrators of the facility contact the leaders of the U.S. law enforcement community to remind them of the price many officers have paid.

Go to: http://www.aphf.org. Write or visit: APHF, 6350 Horizon Drive, Titusville, FL 32780. Phone: 321-264-0911.

National Law Enforcement Officers Memorial

Every fifty-three hours an officer is killed. The National Law Enforcement Officers Memorial in Washington, DC, honors all of America's federal, state and local law enforcers killed in-the-line-of-duty. It also offers an opportunity for officers and their families to grieve for friends and loved ones.

Inscribed on the Memorial's marble walls are the names of more than 18,000 officers, dating back to the first known death in 1792.

To preview the Memorial online or to search the database for friends or loved ones, go to: http://www. nleomf.org and click on OfficerInformation/Search. Phone: 202-737-3400.

Two blocks away from the Memorial is a Visitors' Center and Gift Shop at 605 E Street, NW, Washington, DC 20004. Phone: 866-569-4928. You can view items in the Gift Shop at www.nleomf.org.

Peace Officers Memorial Day and National Police Week

In mid-May, law enforcement officers commemorate Peace Officers Memorial Day. Remembrance ceremonies are held and police officers across the nation wear black mourning bands on their shields or stars to honor fallen officers. During National Police Week, which begins before Memorial Day and continues after it, thousands gather at the National Law Enforcement Officers Memorial for a candlelight vigil.

For information on how officers, their families and the community can participate in Police Week or to see a calendar of the week's activities, go to: http://www. nleomf.com. Call: 202-737-3400.

Vietnam Veterans Memorials

In many U.S. states and in Australia, Canada, New Zealand and Vietnam there are memorials to those who died in the Vietnam War. As well as visiting the Police Memorial, officers who are veterans may also wish to visit "The Wall" and similar memorials.

On the website, the Remembrance Page provides stories, poems, songs, art—anything that honors the dead and comforts the living. The site also connects to memorials around the world, including the National Vietnam Veterans Memorial in Washington, DC.

Go to: http://www.vietvet.org/vietmems.htm.

See also: Veterans of War

For more on Vietnam, World War II, Korean, Gulf War veterans.

*   *   *

Marriage, Mediation and Divorce

Family problems are stressful for everyone. When coping with traumatic stress, officers may finally face marriage troubles or exaggerate the extent of their conflicts.[6] Often marriages can be worked out, but sometimes divorce is inevitable.

Many studies say police officers divorce at a higher rate than most other people, in some cities as high as 75 percent. Other studies report rates at slightly above or even below the national average.[7] As with many issues about police life, statistics vary from city to city, and from precinct to precinct.

What is not under dispute is that unlike many other high-pressure jobs, policing puts additional stress on marriages. The threat of being injured or killed, witnessing human suffering, long and unpredictable hours, shift work, conflicts with bosses, excessive paperwork, an ineffective criminal justice system, attacks by the media, days off spent in court, moonlighting to make ends meet, missed birthdays and anniversaries—all can cause anxiety and friction at home.

Like everybody else, police officers must work at marriages. The Internet has a flood of resources embracing every aspect of marriage, mediation and divorce.

Mediate.com

The Mediate.com website offers publications and referrals to trained mediators throughout the U.S., Canada, UK, Australia and New Zealand. Its services cover every aspect of mediation and divorce including separation, child custody, prenuptial agreements, disputes, conflicts and family issues.

Go to: http://www.mediate.com. Write: Mediate.com, PO Box 51090, Eugene, Oregon 97405. Phone: 541-345-1629.

Divorcenet.com

This popular website provides divorce information, and seeks to empower women and men undergoing divorce. You can access objective divorce-related articles, support communities, interactive tools for managing divorce, and a nationwide directory of divorce lawyers, mediators and financial professionals. It addresses all aspects pertaining to divorce such as alimony and child support. With over 40,000 members, its online communities and special events allow you to participate in real-time discussions with experts and with other people who share similar divorce issues.

Go to: http://www.divorcenet.com. Write: LawTek Media Group, LLC, 321 Walnut Street, Suite 440, Newton, MA 02460. Phone: 800-696-2026.

Divorce Online

Created by the American Divorce Information Network, this electronic magazine is for people involved in or facing the prospect of divorce. The site provides free articles and information concerning financial, legal, psychological, real estate and other aspects of divorce as well as referrals to qualified attorneys.

Go to: http:www.divorce-online.com.

DivorceSource.com

This comprehensive site provides information on the financial, legal, psychological, real estate and other aspects of divorce. It offers, among many other things, live chat rooms, downloads, articles, books, cases, tutorials, divorce kits, agreements, family law links and a directory to help locate professionals throughout the U.S. and Canada. Many of the offerings are free, and others you pay for.

Go to: http://www.divorcesource.com. Write: Divorce Source, P.O. Box 1580, Allentown, PA 18103. Phone: 610-820-8120.

MarriageBuilders.com

MarriageBuilders presents ways to overcome marital conflicts and restore love and caring. As well as many articles, the site offers an online radio show, questionnaires, a discussion forum, books, counseling, and referral to local counselors.

Go to: http://www.marriagebuilders.com.

Marriage Toolbox

An online marriage magazine, this website focuses on many aspects of marriage including how to maintain a healthy one. As well as covering the basics in over 80 pages, the magazine is inspiring and uplifting. It also offers practical suggestions and exercises for maintaining or improving communication and loving in a relationship.

Go to: http://www.marriagetools.com. Call toll-free: 800-691-9477.

Online Guide for Effective Living

Bill Ferguson offers this site for loving, learning and healing. He provides articles and access to workshops, books, tapes and telephone consulting. The articles include divorcing as friends, resolving disputes without conflict and the steps needed to end conflict and restore love in difficult relationships.

Go to: http://www.billferguson.com. Phone: 713-520-5370.

Chapter 16

Support Sources
Issues and Commentaries

N to Z

Panic Attacks And Panic Disorder

Panic attacks are common, and about one-third of Americans experience at least one such attack every year. Although they are the most frequently occurring type of emotional disorder or reaction, they should not be underestimated for their ability to inflict harm. An episode usually begins without warning and can last anywhere from a few minutes to a half hour or longer. Attacks may be characterized by a rapid heartbeat, sweating, trembling, chills, nausea, chest pain, dizziness and other symptoms.[1] Panic attacks are the primary condition in Panic Disorder, as defined by the American Psychiatric Association. Panic attacks are sometimes considered a precondition to PTSD.

For a Panic Disorder Self-Test, please see Appendix 4.

Anxiety Centre.com

This outstanding website is filled with comprehensive information, help and support for those who suffer from anxiety, stress, panic attacks, phobias, depression, and PTSD. It is beautifully assembled by Jim Folk, who suffered extremely debilitating stress and anxiety symptoms including intense panic attacks for more than ten years. As he says, "I went from being an out-going, healthy and excited-about-life type of person to being always sick, almost housebound, and thinking I was losing my mind." Finally, he found a therapist who understood what was happening to him, and he returned to having a normal healthy life.

This website offers not only information, but also personal coaching by a cadre of caring professionals who have personally experienced overwhelming anxiety—so they know what they are talking about. Jim says you don't have to suffer needlessly. You can beat your condition for good.

For an Anxiety Potential Self-Test, see Appendix 2, for a Stress Self-Test, please see Appendix 3, or go to AnxietyCentre.com.

Go to: http://anxietycentre.com. Write: Jim Folk, Anxiety-Centre.com, 70 Rockbluff Close NW, Calgary, Alberta T3G 5B2. Phone: 403-208-0091.

Anxiety Disorders Association of America (ADAA)

The Anxiety Disorders Association of America is the leading nonprofit organization dedicated to increasing awareness and improving the early diagnosis, treatment, and cure of anxiety disorders (such as PTSD and Panic Disorder) through education and research. ADAA offers free educational information and resources about anxiety disorders, local treatment providers, self-help groups, self-tests, clinical trials, and more. ADAA promotes the message that anxiety disorders are real, serious and treatable.

You may wish to complete their "PTSD Self-Test" reproduced in Appendix 5 of this book and their "Panic Disorder Self-Test" in Appendix 4, and show them to your health care professional.

Go to: http://www.adaa.org. Write: ADAA, 8730 Georgia Avenue, Suite 600, Silver Spring, MD 20910. Phone: 240-485-1001.

Anxiety Disorders Education Program

The National Institute of Mental Health (NIMH) features a website that describes symptoms of Panic Disorder, PTSD and other anxiety disorders. Treatment options are also considered.

Go to: http://www.nimh.nih.gov. Click on the "Site Map," and then on the area you wish to access such as Panic Disorder, PTSD, and so on. Write: National Institute of Mental Health (NIMH), Science Writing, Press, and Dissemination Branch, 6001 Executive Blvd., Room 8184, MSC 9663, Bethesda, MD 20892-9663. Phone: 301-443-4513. Toll free: 866-615-6464.

Anxiety/Panic Attack Resource Site

Dedicated to those who suffer from anxiety and panic attacks, this comprehensive site features information on symptoms, medications and treatment. Among other things, it also offers books and a chatroom.

Go to: http://www.anxietypanic.com.

Cyberpsychologist

Created by Dr. Robert Sarmiento who counsels many police officers in his practice, this self-help resource focuses on depression, addictions and relationships. Its information will help those suffering from panic attacks, providing stress management methods. The website discusses therapy for people who don't believe in therapy.

Go to: http://www.cyberpsych.com. Write: Robert F. Sarmiento, Ph.D., 955 Dairy Ashford, Suite 108, Houston, TX 77079. Phone: 281-679-0001.

Descriptions of Panic Attacks and Panic Disorder

For numerous articles and detailed descriptions of symptoms and treatment for panic attacks and Panic Disorder, have a look at Internet Mental Health. Go to: http://www.mentalhealth.com. Search the index for panic attacks.

National Anxiety Foundation (NAF)

The NAF provides information on Panic Disorder, and an online series of handbooks on its causes, cures and care.

Go to: http://www.lexington-on-line.com/naf.html. Write: Stephen M. Cox, M.D., President and Medical Director, NAF, 3135 Custer Drive, Lexington, KY 40517-4001.

Tapir, The Anxiety-Panic Internet Resource

Tapir is a self-help network dedicated to overcoming and curing overwhelming anxiety. As well as detailed information on panic attacks, it provides information on PTSD.

Go to: http://www.algy.com/anxiety.

* * *

Peer Support for Police Officers

Since the 1980s, many law enforcement stress programs have trained police officers to offer support to fellow officers experiencing stress and trauma. Because both "counselors" and officers seeking help wear a badge, a bond of trust is quickly formed. Peer supporters can empathize with situations and feelings other officers undergo. And most important, confidentiality is maintained. Otherwise, the peer support program would fail.

In many police forces they are not called "counselors." They are referred to as "peer supporters." This is perhaps a better depiction of the role, as peer supporters do not usually offer therapy. Instead, they provide comfort, intervention, education and referrals. A peer support program does not replace the services of mental health professionals.

For a detailed description of peer support programs, see pages 56-71 in *Developing A Law Enforcement Stress Program for Officers and Their Families*. To order this book, see *Publications*.

California Peer Support Association (CPSA)

The CPSA is a good example of a support organization for peer support personnel. It is dedicated to the advancement, promotion, and enhancement of peer support and peer support programs for law enforcement, fire, and allied emergency service personnel in the state of California. However, the goals and programs of this organization could be duplicated in any jurisdiction for the betterment of all law enforcement. In addition to training seminars, the CPSA also conducts a conference every year to further the education of peer support people.

Go to: www.californiapeersupport.org. Write: CPSA, PO Box 163, La Mesa, CA 91944.

Cop2Cop Telephone Helpline

Cop2Cop is a confidential telephone helpline for New Jersey police officers. It offers 24 hour/7days a week help from fellow officers who understand what officers are experiencing. The service is staffed by retired officers who are licensed Clinical Social Workers, along with retired officers who are trained as peer supporters. The organization offers peer and clinical support services, clinical assessments, referrals, and critical incident stress management while maintaining confidentiality.

After a number of police suicides in the 1990s, New Jersey community leaders felt that police officers needed a confidential, safe outlet to talk to peers who could understand and provide support without judgment. So they legislated Cop2Cop into law to focus on suicide prevention and mental health support. This is a resource every police department across the country needs, and serves as a model program.

Go to: www.Cop2CopOnline.net. 24-Hour Hotline: 866-267-2267 (866-Cop2Cop). E-mail: cop2cop@umdnj.edu. They will answer emails within 48 hours.

Law Enforcement Educators and Trainers

The International Law Enforcement Educators and Trainers Association (ILEETA) is a professional organization that helps train instructors in criminal justice professions. As well as offering periodicals and training opportunities, it provides an annual international training conference and expo.

Go to: www.ileeta.org. Write: ILEETA, PO Box 1003, Twin Lakes, WI 53181. Phone: 262-279-7879.

Peer Support Training Institute (PSTI)

The Peer Support Training Institute conducts peer support training for New York City's Police Department peer support program, POPPA (Police Officers Providing Peer Assistance). Since the inception of POPPA (originally MAP) in 1995, PSTI has been an integral part of its development and continues to train two new groups of volunteer NYPD officers each year. (See POPPA next). PSTI's program is used as a model for police departments worldwide.

Who are peer supporters? What are they expected to do? These important questions are addressed by Dr. Ronnie M. Hirsh, Director of PSTI, a division of Manhattan Counseling and Psychotherapy Associates, LLC, in the following material:

"At PSTI, peer supporters are trained to be a supportive resource, serving as a friendly sounding board to allow clients to explore feelings, ideas, and alternatives to situations. Peer supporters are taught to help clients identify issues of concern, and refer them to professionals when necessary rather than give advice or try to solve the problems. As a result of training, peer supporters develop greater self-awareness and improved sensitivity to the needs of others as well as increased confidence in their peer support skills."

Dr. Hirsh says that PSTI tailors training programs to the needs of individual law enforcement organizations seeking to develop a peer support program. The training is comprehensive, covering a wide range of topics that peer supporters must know to effectively assist fellow officers. Training programs adhere to the standards set by the IACP (International Association of Chiefs of Police), Psychological Services section. He stresses that the training material is reinforced "by experiential exercises to ensure that peer supporters understand their role and feel comfortable applying their skills." He adds, "A great emphasis is placed on providing peer supporters with helpful communication techniques to create a safe, nonjudgmental, and confidential environment that facilitates trust and openness for those seeking help. The training includes information about depression, suicide prevention, alcohol abuse, relationship problems, critical incident stress, and Posttraumatic Stress Disorder." The training covers additional topics including those dealing with ethical issues and making assessments and referrals. A more comprehensive description of their training model and their peer support training textbook, *Cop to Cop* can be found on their website.

Go to: http://www.peersupport.com. Write: Manhattan Counseling and Psychotherapy Associates, LLC, Peer Support Training Institute, 61 West 9th Street, New York, NY 10011. Phone: 212-477-8050.

Police Organization Providing Peer Assistance (POPPA)

Plagued by twenty-six suicides of police officers in two years, the New York City Patrolmen's Benevolent Association (PBA) formed a peer support organization today known as POPPA. It was created by William Genêt, a PBA union trustee and police officer with thirty-two years experience.

When I met Bill in 1993, he was distressed that troubled, even suicidal officers, rather than seeking help from the administration, preferred to suffer. They didn't believe the administration would support them or maintain confidentiality. By 1996, Bill had realized his dream of forming an intervention, referral and treatment organization run by cops for cops.

Peer support officers (PSOs) in the program emphasize that voluntarily seeking help for personal problems is a sign not of weakness but of strength. POPPA also wants to get help for members early, before problems become insurmountable and possibly lead to suicide.

The POPPA website describes how and why POPPA was formed, and lists New York City area support groups for police officers as well as support groups for police families. Here's how POPPA describes some of what they do:

"The POPPA Organization provides peer support for New York City police officers experiencing personal or professional problems, such as trauma, stress, depression, alcohol abuse, or family problems. The POPPA Organization is an independent, not-for-profit agency, offering entirely confidential services through trained volunteers from the NYPD. Officers calling the POPPA Organization's HelpLine can meet with a fellow officer immediately or the next day. If needed, the POPPA Organization can refer an officer to a mental health professional within the POPPA Organization's network and the officer's own insurance plan, while continuing to provide peer support. The POPPA Organization's services are available 24 hours a day, every day of the year, to any New York City police officer who voluntarily seeks them."

POPPA is a milestone in police circles because it is union initiated. Bill says POPPA can be adapted to any size department, large or small, and he would be happy to assist other unions and departments in creating their own programs. See *Retirement* in chapter 16 for information on POPPA's Retiree Program.

Go to: http://www.poppainc.com. Write: POPPA, Inc, Bill Genêt, Director, 26 Broadway, Room 1640, New York, NY 10004-1898, Phone: 212-298-9111. 24-Hour Member Hotline: 888-267-7267. Retiree HelpLine: 800-599-1085.

Self-Support Group
In New York City, Tony Senft is president of The Police Self-Support Group. It provides comfort for officers who have been wounded physically and are forgotten. It also supports officers who have experienced emotional trauma.

Meeting once a month, members visit officers in the hospital or at home and lecture at the police academy. The group features social functions like barbecues and parties that allow injured officers to remain part of the law enforcement community.

A self-support group can be started in any department, and Tony would be pleased to provide information about how the New York organization is run. Write: Tony Senft, 299 Pond Road, Bohemia, NY 11716-3410. Phone: 516-244-9002.

Why Police Departments Want To Provide Peer Support
Besides providing the public with the best-trained officers, police departments are mostly concerned about the bottom line. Since that's the case, then departments should clamor to provide peer support programs. Why? Because it is cheaper to keep a trained officer than it is to hire a new one. It is cheaper to send officers to counseling than it is to replace them.

To train an officer can cost a department thousands, as much as $500,000 over a five-year period in some jurisdictions. Does a department really want to lose that investment and then spend it all over again to train a new officer? Too many times I've heard that officers were fired or forced out because they developed PTSD or other stress-related illnesses. Rather than send the officer to get help, their department's view seemed to be, *Well, if you can't cut it, get out.*

That attitude is counterproductive and costly to a department. Look at these figures from *Developing a Law Enforcement Stress Program for Officers and their Families*: (p.169)

Example #1:
Barrington Psychiatric Center, Los Angeles, CA
- ➢ Average cost of intervention where posttraumatic stress was diagnosed soon after a critical incident: $8,300 per person.
- ➢ Average cost where treatment delayed: $46,000 per person.
- ➢ Officers who received prompt treatment returned to work in 12 weeks.
- ➢ Officers who received delayed treatment returned to work in 46 weeks.

Example #2:
Philadelphia Police Department
- ➢ A cost benefit study of their peer support program for alcoholic officers found that the program resulted in reduced sick leave, fewer injury days and suspensions.
- ➢ The department more than recovered its costs for the program in 3 years.
- ➢ It estimated a savings of $50,094 for each subsequent year.

Example #3:
Palo Alto Police Department
- ➢ This department found that their stress program cost was absorbed many times over with the prevention of one stress-related disability retirement.
- ➢ Before the peer support program, there were 12 stress-related retirements.
- ➢ After the program began, there was only one (1) stress-related retirement during a period of 16 years.

Example #4:
San Bernardino Sheriff's Department
- ➢ With a peer support program, this department reduced its psychological stress retirements from 8 to 0 over a 6 year period.
- ➢ As a result, it saved $1½ million dollars per officer, or a total savings of $12 million dollars in retirement funds alone.

If you crunch the numbers, you will see that large and small departments cannot afford to let a good officer go. It's more cost effective to create a peer support program.

* * *

Peer Support For Police Officers' Family

A number of departments now provide treatment services and training to officers' families. Support helps to reduce stress in the family, limit stress family members may cause the officer and turn family input into a source of comfort. The International Association of Chiefs of Police suggests that police agencies should offer support through marital counseling, post-shooting trauma debriefing, group discussions, orientation programs and frequent family events.

Some departments provide training for family members while their loved ones attend the academy. The training may consist of several weeks of ridealongs and courses on police work, stress management and weapons practice. Martin Reiser, former director of the LAPD's Behavioral Science Unit, suggests that departments provide periodic stress training after the academy in joint sessions for officers and family members. Further details can be found on pages 137-147 of *Developing a Law Enforcement Stress Program for Officers and Their Families*. See *Publications* for ordering this book.

Police Family Plan

As well as welcoming police officers, New York City's POPPA peer support organization invites police officer families to attend seminars designed solely for them. The family is the most important support unit for cops, and director Bill Genêt wants to be sure family members understand their roles.

Known as the Police Family Plan, the discussion group teaches loved ones, including children, how to identify and work with officers suppressing feelings from trauma. Bill's Peer Support Officers advise family members to encourage police officers to talk about their feelings and experiences, to make talking, usually taboo, acceptable. Vocalizing feelings helps reduce the risk of developing PTSD. See *Retirement* in chapter 16 for information on POPPA's Retiree Program.

Go to: http://www.poppainc.com. Write: POPPA, Inc, Bill Genêt, Director, 26 Broadway, Room 1640, New York, NY 10004-1898, Phone: 212-298-9111.

* * *

Police Dispatcher Trauma

Police Dispatchers are often the forgotten heroes when we talk about police stress, trauma and PTSD. After a critical incident, peer support groups may debrief police officers who were at the crime scene. Sometimes dispatchers who were involved with the call are included, but too often they are overlooked.

In the definition of PTSD, one of the main criteria is that the subject experienced or *witnessed* an event that involved actual or threatened death or serious injury. Police dispatchers witness many scenes of death, mayhem and destruction while talking on the phone to victims. Yet there is little resolution. They often don't know what eventually happened, whether the victims lived or died. When the critical incident involves a police officer such as an officer down call, suicide-by-cop, a shootout, or high-speed pursuit, the dispatchers suffer even more dramatically. They may experience adrenaline rushes, heart palpitations, anxiety, and fear. They may have sleepless nights, get irritable and angry, and develop eating disorders. Only in the past few years has police dispatcher trauma been fully recognized and understood.

Police dispatchers will benefit greatly from the support sources listed for police officers in this book, but here are some sources specifically for police dispatchers.

911 Cares

911 Cares is run by volunteer 9-1-1 professionals who offer emotional support including stress debriefings to emergency communicators during difficult times or events. In addition, the organization awards "Everyday Heroes" within the industry, and provides public and agency education about 9-1-1 issues.

Go to: http://www.911cares.com. Phone: 650-595-5202 ext 102 or 103. E-Mail: Kevin@pstc911.com.

9-1-1 Magazine

9-1-1 Magazine: Managing Emergency Communications is a print magazine for dispatchers that is published nine times a year. It contains a blending of product-related technical, operational, and people-oriented features. The magazine covers provocative issues and major incidents from both a responder and a commun- ications standpoint. In addition, the website offers photo stories, career opportunities, web links, selected stories from past issues, and a 9-1-1 resource directory.

Go to: http://www.9-1-1magazine.com.

Dispatch Monthly Magazine
This online monthly newsmagazine offers a great deal of information dispatchers will be interested in. It connects to news stories that involve 911 dispatchers, provides a forum and bookstore, and addresses issues such as shifts, staffing, training, preparedness and stress management.

Go to://www.911dispatch.com. Contact: Gary Allen. Phone: 877-370-3477. E-mail: editor@911Dispatch.com.

Headsets911
This website is about "helping dispatchers cope with stress," and was founded and developed by one of your own—T. P. McAtamney, who served over ten years in emergency dispatching. The site is filled with articles about what dispatchers do, and how they react to stress, offers links to other helpful sites, free materials, a newsletter, and a weekly podcast. It also offers a seminar that addresses the stressors that affect 911 dispatchers, discusses positive and negative stress, how to cope with stress, PTSD, and nutrition.

Go to: http://www.headsets911.com. Phone: 954-270-8201. E-mail: tpmac@headsets911.com.

Under the Headset
Under the Headset: Surviving Dispatcher Stress (2000, Staggs Publishing) is a book about dispatcher stress and trauma. It was written by Richard Behr, a dispatcher and critical incident stress instructor, and covers the stress process and how to cope with it. It includes some humorous chapters, stories to inspire the dispatcher, prayers, and stories of survival. At just 116 spiral-bound pages, it answers a lot of questions about life on the headset and how to avoid the predictable burn-out after only two to three years.

The book can be found at: http://amazon.com, www.staggs publishing.com, or www.chevronpublishing.com.

* * *

Police Information and Psychological Support
There are many websites on the Internet that offer copious amounts of information for police officers, from news stories and forums to products and training and psychological and emotional support. Included here are some of the more comprehensive sites, as well as more websites for police dispatchers.

Badge of Life—Psychological Survival for Police Officers

The police volunteers at Badge of Life will help you with presentations and training seminars in order to create a better quality of mental health for police officers and to prevent suicide. Their board of directors consists of retired and active cops, a psychiatrist, clinical social worker, a psychiatric nurse and major consultants in the mental health field. The website also provides information for grieving families.

Go to: http://www.badgeoflife.com. Write: Andy O'Hara, Executive Director, Badge of Life, PO Box 2203, Citrus Heights, CA 95611. Phone: 916-212-3144.

CopNet

CopNet links many police sites around the world into one large resource for police officers and anybody interested in police work. It features material on everything from firearms, forensics and psychology to books and equipment. In addition, CopNet features a nationally syndicated radio show where police issues, crime prevention, community relations, and interaction with citizens are discussed.

Go to: http://www.copnet.org.

CopSeek.com

CopSeek.com is an exhaustive website. It is a law enforcement directory, a search engine for all things police, and it offers news, entertainment, columns, grants and funding information, a members network, discussion forums, a gift shop, products of all sorts, a police job center, a directory of over 6,000 police websites, training information, a section for police wives websites, and even the police joke of the day.

Go to: www.copseek.com.

National Criminal Justice Reference Service (NCJRS)

As well as pages and pages of articles about corrections, crime prevention, law enforcement and crime victims, the NCJRS offers links to many websites, statistics, and books. I acquired many studies on the psychological effects of PTSD on law enforcement officers from this service.

Go to: http://www.ncjrs.org/. Write: NCJRS, P.O. Box 6000, Rockville, MD 20849-6000. Call toll-free: 800-851-3420. Phone: 301-519-5500.

National Law Enforcement Officers Memorial Fund

The National Law Enforcement Officers Memorial Fund has been mentioned elsewhere in the support sources, but it shows how significant it is that it falls into several major categories.

Among other things, the NLEOMF collects the names and stories of all law enforcement officers who have been injured or killed in-the-line-of-duty, and during Police Week, the names of those recently deceased are read out, wreaths are placed in their honor, and the names are etched into the Memorial wall in Washington, DC. In addition, on its website and in its newsletter the NLEOMF tells the stories of those officers who gave their lives.

The NLEOMF is also a repository of facts, figures and information about law enforcement trends, issues, and procedures. Its chairman and CEO, Craig Floyd, is an expert in law enforcement. For more than three decades, he has written articles, hosted radio shows, and published books. He is often quoted in the media about issues in the news, and on what officers do, how they are trained, and how they think. His work has been credited with changing America's attitude toward the law enforcement profession, saving police lives, and providing assistance to the survivors of officers killed in-the-line-of-duty.

Go to: http://www.nleomf.org.

Officer.com

This remarkable website attempts to list every worldwide police source on the Internet. Providing a mountain of material, it lists individual departments, officers' personal pages, officers killed on duty, and corrections information. It provides daily news stories related to law enforcement, forums, events, career information, products, articles on police life, leadership, operations and tactics, technology, and much more.

Go to: http://www.officer.com. Write: Officer.com, 11720 Beltsville Drive, Suite 300, Beltsville, MD 20705.

PoliceOne.com

This is one of the most comprehensive law enforcement websites on the Internet. It contains reference sections such as police news articles, products, community, career, training, officer safety, grants, body armor, communications, corrections, firearms, equipment, software, tactical, evidence collection, gangs, investigations, K9, SWAT, terrorism, expert witness, police videos, chat, forums, job postings, and more.

Through PoliceOne.com, you can access one of their divisions called Calibre Press, which offers many law enforcement books, training manuals, and videos.

The Calibre Press *Street Survival Seminar* is also listed with cities and dates when the seminar will be conducted. I have attended two of their seminars, and the instruction is topnotch, the videos exceptional, and you will leave the seminar a changed, safer, and better officer—the Street Survival Seminar is that powerful. Their tee-shirts say: "The Trained Survive," and they mean it.

For PoliceOne.com go to: www.PoliceOne.com. Write: 200 Green Street, 2nd Floor, San Francisco, CA 94111. Phone toll-free: 800-765-4231.

For Calibre Press or the Street Survival Seminar go to: www.CalibrePress.com. Write: 7616 LBJ Freeway, Suite 405, Dallas, TX 75251. Phone toll free: 800-323-0037. Main: 214-545-3060.

* * *

Police Political Groups

Getting officers help for combating PTSD often requires the influence and strength of political organizations. Police groups can negotiate, lobby and fight for better working conditions, training and trauma intervention programs.

Federal Law Enforcement Officers Association (FLEOA)

FLEOA is the largest professional association in the U.S. representing federal law enforcement officers and criminal investigators from over 65 different agencies. Apart from legislative involvement, FLEOA provides legal advice and representation to its many members.

The FLEOA Foundation offers assistance to family members of officers who are killed, provides scholarships to help students interested in criminal justice and administers grants to select charities.

Go to: http://www.fleoa.org. Write: FLEOA, P.O. Box 326, Lewisberry, PA 17339. Phone: 717-938-2300.

Fraternal Order of Police (FOP)

The FOP is the world's largest organization of sworn law enforcement officers with more than 2,100 lodges and over 340,000 members. Besides legislative activities and numerous programs, it encourages the use of intervention methods for police officers who experience trauma.

The National FOP's Critical Incident Committee promotes peer support, analyzes critical incident needs and offers training programs. It is engaged in pre-incident education to prepare law enforcement officers for the effects of trauma. Departments in several states have organized Critical Incident Stress Management (CISM) programs with the assistance of the FOP.

Go to: http://www.grandlodgefop.org. Write: Atnip-Orms Center, National Fraternal Order of Police, 701 Marriott Drive, Nashville, TN 37214. Phone: 615-399-0900.

International Association of Chiefs of Police (IACP)

The IACP is the world's oldest and largest nonprofit membership organization of police executives with over 16,000 members in ninety-four countries. Among its many goals, this group is dedicated to improving the working conditions of the police profession. The IACP has conducted conferences and training about the effects of stress and trauma, and its policy center has developed related model policies to assist the law enforcement community.

With over a century of experience, the organization has credibility in all areas including government, the public and the media. As well as offices in the U.S., the IACP maintains international offices in Europe, India and the Pacific/Asian region.

Go to: http://www.theiacp.org. Write: IACP, 515 N. Washington Street, Alexandria, VA 22314-2357. Call toll-free: 800-843-4227. Phone: 703-836-6767.

International Union of Police Associations (IUPA)

IUPA has become one of the most influential voices for law enforcement in the political arena. The union lobbies in Washington on a wide range of issues, including police officer rights, survivor benefits, overtime pay and armor vest grants.

To combat the impact of trauma, the union retains a renowned police psychologist and expert in the field of police stress to conduct educational stress seminars for IUPA members and their families. The IUPA offers local unions research articles and publications with the latest findings in the area of police stress.

The IUPA has affiliates in Puerto Rico, the Virgin Islands and Canada.

Go to: http://www.iupa.org. Write: IUPA, 1549 Ringling Blvd., Suite 600, Sarasota, FL 34236. Phone: 941-487-2560. National Association of Police Organizations (NAPO)

NAPO represents the interests of more than 2000 police unions and associations, over 238,000 sworn officers and thousands of retired cops. In 1991, NAPO established the Police Research and Education Project (PREP) to promote the well-being of police officers and their families.

Go to: http://www.napo.org. Write: NAPO, 317 South Patrick Street, Alexandria, VA 22314. Phone: 703-549-0775.

National Sheriffs' Association (NSA)

The NSA is involved in many programs to enable sheriffs, their deputies, chiefs of police and others in criminal justice to perform their jobs in the best possible manner. It monitors legislation and provides training for its members.

Go to: http://www.sheriffs.org. Write: National Sheriffs' Association, 1450 Duke Street, Alexandria, VA 22314-3490. Call toll-free: 800-424-7827. Phone: 703-836-7827.

National Trooper's Coalition (NTC)

One of the many goals of the NTC is to assist member state police associations in acquiring the best possible equipment, salaries, pension, fringe benefits and working conditions. The organization is very active in lobbying Washington and conducts seminars on important issues to state troopers.

Go to: http://www.ntctroopers.com. Write: NTC, 1308 9th Street, NW, Washington, DC 20001. Phone: 202-387-1682.

* * *

Police Social Groups

One of the conditions that sets cops up for depression and other onerous stress reactions is isolation. Social groups help reduce the feeling of being alone or abandoned. The following is only a sample of police social groups on the Internet.

International Footprint Association (IFA)

The IFA was formed in 1929 to provide camaraderie and fun for people in law enforcement, as well as to encourage closer cooperation between police agencies. The Association promotes involvement in charitable activities such as helping children, sponsoring boys and girls clubs and awarding scholarships to young people interested in law enforcement.

With over forty-one chapters and over 4,000 members, membership is not only for police officers, but also for citizens from every business and profession sympathetic to good law enforcement.

Go to: http://www.footprinter.org. Write: IFA, PO Box 1652, Walnut, CA 91788. Phone: 877-432-3668.

International Police Association (IPA)

With a membership of over 270,000 serving or retired police officers in more than fifty countries, the IPA offers activities for police families involving travel, hobbies, professional seminars, youth exchanges and sports events. Among countries represented are Australia, Canada, Ireland, New Zealand, South Africa, the UK and the U.S.

For a complete listing of websites worldwide, go to: http://www.ipa-iac.org. Their preferred method of contact is email at isg@ipa-iac.org. Write: International Police Association, International Administration Center, 1 Fox Road, West Bridgford, Nottingham, NG2 6AJ England. Phone: +44 (0) 115 945 5985.

Thin Blue Line

This online haven is difficult to categorize. Not only is it a social, political and support resource, but it also offers information on PTSD and stress, issues in the courts, injured officers, Police Week, memorials and many other subjects.

Go to: http://www.thinblueline.com.

Top Cops On The Internet

Visited by law officers, criminal justice professionals and civilians around the globe, this site offers an exchange of common interests through chat groups and links to many police, software and associated sites. Its electronic newsmagazine in seven languages provides news, views, jokes, heartwarming stories and reports about what it's like being a cop.

Go to: http://www.TopCops.com. Contact Deborah Gulley, publisher and editor, at LawWoman@topcops.com.

* * *

Post-Shooting Trauma (PST)

After a shooting, many officers show symptoms of PST that may include increased alcohol use, nightmares about malfunctioning guns, physical illness, inability to sleep or hold down food, and periods of self-doubt, depression, anger and guilt. A common symptom is rumination or brooding about the shooting. Even if officers do not draw or fire their guns during a frightening confrontation, they may experience symptoms of post-shooting trauma. Untreated, post-shooting trauma could eventually develop into PTSD.

Police administrators may wish to consult *Developing A Law Enforcement Stress Program for Officers and Their Families* (page 131) for help in learning how to respond appropriately to officers with these reactions. To order this book, see *Publications*.

Post-Violent Event Trauma

Shooting expert Massad Ayoob of the Lethal Force Institute has produced a videotape about Post-Shooting Trauma called *Post-Violent Event Trauma* concerning the causes, symptoms and recovery from post-shooting trauma. The tape states that PST is not Posttraumatic Stress Disorder but a reaction to a single cataclysmic event or critical incident.

To order the tape, go to: http://www.ayoob.com. Write: Police Bookshelf, P.O. Box 122, Concord, NH 03302-0122. Call toll-free: 800-624-9049. Phone: 603-224-6814. Contact ayoob@attglobal.net.

Post-Shooting Trauma Studies

To examine psychological studies on post-shooting trauma, check with major medical or science libraries. Most provide access for people who are not doctors or students. Ask the librarians for help.

For online abstracts of studies, go to the website for The National Center for PTSD: http://www.ncptsd.va.gov. Phone: 802-296-5132. They allow free access to their huge *Pilots Database*. Search also The National Criminal Justice Reference Service (NCJRS): http:// www.ncjrs.org/. Call toll-free: 800-851-3420.

*   *   *

PTSD Support Groups

PTSD Support

Although based in the UK, this website is for all those with PTSD, their family, friends and partners, and is focused on offering practical advice for living with the condition. This site was developed by people with PTSD who wanted to establish a reliable source of news and comfort. The site contains information on treatment, coping, personal experiences, and features news articles, videos, publications and a forum.

Go to: http://www.ptsduk.co.uk. PTSD 24-hr. helpline in the UK: 01788-560800.

Trauma Anonymous (TA)

TA focuses on PTSD and recovery. The website provides a discussion board, chatrooms, and many useful links about PTSD. Check the telephone book for groups that may already exist.

Go to: http://www.bein.com/trauma.

* * *

PTSD/Trauma Research and Referral

The following organizations and references will help you in researching PTSD and trauma.

American Academy of Experts in Traumatic Stress/ (AAETS)/National Center for Crisis Management (NCCM)

The American Academy of Experts in Traumatic Stress, in collaboration with the National Center for Crisis Management, are multidisciplinary networks of professionals who are committed to the advancement of intervention for survivors of traumatic events and crisis situations. The Academy and the Center aim to identify expertise among professionals, across disciplines, and provide meaningful standards for those who work regularly with survivors and crisis situations. The Academy's and Center's Traumatic Stress and Crisis Management Library provide publications and practical information for survivors of traumatic events and crisis situations and for professionals who address their needs.

The Academy's and the Center's international membership include individuals from over 200 professions in the health-related fields, emergency services, criminal justice, forensics, law and education. Members have joined these organizations from every U. S. state and from over fifty-eight foreign countries.

AAETS and NCCM provide a standard for those who regularly work with survivors, and have developed certification programs in several specialty areas. The Academy's and Center's official membership directory and referral network may be accessed through their Professional Directory on their websites.

Go to: http://www.aaets.org. or http://www.nc-cm.org. Write: AAETS/NCCM, Administrative Offices, 368 Veterans Memorial Highway, Commack, NY 11725. Phone: 631-543-2217.

Australasian Society for Traumatic Stress Studies (ASTSS)

With chapters in every Australian state, the ASTSS is a body of professionals, researchers and survivors who promotes the advancement of knowledge about the nature, consequences and treatment of reactions to highly stressful experiences. The website provides a description of the Society's activities.

Go to: http://www.astss.org.au/site. Write: ASTSS, PO Box 6227, Halifax St, South Australia. E-mail: davidk@ victimsa.org.

Australian Trauma Web with US and Canadian Resources

Psychologist Grant Devilly has collected trauma sites in Australia, the United Kingdom, Canada and the United States on his website. He provides a self-help resource page, which is a series of handouts for trauma sufferers, professionals and debriefers. Click on *Resources for Psychologists, Assessment Devices, Interview Resources, Free Software,* or *Therapeutic Process Resources.*

Go to: http://www.swin.edu.au/bioscieleceng/neuropsych/ptsd. Write: Grant Devilly, Centre For Neuro-psychology. Swinburne University of Technology, PO Box 218, Hawthorn, Victoria 3122. Australia. Phone: +61 3 9214 5920.

Canadian Traumatic Stress Network (CTSN)

(Reseau Canadien Du Stress Traumatique). The CTSN is a Canadian network for people involved in some way with traumatic stress. Its mission is to provide resources for education, training, public awareness, and research and professional development, as well as to foster communication among those affected by traumatic stress, those alleviating it, and those studying it.

Go to: http://www.ctsn-rcst.ca. Write: David S. Hart, Ph.D., ECPS, Education Faculty, University of British Columbia, 2125 Main Mall Vancouver, BC, Canada. david.hart@ubc.ca Phone: 866-288-2876.

CopShock Video

On July 17, 2001, the A&E Television Network broadcast a program based on the book *CopShock*. Titled "Cop Counselors," it shows the effects of trauma on police officers involved in shootings and the day-to-day stress of the job. It discusses the emotional and psychological impact on police officers, including suicide, and what some police therapists are doing to try to alleviate the pain. The video is often shown in police academies, peer support groups and law enforcement college courses. The program was part of the Investigative Reports series hosted by Bill Kurtis, and features interview pieces with the author of *CopShock*.

Go to: http://store.aetv.com. Enter "Cop Counselors" in the search box. Item number is AAE-73422, 50 minutes.

CopShock Website

Among other things, the *CopShock* website features articles on police suicide and one of the few successful PTSD-based lawsuits filed by a police officer against a police department and health care organization in the United States. From time to time, other articles and resources appear on the website. It also offers help on how you can write your own stories about police life.

Go to: http://www.copshock.com

Dart Center for Journalism and Trauma

At the top of the Dart Center's website, it declares that it is "A global resource for journalists who cover violence," and its purpose is to improve media coverage of trauma, conflict and tragedy.

The Center also addresses the consequences of such coverage for those working in journalism. This is a valuable resource not only for journalists in the traditional media, but also for police (officer) journalists who often cover violent stories. Police journalists suffer emotionally and psychologically from seeing so much violence, and this website offers them an opportunity to learn about themselves and how to combat PTSD, trauma, and other stress illnesses.

Go to: http://www.dartcenter.org. Write: Dart Center for Journalism & Trauma, Department of Communication, 102 Communications Building, PO Box 353740, University of Washington, Seattle, WA 98195. Phone: Toll-free 800-332-0565. 206-616-3223.

The Dart Center is also located in Europe and Australia. In London, write: Dart Centre for Journalism & Trauma, 13 Norfolk Place, London W2 1Q1, UK. Phone: +44 20-8123-3549. The phone number for Melbourne, Australia, is: +61 (0) 419131947.

David Baldwin's Trauma Information Pages

Psychologist David V. Baldwin's trauma site provides an enormous amount of information and resources. He defines Posttraumatic Stress Disorder, Secondary Traumatization and discusses different treatment approaches including reexperiencing/ resolving traumatic experiences and Eye Movement Desensitization and Reprocessing (EMDR).

He provides information on trauma organizations and e-mail discussion groups. The Trauma Pages also include selected articles from professional journals on traumatic stress, references on Critical Incident Stress Debriefing (CISD) and EMDR, and supportive links to many other web-sites.

A visit to this site is a must for everyone, whether police, civilian, or war veteran who suffers from trauma or lives with someone who does.

Go to: http://www.trauma-pages.com. If you live in Eugene, Oregon, phone Dr. Baldwin at: 541-686-2598. Otherwise, e-mail is best: dvb@trauma-pages.com.

European Society for Traumatic Stress Studies (ESTSS)

ESTSS promotes the exchange of research and knowledge about the effects of traumatic stress and the application of this knowledge base into clinical practice and social policy. Represented in this organization are members from all across Europe.

Go to: http://www.estss.org. Write: ESTSS secretariat, Churchilllaan 11, 3527 GV Utrecht, The Netherlands. Telephone: +31 (0)30 – 2968000.

Eye Movement Desensitization and Reprocessing (EMDR)

EMDR is a proven method of psychotherapy that helps many survivors of traumatic events including police officers. Trials and studies have shown its effectiveness in resolving single and multiple traumas. On the website for the EMDR Institute, Dr. Francine Shapiro, creator of EMDR, describes its process and offers information on qualified clinicians.

Go to: http://www.emdr.com. Write: EMDR Institute, Inc., PO Box 750, Watsonville, CA 95077. Phone: 831-761-1204.

Therapist David Grand practices EMDR in New York state. I've talked with several of his clients including police officers who found relief from PTSD symptoms after several EMDR sessions. David's website describes his process. Among other things, his website also provides information on audio tapes and CDs about the work he does.

Go to: http://www.biolateral.com. Write: David Grand, 2415 Jerusalem Avenue, Suite 105, Bellmore, NY 11710. Phone: 516-826-7996.

Gift From Within

Gift From Within is an international nonprofit organization dedicated to those who suffer from Posttraumatic Stress Disorder (PTSD), those at risk for PTSD, and those who care for traumatized individuals. This site features a number of well written and informative articles on PTSD and related topics (grief, recovery from motor vehicle accidents, school trauma and police and emergency rescue trauma), plus a peer support network, coping and inspirational stories, a list of retreats for survivors, support groups, and educational videos, books and other resources.

Go to: http://giftfromwithin.org. Write: Gift from Within, 16 Cobb Hill Rd., Camden, Maine 04843. Phone: 207-236-8858.

International Society for Traumatic Stress Studies (ISTSS)

The ISTSS provides a forum for sharing theory, research, clinical interventions, and public policy related to the consequences of traumatic stress in the U.S. and around the globe. It publishes *The Journal of Traumatic Stress*, accessible on the website.

Go to: http://www.istss.org. Write: ISTSS, 60 Revere Drive, Suite 500, Northbrook, IL 60062. Phone: 847-480-9028.

Internet Mental Health

This website features American and European interpretations of disorders and describes medications, treatments and causes for an extensive list of problems such as alcohol and drug abuse, depression, panic attacks and PTSD. The website also offers online diagnosis.

Go to: http://www.mentalhealth.com. E-mail: internetmental health@telus.net.

Interpsych

Interpsych's forums for academics and clinical practitioners include discussions on addiction, anxiety disorders, dissociative disorders, eating disorders, traumatic stress and secondary or vicarious trauma.

Go to: http://www.isu.edu/~bhstamm/InterPsych. htm.

MentalHelp.Net

With articles, news, book reviews, self-help resources, and much more, Mental Help Net's purpose is to educate the public about mental health and wellness. Run by clinical psychologists, the information is accurate and up-to-date on many subjects such as PTSD, depression, eating disorders, panic disorder and their treatments.

Go to: http://www.mentalhealth.net. To contact them, please use their online form.

National Center for PTSD

The National Center for PTSD's website contains a remarkable amount of information and resources for both professional and nonprofessional readers. The Center conducts research into PTSD, trains VA clinicians, and provides information on PTSD to veterans and their families, researchers, clinicians, and members of the public.

The website's most notable feature is its "PILOTS" database, an electronic worldwide index to thousands of publications on PTSD, with citations and abstracts. There is no charge for using the database, and no account or password is required. Although The

National Center for PTSD is a program of the U.S. Department of Veterans Affairs, the PILOTS database is not limited to literature on PTSD among veterans, but includes information on everyone affected by PTSD, including law enforcement officers.

Go to: http://www.ncptsd.va.gov/ncmain/index.jsp. or to: http://www.ncptsd.org. E-mail: ncptsd@va.gov. Phone: the PTSD Information Line at 802 296-6300 or at 802-296-5132.

If you are in need of immediate crisis counseling, please contact VA's suicide hotline at 1-800-273-TALK; counselors are available 24/7 to help.

NetWellness

Created and evaluated by health care professionals at the University of Cincinnati, Case Western Reserve University and the Ohio State University, NetWellness offers the world's largest base of medical experts who provide online consumer health information. Although slanted toward physical illness, the site provides access to thousands of publications that describe the latest research on PTSD, stress and trauma. Because psychological trauma may provoke physical afflictions, this site offers advice on trauma's effects on the body.

The "Ask An Expert" section features pharmacists, nurses, physicians and other health professionals who provide answers to users' health questions.

Go to: http://www.netwellness.org. Write: NetWellness, 231 Albert Sabin Way, PO Box 670574, University of Cincinnati, Cincinnati, OH 45267. Phone: 513-558-8766.

Police Officers and Posttraumatic Stress Disorder

Created by a former police sergeant with chronic PTSD, this website defines PTSD for law enforcement and other emergency personnel, and offers many links to help PTSD sufferers.

Go to: http://home.socal.rr.com/jpmock/ptsd/ ptsd.htm.

Sidran Foundation

Named for its founding donor, Texas philanthropist Kate Sidran, the Sidran Foundation is a national, nonprofit, charitable organization devoted to education, advocacy and research to benefit people suffering from trauma.

To support people with trauma-generated disorders and to educate the public about them, the Sidran Foundation has developed a number of resources including books, a catalog of the best in trauma literature and videos, a database of therapists, a low-cost clinic and a fund for research.

Go to http://www.sidran.org. Write: Esther Giller, President and Director, The Sidran Foundation, 200 East Joppa Road, Suite 207, Baltimore, MD 21286. For ordering literature, call: 410-825-8888 or toll-free 888-825-8249.

See also: *Counseling*
For more research and referral sources.

* * *

Publications
Many worthwhile publications about the issues in this book are available. The following are but a few.

American Academy of Experts in Traumatic Stress (AAETS)—Traumatic Stress Library
See *National Center for Crisis Management* bookstore.

American Psychiatric Association
The American Psychiatric Association publishes *The Diagnostic and Statistical Manual of Mental Disorders, Fourth Edition, Text Revision (DSM-IV-TR)*, used by mental health professionals to diagnose mental conditions. Among other disorders, the Association describes PTSD symptoms and treatment on its website.

The organization also publishes a pamphlet series covering many areas such as anxiety disorders, depression, eating disorders, Panic Disorder, PTSD, and substance abuse. Click on "Public Information" on the left side menu.

Go to: http://www.psych.org or http://www.healthy minds.org. Write: American Psychiatric Association, 1000 Wilson Boulevard, Suite 1825, Arlington, VA 22209. . Call toll-free: 888-357-7924. From outside the US, call 703-907-7300.

American Psychological Association
The American Psychological Association offers a number of articles on topics such as anger, anxiety, trauma, depression, eating disorders, therapy and PTSD. The website also provides news releases, and access to information about books and abstracts from hundreds of scholarly journals.

Go to: http://www.apa.org/topics. Write: American Psychological Association, Office of Public Affairs, 750 First Street, N.E.,

Washington, DC 20002-4242. Phone: Toll-free 800-374-2721 or 202-336-6123.

Clinical Handbook

A Clinical Handbook/Practical Therapist Manual For Assessing and Treating Adults with Post-Traumatic Stress Disorder (PTSD), written by Donald Meichenbaum, Ph.D., a well-known expert and author on PTSD, covers a great deal of ground.

Primarily for counselors, it includes sections on combat veterans, crime victims, positive outcomes from traumatic events, suicide, flashbacks, substance abuse and stress inoculation. The book describes how to assess PTSD, how to use and modify critical incident stress debriefing methods, and how to conduct different kinds of intervention and treatment.

Voted one of the ten most influential psychotherapists, Dr. Meichenbaum has also written *Stress Inoculation Training, Pain and Behavioral Medicine*, and *Cognitive Behavior Modification: An Integrative Approach*, which is considered a classic in its field. In addition to conducting a private practice, he is Research Director of the Melissa Institute for Violence Prevention.

Write: Dr. D. Meichenbaum, University of Waterloo, Department of Psychology, Waterloo, ON N2L-3G1, Canada. Phone: 519-885-1211, ext. 2551.

Crisis, Stress, Trauma Books and Videos

Chevron Publishing publishes and distributes books and videos which promote the understanding and management of crisis, stress, trauma and violence. They specialize in books relevant to disaster mental health, emergency services, crisis intervention, and rescue professions, including books by the founders of the International Critical Incident Stress Foundation (ICISF), and several of the ICISF faculty members. Please check out their selection of publications online.

Go to: http://www.chevronpublishing.com. Write: Chevron Publishing Corporation, 5018 Dorsey Hall Drive, Suite 104, Ellicott City, MD 21042. Phone: 410-740-0065.

Developing A Law Enforcement Stress Program

The National Criminal Justice Reference Service (NCJRS) provides clearinghouse support for the National Institute of Justice (NIJ) including distribution of NIJ publications. *Developing a Law Enforcement Stress Program for Officers and Their Families* is an invaluable NIJ reference for police administrators, union representatives, peer counselors, police officers and their families.

You can download this book from the NCJRS website or order a photocopy.

Other significant Justice Department reference books that can be ordered free from the NCJRS are _Critical Incidents in Policing, Law Enforcement Families: Issues and Answers_ and _Psychological Services for Law Enforcement._ Important books that may be purchased are _Coping With Police Stress_ and _Preventing Law Enforcement Stress: The Organization's Role._ The contents of some of these books may be found at NCJRS' website, the Justice Information Center.

Go to: http://www.ncjrs.org. Write: NCJRS, Box 6000, Rockville, MD 20849-6000. Call toll-free: 800-851-3420. Phone: 301-519-5500.

Grief, Loss and Healing

Gifts My Father Gave Me: Finding Joy After Tragedy was written by Sharon Knutson-Felix, Executive Director of the 100 Club of Arizona. The 100 Club is a benevolent organization that helps police officer and firefighter families in times of need. At one time, members from this organization knocked on Sharon's door. Her police officer husband had been killed in-the-line-of-duty. Several years before that, her six-year-old son was killed by an impaired driver. The book is a remarkable story about surviving loss and grief, and finding love and joy again. It includes a _Grieving and Healing Guide._ I had the privilege of assisting Sharon in the writing of her book.

Go to://www.giftsmyfathergaveme.com.

It's OK Not To Be OK—_Right Now..._
How to Live Through a Traumatic Experience

It's OK Not To Be OK is a book and separate audio tape written and narrated by Mark D. Lerner, Ph.D. Dr. Lerner provides practical information to help you understand what's happening to you during a crisis and how to regain a sense of control. I advise anyone who has experienced a traumatic incident to read this excellent 5-star book that will ease your emotional pain and teach you how to survive and thrive. The book and audio tape can be ordered separately through Amazon.com or from Dr. Lerner's website.

You will also find on his website a lot of information about stress and trauma, as well as many other publications he has been involved with to help you through a crisis.

Go to: http://www.itsoknottobeok.com.

I Love A Cop, (Revised Edition): What Police Families Need To Know

This easy-to-read self-help book prepares cops and their loved ones to cope with the stress of police life and work. Author Ellen Kirschman, Ph.D., a renowned police psychologist, has worked with police officers and their families for over twenty years.

For reviews and to order *I Love A Cop*, search Amazon.com.

Magazines for Law Enforcement Officers

There are many excellent online and print magazines for law enforcement officers that feature articles that keep you informed about everything from equipment, armor, tactics and weapons to peer support and how to cope with stress. Reading articles by other cops keeps you part of the law enforcement community at times that you feel isolated and alone because of stress and trauma. Here are some of them.

9-1-1 Magazine, managing emergency communications. Go to: www.9-1-1magazine.com.

American Cop: tools and training for real cops. Go to: www. americancopmagazine.com.

Blue Line: Canada's National Law Enforcement Magazine. Go to: www.blueline.ca.

Chief Learning Officer: for academy directors and training supervisors. Go to: www.clomedia.com.

Chief of Police Magazine: subjects that would influence decision-making within police departments. Go to: www.aphf.org/thechief.html.

Corrections Forum Magazine: for senior corrections management. Go to: www.criminaljusticemedia.com.

Corrections Today: a publication of the American Correctional Association. Go to: www.aca.org.

Dispatch Monthly: news and information about public safety communications. Go to: www.911dispatch.com.

Evidence Technology Magazine: for evidence/crime scene technicians or those engaged in forensic analysis. Go to: www.evidencemagazine.com.

FBI Law Enforcement Bulletin: monthly. Go to: www.fbi. gov/publications/leb/leb.htm.

FLETC Journal: an unofficial law enforcement training magazine published by the Federal Law Enforcement Training Center. Go to: www.fletc.gov.

Law & Order Magazine: publication for police management, and everybody else in law enforcement. Go to: www.hendonpub.com/ publications/lawandorder.

Law Officer: tactics, technology and Training for Today's Law Enforcement Officer. Go to: www.policeone.com

Law Enforcement Technology: for law enforcement decision-makers. Go to: www.officer.com/magazines/let.

National Institute of Justice Journal: research, development and evaluation agency of the US Department of Justice. Go to: www.ojp.usdoj.gov/nij/journals.

PI Magazine: professional investigator magazine. Go to: www. pimagazine.com.

Police and Security News: information source for law enforcement and Homeland Security. Go to: www.police andsecuritynews.com.

Police Chief Magazine: official voice of the International Association of Chiefs of Police. Go to: www.policechief magazine.org.

Police Marksman Magazine: tactical excellence in law enforcement training. Go to: www.policeone.com/police marksman.

Police Magazine: for the community of cops. Go to: www.police mag.com.

PORAC Magazine: publication of the Police Officers Research Association of California. Go to: www.porac.org/ news.html.

Police Review: a magazine for UK police published by Jane's, the same people that publish military books. Go to: www. policereview.com

Public Safety IT Magazine. Go to: www.hendonpub.com/ publications/publicsafetyit.

Security Management: a magazine published by ASIS International, an international organization for security professionals. Go to: www.securitymanagement.com.

Sheriff Magazine: publication of the National Sheriff's Association. Go to: www.sheriffs.org/publications.

SWAT Digest: a platform that meshes the tactical skills, training and knowledge of both law enforcement and military special operations. Go to: www.swatdigest.com.

Tactical Response: the publication for Special Enforcement. Go to http://www.hendonpub.com/publications/tacticalresponse.

The Blues Police Newspaper: Texas's oldest and largest police newspaper. Go to: www.thebluesnews.com

Women Police Magazine: official publication of the Inter-national Association of Women Police. Go to: www.iawp.org.

Peer Support Training Manual
On police psychotherapist Nancy Bohl's website, she offers a series of very helpful articles including crisis intervention, critical incident trauma, and trauma in the workplace. She also offers breathing and relaxation techniques and surveys and self-tests for compassion fatigue, depression, work addiction risk, alcoholism, stress and anger.

Go to: http://www.thecounselingteam.com. Write: The Counseling Team, 1881 Business Center Drive, Suites 11 & 12, San Bernardino, CA 92408. Call Toll-free: 800-222-9691. Phone: 909-884-0133.

National Center for Crisis Management Bookstore
The National Center for Crisis Management (NCCM), in collaboration with The American Academy of Experts in Traumatic Stress (AAETS), have an excellent bookstore that distributes books and other resources for the professional and survivor alike.

They offer books that help professionals address crisis situations and the emergent psychological needs of those exposed to traumatic events. Many of the books address traumatic stress and crisis management.

These publications include subjects such as crisis response in our schools, university crisis response, becoming stress-resistant, community response to terrorism, acute traumatic stress management, how to deal with anxiety and nervous fatigue, group crisis support, depression, crisis intervention and many more.

Go to: http://www.aaets.org. or http://www.nc-cm.org. Write: AAETS/NCCM, Administrative Offices, 368 Veterans Memorial Highway, Commack, NY 11725. Phone: 631-543-2217.

Spiritual Survival for Law Enforcement

The book titled _Spiritual Survival for Law Enforcement_ by Cary A. Friedman is a must have for every police officer. Too often we focus on our emotional, psychological and physical wellbeing, but forget that we are primarily spiritual creatures having a physical experience. The book provides spiritual fortification for officers faced with horrific experiences that challenge their most deeply held personal beliefs. Focused on inner peace and finding clarity, this practical guide is jam-packed with exercises, tools, and insights that you can't do without. As Friedman says, it "nourishes the spirit of everyday heroes."

A much admired chaplain and rabbi, Friedman writes about coping with trauma regardless of religious denomination. He is the spirituality consultant to the FBI's Behavioral Science Unit in Quantico, Virginia, and to the law enforcement community in general.

The author of five books, he has also written the book _Wisdom from the Batcave_. In 18 lighthearted chapters, he uses Batman's example to illustrate profound truths such as How to Triumph over Adversity, the Value of Inspiring Others, and A Better Definition of Victory. Focusing on relationships with self, others and the community, the book illustrates how to live a better life, something trauma sufferers want and need.

Go to: http://www.spiritualsurvivalbook.com and to http://www.batwisdom.com. Write: Rabbi Cary A. Friedman, Compass Books, PO Box 3091, Linden, NJ. Phone: 908-868-1023.

Trust After Trauma

One of the most prolific authors on trauma is Aphrodite Matsakis, Ph.D. She has written many easy-to-read books on trauma's aftermath, including _I Can't Get Over It, A Handbook for Trauma Survivors, Second Edition_, and _Trust After Trauma, A Guide To Relationships for Survivors and Those Who Love Them_. Many people consider _I Can't Get Over It_ a bible for trauma sufferers. Her most recent book for law enforcement is titled, _In Harm's Way: Help for the Wives of Military Men, Police, EMTs & Firefighters_. She also wrote the publication titled, _Back from the Front: Combat Trauma, Love, and the Family_.

For descriptions of her books, go to: http://www. amazon.com.

* * *

Rape Support

Although figures vary widely, as many as 300,000 women, children, adolescents and men are raped every year in the U.S. Police officers must be prepared to help these badly traumatized people who are candidates for PTSD.

Sometimes police officers who have suffered rape or sexual assault have unresolved issues. If you have been raped or sexually assaulted, please contact your local rape crisis center.

Brazos County Rape Crisis Center (BCRCC)

Brazos County offers a confidential national hotline for all victims who were raped, sexually abused or assaulted. It's online Information Center features articles on subjects like rape awareness, what to do when attacked, phases of rape trauma, sexual harassment, stalking, the road to recovery, regaining control and date rape drugs.

Go to: http://rapecrisisbv.org. Write: BCRCC, P.O. Box 3082, Bryan, TX 77805. Phone: For help, call their hotline at: 979-731-1000. You can also e-mail them at reaching out@rapecrisisbv.org.

Hope for Healing.org

This website gives survivors of rape a voice. It allows survivors, spouses, friends and men who've been abused to network with each other through chat room and forums. The organization distributes a free quarterly newsletter, provides workshops on prayer journaling as a way to recovery, and a lending library.

The website also provides information about PTSD, depression, eating disorders, and domestic violence.

You've heard of the AIDS Quilt. This group is creating the *Hope Quilt for Victims of Sexual or Domestic Violence.* If you wish to add your "story," please visit the website for details.

Go to: http://www.hopeforhealing.org. Write: Hope for Healing.Org, 153 E. Broadway Blvd., #113, Jefferson City, TN 37760. Phone: 865-933-8769.

If you are looking for counseling, please see the next item called RAINN. If you need a suicide helpline, call 800-273-8255.

Rape, Abuse and Incest National Network (RAINN)

RAINN operates a toll-free twenty-four hour confidential hotline for victims of sexual assault in the U.S. When someone phones, the call is immediately routed to the nearest rape crisis center. RAINN is the nation's largest anti-sexual assault organization, and carries out programs to prevent sexual assault, help victims, and ensure that rapists are brought to justice. On the website are facts, articles and health issues about rape.

Go to: http://rainn.org. Write: RAINN, 2000 L Street, NW, Suite 406, Washington, DC 20036. Phone: 202-544-1034. Hotline: 800-656-4673, extension 3.

Sexual Abuse of Males
Prepared by psychologist Jim Hopper of McLean Hospital and Harvard Medical School, this far-reaching website focuses on sexually abused boys, male survivors of sexual abuse and recovered memories.

Go to: http://www.jimhopper.com. E-mail: drhopper@jim hopper.com.

See also: *Domestic Abuse*
For more resources about rape.

* * *

Religion-Oriented/Faith-Based Support
Chaplains are often trained in counseling officers and their families about the aftermath of trauma.[2] Groups that are affiliated with a particular religious outlook also offer comfort and support.

American Muslim Law Enforcement Officers Association (AMLEOA)
AMLEOA, Inc., is a nationwide effort, within the law enforcement community, dedicated to fostering respectful relationships between the American Muslim community, its attendant institutions, and the law enforcement agencies of the United States of America and its Territories.

The website offers news and events happening in the community, and discusses issues of the day. For better understanding and tolerance, this website provides a much needed resource.

Go to: http://www.amleoa.com. Write: AMLEOA, PO Box 24584, Brooklyn, NY 11202. Phone: 718-998-1549.

Fellowship of Christian Peace Officers
Teaching the Gospel of Jesus, this organization offers training in basic ministry skills. With more than sixty active chapters in the U.S., the Fellowship provides a source of peace and nourishment for the soul.

Go to: http://www.fcpo.org. Write: Grant Wolf, Executive Director, 1801 Bailey Avenue, PO Box 3686, Chattanooga, TN 37404-0686. Phone: 423-622-1234.

International Conference of Police Chaplains (ICPC)

When chaplains work in the police world, they help everyone regardless of religious background including law enforcement officers, their families, other department members, the community and the incarcerated. The ICPC provides information, support and training opportunities to members of the organization and offers assistance to police agencies seeking to start or improve their chaplaincy program.

With members in every U.S. state, numerous Canadian provinces and several other countries, many chaplains are trained in counseling officers and their families affected by trauma. The website provides the e-mail addresses of chaplains in a number of U.S. cities.

The website also mentions a number of important books. Visit www.Amazon.com for descriptions and ordering information for *Chaplaincy in Law Enforcement: What It Is and How To Do It*; *Mastering Law Enforcement Chaplaincy*; and *Law Enforcement Funeral Manual: A Practical Guide for Law Enforcement Agencies*.

Go to: http://www.icpc4cops.org/. Write: ICPC, P.O. Box 5590, Destin, FL 32540-5590. Phone: 850-654-9736.

Jews In Law Enforcement

The National Shomrim Society's purpose is to offer comfort and support to those of the Jewish faith in law enforcement. Their motto back in 1958 was: "*So that police, fire and public safety officers of the Jewish faith may join together for the welfare of all.*" And that guiding principle still rings true. The organization has branches in about 20 states.

The website provides a Jewish Q&A, a chaplain's message, upcoming events, information on their annual convention, a chat room, member news, links to many member chapters, and more.

Go to: http://www.nationalshomrim.org. Write: National Shomrim, c/o Marty Turetzky, 264 East Broadway, #C1905, New York, NY 10002. Phone: 212-777-7809.

A personal website created by a Jewish cop offers support, and explores the meaning, philosophies and ethics behind Jewish cops. It is a call for tolerance and under-standing. Among other things, the site links to Judaism 101, a course in the basics.

Go to: http://www.angelfire.com/on/JodyHomePg/jewish cops.html

With similar aims and objectives of support and under-standing, the United Kingdom has an organization called the Jewish Police Association. Go to: http://www.jewishpolice association.org.uk.

Law Enforcement Chaplaincy Sacramento (LECS)

Founded in 1977, and run by senior chaplains Mindi and Frank Russell, Law Enforcement Chaplaincy Sacramento is a nonprofit organization providing nonsectarian crisis support to law enforcement and the general community around the Sacramento area. As a result of its achievements over the years, the Chaplaincy has been cited as a national model for communities throughout the U.S., and departments wishing to expand their chaplaincy program or start one should check out this website and organization.

The chaplaincy provides chaplains from diverse backgrounds, including Christian, Jewish and Muslim, to help law enforcement officers, first responders, and civilians in crisis.

It offers many programs on what it takes to become a police chaplain. These include classes on stress management, death notification, PTSD, burnout, legal liability, confidentiality, ethics, responding to a crisis situation, the police family, substance abuse, suicide, and officer injury and death.

Go to: http://sacchaplains.com. Write: Law Enforcement Chaplaincy Sacramento, 10399 Rockingham Drive, Sacramento, CA 95827. Phone: 916-857-1801.

Peace Officers for Christ International (POFCI)

The main purpose of the organization is to support cops and their families. As well as an electronic journal, the group offers conferences, couples' retreats and other programs.

Go to: http://www.pofci.org. Write: POFCI, 3000 W. MacArthur Blvd., Suite 426, Santa Ana, CA 92704. Phone: 714-426-7632.

See also: *Publications*

For Chaplain/Rabbi Cary A. Friedman's book, *Spiritual Survival for Law Enforcement.*

* * *

Resiliency

To be resilient means that you adapt well to adverse conditions. Many of us have a natural, some say inborn, resiliency when bad things happen. We spring back from crises. However, our upbringing, genetics, or how we've responded to crises in the past may determine how resilient we are in the future. Nevertheless, no matter how we presently respond to suffering or hardships, we can learn to be more resilient. We can build better coping skills.

Mayo Clinic

On the website for the Mayor Clinic, there are excellent tips for how to build resiliency skills. Such things as building strong relationships with family and friends, using humor and laughter during stressful situations, building on the skills that got you through other tough times, and maintaining perspective. The site also discusses how resiliency offers protection from depression and PTSD.

Go to: http://www.mayoclinic.com/health/resilience/ MH00078

Dr. Michael Norman

Dr. Michael Norman is a highly respected chiropractor and speaker who takes a holistic approach to dealing with trauma and building resiliency. On his website, he discusses how good nutrition, exercise, a finely tuned nervous system, and a positive attitude to life help create resiliency.

His site offers his book, *Above, Down, Inside & Out, Unleashing Your Spiritual Giant Within*, that discusses the relationship between sickness and the subluxated nervous system, among other things. His online Resiliency Quiz (reproduced in *CopShock* in Appendix 1) is the only self-test I've seen that tests not only physical and mental resiliency, but also spiritual resiliency to withstand life's calamities.

As one who has received excellent care from chiropractors for more than 30 years, I highly recommend that you check out this website.

Go to: http://www.DrMichaelNorman.com. Write: 3740 N. Josey Lane, Suite 216, Carrollton, TX 75007. Phone: 972-394-3350.

Resiliency Center

The Resiliency Center website features the work of Dr. Al Siebert, an ex-paratrooper and internationally known researcher into the nature of highly resilient survivors. His book *The Survivor Personality* is world-renowned, and his latest book, *The Resiliency Advantage*, shows how to thrive under pressure and bounce back from setbacks.

On his website, he shares articles about how to develop resiliency, combat stress, and offers resiliency success stories, a learning CD course, books, videotapes, and his free e-newsletter. The website also offers a resiliency quiz that you can fill out on the spot and receive your score.

Go to: http://www.resiliencycenter.com. Write: The Resiliency Center, PO Box 535, Portland, OR 97207. Phone: 503-289-3295.

Trauma and Resiliency Resources

Dr. Eva Usadi is a New York City psychotherapist in practice for more than twenty years who helps people affected by acute and posttraumatic stress and anxiety disorders, which includes PTSD. On September 11th, 2001, she was among the first clinicians to report for duty, organizing support services for those searching for loved ones. As a member of the Red Cross Disaster Mental Health Team, she assisted people at the Armory, and was then deployed to Ground Zero where she counseled rescue/ recovery workers for three months. She has continued to work with first responders in her private office in Manhattan. She is now helping returning troops from Iraq and Afghanistan with PTSD symptoms.

On her website, she features articles for first responders and troops, and also offers links to helpful websites.

Go to: http://www.traumaandresiliencyresources.org. Write: Dr. Eva Usadi, Trauma and Resiliency Resources, Inc., 16 West 9th Street, Suite 5E, New York, NY 10011. Phone: 212-532-6574.

See also: Chapter 14 in *CopShock* about Resiliency, and take the Resiliency quiz in Appendix 1.

* * *

Retirement

A law enforcement officer's retirement is a major life event. Everything he or she is and has worked for seems to suddenly come to an end. This may result in depression and trigger memories of traumatic experiences long buried. An officer must prepare for a successful retirement.

Police Retiree Handbook

Although you may not be part of the Fairfax County Police Officers Retirement System in Virginia, that county's retiree handbook published online is an excellent resource for police retirees everywhere. It provides questions to ask before retirement and what to do after leaving the force.

Go to: http://www.fairfaxcounty.gov/retbrd/PoliceHand book.pdf.

For retirement benefits from Social Security, be sure to call at least three months before retirement: 800-772-1213.

POPPA Retiree Program

POPPA volunteer retirees trained as PSOs answer the 24-hour Retiree Help-Line covering the New York Metro area and other states. They help retirees with stress and trauma related problems and refer them to competent professionals, as PTSD can be debilitating long after retirement.

Go to: http://www.poppainc.com. Phone: 800-599-1085.

Retired Peace Officers Association of California (RPOAC)

All retired peace officers, in or out of California, are eligible for membership in RPOAC, a watchdog organization dedicated to protecting retired peace officers' interests, especially benefits. It operates through the Peace Officers Research Association of California (PORAC) and the National Association of Police Organizations (NAPO) in Washington, DC. PORAC conducts critical incident stress and line-of-duty death seminars.

Go to: http://www.rpoac.org. Write: RPORAC, PO Box 1239, Colfax, CA 95713. Call toll-free: 800-743-7622.

Retirement Pilot Study

Psychologist Daniel A. Goldfarb runs a counseling center for Long Island Law Enforcement. In this pilot study, he attempts to predict retirement satisfaction in police officers. Dr. Goldfarb comments on retired officers who show signs of stress, depression and anxiety.

To examine this study, go to: http://www.heavy badge.com. Then click on the "retirement" button. Dr. Goldfarb says that he is surprised at the level of stress experienced by retiring and retired cops. He is reminded of the old saying: "*If you are what you do, and you don't, you AIN'T!*" But the results are not as bad as they sound. It seems that if officers prepare for their retirement, then things usually go well.

Retirement Test

While reviewing Dr. Goldfarb's study mentioned previously, you will notice a button that says "Take the Test." Go for it, and you may find out how ready you are for retirement. Go to: http://www.heavybadge.com, and click on the "Retirement" button.

10-13 Clubs of America

The 10-13 Club is a national organization of retired New York City police officers. It is dedicated to "protecting, preserving and pursuing the rights" of the retiree.

Go to: http://www.ny10-13amer.org. For New York, write: New York 10-13 Association, 260-09 Hillside Avenue, Floral Park, NY 11004. Phone: 718-343-7271. For Florida, write: 10-13 Clubs of America, P.O. Box 1013, Lecanto, FL 34460. Phone: 352-527-0347.

*   *   *

Stress Management

To control symptoms of PTSD and the everyday pressures of the job, officers need to manage their stress. But how? They can learn a variety of effective techniques and methods that may include rest and relaxation, exercise, nutrition, yoga, deep breathing, hypnosis, massage and meditation. They could involve humor, Tai Chi, time management strategies, assertiveness training, spiritual awakening and establishing support networks.

I once gave myself a gift—once a week for a year I got a massage. And it was the best thing I've ever done to relieve the stress. Bob Hope said that the reason he had lived so long was because he got a massage everyday. In fact, his massage person traveled with him around the world. He was so relaxed he couldn't help being funny. For those of us without Hope's financial resources, every once in awhile is a great thing to do.

There are no rights or wrongs in stress management, only what works for you. The Internet offers an abundance of sources for understanding and employing stress management. Here are just a few of them.

American Institute of Stress (AIS)

Run by health professionals, the AIS serves as a clearing house for information on all stress related subjects. The group can provide a great deal of information on stress in police and law enforcement officials as well as on PTSD. Among the founding members were prominent figures like Hans Selye, Norman Cousins and Linus Pauling.

Online, the organization provides fact sheets and links to other stress resources. Readers can order in-formational packets on stress or health related issues, videos and books.

Members of the AIS Board of Trustees serve on the advisory boards of organizations devoted to understanding PTSD and stress in law enforcement officials. These subjects are regularly addressed in AIS' monthly newsletter, as well as at the annual International Montreux Congress on Stress.

Go to: http://www.stress.org. Write: Director of Communications, The AIS, 124 Park Avenue, Yonkers, NY 10703. Phone: 914-963-1200.

Institute for Stress Management (ISM)

A consulting and training group, the Institute offers free reports, articles and posters online. The articles feature stress management tips, frequently asked questions about sleep as well as other subjects.

Go to: http://www.hyperstress.com. Write: The Institute for Stress Management, 3023 Shannon Lakes, N., #102, Tallahassee, FL 32309. Phone: 850-668-0696.

Self-Help Magazine for Good Mental Health

Among other resources, this online publication offers a free newsletter, articles, and information on how to relax, meditate and manage stress. It provides discussion groups on many topics, including alcohol use, depression, anxiety, eating disorders, terrorism and death of a loved one.

Go to: http://www.selfhelpmagazine.com.

Street Survival Seminar

I mentioned the Street Survival Seminar and Calibre Press, a division of PoliceOne.com, earlier in a different context, but they deserve repeating here. Calibre Press is the world's foremost independent source of law enforcement training materials, books and seminars. Offered around the U.S., its three day Street Survival® Seminar focuses not only on surviving threats on the job and hostility in court, but Day Three concentrates on speeding up emotional recovery from traumatic events, and how to improve family communication at home and on the job to reduce stress.

For Calibre Press or the Street Survival Seminar go to: www.CalibrePress.com. Write: 7616 LBJ Freeway, Suite 405, Dallas, TX 75251. Phone toll free: 800-323-0037. Main: 214-545-3060.

The Stress Doc

Sometimes we take things so seriously we forget to laugh at our own foibles. AOL's and the Internet's "Online Psychotherapist"™ Mark Gorkin, LICSW, a.k.a. The Stress Doc, is a therapist who uses humor as a therapy tool. His website entertains while exploring the management of stress and creatively dealing with conflict. He is the author of *Practice Safe Stress*.

Go to: http://www.stressdoc.com. Write: Mark Gorkin, Stress Doc Enterprises, 9629 Elrod Road, Kensington, MD 20895. Phone: 301-946-0865.

Stress Education Center

John Mason, Ph.D., gives stress relief seminars to many organizations including police and fire departments. His website offers information and articles about coping with stress. His book *Guide To Stress Reduction* and audio stress management tapes are available.

Go to: http://www.dstress.com. Write: L. John Mason, Ph.D., 1258 Eagle Crest Drive, Oak Harbor, WA 98277. Phone: 360-593-3833.

Stress Free Net

Health care professionals at Stress Free allow online visitors to take a free stress vulnerability test. Other features include a therapist directory and stress audit.

Go to: http://www.stressfree.com.

Stress Management

Created by Mark Perloe, M.D., P.C., this web page examines the concepts of optimal stress, managing stress better and eliminating stress.

Go to: http://www.ivf.com/stress.html.

Stress Management from Mind Tools

With over 4,000,000 visitors each year, this popular website offers a great deal of information about what stress is, how to avoid burnout, and what techniques you can use to lessen the negative aspects of stress. It explores the idea of good stress versus bad stress. It offers a burnout self-test, and many worthwhile links.

Go to: http://www.mindtools.com/smpage.html. Write: Mind Tools, Ltd., 2nd Floor, 145-157 St. John Street, London EC1V-4PY United Kingdom

The Web's Stress Management & Emotional Wellness Page

Ernesto A. Randolfi, Ph.D., provides a wealth of information about stress management on his website. His links cover a wide territory, exploring areas such as humor, relaxing your body, crisis intervention and PTSD, stress in the workplace, and emotional self-help links. To access the many links, click on The Web's Stress Management and Emotional Wellness page.

Go to: http://www.OptimalHealthConcepts.com. Write: Optimal Health Concepts, 1250 Kootenai Avenue, Billings, MT 59105-2088. Phone: 406-657-2123 (day) or 406-252-9797 (eve).

* * *

Suicide Support

If you are contemplating suicide, please consult the first few pages of the telephone book under headings like Crisis Counseling, Suicide Prevention or Suicide Hotline. For a national call, dial the 24-hour toll-free National Suicide Lifeline at **800-273-8255** or the National Hopeline Network at **800-784-2433**.

As an option, you may e-mail The Samaritans suicide support organization at: **jo@samaritans.org**. Your message will be answered within twenty-four hours.

More police officers die by their own hand than are killed in-the-line-of-duty. Yet suicide of police officers is rarely talked about. With few support groups for families, friends and coworkers of officers who kill themselves, those left shocked and in pain often feel deserted. But there are many sources they can consult. For police officers feeling depressed or suicidal, they may want to talk to their peer support officers. If the department doesn't offer peer support, you may wish to check out the resources that follow.

American Association of Suicidology (AAS)

More than 31,000 Americans kill themselves every year, and worldwide the figure is around 1,000,000. This leaves millions of devastated loved ones and friends behind wondering why. The number of non-fatal suicide attempts is far greater. The AAS serves as a national clearing house for information about suicide. It offers books and resources such as fact sheets, statistics and public education materials. On the website, the organization describes what steps to take to get help for someone thinking of committing suicide. In addition, the group offers referrals to suicide survivor support groups.

Go to: http://www.suicidology.org. Write: AAS, 5221 Wisconsin Avenue, NW, Washington, DC 20015. Phone: 202-237-2280.

American Foundation for Suicide Prevention (AFSP)

The AFSP provides a considerable amount of information and support online. It offers programs to help survivors cope with loss and features a national directory of survivor support groups in U.S. states for families and friends. The website gives the warning signs that a loved one may be contemplating suicide.

The list of resources includes videos, books, personal stories and studies on suicide.

Go to: http://www.afsp.org. Write: AFSP, 120 Wall Street, 22nd Floor, New York, NY 10005. Call toll-free: 1-888-333-2377. Phone: 212-363-3500.

Befrienders Worldwide

With access in 21 languages, this website and its affiliates sole purpose is to reduce suicide worldwide. It has 31,000 volunteers in almost 40 countries with that one goal. Through hotlines and e-mails, the Befrienders offer a safe and confidential environment to talk about your problems and pain.

There are member centers in Argentina, Armenia, Australia, Barbados, Belgium, Brazil, Canada, China (Hong Kong), Cyprus, Denmark, Egypt, Estonia, France, Hungary, India, Italy, Japan, Kosovo UNMIK, Lithuania, Malaysia, Mauritius, New Zealand, Norway, Poland, Portugal, Russia, Serbia & Montenegro, Singapore, South Africa, South Korea, Sri Lanka, St. Vincent & Grenadines, Sweden, Thailand, Trinidad & Tobago, Ukraine, United Kingdom (& ROI), USA and Zimbabwe.

On the Befrienders website, you can access a list and contact information for centers worldwide.

Affiliated with the Samaritans (see entry later in this section), the organization provides articles and help to those who are bereaved by suicide, who self-harm, who are subject to bullying, who have issues with sexual orientation and gender identity. It has information and advice about depression, suicidal feelings, the warning signs of suicide, and addresses what to do if you are worried about somebody who is suicidal.

Go to://www.befrienders.org. Write: International Officer, Samaritans, Upper Mill, Kingston Road, Ewell, Surrey KT17 2AF, United Kingdom.

Centre for Suicide Prevention (CSP)

The CSP is a large English language suicide information resource center and library located in Canada. Although not a crisis center, it has extensive information on suicide prevention, intervention and trends. It provides pamphlets, information kits, videos and books helpful to organizations and crisis centers in Canada and the United States. There is a charge for some of the publications.

If you are afraid someone might be considering suicide, the CSP website suggests questions to ask and things to say to comfort that person.

Go to: http://www.suicideinfo.ca. Write: Centre for Suicide Prevention, Suite 320, 1202 Centre Street, SE, Calgary, Alberta B T2G 5A5 Canada. Phone: 403-245-3900.

Daniel W. Clark

Clinical psychologist Daniel W. Clark teaches suicide intervention courses for the International Critical Incident Stress Foundation (ICISF). These courses are geared toward first responders, law enforcement officers, firefighters, peer supporters, and therapists. I attended one of his courses and came away with a great deal of information and enlightenment. If you have the opportunity to attend his courses, Dr. Clark is an excellent presenter.

His website contains lots of information concerning suicide, suicide survivors, and suicide intervention.

Go to: http://www.criticalconcepts.org. Phone: 360-786-0292. E-mail: drdan@criticalconcepts.org.

The National Police Suicide Foundation (NPSF)

The mission of the National P.O.L.I.C.E. Suicide Foundation is to provide suicide awareness and prevention training programs and support services that will meet the psychological and spiritual needs of emergency workers and their families. Through quarterly membership newsletters the organization provides information on suicide support group services, seminars, counseling hot lines, statistics, and provide a means of supportive communication for survivors.

In particular, Robert E. Douglas Jr.'s *Police Suicide Awareness Training Program*, and books titled *Hope Beyond the Badge*, and *Death With No Valor* are excellent resources.

Go to: http://psf.org. E-mail: redoug2001@aol.com.

The National Suicide Prevention Lifeline

The National Suicide Prevention Lifeline is a 24-hour, toll-free suicide prevention service available to anyone in suicidal crisis. After you dial the number below, you will be routed to the closest crisis center. With over 120 crisis centers across the US, their mission is to provide immediate assistance. They encourage you to call about yourself or about someone you care about. The call is free and confidential.

Go to: http://www.suicidepreventionlifeline.org. Phone toll-free: 800-273-8255. You can also call 800-800-784-2433.

The Samaritans

For over forty years, The Samaritans have helped people in crisis. As well as offering crisis services, the organization provides training for volunteers. Although it is based in the UK, associated groups have formed in the U.S. and other countries, and people from all over the world use its 24-hour suicide prevention e-mail service.

Many people find it easier to express themselves using computers than talking on the telephone. Please be aware that a response is not provided immediately, but within a day.

Go to: http://www.samaritans.org. For online response, e-mail: jo@samaritans.org.

In an emergency, phone The Samaritans UK: 08457 90 90 90 or in the Republic of Ireland: 1850 60 90 90. For information, write: Chris, P.O. Box 9090, Stirling, FK8 2SA UK.

The Samaritans are also in the United States. Go to: http://www.timesunion.com/communities/samaritans. Write: Samaritans USA, PO Box 5228, Albany, NY 12205. Phone Helpline at: 518-689-4673. E-mail: samaritans@ monad.net.

See also: Befrienders Worldwide earlier in this section for hotlines in many countries and US states.

Suicide Awareness\Voices of Education (SAVE™)

SAVE's mission is to educate about suicide and to speak for suicide survivors. The website focuses on the symptoms of depression as danger signs for suicide. It describes some of the misconceptions about suicide and offers suggestions on how to help someone who is depressed or suicidal. Please see the Depression Checklist provided by SAVE in Appendix 6.

Go to: http://www.save.org. Write: SAVE, 8120 Penn Avenue S., Suite 470, Bloomington, MN 55431. Phone: 952-946-7998. Toll-free hotline: 800-273-8255.

Survivors of Law Enforcement Suicide (SOLES)

In 1989, Teresa Tate lost her police officer husband to suicide and had no where to turn. Not wanting anyone else to feel so abandoned, she created the SOLES support group. An experienced survivor, she offers support and information to people who are suffering this terrible loss.

As well as comforting people who contact her, she publishes a newsletter, provides the names of suicide support groups across the country and teaches people how to create their own support groups. She is active in the organization called *Tears of a Cop (TOAC)*. See website information for TOAC later in this section.

Write: Teresa Tate, 2708 SW 48th Terrace, Cape Coral, FL 33914. Phone: 941-541-1150.

Survivors of Suicide (SOS)

The person who committed suicide is not the only tragedy. The people left behind die a thousand times asking themselves why it happened. The purpose of the Survivors of Suicide website is to help those who have lost a loved one to suicide resolve their grief and pain. This site provides a safe place for survivors and friends of survivors to share their struggle and pain and offer comfort and under-standing to others who have experienced a similar loss. Among other resources on this website are help topics such as understanding suicide, beyond understanding, how to help a survivor heal, and a directory of SOS support groups.

Go to: http://www.survivorsofsuicide.com.

Tears of a Cop

Cheryl Rehl-Hahn's brother killed himself. He was a police officer with the Philadelphia PD, and ever since his death, Cheryl has been asking herself why he did it and what could we do to prevent it from happening to other officers. This website is dedicated to his memory and promotes awareness of the epidemic of police PTSD and suicide. The site offers resources, interviews, articles, books, and information on PTSD and Critical Incident Stress Debriefing techniques.

Go to: http://www.tearsofacop.com. E-mail Cheryl at: badge 000@tearsofacop.com.

* * *

Treatment Centers for PTSD

There are many good treatment facilities available for treating alcohol and drug addiction, depression and eating disorders, among other things. At the same time, they often treat reactions to trauma and PTSD. But ask to be sure that trauma treatment is a priority for them. If you are suffering from drug addiction, you can often just tell them you wish to deal with alcoholism, which is a more acceptable addiction as far as departments are concerned. After you arrive, tell them your problem and you will be treated for drugs, and it will likely be kept confidential.

At one time, there were several treatment centers focused on helping police officers and emergency services personnel exclus-ively. There are two areas of thought on this subject. Many cops don't want to interact with civilians when they are being treated, especially if they would end up mingling with drug addicts who they would typically arrest. They want fellow cops around them who understand what they are going through. On the other hand, many police officers want to get away from being with other cops so they can heal and not feel any peer pressure.

Whatever your feelings on the matter, this conflict has been largely taken out of your hands. After HMOs took over the medical field, most of these treatment centers were forced into diversifying or closing.

There are now only two treatment centers in the United States that cater exclusively to first responders, police, fire, EMS and other human service personnel. Ask your peer support people for their treatment program and facility suggestions. Not every program is suitable for every person, so ask a lot of questions before you consider going.

On-Site Academy—Massachusetts

The On-Site Academy is a non-profit residential treatment and training center for critical incident stress management. The Academy serves emergency service workers who are in distress, and the program is for all law enforcement, fire service, EMS, or other human service personnel who are temporarily overwhelmed by the stress of their jobs, by what they have seen, and what they have been through.

The Massachusetts based Academy helps them get back to the job or to a new beginning and quality of life with the tools necessary to master critical incident stress. The On-Site Academy has a skilled staff of licensed clinicians, CISM Advanced trained peers, national trauma consultants, and additional support staff from Police, Fire and Emergency Medical Services.

Go to: http://onsiteacademy.org. Phone: 978-632-3518. Page: 781-553-0542 or 978-245-1199. E-mail: kims@onsiteacademy.org.

West Coast Post-Trauma Retreat (WCPR)—California

The WCPR program is for first responders whose lives have been impacted by their work experience. The WCPR residential program provides an educational experience designed to help current and retired first responders recognize the signs and symptoms of work-related stress including Posttraumatic Stress Disorder (PTSD) in themselves and in others.

Licensed clinicians, chaplains, and peer support members from police, fire and EMS make up the clinical team and volunteer their services. WCPR's goal is to help emergency service professionals and retirees regain control over their lives and either return to work with a new perspective on stress and coping, move on with their lives if that is a more appropriate decision, or simply enjoy retirement.

I have personally recommended WCPR to a few police officers. They have given me feedback about the program, and were very happy with how they were treated.

Go to: http://www.wcpr2001.org. Phone: 415-721-9789. E-mail: wcpr2001@ aol.com.

* * *

Veterans Of War

Research on Vietnam veterans shows that exposure to combat is the single most important predictor of PTSD.[3]

Combat veterans from any war who become police officers may carry memories of horror into police work. Those with PTSD symptoms might be more comfortable attending veterans support groups than police groups, especially if many issues are combat-related. They may prefer to go to Department of Veterans Affairs (VA) therapists instead of police peer supporters or Behavioral Science Units. Confidentiality is usually assured in the VA setting, but it's important to confirm that it is.

As war veterans, police officers may be eligible for benefits and services not covered by their departments or unions. The most important issue seems to be health care. Be aware, though, that the VA has reduced its counseling services, and the veteran may have to spend time searching for the right therapist.

In addition to checking out the VA, police officers may wish to investigate the many support groups for veterans. The following represents only a few of the resources available.

Department of Veterans Affairs (VA)

The VA's website features sections on health care and benefits, as well as special sections on disabled, homeless, minority and women veterans. Among many other items, they provide a facilities locator for every state, and a directory of service organizations from the African American Post Traumatic Stress Disorder Association, American Ex-Prisoners of War, the United Spinal Association, to the Women's Army Corps Veterans Association. In their list of top information requests, number 1 is prescription drug refills. Number 6 is the suicide prevention Lifeline. The mammoth size of the organization is reflected in the enormity of the website. Be prepared to spend some time at this site.

Go to: http://www.va.gov.

Disabled American Veterans (DAV)

The DAV website provides information on the organization's legislative initiatives, issues that affect disabled veterans and a help program to aid vets with VA claims. The site even offers a mobile office that will come to your door to explain benefits, and information on transportation available for veterans needing to go to a facility for treatment.

Go to: http://www.dav.org. Write: DAV, National Headquarters, P.O. Box 14301, Cincinnati, OH 45250-0201. Phone: 877-426-2838 or 859-441-7300. For information on PTSD in military veterans, enter "PTSD" in the website's search box.

1st Cavalry Division Association

In the chapter titled "Soldiers," Bob McClellan talks about the 1st Cav. Mostly a social group, the "alumni of the first team" share memories and friendship and engage in charitable work. With chapters across the U.S., veterans of the 1st Cav who fought in Vietnam and other wars may appreciate the camaraderie and emotional support.

Go to: http://www.1cda.org/. Write: 1st Cavalry Division Association, 302 North Main Street, Copperas Cove, TX 76522-1799. Phone: 254-547-6537.

Gulf War Veteran Resource Pages

Privately run by volunteers, the best place to start is the Frequently Asked Questions (FAQs) section. The prime focus of Gulf War sites is Gulf War Syndrome (GWS), "most likely a collection of different illnesses with similar or overlapping symptoms." PTSD and other psychological conditions are blamed less on GWS and the trauma from exposure to toxic chemicals and more on mistreatment by the Department of Defense and Department of Veterans Affairs.

These resource pages provide plenty of information and access to a searchable document library, forums, a self-help guide, a locator to track vets you may know, and a referral network.

Go to: http://www.gulfweb.org.

Iraq and Afghanistan Veterans of America (IAVA)

An article on the IAVA website says, "At least one-in-three Iraq veterans and one-in-nine Afghanistan veterans will face a mental health issue like depression, anxiety, or Posttraumatic Stress Disorder (PTSD). Multiple tours and inadequate rest between deployments have increased the stress of combat. PTSD rates for Iraq veterans are already higher than the rates recorded among veterans of Vietnam."

Iraq and Afghanistan Veterans of America is the nation's largest group dedicated to the Troops and Veterans of the wars in Iraq and Afghanistan, and the civilian supporters of those Troops and Veterans. IAVA represents more than 70,000 veteran members and civilian supporters in all 50 states. IAVA's mission is to educate the public about the wars and to improve the lives of Iraq and Afghanistan veterans and their families. IAVA addresses critical issues facing new veterans and their families, including mental health, Traumatic Brain Injury, a stretched VA system, inadequate health coverage for national guardsmen and reserve-ists, and outdated GI Bill educational benefits.

Go to: http://www.iava.org. Write: IAVA, 770 Broadway, 2nd Floor, New York, NY 10003. Phone: 212-982-9699.

Iraq War Veterans Organization

The Iraq War Veterans Organization was created to organize and represent Operation Iraqi Freedom veterans.

The organization provides information and support for: Operation Iraqi Freedom Veterans, Global War on Terror Veterans, Operation Enduring Freedom Veterans, active military personnel and family members related to pre-deployment, deployment, and post-deployment issues, as well as service member and family Operation Iraqi Freedom Deployment Readiness problems, information about PTSD, Health issues and Veterans Benefits. The Iraq War Veterans Organization website has links to information about Veterans Administration health care, readjustment after deployment, education, employment, military discounts, PTSD issues, support-chat forums, family support and deployment information.

Go to: http://www.iraqwarveterans.org. Contact information for individual board members and the executive committee are on the website.

Korean War Project

New wars tend to exacerbate PTSD symptoms in war veterans. Just reading about conflicts like the Iraq War in the newspaper or seeing them on TV news push many veterans into sleepless nights and flashbacks. According to Hal Barker, dealing with PTSD is the driving force behind this website. The site features books, recollections and connections to friends, families, units, reunions and veterans groups. The featured book *Return to Heartbreak Ridge* tells the story of what PTSD can do to a soldier.

Go to: http://www.koreanwar.org. Write: Korean War Project, PO Box 180190, Dallas, TX 75218. Phone: 214-320-0342.

National Veterans Organization of America (NVO)

Many veterans believe the NVO's website is the most informative site on the web dealing with Veterans, POW/ MIA and PTSD issues. It can take as long as two years for a veteran's claim to be acted upon. The NVO wants to change that. This site describes how to handle claims and legal rights as well as offers insights into congressional action.

Go to: http://www.nvo.org. Write: NVOA, PO Box 2510, Victoria, TX 77902. Phone: 361-356-1215.

South African Veterans Association (SAVA)

SAVA's membership is open to veterans of all armed forces in the world. The group appeals to international organizations for help in understanding how PTSD affects their veterans and citizens after many years of bloodshed and turmoil.

Besides articles about the effects of PTSD, the website also features, *Behind the Lines of the Mind, Healing the Mental Scars of War*, a book by Peter Tucker and Marius van Niekerk. It is a soldier's story and handbook on combat-related stress that includes a section on police PTSD.

Go to: http://www.saveterans.org.za. Write: SAVA, P.O. Box 43759, Fishhoek 7974, Cape Town, South Africa. Phone: +27(0)84-843 13 48.

Veterans of Foreign Wars (VFW)

The VFW represents the interests of millions of veterans from World War I, World War II, Korea, Vietnam, Haiti, Somalia, the Persian Gulf, Grenada, Panama, Lebanon, Afghanistan, Iraq and many other areas of conflict. Its main purpose is to secure aid for veterans and their families in need of benefits claims assistance, rehabilitative, educational and employment services. It provides a free brochure about PTSD,

Go to: http://www.vfw.org. Write: VFW National Headquarters, 406 West 34th Street, Kansas City, MO 64111. Phone: 816-756-3390.

Veterans of the Vietnam War (VVNW)

With 90 posts worldwide, the VVNW was formed in 1980, the VVNW's goal is to serve not only Vietnam veterans, but also anyone who served in the Armed Forces of the United States at any time. The group is active in issues concerning veterans health, public awareness of the POW/MIA problem, homeless vets, Agent Orange, PTSD and public education on the Vietnam War.

Go to: http://www.vvnw.org. Write: 805 So. Township Blvd., Pittston, PA 18640. Phone: 570-603-9740.

World War II U.S. Veterans Website

Now that many World War II veterans are retired and have time to reflect, they realize the quality of their lives could be better, free of agonizing flashbacks, nightmares, anger and survivor guilt.

About a quarter million WWII survivors suffer from traumatic stress. Many have PTSD. Among other things, this site helps WWII vets connect with others suffering from the same condition through their forums.

Go to: http://ww2.vet.org.

See also: *Counseling*
For more referral.

*   *   *

Women-Only Police Associations

To address issues that female officers experience on the job, there is a need for women-only groups. Studies show that women officers subjected to sexual harassment, sexism and prejudice are vulnerable to acquiring PTSD.[4] Women officers are more stressed-out and have higher burn-out rates than men. With a high attrition rate, women officers find that hostility in the workplace is making them sick. A San Francisco police department study concludes that they become more physically exhausted and are more jittery and irritated than male cops. They experience more headaches, backaches, stomachaches and sleep problems.

At the same time, studies also show that women are exceptional at defusing potentially violent situations, and save departments money because they are rarely named in excessive use-of-force lawsuits.

International Association of Women Police (IAWP)
Since 1915, the IAWP has advanced the interests of policewomen, visualizing "a world where women working in the criminal justice professions are treated justly, fairly, and equitably by the agencies they serve."

Spanning the globe, the Association provides a network of support and training for every woman in the criminal justice system, as well as mentoring, peer support, scholarships, networking and resources.

Go to: http://www.iawp.org.

National Center for Women & Policing (NCWP)
Although female officers have proven themselves as good defusers of potentially violent situations, women account for only 13 percent of police officers across the country. A division of the Feminist Majority Foundation, the National Center for Women & Policing (NCWP) promotes increasing the numbers of women at all ranks of law enforcement as a strategy to improve police response to violence against women, reduce police brutality and excessive force, and strengthen community policing.

Among the NCWP's projects are training, networking, internships, leadership development, law enforcement assistance programs, research conferences and more.

Go to: http://www.feminist.org/other/ncwp.asp. Write: NCWP, 433 S. Beverly Hills, CA 90212. Phone: 310-556-2526. E-mail: womencops@feminist.org.

Women In Federal Law Enforcement (WIFLE)

WIFLE promotes gender equity through its leadership education center that provides training, research, scholarships, awards, and networking opportunities in partnership with law enforcement agencies, members and supportive sponsors. Among its goals are assisting agencies recruit, retain, train and promote women in federal law enforcement. The website offers the latest news affecting women federal law enforcement, studies, job availability and more.

Go to: http://www.wifle.org. Write: WIFLE, PMB-204, Suite 102, 2200 Wilson Blvd., Arlington, VA 22201. Phone: 703-548-9211.

Women Peace Officers Association (WPOA)

Formed in 1928, the WPOA of California provides a forum of continuing education and training. It cultivates an atmosphere that encourages camaraderie and an open exchange of ideas.

The organization offers scholarships for law enforcement personnel, supports the Peace Officer's Memorial in Sacramento, monitors legislative information and offers awards for professional achievement and valor. This association serves as a model for female officers wishing to form their own groups.

Go to: http://www.wpoaca.com. Write: WPOA, PO Box 589, Sacramento, CA 95812. Phone: 909-698-6216. E-mail: pres78 @wpoaca.com.

Appendix 1

How is Your Resiliency?

This *Resiliency Quiz* can be found at www.drmichaelnorman.com.

Rate yourself from 1 to 5
**1 = very little   2 = below average   3 = okay
4 = good   5 = very strong**

Physical Resiliency

I take care of myself, maintain healthy habits, and know and respect my limits when I approach them.	1 2 3 4 5
I frequently eat healthy food that nourishes me.	1 2 3 4 5
I have a consistent exercise program that strengthens me.	1 2 3 4 5
I am satisfied with the overall flexibility of my muscles and joints.	1 2 3 4 5
When I go to sleep, I get sufficient rest to re-energize myself.	1 2 3 4 5
I view and perceive my overall health to be excellent.	1 2 3 4 5
My finances are currently organized and sufficient, and I have a hopeful expectation of financial growth.	1 2 3 4 5

Physical Resiliency Total

Mental Resiliency

During a crisis, I can remain calm while effectively and creatively drawing upon my problem-solving skills.	1 2 3 4 5
I know and trust myself, and my decisions, and others do not easily sway me.	1 2 3 4 5
I am happy with my overall level of optimism, and I frequently expect things to turn out well.	1 2 3 4 5
When I view the future, I am hopeful and believe that each decade will get better and better.	1 2 3 4 5
Overall, I am pleased with my current state in life.	1 2 3 4 5
I can easily let go of anger, overcome discouragement, and ask for help.	1 2 3 4 5
In my life, I feel like I choose and rationally control a majority of my responses instead of emotionally reacting to situations.	1 2 3 4 5
I am aware of my feelings and can openly and honestly express them when appropriate or suppress them when not appropriate.	1 2 3 4 5
I am aware and accepting of the things I cannot change and the situations out of my control.	1 2 3 4 5
I am in charge of my thoughts, and I give resistance to harmful, negative thoughts.	1 2 3 4 5
I am happy with my current level of self-esteem and self- confidence.	1 2 3 4 5
I am excited and motivated to continuously learn new things and further my "education".	1 2 3 4 5

Mental Resiliency—Subtotal

Mental Resiliency (Continued from previous page)

I have goals and objectives that excite me about my future. If necessary, I am able to live with current ambiguity, uncertainty, and risk in order to reach them.	1 2 3 4 5
I am good at bouncing back and adapting quickly to misfortune and difficulties.	1 2 3 4 5
I believe my past difficulties have made me stronger and better, and I continuously learn from the experiences of others and myself.	1 2 3 4 5

Mental Resiliency—Subtotal

Subtotal from previous page

Mental Resiliency Total

Spiritual Resiliency

I am comforted by a strong faith, and I have a sense of peace with the meaning and philosophy of my life.	1 2 3 4 5
My spiritual faith and belief grows stronger each year.	1 2 3 4 5
My daily life and actions are congruent with my spiritual faith and moral beliefs.	1 2 3 4 5

Spiritual Resiliency—Subtotal

Spiritual Resiliency (Continued from previous page)

I am involved in charitable and specific works which give to others less fortunate, and I receive a sense of fulfillment.	1 2 3 4 5
I have a healthy sense of humor, and I can make others laugh as well as laugh at myself.	1 2 3 4 5
I receive a sense of fulfillment with the good friendships and loving relationships in my life.	1 2 3 4 5
In human interactions, I seek to understand before trying to be understood. I am a good listener.	1 2 3 4 5
I have harmony in my relationships and can easily put myself in others' shoes. I have an open mind with others.	1 2 3 4 5

Spiritual Resiliency—Subtotal

Subtotal from previous page

Spiritual Resiliency Total

Physical Resiliency Total _____
Mental Resiliency Total _____
Spiritual Resiliency Total _____

Total Score

Scoring Results:
140 or higher   Very Resilient!
115 to 139   Better Than Most
90   to 114   You're Adequate
75   to 89   You're Struggling
74   to under   SEEK HELP!

Appendix 2

Anxiety Potential Self-Evaluation Quiz

This self-evaluation quiz is reproduced with permission from AnxietyCentre.com. Copyright © 2008.

If you suspect that you might suffer from anxiety, complete the quiz, and show it to your health care professional, or go to the AnxietyCentre.com web site, fill out the quiz online, and e-mail your answers for a confidential reply.

1. Do you worry?

☐   Yes. I worry quite a bit and about many things.

☐   Yes. There are some things that I worry about regularly.

☐   Yes. I do worry. But not overly.

☐   Yes. I worry about a few things, but not that often.

☐   No. I wouldn't consider myself a worrier.

2. Are you concerned about losing control?

☐   Not really. I don't need to be in control.

☐   Not really. I'm okay with not being in control all the time.

☐   Yes. Sometimes it bothers me when I'm not in control.

☐   Yes. I like to be in control.

☐   Yes. I HAVE to be in control.

3. Do you ever have thoughts that run on and on and you can't seem to stop them?

☐   No.

☐   Yes. That happens to me sometimes.

☐   Yes. That happens on and off.

☐ Yes. Sometimes it gets quite annoying.

☐ Yes. I feel like this a lot of the time.

4. How have you been feeling emotionally lately?

☐ I feel very satisfied and content.

☐ I feel good. No major problems.

☐ I feel okay.

☐ I'm having some issues right now.

☐ I'm having some major issues.

5. Describe your sleep patterns over the last 4 weeks.

☐ I've been sleeping very well (6 – 8 hours per night of sound sleep).

☐ Not too bad (5 – 7 hours per night, some interruptions).

☐ Average (4 – 6 hours per night, regular disruptions).

☐ Not too good (3 – 5 hours per night with restlessness).

☐ Not good (2 – 4 hours per night with a lot of restlessness).

6. How often do you feel overwhelmed?

☐ Rarely (once or twice a year).

☐ Occasionally (once or twice in six months).

☐ Frequently (once or twice a month).

☐ Regularly (once or twice a week).

☐ Almost always (almost everyday, sometimes I don't).

7. Describe your rest/relaxation habits.

☐ I take regular relaxation and rest breaks, including holidays.

☐ I take frequent rest breaks and holidays.

[]   I take some time to rest and the occasional holiday.

[]   I don't take enough rest breaks and seldom holidays.

[]   I don't stop often at all. Who has time for holidays?

8. Describe your daily lifestyle.

[]   I have a nice balance of work, play, and rest.

[]   I have a balance, but could take more time to rest and play.

[]   I'm about average.

[]   I frequently feel out of balance. Too much work and too many responsibilities.

[]   I'm busy all day and everyday. Way too much to do.

9. Select the answer that best describes the events in your life this past year.

[]   It's been a very calm and satisfying year.

[]   It's been good for the most part, however, there have been some pressures or changes.

[]   It's been about average.

[]   It's been kind of hectic and chaotic. Many changes and challenges.

[]   It's been very unsettled. Lots of challenges and pressures.

10. How do you feel about yourself.

[]   I'm very confident and comfortable with who I am.

[]   I feel pretty good about myself.

[]   I'm okay.

[]   I don't feel that good about myself lately.

[]   I don't feel very good about myself at all.

11. In the last two months, have you experienced dizziness, upset stomach, trembling or shaking, or an unusual amount of fear or stress when trying to rest?

[]   No. Not at all.

[]   A couple of times, but not too bad.

[]   Occasionally.

[]   Frequently, and it's getting more and more.

[]   Almost always.

12. Do you avoid social situations or gatherings because of nervousness or fear?

[]   Yes. All the time.

[]   Yes. Frequently.

[]   Yes. Sometimes.

[]   Yes. Very seldomly.

[]   No. I like social situations.

13. Are you afraid that you may get into a place or situation where you may not be able to escape in a hurry?

[]   No. I don't think about that at all.

[]   Occasionally. But not that often.

[]   Yes. It does bother me sometimes.

[]   Yes. I do think about it and do become nervous.

[]   Yes. It is a big fear for me.

14. How often do you feel afraid or worried?

[]   I can't recall the last time I was really afraid or worried.

[]   Not too often, but sometimes.

[]   Frequently.

⬚   Regularly. Things have been very challenging lately.

⬚   Almost all the time. Things have been very difficult.

**15. Do you drink caffeinated drinks (such as coffee,
tea, soft drinks, etc.) or ingest chocolate or sweets regularly?**

⬚   Yes. I have to have my fix everyday. I love it.

⬚   Yes, but only a couple of times a week.

⬚   Yes, but only a couple of times a month.

⬚   Yes, but only once and awhile.

⬚   Not at all.

**16. Do you have a lot of nervous energy (always on the go,
hard to sit down, too much to do)?**

⬚   Yes. I can go all day and then some. No time to rest.

⬚   Yes, I do. But I do rest occasionally.

⬚   I think I'm about average.

⬚   I have some. But I do rest regularly.

⬚   I'm pretty relaxed most of the time.

**17. How do you feel about confrontation (arguing or
having disagreements)?**

⬚   I hate it. When there's a problem, I avoid it at all costs.

⬚   I don't like it. I try to avoid it if I can.

⬚   I don't like it, but I don't run away from it.

⬚   It's all part of interacting with people.

⬚   It doesn't bother me at all.

18. Do you search the Internet, books, or the library in search of answers regarding your anxiety and/or how you are presently feeling?

☐   No. Not at all. If I do it's just for entertainment.

☐   Yes. But not that often.

☐   Yes. Sometimes.

☐   Yes. I look online for answers about how I'm feeling.

☐   Yes. I'm constantly looking for answers about how I'm feeling.

19. Are you concerned about what people think of you?

☐   No.

☐   Not so much, but I do try to be nice and friendly.

☐   Yes, to some degree.

☐   Yes. I do sometimes worry about it.

☐   Yes. It's very important what other people think about me.

20. What kind of parents/guardians did you have when growing up?

☐   They were great.

☐   They were good. Some issues, but not too bad.

☐   They were okay. There were some problems, though.

☐   Things were difficult as a child.

☐   I had a very difficult childhood for so many reasons.

Please show this self-test to your health care professional, or go to the AnxietyCentre.com web site, fill out the quiz online, and email your answers for a confidential reply.

If you or someone you know would like more information on Anxiety, please go to www.anxietycenter.com.

Appendix 3

Stress Test

If you suspect that you might suffer from stress, complete the following stress test, and show it to your health care professional, or go to the AnxietyCentre.com web site, fill out the stress test online, and email your answers for a confidential reply.

Stress is a major factor in illness. Stress is also one of the main factors in the onset of an anxiety disorder or panic attack condition. Take this stress test to see how your stress level is.

Select the "Yes" button for each event that you experienced in the last 12 months.

	No	Yes
Death of spouse	☐	☐
Divorce	☐	☐
Marital separation, major relationship problems	☐	☐
Jail term	☐	☐
Death of a close family member	☐	☐
Experiencing anxiety condition or panic attacks	☐	☐
Significant financial problems	☐	☐

	No	**Yes**
Personal injury, illness, or health Concern	☐	☐
Recent Marriage (within 6 months)	☐	☐
Fired at work	☐	☐
Marital reconciliation	☐	☐
Retirement	☐	☐
Loss (lost or death) of a family pet	☐	☐
Family member illness	☐	☐
Working on a stressful project	☐	☐
Move (home, new city or country) within 6 months	☐	☐
Pregnancy	☐	☐
Sex difficulties	☐	☐
Gain of new family member	☐	☐
Business change (changes of, or at work)	☐	☐
Significant change in financial state	☐	☐
Death of a close friend	☐	☐
Career change / looking for work	☐	☐
Change in number of arguments with spouse	☐	☐
Mortgage over $100,000	☐	☐
Foreclosure of mortgage or loan	☐	☐
Change in responsibilities at work	☐	☐

	No	Yes
Son or daughter leaving home	☐	☐
Trouble with in-laws	☐	☐
Outstanding personal achievement	☐	☐
Spouse begins or stops work	☐	☐
Begin or end school	☐	☐
Medical concern	☐	☐
Change in living conditions	☐	☐
Change of personal habits	☐	☐
Trouble with boss	☐	☐
Change in work hours or conditions	☐	☐
Regularly working more than 10 hours per day	☐	☐
Not taking regular rest breaks or vacations	☐	☐
Change in residence	☐	☐
Change in schools	☐	☐
Christmas (3 months prior to or after)	☐	☐
Trouble with co-worker, friend	☐	☐
Change in recreation	☐	☐
Change church or church activities	☐	☐
Mortgage or loan less than $100,000	☐	☐
Less than 6 hours of sleep on average per night	☐	☐

	No	Yes
Change in number of family get-togethers	☐	☐
Change in eating habits	☐	☐
Vacation	☐	☐
Minor violations of the law	☐	☐

Please show this stress-test to your health care profess-ional, or go to the AnxietyCentre.com web site, fill out the quiz online, and e-mail your answers for a confidential reply.

If you or someone you know would like more information on Stress, please go to www.anxietycenter.com.

Appendix 4

Panic Disorder Self-Test

This Panic Disorder Self-Test is reproduced with permission from the Anxiety Disorders Association of America at www.adaa.org. Copyright © 2008 by ADAA.

After completing the Panic Disorder Self-Test, please show it to your health care professional.

Are you troubled by:

Yes ☐ **No** ☐ Repeated, unexpected "attacks" during which you suddenly are overcome by intense fear or discomfort, for no apparent reason?

During this attack, did you experience any of these symptoms?

Yes ☐ **No** ☐ Pounding heart

Yes ☐ **No** ☐ Sweating

Yes ☐ **No** ☐ Trembling or shaking

Yes ☐ **No** ☐ Shortness of breath

Yes ☐ **No** ☐ Choking

Yes ☐ **No** ☐ Chest pain

Yes ☐ **No** ☐ Nausea or abdominal discomfort

Yes ☐ **No** ☐ "Jelly" legs

Yes ☐ **No** ☐ Dizziness

Yes ☐ **No** ☐ Feelings of unreality or being detached from yourself

Yes ☐ **No** ☐ Fear of dying

Yes ☐ **No** ☐ Numbness or tingling sensations

Yes ☐ **No** ☐ Chills or hot flashes

Yes ☐ **No** ☐ Do you experience a fear of places or situations where getting help or escape might be difficult, such as in a crowd or on a bridge?

Yes ☐ **No** ☐ Does being unable to travel without a companion trouble you?

For at least one month following an attack, have you:

Yes ☐ **No** ☐ Felt persistent concern about having another one?

Yes ☐ **No** ☐ Worried about having a heart attack or going "crazy"?

Yes ☐ **No** ☐ Changed your behavior to accommodate the attack?

Having more than one illness at the same time can make it difficult to diagnose and treat the different conditions. Illnesses that sometimes complicate an anxiety disorder include depression and substance abuse. With this in mind, please take a minute to answer the following questions:

Yes ☐ **No** ☐ Have you experienced changes in sleeping or eating habits?

More days than not, do you feel:

Yes ☐ **No** ☐ Sad or depressed?

Yes ☐ **No** ☐ Disinterested in life?

Yes ☐ **No** ☐ Worthless or guilty?

During the last year, has the use of alcohol or drugs:

Yes ☐ **No** ☐ Resulted in your failure to fulfill responsibilities with work, school, or family?

Yes ☐ **No** ☐ Placed you in a dangerous situation, such as driving a car under the influence?

Yes ☐ **No** ☐ Gotten you arrested?

Yes ☐ **No** ☐ Continued despite causing problems for you and/or your loved ones?

Reference: Diagnostic and Statistical Manual of Mental Disorders, Fourth Edition. Washington, DC, American Psychiatric Association, 1994

Appendix 5

Posttraumatic Stress Disorder Self-Test

This Posttraumatic Stress Disorder Self-Test is reproduced with permission from the Anxiety Disorders Association of America at www.adaa.org. Copyright © 2008 by ADAA.

After completing the Posttraumatic Stress Disorder (PTSD) self-test, please show it to your health care professional.

Yes ☐ **No** ☐   Have you experienced or witnessed a life-threatening event that caused intense fear, helplessness or horror?

Do you re-experience the event in at least one of the following ways?

Yes ☐ **No** ☐   Repeated, distressing memories and/or dreams?

Yes ☐ **No** ☐   Acting or feeling as if the event were happening again (flashbacks or a sense of reliving it)?

Yes ☐ **No** ☐   Intense physical and/or emotional distress when you are exposed to things that remind you of the event?

Do you avoid reminders of the event and feel numb, compared to the way you felt before, in three or more of the following ways:

Yes ☐ **No** ☐   Avoiding thoughts, feelings, or conversations about it?

Yes ☐ **No** ☐   Avoiding activities, places, or people who remind you of it?

Yes ☐ **No** ☐   Blanking on important parts of it?

Yes ☐ **No** ☐   Losing interest in significant activities of you life?

Yes ☐ **No** ☐   Feeling detached from other people?

Yes ☐ **No** ☐   Feeling your range of emotions is restricted?

Yes ☐ **No** ☐   Sensing that your future has shrunk (for example, you don't expect to have a career, marriage, children, or a normal life span)?

Are you troubled by two or more of the following:

Yes ☐ No ☐   Problems sleeping?

Yes ☐ No ☐   Irritability or outbursts of anger?

Yes ☐ No ☐   Problems concentrating?

Yes ☐ No ☐   Feeling "on guard"?

Yes ☐ No ☐   An exaggerated startle response?

Having more than one illness at the same time can make it difficult to diagnosis and treat the different conditions. Illnesses that sometimes complicate an anxiety disorder include depression and substance abuse. With this in mind, please take a minute to answer the following questions:

Yes ☐ No ☐   Have you experienced changes in sleeping or eating habits?

More days than not, do you feel:

Yes ☐ No ☐   Sad or depressed?

Yes ☐ No ☐   Disinterested in life?

Yes ☐ No ☐   Worthless or guilty?

During the last year, has the use of alcohol or drugs:

Yes ☐ No ☐   Resulted in your failure to fulfill responsibilities with work, school, or family?

Yes ☐ No ☐   Placed you in a dangerous situation, such as driving a car under the influence?

Yes ☐ No ☐   Gotten you arrested?

Yes ☐ No ☐   Continued despite causing problems for you and/or your loved ones?

Reference: Diagnostic and Statistical Manual of Mental Disorders, Fourth Edition. Washington, DC, American Psychiatric Association, 1994

Appendix 6

Depression Checklist

After you have completed this checklist, please show it to your health care professional.

Depression

It's normal to feel some of the following symptoms from time to time, but experiencing several or more for more than two or three weeks may indicate the presence of depression or another depressive illness. Remember, you must seek a professional for an accurate diagnosis of depression. This checklist is provided only as a tool to help you talk with your doctor or treatment provider about your concerns and develop an action plan for successful recovery.

Please note: Other illnesses and certain medications can cause symptoms that mimic the symptoms of depression. A complete medical examination should be performed to rule out the presence of other medical conditions potentially causing depressive symptoms.

Yes ☐ **No** ☐ I feel sad.

Yes ☐ **No** ☐ I feel like crying a lot.

Yes ☐ **No** ☐ I'm bored.

Yes ☐ **No** ☐ I feel alone.

Yes ☐ **No** ☐ I don't really feel sad, just "empty".

Yes ☐ **No** ☐ I don't have confidence in myself.

Yes ☐ **No** ☐ I don't like myself.

Yes ☐ **No** ☐ I often feel scared, but I don't know why.

Yes ☐ **No** ☐ I feel mad, like I could just explode!

Yes ☐ **No** ☐ I feel guilty.

Yes ☐ **No** ☐ I can't concentrate.

Yes ☐ **No** ☐ I have a hard time remembering things.

Yes ☐ **No** ☐ I don't want to make decisions—it's too much work.

Yes ☐ **No** ☐ I feel like I'm in a fog.

Yes ☐ **No** ☐ I'm so tired, no matter how much I sleep.

Yes ☐ **No** ☐ I'm frustrated with everything and everybody.

Yes ☐ **No** ☐ I don't have fun anymore.

Yes ☐ **No** ☐ I feel helpless.

Yes ☐ **No** ☐ I'm always getting into trouble.

Yes ☐ **No** ☐ I'm restless and jittery. I can't sit still.

Yes ☐ **No** ☐ I feel nervous.

Yes ☐ **No** ☐ I feel disorganized, like my head is spinning.

Yes ☐ **No** ☐ I feel self-conscious.

Yes ☐ **No** ☐ I can't think straight. My brain doesn't seem to work.

Yes ☐ **No** ☐ I feel ugly.

Yes ☐ **No** ☐ I don't feel like talking anymore - I just don't have anything to say.

Yes ☐ **No** ☐ I feel my life has no direction.

Yes ☐ **No** ☐ I feel life isn"t worth living.

Yes ☐ **No** ☐ I consume alcohol/take drugs regularly.

Yes ☐ **No** ☐ My whole body feels slowed down - my speech, my walk, and my movements.

Yes ☐ **No** ☐ I don't want to go out with friends anymore.

Yes ☐ **No** ☐ I don't feel like taking care of my appearance.

Yes ☐ **No** ☐ Occasionally, my heart pounds, I can't catch my breath, and I feel tingly.

Yes ☐ **No** ☐ My vision feels strange and I feel I might pass out. The feeling passes in seconds, but I'm afraid it will happen again.

Yes ☐ **No** ☐ Sometimes I feel like I'm losing it.

Yes ☐ **No** ☐   I feel "different" from everyone else.

Yes ☐ **No** ☐   I smile, but inside I'm miserable.

Yes ☐ **No** ☐   I have difficulty falling asleep or I awaken between 1 A.M. and 5 A.M. and then I can't get back to sleep.

Yes ☐ **No** ☐   My appetite has diminished—food tastes so bland.

Yes ☐ **No** ☐   My appetite has increased—I feel I could eat all the time.

Yes ☐ **No** ☐   My weight has increased/decreased.

Yes ☐ **No** ☐   I have headaches.

Yes ☐ **No** ☐   I have stomachaches.

Yes ☐ **No** ☐   My arms and legs hurt.

Yes ☐ **No** ☐   I feel nauseous.

Yes ☐ **No** ☐   I'm dizzy.

Yes ☐ **No** ☐   Sometimes my vision seems blurred or slow.

Yes ☐ **No** ☐   I' m clumsy.

Yes ☐ **No** ☐   My neck hurts.

Appendix 7

Please Listen

(Show this to your friends and loved ones.)

When I ask you to listen to me, and you start giving advice, you have not done what I asked, nor heard what I need.

When I ask you to listen to me, and you begin to tell me that I shouldn't feel that way, you are trampling on my *feelings*.

When I ask you to listen to me, and you feel you have to do something to solve my problems, you have failed me—strange as that may seem.

Listen, please! All I asked was that you listen. Not talk nor "do" – *just hear me*. Advice is cheap. Fifty cents gets both *Dear Abby* and astrological forecasts in the same newspaper. That I can do for myself, I'm not helpless, maybe discouraged and faltering—but not helpless.

When you do something for me *that I can and need to do for myself*, you contribute to me seeming fearful and weak. But when you accept as a simple fact that I do feel what I feel, no matter how seemingly irrational, then I can quit trying to convince you and can get about to understanding what's behind what I am saying and doing—to what I am *feeling*.

When that's clear, chances are so will the answers be, and I won't need any advice. (Or then, I'll be able to hear it!) Perhaps that's why, for some people, prayer works, because God is mute, and doesn't give advice or try to fix what we must take care of ourselves.

So, please listen and just hear me. And if you want to talk, let's plan for your turn, and I promise I'll listen to you.

—Anonymous

Notes

Book Cover Quotation

"PTSD is a greater cop killer than all the guns ever fired at police officers." Excerpted from comments made by Lt. James F. Devine (Ret.), CSW, CASAC, CEAP, Executive Director, Long Island Council on Alcohol and Drug Dependence, Director of NYPD Counseling Services (1980-85).

Names

Of the police officers and dispatchers who tell their stories in *CopShock*, three have asked that their real names (and descriptions) not be used because they wish to protect their privacy. Ian Shaw, Hector Rodriguez and Corrine Mossman are assumed names. As indicated in the notes for each chapter, incidental individuals are sometimes not identified by their real names.

Introduction

1. How many present, former and retired police officers does PTSD impair? Perhaps hundreds of thousands. Mann and Neece estimate the incidence of PTSD in police officers at 12 to 35 percent. See Mann, J.P., Neece, J., "Workers' Compensation For Law Enforcement Related Post Traumatic Stress Disorder," *Behavioral Sciences and the Law*, V8, 1990: 447-456.

Martin, McKean and Veltkamp report that 29 percent of officers experience above average or high amounts of stress with 26 percent meeting the criteria for PTSD. See Martin, C.A., McKean, H.E., Veltkamp, L.J., "Post-Traumatic Stress Disorder In Police And Working With Victims: A Pilot Study," *Journal of Police Science and Administration*, V14, N2, 1986: 98-101.

Swann and D'Agostino state that one third of police officers involved in traumatic incidents will experience long-term stress symptoms. See Swann, G.B., D'Agos-tino, C.A., "Post-Shooting Trauma And Domestic Violence: Clinical Observation And Preliminary Data," in *Law Enforcement Families: Issues And Answers*, eds. J.T. Reese, E. Scrivner, C.J. Lent, Washington, DC: U.S. Government Printing Office, 1994: 227-231.

Carlier, et al., reveal a level of 7 percent PTSD in a sample of traumatized police officers, but 34 percent suffer posttraumatic stress symptoms or "subthreshold PTSD." See Carlier, I.V.E., et al., "Risk factors for posttraumatic stress symptomatology in police officers: a prospective analysis," *Journal Of Nervous And Mental Disease*, V185, N8, August 1997: 498-506.

In her book, *I Can't Get Over It, A Handbook For Trauma Survivors, Second Edition*, Oakland, CA: New Harbinger Publications, 1996, trauma specialist Aphrodite Matsakis discusses who may develop PTSD. She reports that "PTSD symptoms are estimated to affect, at the very minimum, some 8 to 9 percent of our population." She refers to recent studies that show that "PTSD develops, on average, in 25 percent of those exposed to a traumatic stressor." (p. 13).

The scope of these studies does not include a portion of the 600,000 security guards, often poorly trained to cope with stress illness, who also acquire PTSD. They do not always reflect on the country's 523,000 corrections officers. The California Correctional Officers Association estimates that almost 40 percent of their members will be assaulted during their career. Thirty percent will be assaulted three to five times. The emotional aftermath of a violent assault may cause PTSD as well as more common reactions like depression. See "Living Targets, A Special Report By The California Correctional Officers Association," 1981.

Those in federal agencies like the FBI, CIA, DEA, ATF, Secret Service and Border Patrol also experience or witness traumatic events that involve "actual or threatened death or serious injury" and respond with "intense fear, helplessness or horror." See the *Diagnostic and Statistical Manual of Mental Disorders, Fourth Edition*, (DSM-IV), Washington, DC: American Psychiatric Association, 1994: 427-428.

Be aware, however, that there is some disagreement about the incidence and prevalence of PTSD, even though "at risk" individuals like police officers exposed to intense trauma seem vulnerable. For a detailed discussion of who may develop PTSD, see Donald Meichenbaum's book, *A Clinical Handbook/Practical Therapist Manual For Assessing And Treating Adults With Post-Traumatic Stress Disorder (PTSD)*, 1994: 22-31.

2. A 1997 survey examines the effects of the 1992 Los Angeles civil unrest on LAPD police officers assigned to a major riot area. Among other things, the survey indicates that 17 percent of the subjects who responded experienced PTSD symptomatology. See Harvey-Lintz, T., Tidwell, R., "Effects Of The 1992 Los Angeles Civil Unrest: Post Traumatic Stress Disorder Symptomatology Among Law Enforcement Officers," *Social Science Journal*, V34, N2, 1997: 171-183.

Events that imitate the conditions of warfare, causing senseless loss of life, may trigger PTSD symptoms in veterans. See Moyers, F., "Oklahoma City Bombing: Exacerbation Of Symptoms In

Veterans With PTSD," *Archives of Psychiatric Nursing*, V10, N1, 1996: 55-59.

Chapter 1: Assaults

1. Honeymooning passengers Dale and Teri Demetropoulos, of Tacoma, Washington, and air hostess Myrna Bonét, the woman who ordered everyone off a seat and used her scarf to arrest the bleeding, were later credited with saving Christine's life. Transit cop Joe McGarry and Dale rushed Christine up the stairs.

2. Christine exhibited symptoms of dissociation. Dissociation may be recognized in "an inability to recall important personal information, usually of a traumatic or stressful nature" (Dissociative Amnesia) or is "characterized by a persistent or recurrent feeling of being detached from one's mental processes..." (Depersonalization Disorder). Dissociation is defined as "a disruption in the usually integrated functions of consciousness, memory, identity, or perception of the environment." See DSM-IV, pp. 477-491.

There is a great deal of interest in dissociative states and disorders in relation to PTSD. Carlier et al conducted a study of police officers with PTSD or partial PTSD. The study concluded that it is quite likely that PTSD predicts dissociation and not the other way around. Carlier argues that "dissociation might occur as a coping mechanism to help a person live with the symptoms of PTSD." (p. 1327).

Mental health professionals are also discussing whether PTSD should be called an anxiety disorder or a dissociative disorder. Wherever this debate leads, it is clear that dissociation often hinders psychological healing. See Carlier et al., "PTSD In Relation To Dissociation In Traumatized Police Officers," *American Journal of Psychiatry*, V153, N10, 1996: 1325-1328.

As time passed, Christine "forgot" many of the details of the assault. Her ability to remember simple and immediate tasks also declined. Often she felt disconnected or detached from herself, the person who had experienced the event. Therapy has helped her regain aspects of her memory.

For further reference on dissociation, see:

Atchison, M. & McFarlane, A.C. "A Review Of Dissociation And Dissociative Disorders," *Australian & New Zealand Journal of Psychiatry*, V28, N4, Dec. 1994: 591-599.

Brady, K.T., "Posttraumatic Stress Disorder And Comorbidity: Recognizing The Many Faces Of PTSD," *Journal of Clinical Psychiatry*, V58 (Suppl. 9), 1997: 12-15.

Bremner, J.D., Brett, E., "Trauma-related Dissociative States And Long-term Psychopathology In Posttraumatic Stress

Disorder," *Journal of Traumatic Stress*, V10, N1, Jan. 1997: 37-49.

Classen, C., Koopman, C., Spiegel, D., "Trauma And Dissociation," *Bulletin of the Menninger Clinic*, V57, N2, Spring 1993: 178-194.

Connors, R., "Self-injury In Trauma Survivors: 1. Functions And Meanings," *American Journal of Orthopsychiatry*, V66, N2, April 1996: 197-206.

Southwick, S.M., et al., "Psychobiologic Research In Post-Traumatic Stress Disorder," *Psychiatric Clinics of North America*, V17, N2, June 1994: 251-264.

Spiegel, D., "Trauma, Dissociation, And Memory," *Annals of the New York Academy of Sciences*, V821, June 21 1997: 225-237.

Sutherland, S.M., Davidson, J.R., "Pharmacotherapy For Post-Traumatic Stress Disorder," *Psychiatric Clinics of North America*, V17, N2, June 1994: 409-423.

van der Kolk, B.A. et al., "Dissociation, Somatization, And Affect Dysregulation: The Complexity Of Adaptation Of Trauma," *American Journal of Psychiatry*, V153, N7 Suppl., July 1996: 83-93.

van der Kolk, B.A., Fisler, R., "Dissociation And The Fragmentary Nature Of Traumatic Memories: Overview And Exploratory Study, *Journal of Traumatic Stress*, V8, N4, Oct. 1995: 505-525.

3. Having conducted over 800 debriefings of officers involved in shootings, police psychotherapist Nancy Bohl, author of several studies and Past Chair for the International Association of Chiefs of Police (IACP), says that in most instances fellow officers blew the details of the stories out of proportion or changed them.

"When cops hear the story told by another cop," she said, "they change the story in their minds in order not to feel vulnerable. All cops do it. They're not mad at the person or trying to make the person look stupid. It's because if they realized you got shot doing everything right, then they're going to be too afraid to do their job. So if they can change the story into something so bizarre that you're to blame, then that won't happen to them."

4. Joseph Wambaugh's book, *The Onion Field*, New York: Dell, 1987, tells the true story of two Los Angeles police officers who give up their guns when confronted by two armed men. One officer is shot to death and the other manages to escape. Right after the shooting, police department supervisors encourage Karl Hettinger, the surviving officer, to go from roll-call room to roll-call room, telling what he did wrong when he doesn't believe he did anything wrong. The effect is blaming the victim. "Now let's hear your opinion about how you guys fouled up. The things each of you did wrong. Or what you *didn't* do and should've done." (p. 216).

With the intentions of trying to save the lives of other officers, the supervisors infer that Hettinger is to blame for his partner's murder. Their actions undermine his confidence before he has a chance to adapt to the mental repercussions of the terrible trauma, and the officer, overwhelmed with guilt, attempts suicide.

5. Not every department insists on mandatory psychological assessment meetings. Many departments believe officers should attend willingly. Forcing officers to attend is not always the best way to get results.

6. Dr. Nancy Bohl says that many departments try never to hospitalize officers for psychiatric reasons. Hospitalization can lead to secondary injury or wounding—psychological damage that may occur after the initial injury as a result of insensitivity or ill-considered efforts by helpers. Besides the loss of control, hospitalized officers are sometimes locked up with the type of people they arrest and this can undermine treatment. Officers would feel betrayed by the department.

Dr. Aphrodite Matsakis says "secondary wounding occurs because people who have never been hurt sometimes have difficulty understanding and being patient with people who have been hurt." (p. 93). She attributes secondary wounding to ignorance, burnout and blaming the victim. See *I Can't Get Over It, A Handbook For Trauma Survivors, Second Edition*, pp. 90-103.

7. Two years later in a letter, therapist Salvatore Conti comments on that confrontation. "Officer McIntyre refused to allow any communication from this office to be sent to her department or to her union representatives. She could not or would not admit to failure. She was operating under the misguided assumption that she could continue to hide and deny her acute distress and still remain on the job." Conti, S., Executive Director, Clinical Psychotherapist, Diagnostic And Counseling Services, New York, in an unpublished, untitled, confidential psychiatric report, January 16, 1991.

8. Among Christine's police officer friends, Kathy Burke, from the Police Self-Support Group, was one of the few who understood Christine's struggles and helped her immeasurably.

9. A psychiatric report looks deeper into Christine's reasons for not soliciting her family's support. "Christine could not bring herself to allow her family to see her in her present weakened state and chose instead to distance herself from them. She did this in order to hide the self-imposed shame of not being able to deal with her injury and the significant changes in her which followed." Conti, S., January 16, 1991.

10. Christine's aversion to leaving the house is an associated feature or disorder that can precede or develop from PTSD. It is sometimes, but not always present. Called Agoraphobia, the condition is a separate anxiety disorder. See DSM-IV, pp. 396-397 and p. 425.

11. In part, here is what Christine tells Dr. Benezra. "All I wanted was to be a good police officer. To try my damned best. (Cries) I know something holds me from doing anything, but I'm getting weaker. I'm afraid that I'll just snap. I don't want to do it. I don't want to hurt anybody. But I'm hurting so much. I really was so strong. And now I feel that my whole life is in ruins. (She hits her leg) I just wish this didn't happen. I just want to lead a normal life.

"I just want to go back to work. I never wanted this to take over my life...and it did. I feel like a worn out towel. I tried. I wanted to be a police officer for years, helping people, entrusted with responsibility. There was the comraderie [*sic*], friendship, excitement." Benezra, J., Psychiatrist, New York, in an unpublished, untitled, confidential psychiatric report, June 15, 1990.

12. Today, hospitalization is a rare occurrence. In critical incidents, debriefers instruct officers that they won't be hospitalized, that they will get help and not experience secondary injuries. Everything is done to protect officers.

13. In Dr. Benezra's December 10, 1990, report on Christine's progress, he quotes her as saying, "I feel so much hatred towards this guy. I want to go and see what life he's leading. I want to see him suffering."

Christine's attacker, calling himself Jack Webb, professing to live in the Empire State Building, was identified as Peter Son, fifty-six. Charged with assault and attempted murder of a police officer, he pleaded guilty. Although insane with a history of previous assaults, he received eight to twenty-five years in prison instead of confinement to a mental institution. Having served the minimum sentence, he's up for parole. Christine is writ-ing letters to keep him in jail.

14. After release from hospital, Christine told Dr. Benezra how she felt. "I'm still paranoid... In conversations I'll forget what I'm saying in the middle of talking... I'll be driving and suddenly I'm lost, don't know where I am. I panic. My mind... it's like I suddenly have Alzheimer's. A blanket over everything." Benezra, J., December 10, 1990.

15. After her European trip, Christine tells Dr. Benezra, "I don't trust anyone. The things I do now—my husband doesn't know me anymore. I don't know me anymore." Later in the transcript, she says, "There's been no sex at all since April. In Europe things were a bit better, but I was reluctant. I had no desire...I keep turning my husband away." Benezra, J., December 10, 1990.

Dr. Cavanagh comments on the state of her marriage at that time. "The patient's marriage became quite turbulent in that her husband, also in the police department, would discuss his various activities and the patient found that she could not bear listening to her husband and his role as a policeman. On a few occasions the patient's husband accompanied her into the interviews. He was not able to 'understand' his wife's problems with dealing with police work for which she was no longer suited." Cavanagh, J.J., Psychiatrist, New York, in an unpublished, confidential psychiatric report addressed to *Workers Compensation Board*, April 28, 1993.

16. About her paranoid state, Christine tells Dr. Benezra, "I think that someone will blast open the door; break open the car door; try to rob me. That I'll be in a store and someone will come in and rob it. I imagine these things. That I'll be someplace and that a violent thing will happen. Noises... especially if I'm alone I'll think that someone is downstairs in the basement. I go down expecting to be attacked." Benezra, J., December 10, 1990.

17. For a pension claim, Dr. Benezra sums up Christine's condition. "All of her symptoms are directly and causally related to the assault. As a result, she is totally unable to function as a police officer. This condition is permanent." Benezra, J., December 10, 1990.

18. Dr. Cavanagh explains to transit doctors the effect they are having on Christine. "The patient had to travel into New York City for periodic evaluations by the Transit Authority. The patient would be in a near panic for days prior to going to New York City. She was not able to travel alone and had to be accompanied by a relative. After the Transit Authority interviews, the patient remained in a state of high agitation for at least a week to two weeks afterward." Cavanagh, J.J., April 28, 1993.

19. In light of the harassing behavior of the transit doctors and documentation that police psychologists who report to the administration that pays them do not maintain confidentiality, although they provide therapy, it is reasonable to conclude that the Transit Authority (TA) may actively encourage their doctors to dismiss claims no matter how just. I have found no written proof of such a policy.

Nonetheless, other police officers I've interviewed recounted similar stories to Christine's. Credit should be given to the Transit Authority, however, for its financial support. Whenever Christine was off work, the TA and Workers' Compensation each paid a percentage of her salary. Although the Transit Authority became part of the New York Police Department several years after

Christine retired, the issue of doctor/patient confidentiality remains a problem for mental health professionals working for the NYPD.

For papers on the dilemma that police department psychologists find themselves in, see Archibald, E.M., "Confidentiality When The Police Psychologist Is Evaluator And Caregiving Practitioner," (pp. 215-217) and see Weiner, B.A., "Confidentiality And The Legal Issues Raised By The Psychological Evaluations Of Law Enforcement Officers," (pp. 97-102). Both papers may be found in *Psychological Services For Law Enforcement*, eds. J.T. Reese, H.A. Goldstein, Washington, DC: U.S. Government Printing Office, 1986.

20. Roan, S., "A Refuge No More," *Los Angeles Times*, August 30, 1994: E-1, 7.

21. Although death rates for police officers appear to be diminishing, the rate of assaults on officers in 2006 was higher than in 1997. In 1997, the rate of assaults was 10.9 per 100 sworn officers. In 2006, the rate of assaults was 11.8 percent per 100 sworn officers (according to Law Enforcement Officers Assaulted—LEOKA 2006 at www.fbi.gov/ucr/killed/2006/officerassaulted.html)

The National Law Enforcement Officers Memorial Fund (NLEOMF) documents a large number of officers assaulted. Averaging a ten year period from 1997 to 2006, it reports that there are, on average, more than 57,558 assaults per year, with 49,779 in 1997, and 59,907 in 2006—with 16,219 injuries per year. The FBI reports that 58,634 officers were assaulted in 2006. The NLEOMF's figures are higher because they include criteria not applied by the FBI, such as assaults and injuries as a result of struggling with prisoners and assaults on military police. Griffiths and McDaniel suggest that a police officer has a 44 percent chance of being assaulted in any one year. (p. 7) See Griffiths, R.F., McDaniel, Q.P., "Predictors Of Police Assaults," *Journal of Police and Criminal Psychology*, V9, N1, 1993: 5-8. See also McMurray, H.L., "Attitudes Of Assaulted Police Officers And Their Policy Implications," *Journal of Police Science and Administration*, V17, N1, 1990: 44-48.

Chapter 2: What Is CopShock?

1. See DSM-IV, p. 424.

2. See Matsakis, A., *I Can't Get Over It, A Handbook For Trauma Survivors, Second Edition*, p. 3.

3. In "War Syndromes And Their Evaluation: From The U.S. Civil War To The Persian Gulf War," *Annals of Internal Medicine*, V125, N5, September 1996: 398-405, Hyams, Wignall, and Roswell discuss the progression of psychological illness on the battlefield.

For further historical perspective, see also Kobrick, F.R., "Reaction Of Vietnam Veterans To The Persian Gulf War," *Health & Social Work*, V18, N3, 1993: p. 166. And see Matsakis, A., *I Can't Get Over It, A Handbook For Trauma Survivors, Second Edition*, p. 14.

4. World War II veterans. See Landsberg, M., "World War II Ghosts Come Back To Haunt Veterans 50 Years Later," *Associated Press*, August 6, 1995: A-1. After many years, World War II veterans are experiencing PTSD symptoms. According to the June 13, 1994 issue of Newsweek, there are an estimated 210,000 survivors of WWII who continue to suffer full blown symptoms of traumatic stress.

Hurricane Andrew. See Clary, M., "Clouds Of Despair Linger In Florida In Andrew's Wake," *Los Angeles Times*, August 23, 1993: A-10, 11. See also "Social Troubles To Follow Andrew," *Santa Barbara News Press*, October 11, 1992.

Kobe, Japan earthquake. See Watanabe, T., "Illness, Mental Problems On Rise After Kobe Quake," *Los Angeles Times*, January 25, 1995: A-1, 22. See also Watanabe, T., "After Kobe, Healing The Psyche Of Japan," *Los Angeles Times*, June 20, 1995: A-1. And see Watanabe, T., "Year After Kobe Quake, Crisis Brings Change," *Los Angeles Times*, December 26, 1995: A-1.

5. Murders in the U.S. In 2006, 17,034 people were murdered in the United States. See *Crime in the United States, 2006*, which contains the most current *Uniform Crime Reports* data published by the U.S. Department of Justice, Federal Bureau of Investigation.

Despite declines in the number of murders, 2006 homicide rates are almost 6 murder victims per 100,000 people. There were an estimated 1,417,745 violent crimes during 2006. The rate of 473.5 violent crimes for every 100,000 inhabitants is the lowest in many years. Since 1997, violent crime rates have fallen 13.3 percent. For details on crime rates, see *Crime in the United States, 2006*, at: http://www.fbi.gov/ucr/cius2006/offenses/violent_crime.

Rape. Accurate figures for rape and sexual assault are hard to obtain. The National Crime Victimization Survey estimates that only 32 percent of rape or sexual assaults are reported. The US Department of Justice document *Criminal Victimization in the United States for 2005* states that 148,110 men, women and children were raped in that year. Other data analysts estimate the actual number of rapes at well over 300,000 per year. Whatever the real number is, most people who are raped are keeping the trauma hidden, setting themselves up for PTSD and other disorders.

Illegals crossing the border. See Zamichow, N., "Latina Immigrants Suffer Post-Traumatic Disorders," *Los Angeles Times*, February 18, 1992: A-3, 24. Many illegal Latina women are so frightened by their trip across the border that they develop PTSD. See also Clary, M., "Depression Often Undetected In Latinos," *Los Angeles Times*, August 10, 1995: B-2.

Monica Seles. See Kirkpatrick, C., "Monica's Dark Odyssey," *Newsweek*, September 4, 1995: 48-49. Tennis star Monica Seles sought treatment for PTSD from Nevada psychologist Jerry R. May. To help herself heal, she regularly visited battered teens and runaways at the House of Hope shelter in Orlando, FL. See also Cart, J. "The Question About Monica," *Los Angeles Times*, May 28, 1995: C-1. And see Cart, J., "A Return To The Light," *Los Angeles Times*, August 18, 1995: C-1.

Counselors need counseling. Counselors at the Oklahoma City bombing needed counseling too. See Knowlton, L., "New Stresses Spark More Burnout For Counselors," *Los Angeles Times*, June 5, 1995: D-10. See also Morell, J., "Sometimes The Listeners Need Compassion Too," *Los Angeles Times*, June 5, 1995: E-1.

6. Waking during surgery. People sometimes wake up during surgery and from the trauma of what they see develop PTSD. See Stevens, J., "Rude Awakening," *Los Angeles Times*, September 13, 1994: E-3, 4.

See also Schwender, D., et al., "Conscious Awareness During General Anaesthesia: Patients' Perceptions, Emotions, Cognition And Reactions," *British Journal of Anaesthesia*, V80, N2, February 1998: 133-139. The authors offer evidence that patients who wake during surgery may suffer from anxiety, fear, nightmares and, in some cases, develop PTSD.

Death of loved ones. See Breslau, N., et al, "Trauma And Posttraumatic Stress Disorder In The Community: The 1996 Detroit Area Survey Of Trauma," *Archives of General Psychiatry*, V55, 1998: 626-631. Breslau et al suggest that sudden unexpected death of a loved one is a greater cause of PTSD in the community than previously imagined. This cause may account for almost one-third of PTSD cases.

Breast cancer hastens PTSD. See Andrykowski, M.A., et al., "Posttraumatic Stress Disorder After Treatment For Breast Cancer: Prevalence Of Diagnosis And Use Of The PTSD Checklist—Civilian Version (PCL-C) As A Screening Instrument," *Journal of Consulting and Clinical Psychology*, V66, N3, June 1998: 586-590. This paper suggests that the diagnosis and treatment of breast cancer precipitates the development of PTSD.

7. See DSM-IV, p. 426. See also Solomon, S.D., Davidson, J.R., "Trauma: Prevalence, Impairment, Service Use, And Cost," *Journal of Clinical Psychiatry*, V58, Suppl., N9, 1997: 5-11.

Recent estimates suggest that 5 percent of men and 10 percent to 12 percent of women suffer from PTSD sometime in their lives. For victims of violent traumas like rape, the rate may increase to 60 percent to 80 percent. Treating the effects of trauma is very costly to victims, society and the health care system.

8. For Epictetus and Hans Selye references, see Everly, G.S., "Familial Psychotraumatology," in *Law Enforcement Families, Issues and Answers,* eds. J.T. Reese, E. Scrivner, C.J. Lent, Washington, DC: U.S. Department of Justice, Federal Bureau of Investigation, 1994: 178.

9. See *Webster's II New Riverside Dictionary, Office Edition,* New York: Berkley Books, 1984: 729-730.

10. See Stotland, E., "Police Stress And Strain As Influenced By Police Self-Esteem, Time On Job, Crime Frequency And Interpersonal Relationships," in *Psychological Services For Law Enforcement,* eds. J. T. Reese, H.A. Goldstein, Washington, DC: U.S. Government Printing Office, 1986: 521. And see Stotland, E., "The Effects of Police Work And Professional Relationships On Health," *Journal Of Criminal Justice,* V19, N4, 1991: 372.

11. In *Emergency Services Stress,* New Jersey: Prentice Hall, 1990, Dr. Jeff Mitchell and Dr. Grady Bray say "PTSD is an anxiety disorder... [It] is called a disorder because it disrupts the normal functions of one's life. The disorder interferes with sleep, activities, relationships with others, and even with one's health... It is listed as an 'anxiety' disorder because some of its chief characteristics are anxiety, fear, apprehension, and avoidance of painful stimuli." (pp. 31-32).

On the consequences of Posttraumatic Stress Disorder, Dr. Mitchell and Dr. George Everly, Jr., said in a Washington, DC, conference on occupational stress in 1992, "PTSD is the most severe and incapacitating form of stress-related disorder, capable of ending its victim's functional life in a matter of moments while changing, forever, the life of the victim's family."

They point out that, "For those in high risk professions, [like police officers], any single traumatic incident could engender symptoms of posttraumatic stress, or fully developed PTSD, at an incidence of anywhere up to 90% or more in those who are primary or secondary victims."

How do police officers suffer physically from PTSD? See Friedman, M.J., "Posttraumatic Stress Disorder," *Journal of Clinical Psychiatry,* V58 Suppl., N9, 1997: 33-66. Victims of PTSD are more vulnerable to medical illnesses.

See also Anson, R.H., Bloom, M.E., "Police Stress In An Occupational Context," *Journal of Police Science and Administration,* V16, N4, Dec. 1988: pp. 229-235. "...police rank high on the consequences of stress (in other words, heart disease, ulcers, drinking, and suicide)..." (p. 232).

See Crank, J.P., Caldero, M., "The Production of Occupational Stress In Medium-Sized Police Agencies: A Survey Of Line Officers In Eight Municipal Departments," *Journal Of Criminal Justice*, V19, 1991: 339-349. "Physical disorders such as hypertension, gastric and duodenal ulcers, and kidney and cardiovascular disease also have been attributed to stress among police personnel." (p. 339).

And see Sigler, R.T., et al., "Police Stress And Teacher Stress At Work And At Home," *Journal of Criminal Justice*, V19, 1991: 361-370. "...police officers experience relatively higher rates than the general public of heart attacks and diabetes and have an increased mortality risk from cancer, particularly for cancers of the colon and liver." (p. 363).

12. See DSM-IV, pp. 427-428.

13. See Anderson, B.J., "Trauma Response Profile," *Trauma Response*, V4, N2, Summer 1998: 5. Dr. Anderson has created the trademarked term "Police Trauma Syndrome®," which explains the cluster of symptoms many officers endure because of their job.

14. Mitchell and Bray in *Emergency Services Stress*, New Jersey: Prentice Hall, 1990, say, "[PTSD] occurs when people cannot (or, in some cases, will not) work through their normal reactions and recover from the awful experience. They get stuck and life for them is changed. They suffer emotionally and sometimes physically as a result of powerful stressors that have invaded their lives." (p. 31).

15. See Finn, P., Tomz, J.E., "IACP Model Policy, Post-Shooting Incident Procedures, Appendix L", in *Developing A Law Enforcement Stress Program For Officers And Their Families*, U.S. Department of Justice, Office of Justice Programs, National Institute of Justice, March 1997. PTSD may be defined as, "An anxiety disorder that can result from exposure to short-term severe stress, or the long-term buildup of repetitive and prolonged milder stress." (p. 207).

See also Paradise, P.R., "DEA Trauma Team," *Law and Order*, V39, N6, June 1991: 97-99. Here PTSD is defined as "a psychological condition that results from exposure to violence. Because of the continuous exposure to violence that is inherent in law enforcement work, PTSD is a constant danger to law enforcement personnel and their families." (p. 97).

16. See DSM-IV, pp. 427-429.

Chapter 3: 9/11

1. Compared to the 72nd precinct, the 75th precinct had three to four times the number of violent crimes. 1995 NYPD CompStat Unit, Police Department City of New York CompStat statistics for 1995 show the 72nd Precinct with an overall number of 3,381 crime complaints. It includes 11 murders, 30 rapes, 690 robberies and 452 fel. Assaults. For the same period, the 75th Precinct had an overall number of 8,031 crime complaints with 44 murders, 144 rapes, 2,397 robberies, and 1,280 fel. Assaults.

2. Housewatch duty as described on the FDNY Engine 10/Ladder 10 website at www.fdnytenhouse.com/ontheweb.htm. Article: What is the FDNY Housewatch?

3. Details of the attack on the World Trade Center complex. FDNY Fire Operations response on September 11, 2001. http://nyc.gov/html/fdny/pdf/mck_report/fire-operations_response.pdf. See also: Wikipedia.org website under Impacts of airliners; World Trade Center collapse; September 11 attacks. See also: National Construction Safety Team (September 2005). Final Report on the Collapse of the World Trade Center Towers. http://wtc.nist.gov/NISTNCSTAR1CollapseofTowers.pdf. Retrieved on 2007-07-10.

4. Brooklyn-Battery Tunnel. http://en.wikipedia.org/wiki/ Brooklyn-Battery_Tunnel.

5. See number 3.

6. In May, 2008, the names of eight police officers who died after 9/11 as a result of illnesses such as lung disease that they developed from working on the pile were added to the NYPD's Wall of Heroes Memorial. Hays, Tom. (5/8/2008). 8 officers who died of post-9/11 illness on NYPD memorial. The Associated Press.

Chapter 4: 9/11, Months or Years Later

1. World War II veterans contend that they did not show symptoms of PTSD until thirty years after the war. Van Dyke C., Zilberg NJ, McKinnon JA (September 1985). Posttraumatic stress disorder: a thirty-year delay in World War II veteran. *American Journal of Psychiatry.* 142(9):1070-3. See also: Herrmann N, Eryavec G. (September 1994). Delayed onset post-traumatic stress disorder in World War II veterans. *Canadian Journal of Psychiatry.* 39(7):439-41.

2. This study describes victims of motor vehicle accidents that showed no symptoms of PTSD until two years after their accidents. Bryant, Richard A. and Harvey, Allison G. (2002) Delayed-onset posttraumatic stress disorder: a prospective evaluation. *Australian and New Zealand Journal of Psychiatry*: Blackwell Synergy.

3. At least 10 percent of Israeli soldiers selected for examination who fought in the 1982 Lebanon War had no symptoms of PTSD until six months to five years later. Solomon Z, Kotler M, Shalev A, Lin R. (November 1989). Delayed onset PTSD among Israeli veterans of the 1982 Lebanon War. *Psychiatry.* 52(4):428-36.

4. Holland, Beth. (2001, November 13). Plane crashes in Queens. *Newsday*: New York. See also: Ibarguen, Diego. (2001, November 13). Plane crashes into Queens, N.Y. *The Associated Press.* See also: Bruinius, Harry. (2001, November 14). Another plane crash rocks a shattered town. Christian Science Monitor.

5. The pile burned for 99 days. See: Levin, Aaron (September 2007). Differences in PTSD prevalence and associated risk factors among World Trade Center disaster rescue and recovery workers. *American Psychiatric Association.* www.ajp.psychiatryonline.org.

6. "Someone with PTSD is at risk for developing other mental health disorders such as panic disorder, phobias, major depressive disorder, and obsessive-compulsive disorder." Posttraumatic Stress Disorder (PTSD). Updated January 2002, Concerned Counseling. http://www.concernedcounseling.com.

7. A ground-breaking study conducted by the University of London in 2007 on delayed PTSD in the military reveals that delayed onsets accounted for almost 40 percent of PTSD in combat troops. It claims that delayed onset PTSD *rarely* came out of the blue, and that there were usually some prior symptoms. Andrews, Bernice et al. (2007, September). Delayed-onset posttraumatic stress disorder: a systematic review of the evidence. *American Journal of Psychiatry.* 164:1319-1326.

8. Superior Court of New Jersey, Appellate Division. Docket No. A-1961-00T3, A-2044-00T3. Respondents: Wildwood Crest Police Department, Lower Township Police Department. Petitioners-Appellants are confidential. Argued: January 10 and 16, 2002. Decided: February 21, 2002. On appeal from the Division of Workers' Compensation. Available online at findlaw.com.

Chapter 5: Drugs

1. John's experiences are highly relevant as cops in small towns make up most of the police officers in the U.S. A small town means a population under 50,000 people. A small department is one that employs fewer than 50 full-time police officers. "Over 85% of the nearly 10,000 municipal police departments employ fewer than 50 full-time officers." (p. 240). See Bartol, C.R., et al., "Women In Small-town Policing: Job Performance And Stress," *Criminal Justice And Behavior*, V19, N3, September 1992: 240-259.

2. Police psychotherapist Nancy Bohl says staying out late with the boys drinking is not as prevalent among young police officers because they want to go home to their families. Many are health nuts and don't smoke. She says that the biggest complaint from seasoned officers is that young troops don't bond. Once cops had to live in the community they worked in, but today most do not. Separated by distance and family obligations, new officers have weakened the philosophy that cops spend time with fellow officers to unwind, compare notes and bond. As with every generalization about police officers, this is not true in every department.

3. "Rose" is not the wounded woman's real name.

4. One of the most common and potentially damaging defense mechanisms is what police psychologist, James T. Reese, calls "isolation of affect." He writes, "Police officers see it in killers and rapists who speak about their crimes expressionlessly. They see it in hospitals where medical and nursing professionals cope with patients with such detachment that they seem cold and indifferent. And they see it in themselves when they stand over a pitiful victim and calmly order an investigation." (p. 353). See Reese, J.T., "Psychological Aspects of Policing Violence," in *Police Psychology: Operational Assistance*, eds. J.T. Reese, J.M. Horn, Washington, DC: U.S. Government Printing Office, 1988: 347-361.

5. See American Medical Association, "Androgens And Anabolic Steroids," *Drug Evaluations, Sixth Edition*, Chicago: Author, 1986: 675-687. And see *Physicians' Desk Reference, 48th Edition*, (PDR) "Deca-Durabolin," (p. 1641), "Anadrol-50," (pp. 2349, 2350), Montvale, NJ: Medical Economics Data Production Company, 1994.

6. Ibid. PDR, 1994. And see *Physicians GenRx*, "Nandrolone Decanoate," (pp. II-1590-1592), Smithtown, NY: Data Pharmaceutica, Inc., 1994.

7. "...denial or suppression of fear can lead to over aggressiveness..." (p. 392) See Solomon, R.M., "Mental Conditioning: The Utilization Of Fear, in *Police Psychology: Operational Assistance*, eds. J.T. Reese, J.M. Horn, Washington, DC: U.S. Government Printing Office, 1988: 391-407.

8. See p. 445, Gilmartin, K.M., "Hypervigilance: A Learned Perceptual Set And Its Consequences On Police Stress," in *Psychological Services For Law Enforcement*, eds. J.T. Reese, H.A. Goldstein, Washington, DC: U.S. Government Printing Office, 1986: 445-448.

9. For more information about the nature of arousal and PTSD, consult Everly, G.S., *A Clinical Guide To The Treatment Of The Human Stress Response*, New York: Plenum Press, 1989.

10. See p. 448, Gilmartin, K.M., "Hypervigilance... and Its Consequences On Police Stress."

11. The name Patrick is a pseudonym.

12. Children of alcoholics may inherit a behavioral or genetic predisposition to heavy drinking or alcoholism. See Dowling, C.,

You Mean I Don't Have To Feel This Way?, New Help For Depression, Anxiety, and Addiction, New York: Scribners, 1991. "...at least 50 percent, and perhaps 'nearly all,' of those treated for alcoholism come from families with histories of the illness." (p. 155). For further reference, see C.R. Cloninger et al., "Inheritance of Alcohol Abuse," *Archives of General Psychiatry*, V38, 1981: 861-68. The National Association for Children of Alcoholics (NACoA) provides similar statistics.

13. The name Mary is a pseudonym.

14. Psychologist Scott W. Allen finds that risk-takers become self-destructive when there is evidence of depression. See Allen, S.W., "Suicide And Indirect Self-destruction Behavior Among Police, in *Psychological Services For Law Enforcement*, eds. J.T. Reese, H.A. Goldstein, Washington, DC: U.S. Government Printing Office, 1986: 413-417.

Dr. Allen says, "Associated most often with depression in ISDB (indirect self-destruction behavior) are the feelings of helplessness and hopelessness which precipitate an overall lack of self-esteem. Adding to the danger of ISDB is the lack of awareness on the individual's part to either realize or care about the effects of his behaviors. Also present is a lack of awareness that his actions may, in fact, be suicidal." (p. 414). John Jenks feels that when he was a police officer he fit Allen's description completely.

15. Keith is not the victim's real name.

16. Kevin Gilmartin's paper on hypervigilance, "Hyper-vigilance... and Its Consequences On Police Stress," suggests that the overly hypervigilant officer may find the family dull compared to his job. He gets depressed. Sometimes he decides to create some excitement away from the job to get out of his depression. Dr. Gilmartin says the officer wants "to recreate the energized feeling or 'high'" he gets from work, often indulging in abusive drinking and promiscuity. (p. 448). Without knowing him, the psychologist had John pegged correctly.

17. The Council on Alcoholism and Drug Abuse provides many pamphlets and papers on the effects of cocaine use. Consult the DSM-IV, pp. 221-229, for cocaine-induced, related disorders and side effects.

See also Najavits, L.M., et al., "Cocaine Dependence With And Without PTSD Among Subjects In The National Institute On Drug Abuse Collaborative Cocaine Treatment Study," *American Journal of Psychiatry*, V155, N2, Feb. 1998: 214-219. Cocaine users were found to have experienced a large number of lifetime traumatic events.

18. Acute Stress Disorder (ASD) features symptoms similar to PTSD. In ASD, symptoms last for at least two days, a maximum of four weeks and occur within four weeks of the traumatic incident.

PTSD is not diagnosed until symptoms last longer than one month. If duration of symptoms is less than three months, the diagnosis is Acute PTSD. If the duration is three months or more, it is Chronic PTSD. If the onset of symptoms is at least six months after the event, as in John Jenks' case, then the diagnosis may be called *PTSD with delayed onset.* For a detailed description of Acute Stress Disorder, consult the DSM-IV, pp. 429-432.

See Classen, C., et al., "Acute Stress Disorder As A Predictor Of Posttraumatic Stress Symptoms," *American Journal of Psychiatry,* V155, N5, May 1998: 620-624. The writers conclude that not only is witnessing extreme violence very stressful, but acute stress reactions predict later posttraumatic stress symptoms.

See also Harvey, A. and Bryant, R.A., "The Relationship Between Acute Stress Disorder And Posttraumatic Stress Disorder: A Prospective Evaluation Of Motor Vehicle Accident Survivors," *Journal of Consulting and Clinical Psychology,* V66, N3, June 1998: 507-512. The authors suggest that only ASD symptoms and not other symptoms are strongly related to the development of chronic PTSD.

19. See Federal Bureau of Investigation, (FBI), *Use Of Unauthorized Force By Law Enforcement Personnel: Problems And Solutions,* Washington, DC: U.S. Government Printing Office, 1991.

Chapter 6: Shootings

1. Ian Shaw is not his real name.

2. The name Charlie is a pseudonym.

3. PTSD was officially catalogued as a mental disorder in the 1980 publication of the *Diagnostic And Statistical Manual Of Mental Disorders, 3rd Edition, DSM-III.* Since that time, its diagnosis has been refined in subsequent editions, namely the DSM-III-R and the DSM-IV. For a number of years, the word "Posttraumatic" in "Posttraumatic Stress Disorder" was spelled "Post-traumatic" or "Post-Traumatic." In the 1994 DSM-IV, its spelling was changed to "Posttraumatic," although some publications have used varied spellings ever since PTSD's inception. Hence, there is an appearance of confusion in the bibliography when comparing previous spellings to the 1994 version and beyond.

A similar situation exists in spelling "posttraumatic" when its meaning refers to a condition other than the disorder, such as in "posttraumatic stress reaction." Past research materials spell the word "post-traumatic" or "post traumatic." Many professional journals have changed to "posttraumatic," which is in line with the DSM-IV's spelling.

4. See Solomon, R.M. and Horn, J.M., "Post-Shooting Traumatic Reactions: A Pilot Study," in *Psychological Services For Law Enforcement*, eds. J.T. Reese, H.A. Goldstein, Washington, DC: U.S. Government Printing Office, 1986: 383-393. "It is a common reaction for people to stare at someone who has been involved in some kind of incident. However, gawking by those around the officers may later reinforce a belief that 'everyone is watching.'" (p. 385).

The psychologists refer to the shooter's perception of being watched as the "Mark of Cain." In the Bible, God protected Cain from his deeds by a mark of immunity. No matter how justified in shooting someone, a cop is often marked by others or marked by himself for violating both God's commandments and the laws of civilized society.

5. Ibid. Solomon and Horn say, "...officers who experience guilt over a shooting may project this feeling to others. They may also assume others blame or shame them." Referring to the feeling that everyone is watching, they add, "Such a perception may readily contribute to further isolation and withdrawal by the officers." (p. 385)

6. New York police officers had a wide range of discretion in using deadly force at this time. They could shoot a suspect to "defend life" or if the suspect was a "fleeing-felon." See Fyfe, J.J., "Administrative Interventions On Police Shooting Discretion: An Empirical Examination," *Journal of Criminal Justice*, V7, 1979: 309-323.

7. The name Eric is a pseudonym.

8. Solomon and Horn's, "Post-Shooting Traumatic Reactions: A Pilot Study," documents the occurrence of nightmares about malfunctioning guns. The study attributes the nightmares to "the fear and vulnerability which were experienced by the officer" and to "emotions we have that have not yet been admitted to consciousness and/or conflicts which have not been resolved." (p. 385).

9. Symptoms for panic attacks and Panic Disorder can be found in the DSM-IV, pp. 393-405.

10. In "Post-Shooting Traumatic Reactions: A Pilot Study," Solomon and Horn describe typical post-shooting reactions. The discussion covers a large array of responses, including a heightened sense of danger, anxiety about future situations, intruding thoughts and flashbacks, isolation and withdrawal, emotional numbing, anger, sleep difficulties, alienation, depression, problems with authority, nightmares, family problems, alcohol abuse and suicidal thoughts.

11. For many years, studies and papers have warned of the damaging effects on police officers from obstructive and overbearing policies, procedures and insensitive police bosses. See Crank & Caldero, "The Production Of Occupational Stress In Medium-sized Police Agencies: A Survey Of Line Officers In Eight Municipal Departments," 1991. Almost 70 percent of police officers interviewed in this survey indicted the police organization for malicious and self-protective behavior and policies. (p. 343).

Other sources include:

Conroy, D.L., Hess, K.M., *Officers At Risk: How To Identify And Cope With Stress*, Placerville, CA: Custom Publishing, 1992: 50-51, 177-179.

Farmer, R.E., "Clinical And Managerial Implications Of Stress Research On The Police," *Journal of Police Science and Administration*, 1990: 209-210.

Finn, P., Tomz, J.E., *Developing A Law Enforcement Stress Program For Officers And Their Families*, Washington, DC: U.S. Department of Justice Programs, National Institute of Justice, 1997: 7-8.

Fishkin, G.L., *Police Burnout: Signs, Symptoms And Solutions*, Harcourt Brace, 1988: 30.

What can administrators do to reduce "organizational stress?" Besides taking sensitivity training, they can create programs to lessen stress. See Farmer, R.E., "Clinical And Managerial Implications Of Stress Research On The Police," p. 215. Farmer describes the need for stress inoculation training, activities to reduce occupational stressors, programs that deal with line-of-duty trauma situations, physical fitness programs, family involvement activities, support groups and wellness programming.

12. Secondary injury creates an additional barrier to healing. It may intensify posttraumatic symptoms. The primary injury is tough enough to deal with, but secondary injury pulls the rug of support out from under officers who are suffering. Ian was suffering from post-shooting trauma, but his bosses injured him again by making him feel worthless.

Dr. Ellen Kirschman discusses "second injury" in *I Love A Cop, What Police Families Need To Know*, pp. 62-67. Dr. Aphrodite Matsakis also describes "secondary wounding" and how to overcome it in *I Can't Get Over It, A Handbook For Trauma Survivors, Second Edition*, New Harbinger Publications, 1996: 90-103

13. Panic Disorder and panic attacks may precede the development of PTSD. The reverse may also be true—PTSD may increase the risk of Panic Disorder. "It is not known to what extent" Panic Disorder and other conditions "precede or follow the onset of Posttraumatic Stress Disorder." See DSM-IV, p. 425.

14. A PTSD diagnosis is based on the number of symptoms per category. For instance, a person must have both symptoms in category A, at least one of five symptoms in category B, three or more in category C, and so on. The description of categories and their symptoms according to the DSM-IV is in the *Appendix.*

15. See Jones, C.E., *After The Smoke Clears: Surviving The Police Shooting—An Analysis Of The Post Officer-involved Shooting Trauma,* Springfield, IL: Charles C. Thomas, 1989. According to the Denver Police Department's Critical Incident Program, 80 percent of officers involved in shootings will leave the force within seven years. (p. 58).

See also Williams, C., "Peacetime Combat: Treating And Preventing Delayed Stress Reactions In Police Officers," in *Post-Traumatic Stress Disorders: A Handbook For Clinicians,* ed. T. Williams, Cincinnati, Ohio: Disabled American Veterans, 1987: 267-292. The departure of officers within seven years after a shooting may be attributed to a delayed reaction, the severity depending on an accumulation of other traumas, how the person handles stress, what's going on in the person's life, previous history and available support. "There's no one to guide the officer through periods of self-doubt, depression, anger and guilt. If unresolved, the trauma can ruin the officer's life." (p. 273, 278-284.)

The figure of 80 percent is not accurate for every department. Departments with good support have much lower figures. Police psychotherapist Nancy Bohl reports that her department experiences a figure of 10 percent because of the good support officers receive.

See Gersons, B.P.R., "Patterns Of PTSD Among Police Officers Following Shooting Incidents: A Two-dimensional Model And Treatment Implications," *Journal of Traumatic Stress,* V2, N3, 1989: 247-257. Gersons implies that almost all police officers who fire their guns will experience posttraumatic stress reactions. Without help, nearly half of them may eventually be diagnosed with Posttraumatic Stress Disorder. (p. 249).

A worthwhile guide for supervisors wishing to help officers involved in shootings can be found in Bettinger, K.J., "After The Gun Goes Off," *State Peace Officers Journal,* V39, N2, Summer 1990: p. 92. The guide is titled: "Steps For Handling Officer-Involved Shootings."

16. See Somodevilla, S.A., "Post-Shooting Trauma: Reactive And Proactive Treatment," in *Psychological Services For Law Enforcement,* eds. J.T. Reese, H.A. Goldstein, Washington, DC: U.S. Government Printing Office, 1986: 397, 398.

Chapter 7: Family

1. Details of the shootout including the number of rounds fired can be found in the lawsuit titled Supreme Court of New York, Appellate Division, First Department: Claude Pierre Lubecki, Plaintiff, et al., versus The City of New York, et al., Defendants, 1413. 304 A.D.2d 224; 758 N.Y.S.2d 610. March 27,2003, Decided and Entered. The text of this lawsuit can be found online at www.aele.org/law/2004LRJAN/lvc.html. See also: McFadden, Robert D. (1993, January 30). Gunman and hostage are killed after Manhattan bank robbery. *New York Times.*

2. Ed showed symptoms of physical and emotional shock, but more likely what is sometimes called an Acute Stress Reaction. These symptoms include feeling dazed or disoriented, agitation, overactivity, depression, withdrawal, amnesia, anxiety symptoms such as sweating, and an increased heart rate. The symptoms begin within minutes of the traumatic event and disappear within days, even hours. "The traumatic events that can lead to an acute stress reaction are of similar severity to those involved in post-traumatic stress disorder." See Acute Stress Reaction 4.8, Management of Mental Disorders, published by *World Health Organization*: Australia, Canada, China, Italy, NZ, UK. Pages 277-281. Edited by Gavin Andrews, MD, UNSW, January 3, 2003. This article may be found online at: www.crufad.com/self_help/trauma-level2.htm. See also: Acute stress reaction at http://en.wiki pedia.org/Acute_stress_reaction. Accessed 6/14/2008. This article states that Acute stress reaction is a variation of PTSD and is the mind's and body's response to feelings of intense helplessness. See also: Mind-Body Interactions at www.merck.com/mmhe/print/sec01/ ch001/ch001f.html.

3. The "hit ratio" for NYPD police officers involved in gunfights varies from year to year, but ranges from 11 percent to 34 percent. Taking away suicide-by-cop encounters and shootings of dogs that attack officers, the rate hovers around 20 to 25 percent. In other words, officers hit their target less than a quarter of the time. With increased adrenaline making both Ed and the gunman tremble, and both of them moving, it's not surprising that they missed each other. See Baker, Al. (2008, May 8). 11 years of police gunfire, in painstaking detail. *New York Times.* See also: Gardiner, Sean. (2006, November 28) Guns gone wild. www.villagevoice.com/news/0649,gardiner,75216,6.html. See also: White, Michael D. (2006). Hitting the target (or not): comparing characteristics of fatal, injurious, and noninjurious police shootings. *Police Quarterly*, V9, N3, 303-330. Sage Publications. White outlines a number of factors that may predict shooting accuracy during a gunfight including distance, suspect actions, officer approach and preparedness, lighting conditions, use of cover, gun type, etc.

4. The term "stress bucket" was coined by psychologist Stephen L. Carson to refer to repressed feelings. "As time passes, our buckets tend to become full. We stuff those feelings with which we do not care to deal into our stress bucket, and they rattle around within us until they emerge, somehow." See Carson, S.L., "Shooting, Death Trauma, And Excessive Force," in *Police Managerial Use of Psycyology And Psychologists*, p 54.

Chapter 8: Soldiers

1. With major base closings and downsizing of personnel, recruitment from the military has diminished. There is not a large pool of soldiers to draw from. But departments still prefer rookies with military background.

2. Vietnam War. See Armfield, F., "Preventing Post-Traumatic Stress Disorder Resulting From Military Operations," *Military Medicine*, V159, N12, 1994: 739-746. Almost 500,000 Vietnam veterans suffer from prolonged cases of PTSD. Another 350,000 struggle with moderate PTSD symptoms. (p. 741). These statistics were compiled not a year or two after the war, but twenty years later.

For further reference, see Kobrick, F.R., "Reaction Of Vietnam Veterans To The Persian Gulf War," *Health & Social Work*, V18, N3, 1993: 167. And see also Kulka, R., et al., *National Vietnam Veterans Readjustment Study*, Research Triangle Park, NC: Research Triangle Institute, 1988.

PTSD causes an increase in drug and alcohol use in Vietnam veterans. See Bremner, J.D., et al., "Chronic PTSD In Vietnam Combat Veterans: Course Of Illness And Substance Abuse," *American Journal of Psychiatry*, V153, N3, March 1996: 373. See also Zaslav, M.R., "Psychology Of Comorbid Posttraumatic Stress Disorder And Substance Abuse: Lessons From Combat Veterans," *Journal of Psychoactive Drugs*, V26, N4, 1994: 393-400.

Fifteen percent of Vietnam veterans showed signs of PTSD twenty years after the war. See Southwick, S.M., et al., "Trauma-Related Symptoms In Veterans Of Operation Desert Storm: A 2-Year Follow-Up," *American Journal of Psychiatry*, V152, N8, August 1995: 1150.

World War II. In World War II prisoners of war, a third to a half suffered from PTSD forty years after imprisonment. See Southwick, S.M., et al., "Trauma-Related Symptoms In Veterans Of Operation Desert Storm: A 2-Year Follow-Up," p. 1150.

Psychiatric evacuations from the battlefield totaled 23 percent in World War II. But only in recent years have soldiers of that war come forward with cases of PTSD. See Kobrick, F.R., "Reaction Of

Vietnam Veterans To The Persian Gulf War," p. 166. See also Buffum, M.D., Wolfe, N.S., "Posttraumatic Stress Disorder And The World War II Veteran," Geriatric Nursing, V16, N6, Nov-Dec. 1995: 266.

Soldiers who saw combat in World War II were likely to experience physical decline or death fifteen years after the war. See Elder, G.H., Shanahan, M.J., Clipp, E.C., "Linking Combat And Physical Health: The Legacy Of World War II In Men's Lives," *American Journal of Psychiatry*, V154, N3, March 1997: 330-336. See also Bursztajn, H.J., "World War II: Its Effects After 50 Years," *American Journal of Psychiatry*, V153, N4, April 1996: 584.

PTSD was triggered in many World War II veterans by the media commemorating the fiftieth anniversary of the end of the war. See Hilton, C., "Media Triggers Of Post-Traumatic Stress Disorder 50 Years After The Second World War," *International Journal of Geriatric Psychiatry*, V12, N8, August 1997: 862-867.

Gulf War. The Gulf War created great stress for veterans of other wars. Media coverage provoked episodes of PTSD in Vietnam and other veterans, as PTSD has a tendency to wax and wan, depending on what stimulates it to appear. See Long, N., et al., "Effect Of The Gulf War On Reactivation Of Adverse Combat-Related Memories In Vietnam Veterans," *Journal of Clinical Psychology*, V50, N2, March 1994: 138-44. See also Southwick, S.M., et al., "Trauma-Related Symptoms In Veterans Of Operation Desert Storm: A 2-Year Follow-Up," p. 1150.

The Gulf War caused an illness that may be PTSD as a reaction to extreme stress or PTSD that resulted from exposure to toxic chemicals or a combination of both theories. See Baker, D.G., et al., "Relationship between posttraumatic stress disorder and self-reported physical symptoms in Persian Gulf War veterans," *Archives Of Internal Medicine*, V157, N18, October 13, 1997: 2076-2078. See also Malone, J.D., et al., "Possibilities For Unexplained Chronic Illnesses Among Reserve Units Deployed In Operation Desert Shield/Desert Storm," *Southern Medical Journal*, V89, N12, December 1996: 1147-1155.

Military and Police Cultures. Military training and experience may set police officers up for failure. See Ryan, A.H., Brewster, M.E., "Post-Traumatic Stress Disorder And Related Symptoms In Traumatized Police Officers And Their Spouses/Mates," in *Law Enforcement Families: Issues And Answers*, eds. J.T. Reese, E. Scrivner, C.J. Lent, Washington, DC: U.S. Government Printing Office, 1994: 217-225.

"...Vietnam veterans' value systems often emphasize justified violence, emotional distancing, suppression of feelings, distrust of the civilian world, reliance on alcohol/substance abuse, and primacy of the work role." (p. 223). Entering police work with these kinds of values would make it harder for veterans/police officers to change their behavior. The military seems to put a stamp of approval on using poor coping tools.

3. The 1st Cav flew "hunter/killer" helicopter teams. A light observation helicopter (LOH) called a loach was the hunter or scout. A Cobra or Huey gunship was called the killer. Commonly, the loach would fly low to flush enemy troops from the undergrowth by drawing fire, and the gunship would then swoop in to attack. The teams were designated colors like red, blue and white. Red was a fire unit like a Cobra gunship, white was the scout and blue was a command ship with ground troopers. Bob often flew in "pink teams," (white plus red equals pink), which might consist of one or more loaches and two Cobras or Hueys. As the machine-gunner, Bob fired a stripped down M-60.

4. Some police studies compare police work to warfare, which on face value might seem to denigrate the problems experienced by combat soldiers. I do not believe this is their intent. See Williams, C., "Peacetime Combat: Treating And Preventing Delayed Stress Reactions In Police Officers," *Post-Traumatic Stress Disorders: A Handbook For Clinicians*, ed. Tom Williams.

"While there are remarkable similarities between the types of stresses on and the responses of [veterans and cops], there is also one crucial difference: for cops, the 'war' never ends—they are out there 24 hours a day, 7 days a week to 'protect and serve,' to fight the criminal—our peacetime enemy." (p. 267).

See also Turco, R.N., "Police Shootings—Psychoanalytic Viewpoints," *International Journal Of Offender Therapy And Comparative Criminology*, V30, N1, 1986: 53-58. "...an officer tends to remain in a state of alertness to function as an officer 24 hours a day. This is the state of so-called 'constant readiness' which contributes to the unusual stresses police officers encounter of [sic] a daily basis." (p. 53).

5. "Five-0" is street language for police, as in the television police series, "Hawaii Five-0."

6. The police administration's insensitivity caused Joe secondary injury. His family experienced it too. Families are often overlooked when officers have been shot, injured, incapacitated or traumatized from violent confrontations. Loved ones experience worry and fear over the initial injury. If police bosses then treat the officers badly, families may be hurt again. Families are also injured from lack of information and support from the department.

See Ryan, A.H., Brewster, M.E., "Post-Traumatic Stress Disorder And Related Symptoms In Traumatized Police Officers And Their Spouses/Mates." Police families may become secondary victims of the trauma that police officers endure. Ryan and Brewster suggest that spouses often experience the same levels of depression and PTSD. (p. 218).

7. "Suicide is neither a disease nor a force but simply a solution to a problem," says S.W. Allen in "Suicide And Indirect Self-Destruction Behavior Among Police," p. 417.

See also McCafferty, et al., "Stress And Suicide In Police Officers: Paradigm Of Occupational Stress," *Southern Medical Journal*, V85, N3, 1992: 233-243. "For those individuals who feel powerless or hopeless, suicide may be a means of taking control over their helplessness." (p. 235).

"With older police officers, suicide is more common, and is apparently related to alcohol, physical illness, or impending retirement and 'burnout.'" (p. 237). "Police officers, because of the stress they endure, are prone to depression, alcoholism, anxiety disorders, posttraumatic stress disorder, all of which are associated with an increased incidence of suicide." (p. 238). The authors of the paper report that "up to 25 percent of officers in some departments have serious problems related to alcohol abuse." (p. 238).

8. See Kroes, W.H., *Society's Victim—The Police, An Analysis Of Job Stress In Policing*, Springfield, IL: Charles C. Thomas, 1985: 27-34. "It is known that the figures on suicide for policemen are artificially low..."

See also Hill, K.Q., Clawson, M., "The Health Hazards of 'Street Level' Bureaucracy: Mortality Among The Police," *Journal of Police Science and Administration*, V16, N4, December 1988: 243-248. Hill and Clawson suggest that police officer suicides are underestimated. "...suicide in their ranks is often covered up by fellow officers." (p. 245).

McCafferty et al, 1992, in "Stress And Suicide In Police Officers: Paradigm Of Occupational Stress," say, "The statistics for suicide rates in police officers are inconsistent, and they vary from department to department. The exact incidence of suicide among police officers is presently unknown, partly because of a desire to keep secret the internal affairs of a particular department, including such an indicator of stress (suicide)." "...it is generally believed that suicides among police officers are frequently made to appear accidental..." (p. 237).

See also Josephson, R.L., Reiser, M., "Officer Suicide In The Los Angeles Police Department: A Twelve-Year Follow-Up," *Journal Of Police Science And Administration*, V17, N3, September 1990: 227-229. LAPD suicide rates in this study were found to be below the national average while Chicago police officers were five times more likely to kill themselves than citizens. (p. 227).

For further reading, see Violanti, J.M., *Police Suicide: Epidemic In Blue*, Springfield, IL: Charles C. Thomas, 1996. The book discusses many issues including prevention and precipitating factors like traumatic stress, alcohol abuse and retirement.

9. Hector Rodriguez is not his real name.

10. Dissociative Amnesia may account for some memory gaps related to traumatic events. See DSM-IV, pp. 478-481. Memory blocks may also be found in subjects suffering from Acute Stress Disorder or PTSD.

Vernon H. Mark, M.D., discusses recovering memory loss in *Reversing Memory Loss, Proven Methods For Regaining, Strengthening, And Preserving Your Memory*, Houghton Mifflin Co, 1992. The chapter on depression and memory loss is enlightening, pp. 48-64.

Memory problems are one of the cognitive signs of critical incident stress. See Ellen Kirschman's, *I Love A Cop*, pp. 81-82, for the signs and symptoms of traumatic response. Aphrodite Matsakis,' *I Can't Get Over It*, pp. 153-159, features exercises on learning how to recall traumatic events.

11. The job took a heavy toll on Hector's home life. See "Peacetime Combat: Treating And Preventing Delayed Stress Reactions In Police Officers," in Tom Williams' *Post-Traumatic Stress Disorders: A Handbook For Clinicians*. Candis Williams says, "The police officer is expected to be combat-ready at all times while remaining 'normal' and socially adaptive away from the job. The psychological toll for many is great, unexpected, and not well understood." (p. 267).

12. Unpublished, confidential medical reports to City of Los Angeles, Worker's Compensation Division, August 27, 1984, by M. Ray Rogers, M.D., and to Department of Pensions, Los Angeles, by Seymour Leshin, M.D., September 1, 1984.

13. Dr. Leshin's report to the Department of Pensions, September 1, 1984.

14. Ibid. The hospital psychiatric report also says that, "His judgment is significantly impaired, and he showed a large amount of unconventional and paranoid ideas." In addition, the report states, "At present, he appeared tensely emotionally aroused with marked anxiety, depression and anger. He appears to feel vulnerable to threats, both real and imagined; and he appears to view his world as dangerous and unpredictable."

Chapter 9: Flashbacks

1. See Iserson, K.V., *Death To Dust, What Happens To Dead Bodies?* Galen Press, 1994: 42.

2. Ibid, pp. 42-43.

3. The trend in many departments is for the person who debriefs the officer not to be the counselor who determines fitness for duty. For example, in the Los Angeles Sheriff's Department, Psychological Services offers supportive roles, but an outside psychologist, not someone who is part of Psychological Services, assesses fitness for duty.

4. There are a number of therapy techniques used in treating PTSD, and a detailed discussion of their efficacy is beyond the scope of this book. I do not recommend one over another, as what works for one person will not necessarily work for everybody. Bill's therapist used a flooding or implosive therapy technique. By recounting the details of his traumatic incidents repeatedly, he became desensitized to their horror. This is not a technique for everyone, as it can recreate the sense of powerlessness and lack of control experienced in the original trauma.

In *I Can't Get Over It*, Aphrodite Matsakis says, "...given our present state of knowledge about flooding, it should be used only as a last resort." (p. 163). Dr. Matsakis also discusses other therapy techniques in her book for remembering and coping with trauma such as Traumatic-incident reduction therapy, EMDR and hypnosis. See pp. 151-166.

As well as using the flooding technique, Bill's therapist also helped him find meaning and "good things" that came out of the bad and to "rescript" the events so they made sense.

Discussions of treatment options can be found under many categories in Chapters 10 and 11, Issues and Support Sources. For therapists and clients, Donald Meichenbaum, Ph.D., provides descriptions of many techniques in *A Clinical Handbook/Practical Therapist Manual For Assessing And Treating Adults With Post-traumatic Stress Disorder (PTSD)*. See the *Publications* section.

5. The name Norman is a pseudonym.

6. Violence against children may cause PTSD symptoms like avoidance. See Schwarz, E., Perry, B.D., "The Post-Traumatic Response In Children And Adolescents," *Psychiatric Clinics of North America*, V17, N2, June 1994: 311-326.

7. A study on trauma in children assesses the significance of denial. "The child cannot make sense of the relevant sensory information and simply shuts it out." See Johnson, K., *Trauma In The Lives Of Children: Crisis And Stress Management Techniques For Counselors And Other Professionals*, Alameda, CA: Hunter House, 1989: 35.

8. See Terr, L.C., "Children Traumatized In Small Groups," in *Post-Traumatic Stress Disorder In Children*, eds. S. Eth, R.S. Pynoos, Washington, DC: American Psychiatric Press, 1985.

9. In his frightened mind, Bill, the child, saw a gun as a solution to his problems. This is not unusual in trauma cases, as the boy's way of looking at resolving problems was distorted. Repeated beatings from his father had prevented Bill from developing normally and making rational decisions. "A psychological trauma can interrupt the normal progress of development, causing more difficult resolution of current life issues and impeding growth." See Johnson, K., *Trauma In The Lives Of Children: Crisis And Stress Management Techniques For Counselors And Other Professionals*, p. 55.

10. Ibid, p. 12. See also Black, C., "Children Of Alcoholics," *Alcohol Health and Research World*, V4, 1979: 23-27.

11. See Johnson, K., *Trauma In The Lives Of children: Crisis And Stress Management Techniques For Counselors And Other Professionals*, pp. 20-23. Along with the physical and psychological abuse as a young boy, Bill was also victimized by his father's excessive drinking. Children of alcoholics do not develop the same way as other kids. "Thus the parental inconsistency, faulty communication, and learned distrust common to alcoholic families force the children to adopt coping strategies that are often maladaptive."

In order to cope with the chaos around them, they take on specific roles, and most of these roles are self-destructive. Bill saw his role as that of "The Responsible One." He took it upon himself to structure a life out of the chaos around him. This has great implications for Bill's life as a police officer. As "responsible children" grow up, they tend to "carry the need to control into their adult lives" and develop shallow relationships or drive away people who care about them.

12. Bill's feelings of frustration and failure led to depression, an associated condition of PTSD. See Conroy, D.L., Hess, K.M., *Officers At Risk: How To Identify And Cope With Stress*, pp. 26, 157. When engaged in debilitating work like death investigations, it's possible a police officer "may well suffer more pervasive trauma than the citizen victim." See Davis, B., "Burnout," *Police Magazine*, V5, N3, 1982: 9-18.

Chapter 10: Not Shooting

1. During a 1993 seminar called "PTSD: A Neurocognitive Therapy," PTSD expert George S. Everly, Jr., said, "Perception is everything." Dr. Everly is author of many publications including *A Clinical Guide To The Treatment Of The Human Stress Response*.

2. Terry's friend didn't realize she had belittled him by minimizing the value of his traumatic reactions, making him feel that his responses were abnormal when they were completely normal. By not being sympathetic, she contributed to his psychological injury, causing a secondary injury.

3. See Pogrebin, M.R., Poole, E.D., "Police And Tragic Events: The Management Of Emotions," *Journal of Criminal Justice*, V19, 1991: 398. "...officers do not want a partner or back-up who cannot be trusted implicitly to act decisively in any situation, because their lives may depend upon it."

4. See Carson, S.L., "Shooting, Death Trauma, And Excessive Force," in *Police Managerial Use Of Psychology And Psychologists*, eds. Harry W. More, Peter C. Unsinger, Springfield, IL: Charles C. Thomas, 1987: 43-62. Dr. Carson says, "...once we have a feeling, it does not go away." He also says, "...once an individual has a feeling it will come out of him in some fashion." (p. 54).

5. Why didn't Terry shoot? Dr. Nancy Bohl says, "sometimes there is no answer. But does there need to be one? This happens a lot with cops. Too much has gone on" to ever come to a conclusion.

6. Around the time Terry foiled the robbery, Canadian police forces seemed to use alcohol more often than American forces as a coping tool. In 1986, "the Health Directorate of Ottawa, Canada, suggested that perhaps as many as 30 percent of all police officers abused alcohol." See Hepp, C., "Drinking And The Police: It Seems More Common In Blue," *Police Stress*, V8, N1, 1987: 27-28.

7. See Pogrebin, M.R., Poole, E.D., "Police And Tragic Events: The Management Of Emotions," p. 397. "Stratton (1984) noted that from the beginning of their law enforcement careers officers are socialized to repress their emotions on the job in order to maintain a professional image in the eyes of both the public and their fellow officers. Police come to view their own emotions as an occupational weakness or hazard, with the potential to impair their ability to perform their duties effectively. Thus officers have difficulty dealing with the normal emotions that individuals are expected to experience in the face of tragic events." See also Stratton, J.G., *Police Passages*, Manhattan Beach, CA: Glennon, 1984.

8. The term "stress bucket" was coined by psychologist Stephen L. Carson to refer to repressed feelings. "As time passes, our buckets tend to become full. We stuff those feelings with which we do not care to deal into our bucket, and they rattle around within us until they emerge, somehow." See Carson, S.L., "Shooting, Death Trauma, And Excessive Force," in *Police Managerial Use Of Psychology And Psychologists*, p. 54.

9. See Conroy, D.L., Hess, K.M., *Officers At Risk: How To Identify And Cope With Stress*, p. 73. "...you can respond to only so much stress. Each person has a limit. If you are close to that limit when another traumatic event occurs, you are more likely to go over the edge. Additional stress may be too much for you."

10. See Pogrebin, M.R., Poole, E.D., "Police And Tragic Events: The Management Of Emotions," p. 398. "Merely talking about pain, guilt, or fear has been considered taboo. If an officer has to talk about his/her personal feelings, that officer is seen as not really able to handle them—as not being fully in control of his/her emotional responses."

Chapter 11: Bomb Squad

1. See Ragonese, P., Stainback, B., *The Soul Of A Cop*, New York: St. Martin's Press, 1991. A bomb squad instructor describes the value of the bomb resistant suit. "About all that suit will do if a bomb goes off on you is keep you from being blown all over the landscape. In other words, the Safco suit is not unlike a body bag." (pp. 251-252).

2. The United States can expect more terrorist acts, both from domestic and foreign sources. See Perry, S., "Terrorism: A Frightening New Perspective," Office of International Criminal Justice, undated, available at: http://nsi.org/Library/Terrorism/110501.htm.

See also Riley, K.J., Hoffman, B., "Domestic Terrorism: A National Assessment Of State And Local Preparedness," Rand, 1995, partly available at: http://www.rand.org/publications/MR/MR505.

And see Sloan, S., "Terrorism: How Vulnerable Is The United States," in *Terrorism: National Security Policy And The Home Front*, ed. Stephen Pelletiere, The Strategic Studies of the U.S. Army War College, May 1995, available at: http://nsi.org/Library/Terrorism/usterror.htm.

For more sources, go to The Terrorism Research Center at: http://www.terrorism.com/.

3. Visiting the National Law Enforcement Officers Memorial often has positive effects on those with PTSD. But some Vietnam veterans have had negative reactions while visiting the Vietnam War Memorial. See Watson, C.G., et al., "Effects Of A Vietnam War Memorial Pilgrimage On Veterans With Posttraumatic Stress Disorder," *Journal of Nervous & Mental Disease*, V183, N5, May 1995: 315-316.

4. Recruits tend to pay little heed to stories of psychological injury. Perhaps they don't believe anything can happen to them. "The stress that the individual police officer encounters is extraordinary. The effect of this overwhelming stress on the police officer is a demoralization and brutalization in which former values become meaningless. The exposure to carnage, death, and hostility results in a loss of one's sense of immortality, with the consequent development of an expectation of a foreshortened future."

"It would be impossible to adequately prepare an individual in the police academy for the stress encountered on the street." See McCafferty, F.L., et al., "Stress And Suicide In Police Officers: Paradigm Of Occupational Stress," p. 236. Meeting officers who have been injured physically and mentally may encourage recruits to start practicing stress reduction techniques early in their careers.

Chapter 12: Police Dispatchers

1. Stress factors that police dispatchers experience. See: Burke, Tod W. (2004, 1995, October). Dispatcher stress—police dispatchers. FBI Law Enforcement Bulletin. FBI 1995; Gale Group 2004. See also: Behr, Richard (2000, March 1) Under the Headset: Surviving Dispatcher Stress is a book about dispatcher stress and trauma. It was written by Richard Behr, a dispatcher and critical incident stress instructor, and covers the stress process and how to cope with it. It includes some humorous chapters, stories to inspire the dispatcher, prayers, and stories of survival. 116 spiral-bound pages. Staggs Publishing. www.headsets911.com. See also: Holt, Francis X. The top 10 things you should know about dispatcher stress. www.9-1-1magazine.com/magazine/1997/1197/features/holt.html.

2. Burnout factors. See Recognizing the signs of dispatcher burnout by Richard Behr www.headsets911.com/signs. See also: Burke, Tod W. (2004, 1995, October). Dispatcher stress—police dispatchers. FBI Law Enforcement Bulletin. FBI 1995; Gale Group 2004.

3. Corrine Mossman is not her real name, nor is her department in the mid-west. She is still on the job and wants to protect her privacy.

Chapter 13: What To Do About CopShock

1. Many sufferers feel there is no hope, no cure for PTSD. Keep in mind that PTSD and the whole trauma field is relatively new and changing. Dr. Aphrodite Matsakis says, "It bears repeating that PTSD is not incurable. Healing is possible." See Matsakis, A., *I Can't Get Over It, A Handbook For Trauma Survivors, Second Edition*, p. 37.

2. Signs of trauma are adapted from Mitchell, J., Bray, G., *Emergency Services Stress, Guidelines For Preserving The Health And Careers Of Emergency Services Personnel*, pp. 42-43, 52-56; Williams, C., "The Veteran System With A Focus On Women Partners," *Post-Traumatic Stress Disorders: A Handbook For Clinicians*, ed. Williams, T., pp. 186-187, 206; papers from Critical Incident Stress Seminar conducted by Mitchell, J.T. and Everly,

G.S., January 1993, including "Hidden Injury" by Johnson, K., Ph.D., "Reactions," and "Critical Incident Stress Debriefing Team Training."

3. Some of these questions were inspired by Ellen Kirschman's book, *I Love A Cop, What Police Families Need To Know.* See pp. 108-121 of her book for more considerations.

4. Critical Incident Stress Management description adapted from Mitchell, J., Bray, G., *Emergency Services Stress, Guidelines For Preserving The Health And Careers Of Emergency Services Personnel,* pp. 132-151; Williams, C., "Peacetime Combat: Treating And Preventing Delayed Stress Reactions In Police Officers," *Post-Traumatic Stress Disorders: A Handbook For Clinicians,* ed. Williams, T., pp. 278-285; papers from Critical Incident Stress Seminar conducted by Mitchell, J.T. and Everly, G.S., January 1993, including "Hidden Injury" by Johnson, K., Ph.D., "Reactions," and "Critical Incident Stress Debriefing Team Training."

Chapter 14: Resiliency

1. *Corrections and Law Enforcement Family Support Solicitation for the Implementation of the Corrections Field Test,* Julie E. Samuels, National Institute of Justice, 2001. www.ncjrs.gov/pdffiles1/nij/fy01-clefs-corrections.pdf

2. Documents from apahelpcenter.org may be reprinted in their entirety with credit given to the American Psychological Association. Exceptions, including requests to excerpt or paraphrase documents from apahelpcenter.org, must be presented in writing to helping@apa.org.

Chapter 15: Issues and Support Sources, A to M

1. Police psychologists realize they are in a dilemma. Even though many tell police officer clients that therapy sessions will be reported to administrators, once sessions begin, clients quickly forget. If therapy sessions are not confidential, what is their value? Is reporting not a violation of trust? See D'Agostino, C., "Police Psychological Services: Ethical Issues," in *Psychological Services For Law Enforcement,* eds. J.T. Reese, H.A. Goldstein, Washington, DC: U.S. Government Printing Office, December 1986: 241-247. See also Notes, Chapter 1: Assaults, note 19, pp. 360-361.

2. According to the NLEOMF, 2007 showed an unexpected surge in murders of police officers, but for the first six months of 2008, the numbers have plummeted by 41 percent, especially in the number of fatal shootings. Traffic related deaths were also down. By comparison, 100 officers died in-the-line-of-duty during the first six months of 2007. By the end of 2007, 181 officers lost their lives while on the job, which was 20 percent higher than the previous year. In the first six months of 2008, 59 officers died. Although the preliminary statistics for 2008 offer little comfort to the loved ones and fellow officers of those who died, this dramatic decrease is encouraging. The decline is attributed to better training, better equipment, and officers' awareness of safety issues. For more information, see Law Enforcement Officers Killed—LEOKA 2007 at www.fbi.gov/ucr/killed/2007/feloniously killed.html and go to the NLEOMF website and click on statistics and media for 2007 and 2008 statistics.

See Violanti, J.M., "The Impact Of Cohesive Groups In The Trauma Recovery Context: Police Spouse Survivors And Duty-Related Death," *Journal Of Traumatic Stress*, V9, N2, April 1996: 379-386. Support by police groups lowers distress for spouses after the death of a loved one. Police departments may wish to formulate policy to offer long-term contact and assistance to grieving relatives and friends.

See also Williams, M.B., "Impact Of Duty-Related Death On Officers' Children: Concepts Of Death, Trauma Reactions And Treatment," in *Law Enforcement Families: Issues And Answers*, eds. J.T. Reese, E. Scrivner, Washington, DC: U.S. Government Printing Office, 1994: 251-260.

3. See Danieli, Y., "Trauma To The Family: Intergenerational Sources Of Vulnerability And Resilience," pp. 163-175. "...about 50 % of all Vietnam veterans' wives that they treat have been battered." (p. 167.)

See Honig, L.A., White, E.K., "Violence And The Law Enforcement Family," pp. 101-109. Estimated to occur in about 60 percent of police marriages, here domestic violence is defined as: "...any behavior that results in physical harm to a relationship partner." It includes also, "...any behavior that arouses fear of one's physical safety or prevents a relationship partner from exercising free will." (p. 101).

See Neidig, P.H., Russell, H.E., Seng, A.F., "Observations And Recommendations Concerning The Prevention And Treatment Of Interspousal Aggression In Law Enforcement Families," pp. 353-358. "...annual rates of physical marital aggression ranging from 24%... to 41%..." (pp. 353-354). "Law enforcement rates of physical aggression are also considerably higher than the rates obtained in comparable studies of U.S. military personnel..." (p. 354) "...marital violence in law enforcement families can be understood, in part, as a result of the demands of the profession..." (p. 354).

See Swann, G.B., D'Agostino, C.A., "Post-Shooting Trauma And Domestic Violence: Clinical Observation And Preliminary Data," pp. 227-231. "...domestic violence may increase in some police families after a shooting incident." (p. 228).

The above papers are compiled in *Law Enforcement Families: Issues And Answers*, eds. J.T. Reese, E. Scrivner, C.J. Lent, Washington, DC: U.S. Government Printing Office, 1994.

4. See Watson, C.G., et al., "Effects Of A Vietnam War Memorial Pilgrimage On Veterans With Posttraumatic Stress Disorder," pp. 315-316. "It does not appear that real-life exposure to trauma reminders, such as combat helicopters, battlefields, rape scenes, or memorials, can be assumed to generate more long-term positive than negative effects on PTSD symptoms at this time." (p. 318).

5. The National Law Enforcement Officers Memorial Fund (NLEOMF) reports that 1,671 law enforcement officers were killed while on duty during the past ten years. On average, there is one death every 53 hours or 167 per year. There were 181 officers killed in 2007. Since the first recorded police death in 1792, there have been more than 18,200 law enforcement officers killed in-the-line-of-duty. This information was updated on the NLEOMF website in March, 2008. The NLEOMF includes criteria not applied by the *Uniform Crime Reports*, such as deaths and injuries as a result of heart attacks, struggling with prisoners and attacks on military police. See www.nleomf.com/TheMemorial/Facts/polfacts.htm.

6. After a shooting, for instance, officers tend to finalize decisions they were trying to make before the incident. "It is almost as if they decide that life is too short, and they need to make the decisions that will bring them the most happiness and contentment." See Carson, S.L., "Shooting, Death trauma, And Excessive Force," p. 54.

7. See Bettinger, K.J., "After The Gun Goes Off," *State Peace Officers Journal*, p. 91. "...20 percent of officers involved in a shooting are divorced within one year."

See Bohl, N., Solomon, R.M., "Male Law Enforcement Officers' And Their Spouses' Perceptions To Post-Shooting Reactions," in *Law Enforcement Families: Issues And Answers*, eds. J.T. Reese, E. Scrivner, C.J. Lent, Washington, DC: U.S. Government Printing Office, 1994: 155-161. Critical incidents tend to place "considerable strain" on police marriages. Some "spouses perceive greater distress than the officer experiences."

The Bohl report adds, "Conversely, while some officers reported much distress, their wives perceived and/or reported that they were largely unaffected by the critical incident." (p. 159) Why the contradiction? Perhaps the officer is not sharing feelings or the spouse is not willing to admit what is actually happening. Miscommunication strains a marriage.

See Bryant, C., "Law Enforcement Stress: I Need Help," *National F.O.P. Journal*, V19, N2, Spring 1990: 10-11, 57-58. "While statistics differ, divorce rates in law enforcement families may reach as high as 75%." (p. 58).

See Conroy, D.L., Hess, K.M., *Officers At Risk: How To Identify And Cope With Stress.* "Marital difficulties are frequently related to post-traumatic stress disorder..." (p. 75). "The job may become so all-consuming your spouse may give an ultimatum: 'Me or the job.' In looking at officers' exceptionally high divorce rare, the decision of many is apparent." (p. 144).

See Farmer, R.E., "Clinical And Managerial Implications Of Stress Research On The Police," pp. 205-218. "...police divorce rates do not differ from that of the general population..." (p. 213).

See Gentz, D., Taylor, D., "Marital Status And Attitudes About Divorce Among Veteran Law Enforcement Officers," in *Law Enforcement Families: Issues And Answers,* eds. J.T. Reese, E. Scrivner, C.J. Lent, Washington, DC: U.S. Government Printing Office, 1994: 67-71. In this study, 51 percent of officers sampled had divorced at least once, not more than the national average for the civilian population. "...there is a prevalent belief among veteran officers that there is a strong relationship between a career in law enforcement and marital problems that could lead to divorce." (p. 69).

Chapter 16: Issues and Support Sources, N to Z

1. See DSM-IV, pp. 394-395.

2. See Weaver, et al., "Posttraumatic Stress, Mental Health Professionals, And The Clergy: A Need For Collaboration, Training, And Research," *Journal Of Traumatic Stress,* V9, N4, October 1996: 847-856. As millions of people seek help from clergy, there is a need for collaboration between mental health professionals and clergy.

3. See Matsakis, A., *I Can't Get Over It, A Handbook For Trauma Survivors, Second Edition.* "The critical variable in the development of PTSD was the degree of exposure to combat—the amount of stress to which the soldier had been exposed." (p. 15). In reference to the DSM-IV definition of PTSD, Dr. Matsakis says, "The PTSD diagnosis is also the only one that recognizes that, subject to enough stress, any human being has the potential for developing PTSD or PTSD symptoms." (p. 15).

4. See Curran, S.F., "Sexual Harassment Of The Female Officer: Effects On The Police Family," in *Law Enforcement Families: Issues And Answers,* eds. J.T. Reese, E. Scrivner, C.J. Lent, Washington, DC: U.S. Government Printing Office, 1994: 271-274. The effects of sexual harassment "...suggest the psychological response is consistent with post-traumatic stress disorder (American Psychiatric Association, 1987). These effects include a wide range of symptoms associated with arousal, avoidance, and reexperiencing the harassment." (p. 272).

See Bartol, C.R., et al., "Women In Small-Town Policing: Job Performance And Stress," pp. 240-259. This study suggests that sexual harassment is wide spread. Fifty-three percent of female police officers indicated they had been sexually harassed by male officers and more often by male department supervisors. (p. 252). This results in a high turnover among female officers. (p. 257)

See also Fontana, A., Rosenheck, R.A., "Duty-related And Sexual Stress In The Etiology Of PTSD Among Women Veterans Who Seek Treatment," *Psychiatric Services*, V49, N5, May 1998: 658-662. Although this study examined women veterans, it may equally apply to female police officers. The authors concluded that women's exposure to sexual stress is toxic for the development of PTSD.

Bibliography

Alexander, D.A. (1993, Dec.). Stress among police body handlers: a long-term follow-up. *British Journal of Psychiatry*, 163, 806-808.

Alexander, D.A. & Wells, A. (1991, Oct.). Reactions of police officers to body-handling after a major disaster: a before-and-after comparison. *British Journal of Psychiatry*, 159, 547-555.

Allen, S.W. (1986). Suicide and indirect self-destruction behavior among police. In J.T. Reese & H.A. Goldstein (Eds.), *Psychological services for law enforcement* (pp. 413-417). Washington, DC: U.S. Government Printing Office.

American Medical Association (1986). Androgens and anabolic steroids. *Drug evaluations, Sixth ed.* (pp. 675-687). Chicago: Author.

American Psychological Association. Resiliency. Accessed July 9, 2008. www.apahelpcenter.org/featuredtopics.

American Psychiatric Association. (1994). *Diagnostic and statistical manual of mental disorders*, DSM-IV, (Fourth ed.). Washington, DC: Author.

Anderson, B.J. (1998, Summer). Trauma Response profile. *Trauma Response*, 4(2), 4-6.

Anderson, W., Swenson, D., Clay, D. (1994, Oct.). Stress Management for Law Enforcement Officers. Prentice Hall.

Andrews, Bernice et al. (2007, Sept.). Delayed-onset posttraumatic stress disorder: a systematic review of the evidence. *American Journal of Psychiatry*. 164:1319-1326.

Andrykowski, M.A., et al. (1998, June). Posttraumatic stress disorder after treatment for breast cancer: prevalence of diagnosis and use of the PTSD checklist—civilian version (PCL-C) as a screening instrument. *Journal of Consulting and Clinical Psychology*, 66(3), 586-590.

Anson, R.H. and Bloom, M.E. (1988, Dec.). Police stress in an occupational context. *Journal of Police Science and Administration*, 16(4), 229-235.

Archibald, E.M. (1986). Confidentiality when the police psychologist is evaluator and caregiving practitioner. In J.T. Reese & H.A. Goldstein (Eds.), *Psychological services for law enforcement* (pp. 215-217). Washington, DC: U.S. Government Printing Office.

Armfield, F. (1994, Dec.). Preventing post-traumatic stress disorder resulting from military operations. *Military Medicine*, 159(12), 739-746.

Atchison, M. & McFarlane, A.C. (1994, Dec.). A review of dissociation and dissociative disorders. *Australian & New Zealand Journal of Psychiatry*, 28(4), 591-599.

Back, S.E., Brady, K.T., Sonne, S.C., Verduin, M.L. (2006) Symptom improvement in co-occurring PTSD and alcohol dependence. *Journal of Nervous and Mental Disorders*. 194(9), 690-696.

Baker, Al. (2008, May 8). 11 years of police gunfire, in painstaking detail. *New York Times*.

Baker, D.G., et al. (1997, Oct. 13). Relationship between posttraumatic stress disorder and self-reported physical symptoms in Persian Gulf War veterans. *Archives Of Internal Medicine*, 157(18), 2076-2078.

Bartol, C.R., et al. (1992, Sept.). Women in small-town policing: Job performance and stress. *Criminal Justice and Behavior*, 19(3), 240-259.

Bass, M. (1982). Stress—a woman officer's view. *Police Stress*, 5(1).

Behr, Richard (2000, March 1) Under the Headset: Surviving Dispatcher Stress. Staggs Publishing.

Beil, L. (1994, Jan. 2). Shooting survivors suffering stress disorder, doctors claim. *Santa Barbara News-Press*.

Benezra, J. (1990, June 15). Psychiatrist, New York. In an unpublished, untitled, confidential psychiatric report.

Benezra, J. (1990, Dec. 10). Psychiatrist, New York. In an unpublished, untitled, confidential psychiatric report.

Berger, L. (1993, Oct. 9). Women's panel finds ingrained sexism in LAPD. *Los Angeles Times*, B1, B4.

Bettinger, K.J. (1990, Summer) After the gun goes off. *State Peace Officers Journal*, 39(2), 90-93, 95

Black, C. (1979). Children of alcoholics. *Alcohol Health and Research World*, 4, 23-27.

Blair, D.T. & Ramones, V.A. (1996, Nov.). Understanding vicarious traumatization. *Journal of Psychosocial Nursing & Mental Health Services*, 34(11), 24-30.

Bohl, N. & Solomon, R.M. (1994). Male law enforcement officers' and their spouses' perceptions to post-shooting reactions. In J.T. Reese, E. Scrivner & C.J. Lent (Eds.), *Law enforcement families: issues and answers* (pp. 155-161). Washington, DC: U.S. Government Printing Office.

Bonanno, G.A., Galea, S., Bucciarelli, A., Viahov, D. (2007). What predicts psychological resilience after disaster? The role of demographics, resources, and life stress. *Journal of Consulting and Clinical Psychology*, 75(5), 671-682.

Bonanno, G.A., Galea, S., Bucciarelli, A., Vlahov, D. (2006) Psychological resilience after disaster—New York City in the aftermath of the September 11th terrorist attack. _Psychological Science_, 17(3), 181-186.

Bonanno, G.A., Rennicke, C., Dekel, S. (2005). Self-enhancement among high-exposure survivors of the September 11th terrorist attack: Resilience or social maladjustment? _Journal of Personality and Social Psychology_. 88(6), 984-998.

Boscarino, J.A. (2006) Posttraumatic stress disorder and mortality among US army veterans 30 years after military service. _Annals of Epidemiology_, 16(4), 248-256.

Bourne, E.J. (2000, Nov.). The Anxiety & Phobia Workbook, 3rd Edition. New Harbinger Publications.

Bouza, A.V. (1990). _The police mystique_. New York, London: Plenum Press.

Brady, K.T. (1997). Posttraumatic stress disorder and comorbidity: recognizing the many faces of PTSD. _Journal of Clinical Psychiatry_, 58(Suppl. 9), 12-15.

Braxton, G. (1995, June 23). A patient ear for those in anguish. _Los Angeles Times_, E4.

Bremner, J.D. & Brett, E. (1997, Jan.). Trauma-related dissociative states and long-term psychopathology in posttraumatic stress disorder. _Journal of Traumatic Stress_, 10(1), 37-49.

Bremner, J.D. et al. (1996 March). Chronic PTSD in Vietnam combat veterans: Course of illness and substance abuse. _American Journal of Psychiatry_, 153(3), 369-375.

Brende, J.O. (1991). _Trauma recovery for victims and survivors, a twelve step recovery program workbook for group leaders and participants_. Columbus, Georgia: Trauma Recovery Pubs.

Breslau, N., et al. (1998, July). Trauma and posttraumatic stress disorder in the community; the 1996 Detroit Area Survey of Trauma. _Archives of General Psychiatry_, 55, 626-631.

Brown, S. (1994, Oct-Dec.). Alcoholism and trauma: a theoretical overview and comparison. _Journal of Psychoactive Drugs_, 26(4), 345-355.

Brownstein, R. (1997, June). Many big cities face woes of rising poverty. _Arizona Republic_, A8.

Bruinius, Harry. (2001, November 14). Another plane crash rocks a shattered town. Christian Science Monitor.

Bryant, C. (1990, Spring). Law enforcement stress: I need help. _National F.O.P. Journal_, 19(2), 10-11, 57-58.

Bryant, Richard A. and Harvey, Allison G. (2002) Delayed-onset posttraumatic stress disorder: a prospective evaluation. _Australian and New Zealand Journal of Psychiatry_. Blackwell Synergy.

Buffum, M.D. & Wolfe, N.S. (1995, Nov.-Dec.) Posttraumatic stress disorder and the World War II veteran. _Geriatric Nursing_, 16(6), 264-270.

Bullman, T.A. & Kang, H.K. (1994, Nov.). Posttraumatic stress disorder and the risk of traumatic deaths among Vietnam veterans. *Journal of Nervous & Mental Disease*, 182(11), 604-610.

Bureau of Justice Statistics. (1996). *Criminal victimization, general.* U.S. Department of Justice.

Burke, R.J. (1997). Toward an understanding of psychological burnout among police officers. *International Journal of Stress Management*, 4(1), 13-27.

Burke, Tod W. (2004, 1995, Oct.). Dispatcher stress—police dispatchers. *FBI Law Enforcement Bulletin.* FBI 1995; Gale Group 2004.

Bursztajn, H.J. (1996, April). World War II: Its effects after 50 years. *American Journal of Psychiatry*, 153(4), 584.

Carlier, I.V.E., Lamberts, R.D., Fouwels, A.J. & Gersons, B.P.R. (1996, Oct.). PTSD in relation to dissociation in traumatized police officers. *American Journal of Psychiatry*, 153(10), 1325-1328.

Carlier, I.V.E., Lamberts, R.D. & Gersons, B.P.R. (1997, Aug.). Risk factors for posttraumatic stress symptomatology in police officers: a prospective analysis. *Journal of Nervous And Mental Disease*, 185(8), 498-506.

Carlier, I.V.E., Lamberts, R.D., Van Uchelen, A.J., & Berthold, P.R. (1998, July). Disaster-related post-traumatic stress in police officers: a field study of the impact of debriefing. *Stress Medicine*, 14(3), 143-148.

Carlson, J.G., et al. (1998). Eye movement desensitization and reprocessing (EMDR) treatment for combat-related posttraumatic stress disorder. *Journal of Traumatic Stress*, 11(1), 3-24.

Carlson, N.R. (1992). *Foundations of physiological psychology, second edition.* New York: Simon & Schuster.

Carson, S.L. (1987). Shooting, death trauma, and excessive force. In Harry W. More, Peter C. Unsinger, (Eds.), *Police managerial use of psychology and psychologists* (pp. 43-62). Springfield, Illinois: Charles C. Thomas.

Cart, J. (1995, May 28). The question about Monica. *Los Angeles Times*, C1.

Cart, J. (1995, Aug. 18). A return to the light. *Los Angeles Times*, C1

Carty, J., O'Donnell, M.L., Creamer, M. (2006). Delayed-onset PTSD: a prospective study of injury survivors. *Journal of Affective Disorders*, 90(2-3), 257-261.

Cavanagh, J.J. (1993, April 28). Psychiatrist, New York. In an unpublished, confidential psychiatric report addressed to *Workers Compensation Board.*

Centers for Disease Control and Prevention, National Center for Health Statistics. 1996 homicide figures for U.S. *Monthly Vital Statistics Report*, 46(1), Suppl. U.S. Department of Health and Human Services.

Clary, M. (1993, Feb. 24). Hurricane battered Florida city—but not its spirit of renewal. *Los Angeles Times*, A5.

Clary, M. (1993, Aug. 23). Clouds of despair linger in Florida in Andrew's wake. *Los Angeles Times*, A10-A11.

Clary, M. & Simon, R. (1995, April 23). Grim hunt goes on in shattered building as storm adds woes. *Los Angeles Times*.

Clary, M. (1995, Aug. 10). Depression often undetected in Latinos. *Los Angeles Times*, B2.

Classen, C., Koopman, C. & Spiegel, D. (1993, Spring). Trauma and dissociation. *Bulletin of the Menninger Clinic*, 57(2), 178-194.

Classen, C., et al. (1998, May). Acute stress disorder as a predictor of posttraumatic stress symptoms. *American Journal of Psychiatry*, 155(5), 620-624.

Connors, R. (1996, April). Self-injury in trauma survivors: 1. Functions and meanings, 197-206. 2. Levels of clinical response, 207-216. *American Journal of Orthopsychiatry*, 66(2).

Conroy, D.L. & Hess, K.M. (1992). *Officers at risk: how to identify and cope with stress.* Placerville, CA: Custom Publishing Co.

Conti, S. (1991, Jan. 16). Executive Director, Clinical Psychotherapist, Diagnostic And Counseling Services, New York. In an unpublished, untitled, confidential psychiatric report.

Copes, H. (2004, July). Policing and Stress. Prentice Hall.

Cowie, H, Wallace, P. (2001, February). Peer Support in Action: From Bystanding to Standing By. Sage Productions Ltd.

Crank, J.P., & Caldero, M.(1991). The production of occupational stress in medium-sized police agencies: a survey of line officers in eight municipal departments. *Journal of Criminal Justice*, 19(4), 339-349.

Curran, S. F. (1994). Sexual harassment of the female officer: effects on the police family. In J.T. Reese, E. Scrivner & and C.J. Lent, (Eds.), *Law enforcement families: issues and answers* (pp. 271-274). Washington, DC: U.S. Government Printing Office.

D'Agostino, C. (1986). Police psychological services: ethical issues. In J.T. Reese, H.A. Goldstein, (Eds.), *Psychological services for law enforcement* (pp. 241-247). Washington, DC: U.S. Government Printing Office.

Danieli, Y. (1994). Trauma to the family: intergenerational sources of vulnerability and resilience. In J.T. Reese, E. Scrivner & C.J. Lent, (Eds.), *Law enforcement families: issues and answers* (pp. 163-175). Washington, DC: U.S. Government Printing Office.

Davies, M.I. & Clark, D.M. (1998, June). Thought suppression produces a rebound effect with analogue post-traumatic intrusions. *Behaviour Research and Therapy*, 36(6), 571-582.

Davis, B. (1982). Burnout. *Police Magazine*, 5(3), 9-18.

De Turenne, V. (1995, June 7). Life brings stress, learn to live with it. *Arizona Republic*.

Donziger, S.R., Editor. (1996). *The real war on crime: the report of the national criminal justice commission*. New York: Harper Collins.

Dowling, C. (1991). *You Mean I Don't Have To Feel This Way? New Help for Depression, Anxiety, and Addiction*. New York: Charles Scribner's Sons.

D'Souza, D. (1995, Nov-Dec.) Post-traumatic stress disorder—a scar for life. *British Journal of Clinical Practice*, 49(6), 309-313.

Elder, G.H., Shanahan, M.J. & Clipp, E.C. (1997, March). Linking combat and physical health: the legacy of World War II in men's lives. *American Journal of Psychiatry*, 154(3), 330-336.

Ellard, J.H. (1997, Jan. 20). The epidemic of post-traumatic stress disorder: a passing phase? *Medical Journal of Australia*, 166(2), 84-87.

Ellison, K.W. (1986). Development of a comprehensive selection procedure for a medium sized police department. In J.T. Reese and H.A. Goldstein, (Eds.), *Psychological services for law enforcement* (pp. 23-27). Washington, DC: U.S. Government Printing Office.

Ellison, K. & Genz, J.L. (1983). *Stress and the police officer*. Springfield, Illinois: Charles C. Thomas.

Engine 10/Ladder 10 (2008). What is the FDNY Housewatch? Fire Department New York, www.fdnytenhouse.com/ontheweb as accessed 2/9/2008.

Everly, G.S., & Mitchell, J.T. (1992, Nov. 19-22). The prevention of work-related post traumatic stress: the critical incident stress debriefing process (CISD), presented to *Second APA and NIOSH conference on occupational stress*: Washington, DC.

Everly, G.S. (1989). *A clinical guide to the treatment of the human stress response*. New York: Plenum Press.

Farmer, R.E. (1990, Sept.). Clinical and managerial implications of stress research on the police. *Journal of Police Science and Administration*, 17(3).

FDNY Fire Operations response on September 11, 2001. http://nyc.gov/html/fdny/pdf/mck_report/fire-operations_ response.pdf

Federal Bureau of Investigation (FBI). (1991). *Use of unauthorized force by law enforcement personnel: Problems and solutions*. Washington, DC: U.S. Government Printing Office.

Figley, C.R. (1994). Compassion fatigue among law enforcement therapists. In J.T. Reese, E. Scrivner, C.J. Lent (Eds.),

Law enforcement families: issues and answers (pp. 387-400). Washington, DC: U.S. Government Printing Office.

Finn, P. & Tomz, J.E. (1997). *Issues and practices in criminal justice: Developing a law enforcement stress program for officers and their families.* Washington, DC: U.S. Department of Justice, Office of Justice Programs, National Institute of Justice.

Fishkin, G.L. (1988). *Police burnout: signs, symptoms and solutions.* Gardena, CA: Harcourt Brace Jovanovich.

Foa, E.B. (1997). Trauma and women: course, predictors, and treatment. *Journal of Clinical Psychiatry,* 58(9), Suppl., 25-28.

Foa, E.B. & Meadows, E.A. (1997). Psychosocial treatments for posttraumatic stress disorder: a critical review. *Annual Review of Psychology,* 48, 449-480.

Fontana, A. & Rosenheck, R.A. (1998, May). Duty-related and sexual stress in the etiology of PTSD among women veterans who seek treatment. *Psychiatric Services,* 49(5), 658-662.

Fontana, A. & Rosenheck, R.A. (1998, July). Psychological benefits and liabilities of traumatic exposure in the war zone. *Journal of Traumatic Stress,* 11(3), 485-503.

Ford, W.D. (1998, July). Managing Police Stress. Book and cassette. Management Advantage.

Frankel, F.H. (1994, Oct.). The concept of flashbacks in historical perspective. *International Journal of Clinical & Experimental Hypnosis,* 42(4), 321-336.

Friedman, M.J. (1994, June). Post-traumatic stress disorder in the military veteran. *Psychiatric Clinics of North America,* 17(2), 265-277.

Friedman, M.J. (1997). Posttraumatic stress disorder. *Journal of Clinical Psychiatry,* 58(9), Suppl. 33-36.

Fyfe, J.J. (1979). Administrative interventions on police shooting discretion: an empirical examination. *Journal of Criminal Justice,* 7, 309-323).

Gardiner, Sean. (2006, November 28) Guns gone wild. www.village voice.com/news/0649,gardiner,75216,6.html.

Gersons, B.P.R. (1989). Patterns of PTSD among police officers following shooting incidents: a two-dimensional model and treatment implications. *Journal of Traumatic Stress,* 2(3), 247-257).

Gilmartin, K.M. (1986). Hypervigilance: a learned perceptual set and its consequences on police stress. In J.T. Reese & H.A. Goldstein, (Eds.) *Psychological services for law enforcement* (pp. 445-448). Washington DC: U.S. Government Printing Office.

Golembiewski, R.T. & Kim, B.S. (1990, Summer). Burnout in police work: stressors, strain, and the phase model. *Police Studies,* 13(2), 74-80).

Goodman, M. & Weiss, D.S. (1998, Jan.). Double trauma: a group therapy approach for Vietnam veterans suffering from war and childhood trauma. *International Journal of Group Psychotherapy*, 48(1), 39-54.

Goolkasian, G.A., Geddes, R.W., & DeJong, W. (1985). *Coping with police stress*. Washington, DC: National Institute of Justice.

Griffiths, R.F. & McDaniel, Q.P. (1993, March). Predictors of police assaults. *Journal of Police and Criminal Psychology*, 9(1).

Grisham, J. (1994). *The client*. New York: Dell.

Hart, L., Shogren, E. & Clary, M. (1995, April 23). Silent scars, haunting memories. *Los Angeles Times*, A1, A18-20, A23.

Harvey, A.G. & Bryant, R.A. (1998, June). The relationship between acute stress disorder and posttraumatic stress disorder: a prospective evaluation of motor vehicle accident survivors. *Journal of Consulting and Clinical Psychology*, 66(3), 507-512.

Harvey-Lintz, T. & Tidwell, R. (1997). Effects of the 1992 Los Angeles civil unrest: Post traumatic stress disorder symptomatology among law enforcement officers. *Social Science Journal*, 34(2), 171-183.

Hays, T. (5/8/2008). 8 officers who died of post-9/11 illness on NYPD memorial. *The Associated Press*.

Healy, D. (1993). *Images of trauma, From hysteria to posttraumatic stress disorder*. London, Boston: Faber and Faber.

Henry, V.E. (1995, Winter). The police officer as survivor: death confrontations and the police subculture. *Behavioral Sciences and the Law*, 13(1), 93-112.

Hepp, C. (Winter, 1987). Drinking and the police: it seems more common in blue. *Police Stress*, 8(1), 27-28. Reprinted from *Philadelphia Enquirer*.

Herman, J.L. (1992). *Trauma and recovery, the aftermath of violence—from domestic abuse to political terror*. New York: Basic Books.

Herrmann N, Eryavec G. (September 1994). Delayed onset posttraumatic stress disorder in World War II veterans. *Canadian Journal of Psychiatry*. 39(7):439-41.

Hill, K.Q. & Clawson, M. (1988, Dec.). The health hazards of "street level" bureaucracy: mortality among the police. *Journal of Police Science and Administration*, 16(4), 243-248).

Hilton, C. (1997, Aug.) Media triggers of post-traumatic stress disorder 50 years after the Second World War. *International Journal of Geriatric Psychiatry*, 12(8), 862-867.

Hoge, E.A., Austin, E.D., Pollack, M.H. (2007). Resilience: Research evidence and conceptual considerations for posttraumatic stress disorder. *Depression and Anxiety*, 24(2), 139-152.

Hoge, C.W., Auchterlonie, J.L., Milliken, C.S. (2006). Mental health problems, use of mental health services, and attrition from military service after returning from deployment to Iraq or Afghanistan. *Jama-Journal of the American Medical Association*, 295(9), 1023-1032.

Holland, Beth. (2001, November 13). Plane crashes in Queens. *Newsday*: New York.

Holt, Francis X. The top 10 things you should know about dispatcher stress. www.9-1-1magazine.com/magazine/1997/1197/features/holt.html. Accessed 1/13/2008.

Honig, A.L. & White, E.K. (1994). Violence and the law enforcement family. In J.T. Reese, E. Scrivner & C.J. Lent, (Eds.), *Law enforcement families: issues and answers* (pp. 101-109). Washington, DC: U.S. Government Printing Office.

Horowitz, M.J. (1992). *Stress response syndromes, 2nd edition*. New Jersey: Jason Aronson.

Hurricane survivors still reliving 'war'. (1993, January 10). *Santa Barbara News-Press*.

Hyams, K.C., Wignall, F.S. & Roswell, R. (1996). War syndromes and their evaluation: from the U.S. Civil War to the Persian Gulf War. *Annals of Internal Medicine*, 125(5), 398-405.

Ibarguen, Diego. (2001, November 13). Plane crashes into Queens, N.Y. *The Associated Press*.

Iserson, K.V. (1994) *Death to dust. What happens to dead bodies?* Tucson, Arizona: Galen Press.

Jackson, R.L. (1993, May 27). Dangers to prison guards rise as inmate conditions worsen. *Los Angeles Times*, A5.

Janik, J. (1994). Sin eaters. In J.T. Reese, E. Scrivner, C.J. Lent (Eds.), *Law enforcement families: issues and answers* (pp. 401-404). Washington, DC: U.S. Government Printing Office.

Jenkins, M.A., et al. (1998, Feb.). Learning and memory in rape victims with posttraumatic stress disorder. *American Journal of Psychiatry*, 155(2), 278-279.

Jones, C.E. (1989). An analysis of the post officer-involved shooting trauma. *After the smoke clears: surviving the police shooting* (pp. 19,38,58.). Springfield, Illinois: Charles C. Thomas.

Johnson, K. (1989). *Trauma in the lives of children: Crisis and stress management techniques for counselors and other professionals*. Alameda, CA: Hunter House.

Josephson, R.L. & Reiser, M. (1990, Sept.). Officer suicide in the Los Angeles police department: a twelve-year follow-up. *Journal of Police Science and Administration*, 17(3), 227-229.

Kaczala, A. (1984, April). Clinical psychologist, San Antonio Community Hospital. In an April, 1994, unpublished, confidential psychiatric assessment as reported by Dr. S.

Leshin, psychiatrist, Montebello, California, in a letter addressed to *Department of Pensions, Los Angeles.*

Katz, R., Cohen, D.I., Hirsh, R.M. (2000, January 1) Cop to Cop: A Peer Support Training Manual for the Law Enforcement Officer, 2nd Edition.

Keane, T.M., Kaloupek, D.G. (1997, June 21). Comorbid psychiatric disorders in PTSD. Implications for research. *Annals of the New York Academy of Sciences,* 821, 24-34.

Kellogg, T. & Harrison, M. (1991, July). Law enforcement and post traumatic stress disorder—the echoes Of violence. *The Narc Officer,* 24-25.

Kirkpatrick, C. (1995, Sept. 4). Monica's dark odyssey. *Newsweek,* 48-49.

Kirschman, E. (1997). *I love a cop.* New York, London: Guilford Press.

Kleim, B., Ehlers, A., Glucksman, E. (2007). Early predictors of chronic post-traumatic stress disorder in assault survivors. *Psychological Medicine,* 37(10), 1457-1467.

Knowlton, L. (1995, June 5). New stresses spark more burnout for counselors. *Los Angeles Times,* D10.

Kobrick, F.R. (1993, Aug.). Reaction of Vietnam veterans to the Persian Gulf War. *Health & Social Work,* 18(3), 165-171.

Koenen, K.C., Hitsman, B., Lyons, M.J., Niaura, R., McCaffery, J., Goldgerg, J., et al. (2005). A twin registry study of the relationship between posttraumatic stress disorder and nicotine dependence in men. *Archives of General Psychiatry,* 62(11), 1258-1265.

Koenenn, C. (1995, July 20). Just how dangerous is your job, anyway? *Los Angeles Times,* E1.

Kofoed, L., Friedman, M.J., Peck, R. (1993, Summer). Alcoholism and drug abuse in patients with PTSD. *Psychiatric Quarterly,* 64(2), 151-171.

Kopel, H. & Friedman, M. (1997, April). Posttraumatic symptoms in South African police exposed to violence. *Journal of Traumatic Stress,* 10(2), 307-317.

Kroes, W.H. (1985). *Society's victim—the police, an analysis of job stress in policing* (pp. 27-34). Springfield, Illinios: Charles C. Thomas.

Kulka, R. et al. (1988). *National Vietnam veterans readjustment study.* Research Triangle Park, NC: Research Triangle Institute.

Lamarche, L.J., De Koninck, J. (2007). Sleep disturbance in adults with posttraumatic stress disorder: a review. *Journal of Clinical Psychiatry,* 68(8), 1257-1270.

Landsberg, Mitchell (1995, August 6). World War II ghosts come back to haunt veterans 50 years later. *Los Angeles Times,* A1.

Leshin, S. (1984, Sept. 1). Psychiatrist, Montebello, California. In an unpublished, confidential psychiatric report addressed to *Department of Pensions, Los Angeles.*

Levin, Aaron (2007, Sept.). Differences in PTSD prevalence and associated risk factors among World Trade Center disaster rescue and recovery workers. *American Psychiatric Association.* www.ajp.psychiatryonline.org.

Lippert, W.W. (1991). Police officer suicide or homicide: treating the affected department. In J.T. Reese, J.M. Horn, & C. Dunning, (Eds.), *Critical incidents in policing* (rev.) (pp. 179-190). Washington, DC: FBI.

Living Targets. (1981). A special report by the *California Correctional Officers Association.*

Long, N., Chamberlain, K. & Vincent, C. (1994, March). Effect of the Gulf War on reactivation of adverse combat-related memories in Vietnam veterans. *Journal of Clinical Psychology*, 50(2), 138-144.

Lubecki, Claude Pierre, Plaintiff, et al. versus The City of New York, et al., Defendants. Supreme Court of New York, Appellate Division, First Department. 1413. 304 A.D.2d 224; 758 N.Y.S.2d 610. March 27,2003, Decided and Entered. The text of this lawsuit can be found online at www.aele.org/ law/2004LRJAN/lvc.html.

Lynch, R. (1994, Jan. 24). Rape suspect's murder trial tests legal limits. *Los Angeles Times*, A3, A28.

Malone, J.D. et al. (1996, Dec.) Possibilities for unexplained chronic illnesses among reserve units deployed in Operation Desert Shield/Desert Storm. *Southern Medical Journal*, 89(12), 1147-1155.

Management of Mental Disorders. (2003, Jan. 3) Acute Stress Reaction 4.8, published by *World Health Organization:* Australia, Canada, China, Italy, NZ, UK. Pages 277-281. Edited by Gavin Andrews, MD, UNSW. www.crufad.com/ self_help/trauma-level2.htm.

Mann, J.P., Neece, J. (1990). Workers' compensation for law enforcement related post traumatic stress disorder. *Behavioral Sciences and the Law*, 8, 447-456.

Marcus, S.V., Marquis, P. & Sakai, C. (1997, Fall). Controlled study of treatment of PTSD using EMDR in an HMO setting. *Psychotherapy*, 34(3), 307-315.

Mark, V.H. & Mark, J.P. (1992). *Reversing Memory Loss, proven methods for regaining, strengthening, and preserving your memory.* New York: Houghton Mifflin Company.

Martin, C.A., McKean, H.E. & Veltkamp, L.J. (1986). Post-traumatic stress disorder in police and working with victims: a pilot study. *Journal of Police Science and Administration*, 14(2), 98-101.

Matsakis, A. (2005, Aug.) In harm's way: Help for the wives of military men, police, EMTs & Firefighters. New Harbinger Pubs.

Matsakis, A. (1996). *I can't get over it, a handbook for trauma survivors*, second edition. Oakland, CA: New Harbinger Pubs.

McCafferty, F.L., Domingo, G.D. & McCafferty, E.A. (1990, May). Posttraumatic stress disorder in the police officer: paradigm of occupational stress. *Southern Medical Journal*, 83(5), 543-547.

McCafferty, F.L. et al. (1992). Stress and suicide in police officers: paradigm of occupational stress. *Southern Medical Journal*, 85(3), 233-243.

McCulloch, M., Jones, C. & Bailey, J. (1995, Oct.). Post traumatic stress disorder: turning the tide without opening the floodgates. *Medicine, Science & the Law*, 35(4), 287-293.

McFadden, Robert D. (1993, January 30). Gunman and hostage are killed after Manhattan bank robbery. *New York Times*.

McMains, M.J. (1986). Post shooting trauma: principles from combat. In J.T. Reese & H.A. Goldstein (Eds.), *Psychological services for law enforcement* (pp. 365-368). Washington, DC: U.S. Government Printing Office.

McMurray, H.L. (1990). Attitudes of Assaulted Police Officers and Their Policy Implications. *Journal of Police Science and Administration*, 17(1).

Meichenbaum, D. (1994, Sept.). *A clinical handbook/practical therapist manual for assessing and treating adults with post-traumatic stress disorder (PTSD)*. Waterloo, ON: Institute Press.

Mellman, T.A. (1997, June 21). Psychobiology of sleep disturbances in posttraumatic stress disorder. *Annals of the New York Academy of Sciences*, 821, 142-149.

Mendelsohn, B. (1976). Victimology and contemporary society's trends. In E.C. Viano (Ed.), *Victims and society* (pp. 7-28). Washington, DC: Visage Press.

Mills, K.L. Teesson, M., Ross, J., Peters, L. (2006). Trauma, PTSD, and substance use disorders: Findings from the Australian National Survey of mental health and well-being. *American Journal of Psychiatry*, 163(4), 652-658.

Mitchell, J.T. & Bray, G.P. (1990). *Emergency services stress: guidelines for preserving the health and careers of emergency services personnel*. Engle-wood Cliffs, NJ: Prentice Hall.

Monahan, J. & Steadman, H.J., Editors. (1994) *Violence and mental disorder: developments in risk assessment*. Chicago, London: University of Chicago Press.

More, H.W. (1992). Reaction to police work: stress and its consequences. *Special topics in policing* (pp. 171-218). Cincinnati, Ohio: Anderson Publishing Company.

Morell, J. (1995, June 19). Sometimes the listeners need compassion too. *Los Angeles Times*, E1.

Morgan, C.A., et al. (1998, Jan.). Anniversary reactions in Gulf War veterans: a naturalistic inquiry 2 years after the Gulf War. *Journal of Traumatic Stress*, 11(1), 165-171.

Moyers, F. (1996, Feb.) Oklahoma City bombing: exacerbation of symptoms in veterans with PTSD. *Archives of Psychiatric Nursing*, 10(1), 55-59.

Muss, D.C. (1991). A new technique for treating post-traumatic stress disorder. *British Journal of Clinical Psychology*, 30, 91-92. Birmingham, UK: The British Psychological Society.

Najavits, L.M., et al. (1998, Feb.). Cocaine dependence with and without PTSD among subjects in the National Institute On Drug Abuse Collaborative Cocaine Treatment Study. *American Journal of Psychiatry*, 155(2), 214-219.

National Construction Safety Team (September 2005). Final Report on the Collapse of the World Trade Center Towers. http://wtc.nist.gov/NISTNCSTAR1CollapseofTowers.pdf. Retrieved on 2007-07-10.

Neidig, P.H., Russell, H.E. & Seng, A.F. (1994). Observations and recommendations concerning the prevention and treatment of interspousal aggression in law enforcement families. In J.T. Reese, E. Scrivner, C.J. Lent, (Eds.), *Law enforcement families: issues and answers* (pp. 353-358). Washington, DC: U.S. Government Printing Office.

Neria, Y., Gross, R., Litz, B., Maguen, S., Insel, B., Seirmarco, G., et al. (2007). Prevalence and psychological correlates of complicated grief among bereaved adults 2.5-3.5 years after September 11th attacks. *Journal of Traumatic Stress*, 20(3), 251-262.

Newton, J., Boxall, B. & Krikorian, G. (1994, March 3). Sexual harassment a tough LAPD problem. *Los Angeles Times*, A1, A18, A19.

Nielsen, E. (1986). Understanding and assessing traumatic stress reactions. In J.T. Reese & H.A. Goldstein (Eds.), *Psychological services for law enforcement* (pp. 369-364). Washington, DC: U.S. Government Printing Office.

North, C.S., Pfefferbaum, B., Narayanan, P., Thielman, S., McCoy, G., Dumont, C., et al. (2005). Comparison of post-disaster psychiatric disorders after terrorist bombings in Nairobi and Oklahoma City. *British Journal of Psychiatry* (186), 487-493.

NYPD CompStat Unit. (1995). *Police Department City of New York CompStat Crime Complaints*: 72nd Precinct, V15, N24.

NYPD CompStat Unit. (1995). *Police Department City of New York CompStat Crime Complaints*: 75th Precinct, V15, N24.

O'Donnell, M.L. Creamer, M., Pattison, P. (2004). Posttraumatic stress disorder and depression following trauma: understanding comorbidity. American Journal of Psychiatry, 161: 1390-1396.

Orth, U., Wieland, E. (2006). Anger, hostility, and posttraumatic stress disorder in trauma-exposed adults: a meta-analysis. *Journal of Consulting and Clinical Psychology.* 74(4), 698-706.

Paradise, P.R. (1991, June). DEA trauma team. *Law and Order*, 39(6), 97-99. Wilmette, Illinois: Hendon.

Paton, D. & Violanti, J. (1996). *Traumatic stress in critical occupations: Recognition, consequences and treatment.* Springfield, IL: Charles C. Thomas.

Patterson, B.L. (1992, Sept.). Job experience and perceived job stress among police, correctional, and probation/parole officers. *Criminal Justice And Behavior*, 19(3), 260-285.

Perrin, M.A., Digrande, L., Wheeler, K., Thorpe, L., Farfel, M., Brackbill, R. (2007). Differences in PTSD prevalence and associated risk factors among World Trade Center disaster rescue and recovery workers. *American Journal of Psychiatry*, 164(9), 1385-1394.

Perry, T. (1995, Jan. 1). Rape victim fights back and takes story public. *Los Angeles Times*, A1, A32.

Physicians' Desk Reference (PDR, 1994), 48th Edition. Deca-Durabolin, (p. 1641). Anadrol-50, (pp. 2349, 2350). Montvale, NJ: Medical Economics Data Production Co.

Physicians GenRx (1994). Nandrolone Decanoate, (pp. II-1590-1592). Smithtown, NY: Data Pharmaceutica.

Pogrebin, M.R. & Poole, E.D. (1991). Police and tragic events: the management of emotions. *Journal of Criminal Justice*, 19, 395-403.

Ragonese, P. & Stainback, B. (1991). *The soul of a cop.* New York: St. Martin's Press.

Reese, J.T. (1988). Psychological aspects of policing violence. In J.T. Reese & J.M. Horn (Eds.), *Police psychology: operational assistance* (pp. 347-361). Washington, DC: U.S. Government Printing Office.

Rhead, C., Abrams, A., Trasman, H., & Margolis, P. (1968). The psychological assessment of police candidate. *American Journal of Psychiatry*, 124, 1575-1580.

Riley, K.J., Hoffman, B., (1995). *Domestic terrorism: a national assessment of state and local preparedness.* Rand.

Roan, S. (1994, Aug. 30). A refuge no more. *Los Angeles Times*, E1, E7.

Robinson, H.M., Sigman, M.R. & Wilson, J.P. (1997, Dec.). Duty-related stressors and PTSD symptoms in suburban police officers. *Psychological Reports*, 81(3), Part 1, 835-845.

Rogers, L.K. (2000, Jan.) Post Traumatic Stress Disorder: A Police Officers Report. First Page Publications.

Rourke, M. (1995, July 19). Forgive—but not forget. *Los Angeles Times*, E1.

Ryan, A.H., & Brewster, M.E. (1994). Post-traumatic stress disorder and related symptoms in traumatized police officers and their spouses/mates. In J.T. Reese, E. Scrivner & C.J. Lent (Eds.), *Law enforcement families: issues and answers* (pp. 217-225). Washington, DC: U.S. Government Printing Office.

Samaha, J. (1988). *Criminal justice*. St. Paul, MN: West Pub. Co.

Samuels, J.E. (2001, Jan.) Corrections and law enforcement family support solicitation for the implementation of the corrections field test. *National Institute of Justice*. www.ncjrs.gov/pdffiles1/nij/fy01-clefs-corrections.pdf.

Scanlon, R.A. (1990, April). Police enemy #1: stress. *Law Enforcement Technology*, 17(4), 18-21). New York: PTN Pub.

Scheck, M.M., Schaeffer, J.A. & Gillette, C. (1998). Brief psychological intervention with traumatized young women: the efficacy of eye movement desensitization and reprocessing. *Journal of Traumatic Stress*, 11(1), 25-44.

Schiraldi, G.R. (2000, January 1). Post-Traumatic Stress Disorder Sourcebook. McGraw-Hill.

Schwarz, E.D., and Perry, B.D. (1994, June). The post-traumatic response in children and adolescents. *Psychiatric Clinics of North America*, 17(2), 311-326.

Schwender, D., et al. (1998 Feb.). Conscious awareness during general anaesthesia: patients' perceptions, emotions, cognition and reactions. *British Journal of Anaesthesia*, 80(2), 133-139.

Shalev, A.Y., Tuval, R., Frenkiel-Fishman, S., Hadar, H., Eth, S. (2006) Psychological responses to continuous terror: a study of two communities in Israel. *American Journal of Psychiatry*. 163(4), 667-673.

Shalev, A.Y., et al. (1998, June). A prospective study of heart rate response following trauma and the subsequent development of posttraumatic stress disorder. *Archives of General Psychiatry*, 55(6), 553-559.

Sigler, R.T., Wilson, C.N. & Allen, Z. (1991). Police stress and teacher stress at work and at home. *Journal of Criminal Justice*, 19, 361-370).

Sloan, S. (1995, May). Terrorism: how vulnerable is the United States. In Stephen Pelletiere (Ed.), *Terrorism: National security policy and the home front*. The Strategic Studies of the U.S. Army War College.

Smith, V.E., et al. (1997, June 2). NYPD black and blue. *Newsweek*, 64, 68.

Snell, M.E., Janney, R., Vogtle, L.K., Colley, K.M., Delano, M. (2000, February 1). Social Relationships and Peer Support (Teachers' Guides to Inclusive Practices.) Brookes Publishing Company.

Social troubles to follow Andrew. (1992, Oct. 11). *Santa Barbara News-Press*.

Solomon, R.M. (1988). Mental conditioning: the utilization of fear. In J.T. Reese & J.M. Horn (Eds.), *Police psychology: operational assistance* (pp. 391-407). Washington, DC: U.S. Government Printing Office.

Solomon, R.M. (1989). The dynamics of fear in critical incidents. *The Training Key*, #399. Arlington, Virginia: International Association of Chiefs of Police.

Solomon, R.M. & Horn, J.M. (1986). Post-shooting traumatic reactions: a pilot study. In J.T. Reese & H.A. Goldstein (Eds.), *Psychological services for law enforcement* (pp. 383-393). Washington, DC: U.S. Government Printing Office.

Solomon, S.D. & Davidson, J.R. (1997). Trauma: prevalence, impairment, service use, and cost. *Journal of Clinical Psychiatry*, 58(9), Suppl., 5-11.

Solomon, Z., Mikulincer, M. (2006). Trajectories of PTSD: A 20-year longitudinal study. *American Journal of Psychiatry*. 163(4), 659-666.

Solomon Z, Kotler M, Shalev A, Lin R. (November 1989). Delayed onset PTSD among Israeli veterans of the 1982 Lebanon War. *Psychiatry*. 52(4):428-36.

Somodevilla, S.A. (1986). Post-shooting trauma: reactive and proactive treatment. In J.T. Reese & H.A. Goldstein (Eds.), *Psychological services for law enforcement* (pp. 395-398). Washington, DC: U.S. Government Printing Office.

Southwick, S.M., et al. (1993, Oct.) Trauma-related symptoms in veterans of Operation Desert Storm: a preliminary report. *American Journal of Psychiatry*, 150(10), 1524-1528.

Southwick, S.M., et al. (1994, June). Psychobiologic research in post-traumatic stress disorder. *Psychiatric Clinics of North America*. 17(2), 251-264.

Southwick, S.M., et al. (1995, Aug.) Trauma-related symptoms in veterans of Operation Desert Storm: a 2-year follow-up. *American Journal of Psychiatry*, 152(8), 1150-1155.

Spiegel, D. (1997, June 21). Trauma, dissociation, and memory. _Annals of the New York Academy of Sciences_, 821, 225-237.

Stephens, C., Long, N. & Miller, I. (1997). The impact of trauma and social support on posttraumatic stress disorder: a study of New Zealand police officers. _Journal of Criminal Justice_, 25(4), 303-314.

Stevens, J. (1994, Sept. 13). Rude awakening. _Los Angeles Times_, E3-E4.

Stewart, S.H. (1996, July). Alcohol abuse in individuals exposed to trauma: a critical review. _Psychological Bulletin_, 120(N), 83-112.

Stone, V. (1999, June). Cops Don't Cry: a book of help and hope for police families. Creative Bound.

Stotland, E. (1986). Police stress and strain as influenced by police self-esteem, time on job, crime frequency And interpersonal relationships. In J.T. Reese & H.A. Goldstein (Eds.), _Psychological services for law enforcement_ pp. 521-525. Washington DC: U.S. Government Printing Office.

Stotland, E., Pendleton, M. & Schwartz, R. (1989). Police stress, time on the job, and strain. _Journal of Criminal Justice_, 17, 55-60.

Stotland, E. (1991). The effects of police work and professional relationships on health. _Journal of Criminal Justice_, 19(4), 371-379).

Stratton, J.G. (1984). _Police passages_. Manhattan Beach, CA: Glennon.

Stratton, J.G., Parker, D.A. & Snibbe, J.R. (1984). Post-traumatic stress: study of police officers involved in shootings. _Psychological Reports_, 55, 127-131.

Stretch, R.H., et al. (1996, July). Post-traumatic stress disorder symptoms among Gulf War veterans. _Military Medicine_, 161(7), 407-410.

Sutherland, S.M. & Davidson, J.R. (1994, June). Pharmaco-therapy for post-traumatic stress disorder. _Psychiatric Clinics of North America_, 17(2), 409-423.

Swann, G.B. & D'Agostino, C.A. (1994). Post-shooting trauma and domestic violence: clinical observation and preliminary data. In J.T. Reese, E. Scrivner & C. Lent (Editors), _Law enforcement families: issues and answers_ (pp. 227-231). Washington, DC: U.S. Government Printing Office.

Tarnopolsky, A. & Shammi, C. (1995, Oct.). Post-traumatic stress disorder: personal disability, social cost, and prevention. _Canadian Journal of Psychiatry_, 40(8), 496-497.

Terr, L.C. (1985). Children traumatized in small groups. In S. Eth & R.S. Pynoos (Eds.), _Post-traumatic stress disorder in children_. Washington, DC: American Psychiatric Press.

Thompson, J.A. (1993, Nov.). Psychological impact of body recovery duties. *Journal of the Royal Society of Medicine*, 86(11), 628-629.

Turco, R.N. (1986). Police shootings—psychoanalytic viewpoints. *International Journal of Offender Therapy and Comparative Criminology*, 30(1), 53-58. Portland, Oregon: Oregon Health Sciences University.

Uniform Crime Reports, FBI. (2006). *Killed in the line of duty: a study of selected felonious killings of law enforcement officers.* Washington, DC: United States Department of Justice.

Uniform Crime Reports, FBI. (2006). *Crime in the United States, 2006.* Washington, DC: United States Department of Justice.

Uniform Crime Reports, FBI. (2006). *Law enforcement officers killed and assaulted.* Washington, DC: United States Department of Justice.

van der Kolk, B.A. et al. (1996, July). Dissociation, somatization, and affect dysregulation: the complexity of adaptation of trauma. *American Journal of Psychiatry*, 153(7) Suppl., 83-93.

Van der Kolk, B.A., McFarlane, A.C., Weisaeth, L. (1996, May). Traumatic Stress: The Effects of Overwhelming Experience on Mind, Body, and Society. Guilford Press.

van der Kolk, B.A., Fisler, R. (1993, June). The biologic basis of posttraumatic stress. *Primary Care; Clinics in Office Practice*, 20(2), 417-432.

van der Kolk, B.A., Fisler, R. (1994, Spring). Childhood abuse and neglect and loss of self-regulation. *Bulletin of the Menninger Clinic*, 58(2), 145-168.

van der Kolk, B.A., Fisler, R. (1995, Oct.). Dissociation and the fragmentary nature of traumatic memories: overview and exploratory study. *Journal of Traumatic Stress*, 8(4), 505-525.

Van Dyke C., Zilberg NJ, McKinnon JA (September 1985). Posttraumatic stress disorder: a thirty-year delay in World War II veteran. American Journal of Psychiatry. 142(9):1070-3.

Violanti, J.M. (1983). Stress patterns in police work: a longitudinal study. *Journal of Police Science and Administration*, 11(2), 211-216.

Violanti, J.M. (1996). *Police suicide: epidemic in blue.* Springfield, IL: Charles C. Thomas.

Violanti, J.M. (1996, April). The impact of cohesive groups in the trauma recovery context: police spouse survivors and duty-related death. *Journal of Traumatic Stress*, 9(2), 379-386.

Wambaugh, J. (1987) *The onion field.* New York: Dell.

Wang, S., Wilson, J.P. & Mason, J.W. (1996, July-Sept.). Stages of decompensation in combat-related posttraumatic stress disorder: a new conceptual model. _Integrative Physiological & Behavioral Science_, 31(3), 237-253.

Warrick, P. (1994, Jan. 31). Running the risk. _Los Angeles Times_, E1-E2.

Washington, B. (1981). Stress and the female officer. In L. Territo & H. Vetter, (Eds.), _Stress and Police Personnel_. Boston: Allyn & Bacon.

Watanabe, T. (1995, Jan. 25). Illness, mental problems on rise after Kobe quake. _Los Angeles Times_, A1, A22.

Watanabe, T. (1995, June 20). After Kobe, healing the psyche of Japan. _Los Angeles Times_, A1.

Watanabe, T. (1995, Dec. 26). Year after Kobe quake, crisis brings change. _Los Angeles Times_, A1.

Watson, C.G. et al. (1995, May). Effects of a Vietnam War Memorial Pilgrimage on veterans with posttraumatic stress disorder. _Journal of Nervous & Mental Disease_, 183(5), 315-319.

Weaver, A.J., Koenig, H.G. & Ochberg, F.M. (1996, Oct.). Posttraumatic stress, mental health professionals, and the clergy: a need for collaboration, training, and research. _Journal of Traumatic Stress_, 9(4), 847-856.

Webster's Third New International Dictionary (1986, 1961). P. B. Gove (Editor in chief), (pp. 2260, 2432) Springfield, Massachusetts: Merriam-Webster, Inc.

Webster's II New Riverside Dictionary, Office Edition (1984). New York: Berkley Books, (pp. 729-730).

Weiner, B.A. (1986). Confidentiality and the legal issues raised by the psychological evaluations of law enforcement officers. In J.T. Reese & H.A. Goldstein (Eds.), _Psychological services for law enforcement_ (pp. 97-102). Washington, DC: U.S. Government Printing Office.

White, Michael D. (2006). Hitting the target (or not): comparing characteristics of fatal, injurious, and noninjurious police shootings. _Police Quarterly_, V9, N3, 303-330. Sage Pubs.

Wildwood Crest Police Department; Lower Township Police Department—Respondents. (2002). Superior Court of New Jersey, Appellate Division. Docket No. A-1961-00T3, A-2044-00T3. Petitioners-Appellants' names are confidential. Argued: January 10 and 16, 2002. Decided: February 21, 2002. On appeal from the Division of Workers' Compensation. Available online at www.findlaw.com.

Williams, M.B., Poijula, S. (2002, May 15). The PTSD Workbook: Simple, Effective Techniques for Overcoming Traumatic Stress Symptoms. New Harbinger Publications.

Williams, M.B. (1994). Impact of duty-related death on officers' children: concepts of death, trauma reactions, and treatment. In J.T. Reese, E. Scrivner & C.J. Lent (eds.)

Law enforcement families: issues and answers (pp. 251-260). Washington, DC: U.S. Government Printing Office.

Wilson, S.A., Becker, L.A. & Tinker, R.H. (1995). Eye movement desensitization and reprocessing (EMDR) treatment for psychologically traumatized individuals. *Journal of Consulting and Clinical Psychology*, 63(6), 928-937.

Wilson, S.A., Becker, L.A. & Tinker, R.H. (1997). Fifteen-month follow-up of eye movement desensitization and reprocessing (EMDR) treatment for posttraumatic stress disorder and psychological trauma. *Journal of Consulting and Clinical Psychology*, 65(6), 1047-1056.

White, J.W., Lawrence, P.S., Grubb, T.D. (1985, March). Factors of stress among police officers. *Criminal Justice and Behavior*, 12(1).

Williams, C.M. (1987). Peacetime combat. In Williams, T. (Ed.) *Post-traumatic stress disorders: a handbook for clinicians* (pp. 267-291). Cincinnati, OH: Disabled American Veterans.

Williams, T., Editor. (1987). *Post-traumatic stress disorders: a handbook for clinicians.* Cincinnati, OH: Disabled American Veterans.

Wolf, M.E. & Mosnaim, A.D., Editors. (1990). *Posttraumatic stress disorder: etiology, phenomenology, and treatment.* Washington, DC: American Psychiatric Press.

Workers face post-shooting trauma. (1993, July 4). *Santa Barbara News-Press.*

Yehuda, R. (2004). Risk and resilience in posttraumatic stress disorder. *Journal of Clinical Psychiatry*, 65: 29-36.

Yehuda, R., Southwick, S.M., & Giller, E.L. (1992, March). Exposure to atrocities and severity of chronic posttraumatic stress disorder in Vietnam combat veterans. *American Journal of Psychiatry*, 149(3), 333-336.

Zamichow, N. (1992, Feb. 18). Latina immigrants suffer post-traumatic disorders. *Los Angeles Times*, A3, A24.

Zaslav, M.R. (1994, Oct-Dec.). Psychology of comorbid posttraumatic stress disorder and substance abuse: lessons from combat veterans. *Journal of Psychoactive Drugs*, 16(4), 393-400.

Zweben, J.E., Clark, H.W. & Smith, D.E. (1994, Oct-Dec.). Traumatic experiences and substance abuse: mapping the territory. *Journal of Psychoactive Drugs*, 26(4), 327-344.

Subject Index

Support Sources Index

Acknowledgments

This book was written in collaboration with men and women who demonstrated unlimited generosity and kindness.

More than a hundred law enforcement officers, their spouses, police administrators, union representatives and police peer supporters have provided stories, encouragement, information and wisdom. Most wish to remain anonymous, aware that an admission of being unable to cope with trauma can cause disgrace in many police circles. I offer my gratitude to those silent contributors and to all the others who were willing to share with me the most traumatic moments of their lives.

Without Detective Bill Martin, *CopShock* would never have been written. His courage in facing life's adversities and commitment to helping law enforcement officers have inspired and humbled me. With my deep respect and affection, I hope this book is everything he wanted it to be.

This book would also not have been written without John Jenks, Joseph Kroon, Bob McClellan, Christine McIntyre, Terry Nunn, Hector Rodriguez, Tony Senft, Ian Shaw, Jimmy Brown, Jonathan Figueroa, Ed Brown, Ann Marie Brown, Jan Myers, and Corrine Mossman. Speaking of their traumatic experiences put a lot of stress on them. Their insistence on getting every word right regardless of what terrible images tormented them afterwards does credit to law enforcement officers everywhere. To the officers in this book, honor and truth are not just words. They are virtues that define their character and calling.

Nancy K. Bohl, Ph.D., Past Chair of the IACP, Ellen Kirschman, Ph.D., author of *I Love A Cop*, and Aphrodite Matsakis, Ph.D., author of *Trust After Trauma* and *I Can't Get Over It*, were unselfish with their time and knowledge, spending many hours reviewing portions of the manuscript for the first edition of *CopShock*. Early in the research and writing, I told Ebrahim Amanat, M.D., Coordinator of the PTSD Clinical Team at the Veterans Affairs Outpatient Clinic, Commerce, CA, of my goals for the book. He said, "No matter what, you must write this book." His encouragement helped sustain me during the long process.

For critiquing specific chapters or the entire first edition manuscript, I thank George S. Everly, Jr., Ph.D., International Critical Incident Stress Foundation; Sam Klarreich, Ph.D., consultant to the Toronto Police Service; Mark D. Lerner, Ph.D., former President, American Academy of Experts in Traumatic Stress; and Jeffrey T. Mitchell, Ph.D., former President, International Critical Incident Stress Foundation. In addition to reviewing the manuscript, Bennett A. Jennings, Ph.D., of the Tucson Veterans Affairs Medical Center PTSD Clinical Team, was patient and gracious in answering my many questions.

I am grateful for insights into the manuscript from John J. Carr; Lt. James F. Devine (Ret.), Bill Genêt, Director of Police Officers Providing Peer Assistance (POPPA), who spent many days helping me conduct research in New York city, and critiqued both the first edition text and the new chapters for the second edition; Rod "Doc" Kane, combat veteran and author of *Veteran's Day*; and Kathleen Koepplin, therapist, RN, MFCC.

For their acute perceptions, I thank Sgt. Kieth Wm. Moreland, LAPD Chemical Dependency Supervisor; Jaan Schaer, former Director, Employee and Family Assistance Program, Toronto Police Service; Peter Schweitzer, former Law Enforcement Coordinator, Seafield Center; E. Joseph Shoben, Jr., Ph.D., (deceased); police officer Aaron J. Westrick, Ph.D., police sociologist, who was unstinting in providing research materials and contacts; and Sue Woods, Executive Director, Spouses of Police Officers.

For special assistance, I thank librarian Hannah Fisher, RN, MLS, of the Arizona Health Sciences Library, University of Arizona; the National Criminal Justice Reference Service; the librarians at the University of California, Santa Barbara; book cover designers and illustrators Shannon Bodie and Bob Swingle, Lightbourne Images; website designer Sandra Ryan, the Patrolmen's Benevolent Association of New York City; and my attorney Chuck Hurewitz, who never gave up on me.

My Goddard College writing advisors helped me develop the discipline and writing skills necessary to write this book. They made me understand that real writing is rewriting. My thanks to Victoria Redel, Sarah Schulman, Paul Selig and Marina Budhos.

For their encouragement and advice, I thank Greg and Jean Brown, Bill Cushing, Ron Gallagher, Robert and Sarah Graziani, Leo Grillo, Carmen Leal, Sydney Perlmutter, Dan Poynter, Joanne Sears, Webster Watnik, Bob Young, and the American Academy of Experts in Traumatic Stress.

Lastly, I mention two people who have influenced my life greatly. Teresa Ramirez Boulette, Ph.D., was my therapist for several years. Treating me with kindness and skill, she taught me coping skills I still use today. Wildlife artist Sherry Bryant is my best friend. When my goals seemed impossible to achieve, she surrounded me with love and affection, and insisted that I follow my dream.

"It is not the strongest of the species that survive, nor the most intelligent, but the one most responsive to change."

—Darwin

About W. H. Martin

For over thirty-three years, Detective William H. Martin served as an emergency services provider—two years in ambulance service, two years in volunteer fire service, four years in the United States Coast Guard as a medic, two years as an LAPD patrol officer, two years in the LAPD's Scientific Investigation Division, Latent Print Section, and twenty-one years as a detective.

Photo by Baron Erik Spafford

For eight of those years as a detective, he was the coordinator for the Drug and Alcohol Rehabilitation Program, Los Angeles Police Department.

After retiring from the department, Bill became a chemical dependency and intervention counselor. He is a Licensed Alcohol and Drug Abuse Counselor (LADAC), Certified Employee Assistance Professional/Substance Abuse Professional (CEAP/SAP), Certified Criminal Justice Specialist (CCJS) and a Certified Addictions Specialist (CAS).

He is in private practice in Farmington, New Mexico, and lives in Blanco with his wife Bobbi.